# Contents

# *Foreword*

If the listed option is an investment tool—and there should be no question in anyone's mind that it is—this book will become a bible to any investment manager.

Lucidity is the hallmark of this book. It takes you step by step from the simplest tactic to the most sophisticated. From the simple buying of a call to a "box." The exposition is clear and simple. Like any commander in the field, once you have established your strategy, you then select the proper tactic. This book is an absolute must in the selection of the proper tactic.

In any investment strategy, risk-reward is the keystone. Each tactic that Mr. McMillan explains, has its own risk-reward; however, the key to successful money management using listed options is to establish the risk-reward for the account as a whole. Risk-reward is obviously not the same for each account. The profile of the account will determine the risk-reward. A tax-free account will be different from a taxable account. A corporate account will be different from a personal account. The size of the acount will have its own dynamics. This book addresses itself commendably toward this end.

It should not be forgotten that the listed option is a derivative security. What the underlying security does or does not do, will determine what the option will do. There is no magic in listed options, per se. There could be magic in the artful use—or non-use—of the listed option.

One must remember that just because an investment tool is available, it does not mean that it must be used, or it is wise to use; however, how could one make such a decision—go or not go—unless one knows the tool? This book gives you the basis for understanding the tool.

The development of puts has been a giant stride in the use of listed options. It expands the horizon for the investor. When there is a listed put for each listed call, the American investor will have in his or her capacity the ability to maneuver successfully in all kinds of markets.

LEON POMERANCE

# Preface

When the listed option market originated in April, 1973, a new world of investment strategies was opened to the investing public. The standardization of option terms and the formation of a liquid secondary market created new investment vehicles that, adapted properly, can enhance almost every investment philosophy, from the conservative to the speculative. This book is about those option strategies—which ones work in which situations and why they work.

Some of these strategies are traditionally considered to be "complex," but, with the proper knowledge of their underlying principles, most investors can understand them. While this book contains all the basic definitions concerning options, little time or space is spent on the most elementary definitions. For example, the reader should be familiar with what a call option is, what the CBOE is, and how to find and read option quotes in a newspaper. In essence, everything is contained here for the novice to build on, but the bulk of the discussion is above the beginner level. The reader should also be somewhat familiar with technical analysis—understanding at least the terms "support" and "resistance."

Certain strategies can be, and have been, the topic of whole books—call buying, for example. While some of the strategies discussed in this book receive a more thorough treatment than others, this is by no means a book about only one or two strategies. Current literature on stock options generally does not treat covered call writing in a great deal of detail, even though it is one of the most widely used option strategies by the investing public. Therefore, call writing is the subject of one of the most in-depth discussions presented here. Another writing strategy—straddle writing—receives a great deal of attention. The material presented herein on call and put buying is not particularly lengthy, although much of it is of an advanced nature and should be useful even to sophisticated traders.

In discussing each strategy, particular emphasis is given to showing why one would want to implement the strategy in the first place and to demonstrating under which market scenarios the strategy works and under which ones it does not. The full details of each strategy are presented, including many graphical and tabular layouts of the profit and loss potentials, margin requirements, and criteria for the selection of a position. A great deal of attention is also given to follow-up action. It is often easier to decide to establish a position than it is to take action to limit loss or take profits. Therefore, in the cases where follow-up action applies, many of the reasonable alternatives are spelled out in detail, with examples. Comparisons among similar strategies are also made. An investor who is bullish, for example, may want to implement a variety of strategies. A comparison of the benefits and deficiencies of similar strategies helps the investor decide which one is right for his or her particular case. Pitfalls that should be avoided are also pointed out.

I have used the fictional stock XYZ to illustrate the examples, rather than naming actual stocks. Many of the examples are drawn from actual prices that existed. It is, however, rather pointless to give an example starting Bally at 60 when it might easily be 20 or 200 by the time the reader peruses the example. The purpose of examples is to illustrate concepts, not record history. XYZ fits this purpose best since it is very versatile: It can, as the need arises, be low-priced or high-priced, volatile or nonvolatile; and it changes price at will in order to illustrate follow-up strategies.

Call option strategies are presented in the first part of the book, and put option strategies are in the latter portion. While this order of presentation may interrupt the purely strategic flow a bit—for example, bear spreads are discussed using call options in the first part of the book and then are discussed again later using put options—this format is designed to aid the novice and intermediate option investor in that they are more familiar with calls than puts. For the majority of option investors, the development of the strategies in the more familiar environment of calls should make them more understandable. Then the application of the concepts to put options is easier. Put option strategies are not slighted, however. Their applications are necessary for strategists to have a full range of possibilities at their command, and such strategies therefore occupy a sizable amount of text. Certain special subjects are treated as well, such as computer models and their applications, how to use options in arbitraging, and how the actions of market makers and arbitrageurs affect the public option investor.

I am certain that many readers of this book expect to learn what the "best" option strategy is. While there is a section discussing this subject, there is no definitively "best" strategy. The optimum strategy for one investor may not be best for another. Option professionals who have the time to closely monitor positions may be able to utilize an array of strategies that could not possibly be operated diligently by a public customer employed in another full-time occupation. Moreover, one's particular investment philosophy must play an important part in determining which strategy is best for him. Those willing to accept little or no risk other than that of owning stock may prefer covered call writing. More speculative strategists may feel that low-cost, high-profit potential situations suit them best.

Every investor must read the Options Clearing Corporation Prospectus before trading in listed options. Options may not be suitable for every investor. There are risks involved in any investment, and certain option strategies may involve large risks. The reader must determine whether his or her financial situation and investment objectives are compatible with the strategies described. The only way in which an investor can reasonably make a decision on his or her own suitability to trade options is to attempt to acquire a knowledge of the subject.

Several years ago, I wrote that "the option market shows every sign of becoming a stronger force in the investment world. Those who understand it will be able to benefit the most." Nothing has happened in the interim to change the truth of that statement, and, in fact, it could probably be even more forcefully stated today. The universal purpose of this book is to provide the reader with that understanding of options.

I would like to express my appreciation to several people who helped make this book possible: to Ron Dilks and Howard Whitman, who brought me into the brokerage business; to Art Kaufman, whose broad experience in options helped to crystalize many of these strategies; to Peter Kopple for his help in reviewing the chapter on arbitrage; and to Ben Russell and Fred Dahl for their suggestions on format and layout.

Special thanks go to Bruce Nemirow for his invaluable assistance, especially for comprehensively reading and critiquing the entire manuscript. Most of all, I am grateful to my wife, Janet, who typed the manuscript, and to Karen and Glenn, our children, all of whom graciously withstood the countless hours of interrupted family life that were necessary in order to complete this work.

Lawrence G. McMillan

# PART I

# Basic Properties of Stock Options

# Prolog

Each chapter in this book presents information in a logically sequential fashion. Many chapters build on the information presented in preceding chapters. One should therefore be able to proceed from beginning to end without constantly referring to the glossary or index. However, the reader who is using the text as a reference—perhaps scanning one of the later chapters—may find that he is encountering terms that have been defined in an earlier chapter. In this case, the extensive glossary at the back of the book should prove useful. The index may provide aid as well, since some subjects are described, in varying levels of complexity, in more than one place in the book. For example, call buying is discussed initially in Chapter 3; and mathematical applications, as they apply to call purchases, are described in Chapter 28. The latter chapters address more complex topics than do the early chapters. When perusing these more difficult subjects, the reader may find the index and glossary useful in reviewing basic concepts.

# Definitions 1

## *THE NEED TO KNOW*

The successful implementation of various investment strategies necessitates a sound working knowledge of the fundamentals of options and option trading. The option strategist must be familiar with a wide range of the basic aspects of stock options—how the price of an option behaves under certain conditions or how the markets function. A thorough understanding of the rudiments and of the strategies helps the investor who is not familiar with options to decide not only whether a strategy seems desirable, but also—and more important— *whether it is suitable.* Determining suitability is nothing new to stock market investors, for stocks themselves are not suitable for every investor. For example, if the investor's primary objectives are income and safety of principal, then bonds, rather than stocks, would be more suitable. The need to assess the suitability of options is especially important: Option buyers can lose their entire investment in a short time, and uncovered option writers may be subjected to large financial risks. Despite follow-up methods designed to limit risk, the individual investor must decide whether option trading is suitable for his or her financial situation and investment objective.

## ELEMENTARY DEFINITIONS

A *stock option* is the right to buy or sell a particular stock at a certain price for a limited period of time. The stock in question is called the *underlying security*. A *call option* gives the owner (or holder) the right to buy the underlying security, while a *put option* gives the holder the right to sell the underlying security. The price at which the stock may be bought or sold is the *exercise price*, also called the *striking price*. (In the listed options market, "exercise price" and "striking price" are synonymous; in the older, over-the-counter options market, they have different meanings.) A stock option affords this right to buy or sell for only a limited period of time; thus, each option has an *expiration date*. Throughout the book, the term "options" is always understood to mean *listed stock options*, that is, options traded on national option exchanges where a secondary market exists. Unless specifically mentioned, the older type of option, the over-the-counter (OTC) option, is not included in any discussion.

### Describing Options

Four specifications uniquely describe any option contract:

1. the type (put or call),
2. the underlying stock name,
3. the expiration date, and
4. the striking price.

As an example, an option referred to as an "XYZ July 50 call" is an option to buy (a call) 100 shares (normally) of the underlying XYZ stock for $50 per share. The option expires in July. The price of a listed option is quoted on a per-share basis, regardless of how many shares of stock can be bought with the option. Thus, if the price of the XYZ July 50 call is quoted at $5, buying the option would ordinarily cost $500 ($5 × 100 shares), plus commissions.

### The Value of Options

An option is a "wasting" asset; that is, it has only an initial value that declines (or "wastes" away) as time passes. It may even expire worthless, or the holder may have to exercise it in order to recover some value before expiration. Of course, the holder may sell the option in the listed option market *before* expiration.

An option is also a security by itself, but it is a derivative security. The option is irrevocably linked to the underlying stock; its price fluctuates as the price of the underlying stock rises or falls. Splits and stock dividends in the underlying stock affect the terms of listed options, although cash dividends do not. The holder of a call does not receive any cash dividends paid by the underlying stock.

### Standardization

The listed option exchanges have standardized the terms of option contracts. The *terms* of an option constitutes the collective name that includes all of the four descriptive specifications. While the type (put or call) and the underlying stock are self-evident and essentially standardized, the striking price and expiration date require more explanation.

*Striking Price.* Striking prices are generally spaced 5 points apart for stocks selling at or under $60 per share, 10 points apart for stocks up to $200 per share, and 20 points apart for stocks over $200 per share. A $25 stock might, for example, have options with striking prices, or "*strikes*," of 20, 25, and 30, while a $75 stock might have one at 70 and one at 80.

These striking price guidelines are not iron-clad, however. Exchange officials may alter the intervals to improve depth and liquidity, perhaps spacing the strikes 5 points apart on a nonvolatile stock even if it is selling for more than $50. For example, options on a slow-moving, nonvolatile stock such as AT&T might have striking prices of 50, 55, 60, and 65, even though the stock is selling in excess of $60 per share. However, a more volatile stock, such as Texas Instruments, would have striking prices of perhaps 60, 70, and 80 if it were over $60 per share. In addition, very low priced stocks (near $20 per share) may have striking prices spaced only 2½ points apart, such as 15, 17½, and 20.

*Expiration Dates.* Options have expiration dates in one of three fixed *cycles*:

1. the January/April/July/October (the major) cycle,
2. the February/May/August/November cycle, or
3. the March/June/September/December cycle.

Obviously, each cycle uses 4 calendar months spaced 3 months apart.

However, at any given time, the longest-term expiration dates can be
no farther away than 9 months. Hence in any cycle, options may
expire in only 3 of the 4 months (series). For example, on February 1
of any year, XYZ options may expire only in April, July, and
October—not in January. The April option (the closest series) is the
*short-* or *near-term* option; the July, the *middle-term;* and the October, the *far-* or *long-term* option.

The exact date of expiration is fixed within each month. The last
trading day for an option is the third Friday in the expiration month.
Although the option actually does not expire until the following day
(the Saturday following), a public customer must invoke the right to
buy or sell stock by 5:30 P.M., New York time, on the last day of
trading.

### The Option Itself: Other Definitions

*Classes and Series.* A *class* of options refers to all put and call
contracts on the same underlying security. For instance, all IBM
options—all the puts and calls at various strikes and expiration
months—form one class. A *series,* a subset of a class, consists of all
contracts of the same class (IBM, for example) having the same
expiration date and striking price.

*Opening and Closing Transactions.* An *opening transaction* is
the initial transaction, either a buy or a sell. For example, an opening
buy transaction creates or increases a long position in the customer's
account. A *closing transaction* reduces the customer's position.
Opening buys are often followed by closing sales; correspondingly,
opening sells often precede closing buy trades.

*Open Interest.* The option exchanges keep track of the amount
of opening and closing transactions in each option series. This is called
the *open interest.* Each opening transaction adds to the open interest
and each closing transaction decreases the open interest. The open
interest is expressed in number of option contracts, so that one order
to buy 5 calls opening would increase the open interest by 5. Note that
the open interest does not differentiate between buyers and sellers—
there is no way to tell if there is a preponderance of either one. While
the magnitude of the open interest is not an extremely important piece
of data for the investor, it is useful in determining the liquidity of the
option in question. If there is a large open interest, then there should be
little problem in making fairly large trades. However, if the open
interest is small—only a few hundred contracts outstanding—then

there might not be a reasonable secondary market in that option series.

*The Holder and Writer.* Anyone who buys an option as the initial transaction—that is, *buys opening*—is called the *holder.* On the other hand, the investor who sells an option as the initial transaction—an *opening sale*—is called the *writer* of the option. Commonly, the writer (or seller) of an option is referred to as being *short* the option contact. The term "writer" dates back to the over-the-counter days, when a direct link existed between buyers and sellers of options; at that time, the seller was the *writer* of a new contract to buy stock. In the listed option market, however, the issuer of all options is the Options Clearing Corporation, and contracts are standardized. This important difference makes it possible to break the direct link between the buyer and seller, paving the way for the formation of the secondary markets that now exist.

*Exercise and Assignment.* An option owner (or *holder*) who invokes the right to buy or sell is said to *exercise* the option. Call option holders exercise to buy stock; put holders exercise to sell. The holder may exercise the option any time after taking possession of it up until 8:00 P.M. on the last trading day; the holder does not have to wait until the expiration date itself before exercising. Whenever a holder exercises an option, somewhere a writer is *assigned the obligation* to fulfill the terms of the option contract: Thus, if a call holder exercises the right to buy, a call writer is assigned the obligation to sell; conversely, if a put holder exercises the right to sell, a put writer is assigned the obligation to buy. A more detailed description of the exercise and assignment of call options follows later in this chapter; put option exercise and assignment are discussed in the second half of the book.

### Relationship of the Option Price and Stock Price

*In- and Out-of-the-Money.* Certain terms describe the relationship between the stock price and the option's striking price. A call option is said to be *out-of-the-money* if the stock is selling below the striking price of the option. A call option is *in-the-money* if the stock price is above the striking price of the option. (Put options work in a converse manner, which is described later.)

*Example:* XYZ stock is trading at $47 per share. The XYZ July 50 call option is out-of-the-money, just like the XYZ October 50 call and the XYZ July 60 call. However, the XYZ July 45 call, XYZ October 40, or XYZ January 35 is in-the-money.

The *intrinsic value* of an in-the-money call is the amount by which the stock price exceeds the striking price. If the call is out-of-the-money, its intrinsic value is zero. The price that an option sells for is commonly referred to as the *premium*. The premium is distinctly different from the *time value premium* (called *time premium*, for short), which is the amount by which the option premium itself exceeds its *intrinsic value*. The time value premium is quickly computed by the following formula for an in-the-money call option:

*Call time value premium* = call option price + striking price − stock price

> *Example:* XYZ is trading at 48, and XYZ July 45 call is at 4. The premium—the total price—of the option is 4. With XYZ at 48 and the striking price of the option at 45, the in-the-money amount (or *intrinsic value*) is 3 points (48 − 45), and the time value is 1 (4 − 3).

If the call is out-of-the-money, then the premium and the time value premium are the same.

> *Example:* With XYZ at 48 and an XYZ July 50 call selling at 2, both the premium and the time value premium of the call are 2 points. The call has no intrinsic value by itself with the stock price below the striking price.

An option normally has the largest amount of time value premium when the stock price is equal to the striking price. As an option

**TABLE 1-1.** *Changes in the time value premium.*

| XYZ Stock Price | XYZ July 50 Call Price | Intrinsic Value | Time Value Premium |
|---|---|---|---|
| 40 | ½ | 0 | ½ |
| 43 | 1 | 0 | 1 |
| 45 | 2 | 0 | 2 |
| 47 | 3 | 0 | 3 |
| **50** | **5** | **0** | **5** |
| 53 | 7 | 3 | 4 |
| 55 | 8 | 5 | 3 |
| 57 | 9 | 7 | 2 |
| 60 | 10½ | 10 | ½ |
| 70 | 19½ | 20 | −½[a] |

[a]    Simplistically, a deeply in-the-money call may actually trade at a discount from intrinsic value, because call buyers are more interested in less expensive calls that might return better percentage profits on an upward move in the stock. This phenomenon is discussed in more detail when arbitrage techniques are examined.

becomes deeply in- or out-of-the-money, the time value premium shrinks substantially. Table 1-1 illustrates this effect. Note how the time value premium increases as the stock nears the striking price (50) and then decreases as it draws away from 50.

*Parity.* An option is said to be trading *at parity* with the underlying security if it is trading for its intrinsic value. Thus, if XYZ is 48 and the XYZ July 45 call is selling for 3, the call is *at parity.* A common practice of particular interest to option writers (as shall be seen later) is to refer to the price of an option by relating how close it is to parity with the common stock. Thus, the XYZ July 45 call is said to be a half-point over parity in any of the cases shown in Table 1-2.

**TABLE 1-2.** *Comparison of XYZ stock and call prices.*

| Striking Price | + | XYZ July 45 Call Price | − | XYZ Stock Price | = | Over Parity |
|---|---|---|---|---|---|---|
| (45 | + | 1 | − | 45½) | = | ½ |
| (45 | + | 2½ | − | 47 ) | = | ½ |
| (45 | + | 5½ | − | 50 ) | = | ½ |
| (45 | + | 15½ | − | 60 ) | = | ½ |

## *FACTORS INFLUENCING THE PRICE OF AN OPTION*

An option's price is the result of several properties of both the underlying stock and terms of the option. The major quantifiable factors influencing the price of an option are the:

1. price of the underlying stock,
2. striking price of the option itself,
3. time remaining until expiration of the option,
4. volatility of the underlying stock,
5. the current risk-free interest rate (such as for 90-day Treasury bills), and
6. dividend rate of the underlying stock.

The first four items are the major determinants of an option's price, while the latter two are generally less important, although the dividend rate can be influential in the case of high-yield stock.

## The Four Major Determinants

Probably the most important influence on the option's price is the stock price, because if the stock price is far above or far below the striking price, the other factors have little influence. Its dominance is obvious on the day that an option expires. On that day, only the stock price and the striking price of the option determine the option's value; the other four factors have no bearing at all. At this time, an option is worth only its intrinsic value.

*Example:* On the expiration day in July, with no time remaining, an XYZ July 50 call has the value shown in Table 1-3; each value depends on the stock price at the time.

**TABLE 1-3.** *XYZ option's values on the expiration day.*

| XYZ Stock Price | XYZ July 50 Call (Intrinsic) Value at Expiration |
|---|---|
| 40 | 0 |
| 45 | 0 |
| 48 | 0 |
| 50 | 0 |
| 52 | 2 |
| 55 | 5 |
| 60 | 10 |

*The Call Option Price Curve.* The *call option price curve* is a curve that plots the prices of an option against various stock prices. Figure 1-1 shows the axes needed to graph such a curve. The vertical axis is called "Option Price." The horizontal axis is for Stock Prices. This figure is a graph of the intrinsic value. When the option is either out-of-the-money or equal to the stock price, the intrinsic value is *zero.* Once the stock price passes the striking price, it reflects the increase of intrinsic value as the stock price goes up. Since a call is usually worth at least its intrinsic value at any time, the graph thus represents the minimum price that a call may be worth.

When a call has time remaining to its expiration date, its total price consists of its intrinsic value plus its time value premium. The resultant call option price curve takes the form of an inverted arch that stretches along the stock price axis. If one plots the data from Table 1-4 on the grid supplied in Figure 1-2, the curve assumes two characteristics:

**FIGURE 1-1** *The value of an option at expiration, its intrinsic value*

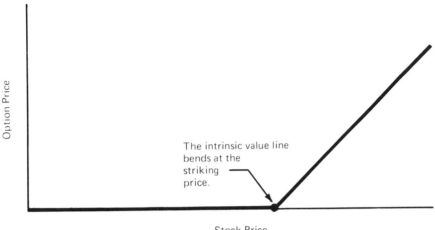

1. The time value premium (the shaded area) is greatest when the stock price and the striking price are the same.
2. When the stock price is far above or far below the striking price (near the ends of the curve), the option sells for nearly its intrinsic value. As a result, the curve nearly touches the intrinsic value line at either end. [Figure 1-2 thus shows both the intrinsic value and the option price curve.]

**FIGURE 1-2.** *Six-month July call option (see Table 1-4).*

**TABLE 1-4.** *The prices of a hypothetical July 50 call with 6 months of time remaining, plotted in Figure 1-2.*

| XYZ Stock Price (Horizontal Axis) | XYZ July 50 Call Price (Vertical Axis) | Intrinsic Value | Time Value Premium (Shading) |
|---|---|---|---|
| 40 | 1 | 0 | 1 |
| 45 | 2 | 0 | 2 |
| 48 | 3 | 0 | 3 |
| → **50** | **4** | **0** | **4** |
| 52 | 5 | 2 | 3 |
| 55 | 6½ | 5 | 1½ |
| 60 | 11 | 10 | 1 |

This curve, however, shows only how one might expect the XYZ July 50 call prices to behave with 6 months remaining until expiration. As the time to expiration grows shorter, the arched line drops lower and lower, until, on the final day in the life of the option, it merges completely with the intrinsic value line. In other words, the call is worth only its intrinsic value at expiration. Examine Figure 1-3, which depicts three separate XYZ calls. At any given stock price (a fixed point on the stock price scale), the longest-term call sells for the highest price and the nearest-term call sells for the lowest price. At the striking price, the actual differences in the three option prices are the greatest. Near either end of the scale, the three curves are much closer together, indicating that the actual price differences from one option to another are small. For a given stock price, therefore, option prices decrease as the expiration date approaches.

**FIGURE 1-3.** *Price curves for the 3-, 6-, and 9-month call options.*

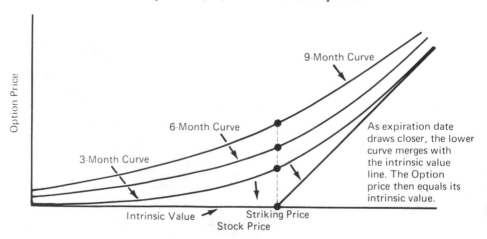

*Example:* On January 1, XYZ is selling at 48. An XYZ July 50 call will sell for more than an April 50 call, which in turn will sell for more than a January 50 call.

This statement is true no matter what the stock price is. The only reservation is that with the stock deeply in- or out-of-the-money, the actual difference between the January, April, and July calls will be smaller than with XYZ stock selling at the striking price of 50.

*Time Value Premium Decay.* In Figure 1-3, notice that the price of the 9-month call is not three times that of the 3-month call. Note next that the curve in Figure 1-4 for the decay of time value premium is not straight; that is, *the rate of decay of an option is not linear.* An option's time value premium decays much more rapidly in the last few weeks of its life (that is, in the weeks immediately preceding expiration) than it does in the first few weeks of its existence. The rate of decay is actually related to the square root of the time remaining. Thus a 3-month option decays (loses time value premium) at twice the rate of a 9-month option, since the square root of 9 is 3. Similarly, a 2-month option decays at twice the rate of a 4-month option ($\sqrt{4} = 2$).

This graphic simplification should not lead one to believe that a 9-month option necessarily sells for twice the price of a 3-month option, because the other factors also influence the actual price relationship between the two calls. Of those other factors, the *volatility* of the underlying stock is particularly influential. *More volatile underlying stocks have higher options prices.* This relationship is logical,

**FIGURE 1-4.** *Time value premium decay, assuming the stock price remains constant*

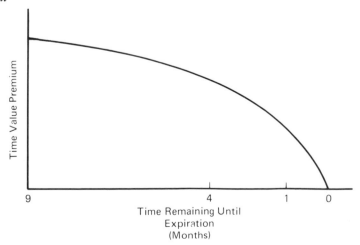

because if a stock has the ability to move a relatively large distance upward, buyers of the calls are willing to pay higher prices for the calls—and sellers demand them as well. For example, if AT&T and Xerox sell for the same price (as they have been known to do), the Xerox calls would be more highly priced than the AT&T calls because Xerox is a more volatile stock than AT&T.

The interplay of the four major variables—stock price, striking price, time, and volatility—can be quite complex. While a rising stock price (for example) is directing the price of a call upward, decreasing time may be simultaneously driving the price in the opposite direction. Thus the purchaser of an out-of-the-money call may wind up with a loss even after a rise in price by the underlying stock, because time has eroded the call value.

### The Two Minor Determinants

*The Risk-Free Interest Rate.* This rate is generally construed as the current rate of 90-day Treasury bills. Higher interest rates imply slightly higher option premiums, while lower rates imply lower premiums. Although members of the financial community disagree as to the extent that interest rates actually affect option price, they remain a factor in most mathematical models used for pricing options. (These models are covered much later in this book.)

*The Cash Dividend Rate of the Underlying Stock.* Though not classified as a major determinant in option prices, this rate can be especially important to the writer (seller) of an option. If the underlying stock pays no dividends at all, then a call option's worth is strictly a function of the other five items. *Dividends, however, tend to lower call option premiums: the larger the dividend of the underlying common stock, the lower the price of its call options.* One of the most influential factors in keeping option premiums low on high-yielding stock is the yield itself.

> *Example:* XYZ is a relatively low-priced stock with low volatility selling for $25 per share. It pays a large annual dividend of $2 per share in four quarterly payments of $.50 each. What is a fair price of an XYZ call with striking price 25?
>
> A prospective buyer of XYZ options is determined to figure out a fair price. In six months XYZ will pay $1 per share in dividends, and the stock price will thus be reduced by $1 per share when it goes ex-dividend over that time period. In that case, if XYZ's price remains unchanged except for the ex-dividend reductions, it will then be $24.

Moreover, since XYZ is a nonvolatile stock, it may not readily climb back to 25 after the ex-dividend reductions. Therefore, the call buyer makes a low bid—even for a 6-month call—because the underlying stock's price will be reduced by the ex-dividend reduction, and the call holder does not receive the cash dividends.

This particular call buyer calculates the worth of the XYZ July 25 call in terms of what it is worth with the stock discounted to 24—not at 25. He knew for certain that the stock was going to lose 1 point of value over the next 6 months, providing the dividend rate of XYZ stock did not change. In actual practice, option buyers tend to discount the upcoming dividends of the stock when they bid for the calls. However, not all dividends are discounted fully; usually the nearest dividend is discounted more heavily than are dividends to be paid at a later date. The less-volatile stocks with the higher dividend payout rates have lower call prices than volatile stocks with low payouts. In fact, in certain cases, an impending large dividend payment can substantially increase the probability of an exercise of the call in advance of expiration. (This phenomenon is discussed more fully in the following section.) In any case, to one degree or another, dividends are an important influence on the price of some calls.

### Other Influences

These six factors, major and minor, are only the quantifiable influences on the price of an option. In practice, nonquantitative market dynamics—investor sentiment—can play various roles as well. In a bullish market, call premiums often expand because of increased demand. In bearish markets, call premiums may shrink due to increased supply or diminished demand. These influences, however, are normally short-lived and generally come into play only in dynamic market periods when emotions are running high.

## EXERCISE AND ASSIGNMENT: THE MECHANICS

The holder of an option can *exercise* his right at any time during the life of an option: Call option holders exercise to buy stock, while put option holders exercise to sell stock. In the event that an option is exercised, the writer of an option with the same terms is *assigned an obligation* to fulfill the terms of the option contract.

### Exercising the Option

The actual mechanics of exercise and assignment are fairly simple, due to the role of the Options Clearing Corporation (OCC). As the issuer of all listed option contracts, it controls all listed option exercises and assignments. Its activities are best explained by an example.

*Example:* The holder of an XYZ January 45 call option wishes to exercise his right to buy XYZ stock at $45 per share. He instructs his broker to do so. The broker then notifies the administrative section of the brokerage firm that handles such matters. The firm then notifies the OCC that they wish to exercise one contract of the XYZ January 45 call series.

Now the OCC takes over the handling. OCC records indicate which member (brokerage) firms are short or which have written and not yet covered XYZ Jan 45 calls. The OCC selects, at random, a member firm who is short at least one XYZ Jan 45 call, and it notifies the short firm that it has been assigned. That firm must then deliver 100 shares of XYZ at $45 per share to the firm who exercised the option. The assigned firm, in turn, selects one of its customers who is short the XYZ January 45 call. This selection for the assignment may be either:

1. at random,
2. on a first-in/first-out basis, or
3. on any other basis that is fair, equitable, and approved by the appropriate exchange.

The selection of the customer who is short the XYZ January 45 completes the exercise/assignment process. (If one is an option writer, he should obviously determine exactly how his brokerage firm assigns its option contracts.)

### Honoring the Assignment

The assigned customer *must* deliver the stock—he has no other choice. It is too late to try buying the option back in the option market. He must, without fail, deliver 100 shares of XYZ stock at $45 per share. The assigned writer does, however, have a choice as to how to fulfill the assignment. If he happens to be already long 100 shares of XYZ in his account, he merely delivers that 100 shares as fulfillment of the assignment notice. Alternatively, he can go into the stock market and buy XYZ at the current market price—presumably something higher than $45—and then deliver the newly purchased stock as fulfillment. A third alternative is merely to notify his brokerage firm that he wishes to go short XYZ stock and to ask them to deliver the 100 shares of XYZ at 45 out of his short account. At times, borrowing stock to go short may not be possible; so this third alternative is not always available on every stock.

*Margin Requirements.* If the assigned writer purchases stock to fulfill a contract, reduced margin requirements generally apply to the transaction, so that he would not have to fully margin the purchased stock merely for the purpose of delivery. Generally, the customer only has to pay a day-trade margin of the difference between the current price of XYZ and the delivery price of $45 per share. If he goes short to honor the assignment, then he has to fully margin the short sale at the current rate for stock sold short on a margin basis.

### After Exercising the Option

The OCC and the customer exercising the option are not concerned with the actual method in which the delivery is handled by the assigned customer. They want only to ensure that the 100 shares of XYZ at 45 are, in fact, delivered. The holder who exercised the call can keep the stock in his account if he wants to, but he has to margin it fully or pay cash in a cash account. On the other hand, he may want to sell the stock immediately in the open market, presumably at a higher price than 45. If he has an established margin account, he may sell right away without putting out any money. If he exercises in a cash account, however, the stock must be paid for in full—even if it is subsequently sold on the same day. Alternatively, he may use the delivered stock to cover a short sale in his own account if he happens to be short XYZ stock.

### Commissions

Both the buyer of the stock via the exercise and the seller of the stock via the assignment are charged a full stock commission on 100 shares, unless a special agreement exists between the customer and the brokerage firm. Generally, option holders incur higher commission costs through assignment than they do selling the option in the secondary market. So *the public customer who holds an option is better off selling the option in the secondary market than exercising the call.*

*Example:* XYZ is $55 per share. A public customer owns the XYZ January 45 call option. He realizes that exercising the call, buying

XYZ at 45, and then immediately selling it at 55 in the stock market would net a profit of 10 points—or $1,000. However, the combined stock commissions on both the purchase at 45 and the sale at 55 might easily exceed $150. The net gain would actually be only $850.

On the other hand, the XYZ January 45 call is worth (and it would normally sell for) at least 10 points in the listed options market. The commission for selling one call at a price of 10 is roughly $30. The customer therefore decides to sell his XYZ January 45 call in the option market. He receives $1,000 (10 points) for the call and pays only $30 in commissions—for a net of $970. The benefit of his decision is obvious.

Of course, sometimes a customer *wants* to own XYZ stock at $45 per share, despite the stock commissions. Perhaps the stock is an attractive addition that will bring greater potential to a portfolio. Or if the customer is already short the XYZ stock, he is going to have to buy 100 shares and pay the commissions sooner or later in any case; so exercising the call at the lower stock price of 45 may be more desirable than buying at the current price of 55.

### Anticipating Assignment

The writer of a call often prefers to buy the option back in the secondary market, rather than fulfill the obligation via a stock trans- action. It should be stressed again that once the writer receives an assignment notice, it is too late to attempt to buy back (cover) the call. The writer must buy *before* assignment, or live up to the terms upon assignment. The writer who is aware of the circumstances that gener- ally cause the holders to exercise can anticipate assignment with a fair amount of certainty. In anticipation of the assignment, the writer can then close the contract in the secondary market. As long as the writer covers the position any time during a trading day, he cannot be assigned on that option. Assignment notices are determined on open positions as of the *close* of the trading each day. The crucial question then becomes, "How can the writer anticipate assignment?" Several circumstances signal assignments:

1. a call that is in-the-money at expiration,
2. an option trading at a discount prior to expiration, and
3. the underlying stock paying a large dividend and about to go ex- dividend.

*Automatic Exercise.* Assignment is all but certain if the stock is in-the-money at expiration. Should the stock close even a half-point above the striking price on the last day of trading, the holder will exercise to take advantage of the half-point rather than let the option expire. Assignment is nearly inevitable even if a call is only one-eighth of a point in-the-money at expiration. In fact, even if the call trades in-the-money *at any time* during the last trading day, assignment may be forthcoming. Even if a holder forgets that he owns an option and fails to exercise, the OCC automatically exercises any call that is ¾-point in-the-money at expiration, unless the individual brokerage firm whose customer is long the call gives specific instructions *not* to exercise. This *automatic exercise* mechanism ensures that no investor throws away money through carelessness.

> *Example:* XYZ closes at 51 on the third Friday of January (the last day of trading for the January option series). Since options don't expire until Saturday, the next day, the OCC and all brokerage firms have the opportunity to review their records to issue assignments and exercises and to see if any options could have been profitably exercised but were not. If XYZ closed at 51 and a customer who owned a January 45 call option failed to either sell or exercise it, it is automatically exercised. Since it is worth $600, this customer stands to receive a substantial amount of money back, even after stock commissions.

In the case of an XYZ January *50* call option, the automatic exercise procedure is not as clearcut with the stock at 51. Though the OCC wants to exercise the call automatically, they cannot identify a specific owner. They know only that one or more XYZ January calls are still open on the long side. When the OCC checks with the brokerage firm, it may find that the firm does not wish to have the XYZ January 50 call exercised automatically, because the customer would lose money on the exercise after incurring stock commissions. Yet the OCC must attempt to exercise automatically any in-the-money calls because the holder may have overlooked a long position.

When the public customer sells a call in the secondary market on the last day of trading, the buyer on the other side of the trade is very likely a market-maker. Thus, when trading stops, much of the open interest in in-the-money calls held long belongs to market-makers. Since they can profitably exercise even for an eighth of a point, they do so. Hence the writer may receive an assignment notice even if the stock has been only slightly above the strike price on the last trading day before expiration.

Any writer who wishes to avoid an assignment notice should

always buy back (or cover) the option if it appears the stock will be above the strike at expiration. The probabilities of assignment are extremely high if the option expires in-the-money.

*Early Exercise Due to Discount.* When options are exercised *prior to expiration,* this is called *early, or premature, exercise.* The writer can usually expect an early exercise when the call is trading at or below parity. A parity or discount situation in advance of expiration may mean that an early exercise is forthcoming, even if the discount is slight. A writer who does not want to deliver stock should buy back the option prior to expiration if the option is apparently going to trade at a discount to parity. The reason is that arbitrageurs (floor traders or member firm traders who pay only minimal commissions) can take advantage of discount situations. (Arbitrage is discussed in more detail later in the text, but here it shows why early exercise often occurs in a discount situation.)

> *Example:* XYZ is bid at $50 per share, and an XYZ January 40 call option is offered at a discount price of 9¾. The call is actually "worth" 10 points. The arbitrageur can take advantage of this situation through the following actions, all on the same day:
>
> 1. Buy the January 40 call at 9¾.
> 2. Sell short XYZ common stock at 50.
> 3. Exercise the call to buy XYZ at 40.
>
> The arbitrageur makes 10 points from the short sale of XYZ (steps 2 and 3), from which he deducts the 9¾ points he paid for the call. Thus his total gain is a quarter-point—the amount of the discount. Since he pays only a minimal commission, this transaction results in a net profit.

Also, if the writer can expect assignment when the option has *no* time value premium left in it, then conversely the option will usually *not* be called if time premium *is* left in it.

> *Example:* Prior to the expiration date, XYZ is trading at 50½, and the January 50 call is trading at 1. The call is not necessarily in imminent danger of being called, since it still has half a point of time premium left.

$$\frac{\text{Time value}}{\text{premium}} = \frac{\text{Call}}{\text{price}} + \frac{\text{Striking}}{\text{price}} - \frac{\text{Stock}}{\text{price}}$$

$$= 1 + 50 - 50\tfrac{1}{2}$$

$$= \tfrac{1}{2}$$

*Early Exercise Due to Dividends on the Underlying Stock.* Sometimes the market conditions create a discount situation, and sometimes a large dividend gives rise to a discount. Since the stock price is almost invariably reduced by the amount of the dividend, the option price is also most likely reduced after the ex-dividend. Since the holder of a listed option does not receive the dividend, he may decide to sell the option in the secondary market before the ex-date in anticipation of the drop in price. If enough calls are sold because of the impending ex-dividend reduction the option may come to parity or even to a discount. Once again the arbitrageurs may move in to take advantage of the situation by buying these calls and exercising them.

If assigned prior to the ex-date, the writer does not receive the dividend for he no longer owns the stock on the ex-date. Furthermore, if he receives an assignment notice *on* the ex-date, he must deliver the stock *with* the dividend. It is therefore very important for the writer to watch for discount situations on the day prior to the ex-date.

A word of caution: Do not conclude from this discussion that a call will be exercised for the dividend if the dividend is larger than the remaining time premium. It won't. An example will show why.

*Example:* XYZ stock, at 50, is going to pay a $1 dividend with the ex-date set for the next day. An XYZ January 40 call is selling at 10¼; it has a quarter-point of time premium. (TVP = 10¼ + 40 − 50 = ¼). The same type of arbitrage will not work. Suppose that the arbitrageur buys the call at 10¼ and exercises it: He now owns the stock for the ex-date, and he plans to sell the stock immediately at the opening on the ex-date, the next day. On the ex-date, XYZ opens at 49, because it goes ex-dividend by $1. The arbitrageur's transactions thus consist of:

1. Buy the XYZ January 40 call at 10¼.
2. Exercise the call the same day to buy XYZ at 40.
3. On the ex-date, sell XYZ at 49 and collect the $1 dividend.

He makes 9 points on the stock (steps 2 and 3), and he receives a 1-point dividend for a total cash inflow of 10 points. However, he loses 10¼ points paying for the call. *The overall transaction is a loser* and the arbitrageur would thus not attempt it.

A dividend payment that exceeds the time premium in the call, therefore, does not imply that the writer will be assigned.

More of a possibility, but a much less certain one, is that the arbitrageur may attempt a "risk arbitrage" in such a situation. *Risk arbitrage* is arbitrage in which the arbitrageur runs the risk of a loss in order to try for a profit. The arbitrageur may suspect that the stock will not be discounted the full ex-dividend amount or that the call's time premium will increase after the ex-date. In either case (or both), he might make a profit: If the stock opens down only five-eighths or if the option premium expands by three-eighths, the arbitrageur could profit on the opening. In general, however, arbitrageurs do not like to take risks and therefore avoid this type of situation. So the probability of assignment as the result of a dividend payment on the underlying stock is small, *unless* the call trades at parity or at a discount.

Of course, the anticipation of an early exercise assumes rational behavior on the part of the call holder. If time premium is left in the call, the holder is always better off financially to sell that call in the secondary market rather than to exercise it. However, the terms of the call contract give a call holder the right to go ahead and exercise it anyway—even if exercise is not the profitable thing to do. In such a case, a writer would receive an assignment notice quite unexpectedly. Though not often, financially unsound early exercises *do* happen, and an option writer must realize that, in a very small percentage of cases, he could be assigned under very illogical circumstances.

## THE OPTION MARKETS

The trader of stocks does not have to become very familiar with the details of the way the stock market works in order to make money. Stocks don't expire, nor can an investor be pulled out of his investment unexpectedly. However, the option trader is required to do more homework regarding the operation of the option markets. In fact, the option strategist who does not know the details of the working of the option markets will likely find that he or she eventually loses some money due to ignorance.

### Market-Makers

In at least one respect, stock and listed option markets are similar. Stock markets use specialists to do two things: First, they are required to make a market in a stock by buying and selling from their own inventory, when public orders to buy or sell the stock are absent. Second, they keep the public book of orders, consisting of limit orders to buy and sell, as well as stop orders placed by the public. When listed option trading began, the Chicago Board Options Exchange (CBOE) introduced a similar method of trading, the market-maker and the board broker system. The CBOE assigns several *market-makers* to each optionable stock to provide bids and offers to buy and sell options in the absence of public orders. Market-makers cannot handle public orders; they buy and sell for their own accounts only. A separate person, the board broker, keeps the book of limit orders. The board broker, who cannot do any trading, opens the book for traders to see how many orders to buy and sell are placed nearest to the current market (consisting of the highest bid and lowest offer). (The specialist on the stock exchange keeps a more closed book; he is not required to formally disclose the size and price of the public orders.)

In theory, the CBOE system is more efficient. With several market-makers competing to create the market in a particular security, the market should be a more efficient one than a single specialist can provide. Also, the somewhat open book of public orders should provide a more orderly market. In practice, whether the CBOE has a more efficient market is usually a subject for heated discussion. The strategist need not be concerned with the question.

The American Stock Exchange uses specialists for its option trading, but it also has floor traders who function similarly to market-makers. The regional option exchanges use combinations of the two systems; some use market makers, while others use specialists.

## DETAILS OF OPTION TRADING

The facts that the strategist should be concerned with are included in this section. They are not presented in any particular order of importance, and this list is not necessarily complete. Many more details are given in the discussion of specific strategies throughout this text.

1. *Options expire on the Saturday following the third Friday of the expiration month, although the third Friday is the last day of trading.* Trading in the expiring series of options actually ceases at 3 P.M. New York time. In general, however, waiting past 2:30 P.M. on that day to place orders to buy or sell the expiring options is not advisable. In the "crush" of orders during the final minutes of trading, even a market order may not have enough time to be executed.

2. *Option trades have a one-day settlement:* The trade settles on the next business day after the trade. Purchases must be paid for in full, and the credits from sales "hit" the account on the settlement day.

Some brokerage firms require settlement on the same day as the trade, when the trade occurs on the last trading day of an expiration series.

3. *Options are opened for trading in rotation.* When the underlying stock opens for trading on any exchange, regional or national, the options on that stock then go into opening rotation on the corresponding option exchange. The rotation system also applies if the underlying stock halts trading and then reopens during a trading day; options on that stock reopen via a rotation.

In the rotation itself, interested parties make bids and offers for each particular option series—the XYZ January 45 call, the XYZ January 50 call, and so on—until all the puts and calls at various expiration dates and striking prices have been opened. Trades do not necessarily have to take place in each series, just bids and offers. Orders, such as spreads, that involve more than one option are not executed during a rotation.

4. *When the underlying stock splits or pays a stock dividend, the terms of its options are adjusted.* Such an adjustment may result in fractional striking prices and in options for other than 100 shares per contract. No adjustments in terms are made for cash dividends. The actual details of splits, stock dividends, and rights offerings, along with their effects on the option terms, are always published by the option exchange that trades those options. Notices are sent to all member firms, who then make that information available to their brokers for distribution to clients. In actual practice, the option strategist should ascertain from the broker the specific terms of the new option series, in case the broker has overlooked the information sent.

*Example 1:* XYZ is a $50 stock with option striking prices of 45, 50, and 60 for the January, April, and July series. It declares a 2-for-1 stock split. Usually, in a 2-for-1 split situation, the number of outstanding option contracts are doubled and the striking prices halved. The owner of 5 XYZ January 60 calls becomes the owner of 10 XYZ January 30 calls. Each call is still for 100 shares of the underlying stock.

If *fractional striking prices* arise, the exchange also publishes the quote symbol that is to be used to find the price of the new option. The XYZ July 45 call has a symbol of XYZGI: G stands for July and I is for 45. After the 2-for-1 split, one July 45 call becomes 2 July 22½ calls. The strike of 22½ is assigned one of the letters between U and Z for this stock only. Assuming that the letter U has been designated to be the symbol for the 22½ strike, the XYZ July 22½ call is quoted with the symbol XYZGU.

After the split, XYZ has options with strikes of 22½, 25, and 30. In some cases, the option exchange officials may introduce another strike if they feel such a strike is necessary; in this example, they might introduce a striking price of 20.

*Example 2:* UVW Corp. is now trading at 40 with strikes of 35, 40, and 45 for the January, April, and July series. UVW declares a 2½ percent stock dividend. The contractually standardized 100 shares is adjusted up to 102, and the striking prices are reduced by 2 percent (rounded to the nearest eighth). Thus, the "old" 35 strike becomes a "new" strike of 34⅜: 1.02 divided into 35 equals 34.314, which is 34⅜ when rounded to the nearest eighth. The "old" 40 strike becomes a "new" strike of 39¼, and the "old" 45 strike becomes 44⅛. Since these new strikes are all fractional, they are given special symbols—probably U, V, and W. Thus the "old" symbol UVWDH (UVW April 40) becomes the "new" symbol UVWDV (UVW April 39¼).

After the split, the exchange usually opens for trading new strikes of 35, 40, and 45—each for 100 shares of the underlying stock. For a while, there are 6 striking prices for UVW options. As time passes, the fractional strikes are eliminated as they expire. Since they are not reintroduced, they eventually disappear as long as UVW does not issue further stock dividends.

5. *All options are quoted on a per-share basis,* regardless of how many shares of stock the option involves. Normally the quote assumes 100 shares of the underlying stock. However, in such a case as that of UVW options just described, a quote of 3 for the UVW April 39¼ means a dollar price of $306 ($3 × 102).

6. *Changes in the price of the underlying stock can also* bring about *new striking prices.* XYZ is a $47 stock with striking prices of 45 and 50. If the price of XYZ stock falls to $40, the striking prices of 45 and 50 do not give option traders enough opportunities in XYZ. So the exchange might introduce a new striking price of 40. In practice, a new series is generally opened when the stock trades at the lowest (or highest) existing strike in any series. For example, if XYZ is falling, as soon as it traded at or below 45 —the striking price of 40 may be introduced. The officials of the option

exchange that trades XYZ options make the exact decision as to the day when the new strike begins trading.

### Position Limit and Exercise Limit

7. *An investor or a group of investors cannot be long or short more than* 2,000 *contracts in one stock on the same side of the market.* So, if one were long 2,000 XYZ call options, he cannot at the same time be short *any* XYZ put options. But he can be "on the same side of the market" even with a mixture of puts and calls. Long calls and short puts are on the same side of the market; that is, both are bullish positions. Similarly, long puts and short calls are both on the same side of the market. While these *position limits* generally exceed by far any position that an individual investor normally attains, the limits apply to "related" accounts. For instance, a money manager or investment advisor, who is managing many accounts, cannot exceed the limit when all the accounts' positions are combined.

8. *The number of contracts that can be exercised in a particular period of time is also limited.* This *exercise limit* prevents an investor or group from "cornering" a stock by repeatedly buying 2,000 calls one day and exercising them day after day. *Option exchanges set exact limits, which are subject to change.*

## ORDER ENTRY

### Order Information

Of the various types of orders, each specifies:

1. whether the transaction is a buy or sell,
2. the option to be bought or sold,
3. whether the trade is opening or closing a position,
4. whether the transaction is a spread (discussed later), and
5. the desired price.

### *Types of Orders*

Many types of orders are acceptable for trading options, but not all are acceptable on all exchanges that trade options. Since regulations change, information regarding which order is valid for a given exchange is best supplied by the broker to the customer. The following orders are acceptable on all option exchanges:

*Market Orders.* These are simple orders to buy or sell the option at the best possible price as soon as the order gets to the exchange floor.

*Market Not Held Order.* The customer who uses this type of order is giving the floor broker discretion in executing the order. The floor broker is not held responsible for the final outcome. For example, if a floor broker has a "market not held" order to buy, and he feels that the stock will "downtick" (decline in price) or that there is a surplus of sellers in the crowd, he may often hold off on the execution of the buy order, figuring that the price will decline shortly and that the order can then be executed at a more favorable price. In essence, the customer is giving the floor broker the right to use some judgment regarding the execution of the order. If the floor broker has an opinion and that opinion is correct, the customer will probably receive a better price than if he had used a regular market order. If the opinion used is wrong, however, the price of the execution may be worse than a regular market order.

*Limit Orders.* The limit order is an order to buy or to sell at a specified price—the limit. It may be executed at a better price than the limit—a lower one for buyers and a higher one for sellers. However, if the limit is never reached, the order may never be executed.

Sometimes a limit order may specify a discretionary margin for the floor broker. In other words, the order may read "buy at 5 with ⅛ discretion." This instruction enables the floor broker to execute the order at 5⅛, if he feels that the market will never reach 5. Under no circumstances, however, can the order be executed at a price higher than 5⅛.

Other orders may or may not be accepted on some option exchanges.

*Stop Order.* This order is not always valid on all option exchanges. A stop order becomes a market order when the security trades through the price specified on the order. Buy-stop orders are placed above the current market price, and sell-stop orders are entered below the current market price. Such orders are used to either limit loss or protect a profit. For example, if a holder's option is selling for 3, a sell-stop order for 2 is activated if the market dropped down below the 2 level, whereupon the floor broker would execute the order as soon as possible. The customer, however, is not guaranteed that the trade will be exactly at 2.

*Stop-Limit Order.* This order becomes a limit order when the specified price is reached. Whereas the stop order has to be executed as soon as the stop price is reached, the stop-limit may or may not be filled, depending on market behavior. For instance, if the option is trading at 3 while a stop-limit order is put in for 2, the floor broker may not be able to get a trade exactly at 2. If the option continues to decline through 2—1⅞, 1¾, 1½, and so on—without ever regaining the 2 level, then the broker's hands are tied. He may not execute what is now a limit order unless the call trades at 2.

*Good-until-Canceled Order.* A limit, stop, or stop-limit order may be designated "good until canceled." If the conditions for the order execution do not occur, the order remains valid for 6 months without renewal by the customer.

## PROFITS AND PROFIT GRAPHS

A visual presentation of the profit potential of any position is important to the overall understanding and evaluation of it. In option trading, the many multi-security positions especially warrant strict analysis: stock versus options (as in covered or ratio writing) or options versus options (as in spreads). Some strategists prefer a table listing the outcomes of a particular strategy for the stock at various prices; others feel the strategy is more clearly demonstrated by a graph. In the rest of the text, both a table and a graph will be presented for each new strategy discussed.

*Example:* A customer wishes to evaluate the purchase of a call option. The potential profits or losses of a purchase of an XYZ July 50 call at 4 can be arrayed in either a table or a graph of outcomes at expiration. Both Table 1-5 and Figure 1-5 depict the same information; the graph is merely the line representing the column marked "Profit or Loss" in the table. The vertical axis represents dollars of profit or loss, and the horizontal axis shows the stock price at expiration. In this case, the dollars of profit and the stock price are *at the expiration date*. Often the strategist wants to determine what the potential profits and losses will be before expiration, rather than at the expiration date itself. Tables and graphs lend themselves well to the necessary analysis, as will be seen in detail in various places later on.

**TABLE 1-5.** *Potential profits and losses for an XYZ call purchase.*

| XYZ Price at Expiration | Call Price at Expiration | Profit or Loss |
|---|---|---|
| 40 | $ 0 | −$ 400 |
| 45 | 0 | − 400 |
| 50 | 0 | − 400 |
| 55 | 5 | + 100 |
| 60 | 10 | + 600 |
| 70 | 20 | + 1,600 |

**FIGURE 1-5.** *Graph of potential profits for an XYZ call purchase.*

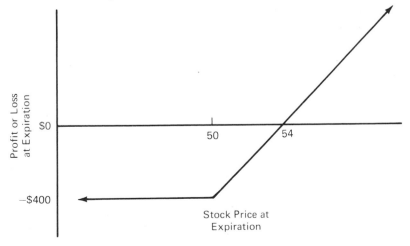

In practice, such an example is too simple to require a table or a graph—certainly not both—to evaluate the potential profits and losses of a simple call purchase held to expiration. However, as more complex strategies are discussed, these tools become ever more useful for quickly determining such things as where a position makes money and where it loses, or how fast one's risk increases at certain stock prices.

# *Call Option* **II**
# *Strategies*

The average person dealing in option trading utilizes primarily one of two option strategies—call buying or covered call writing. These strategies are, at face value, simple, and they are therefore the ones most often tried. There are many more strategies involving the use of call options, many of which will be described later in Part II. However, the next two chapters will deal with these more fundamental call option strategies.

Both covered call writing and call buying *are* relatively simple strategies, but, like any investment, they can be employed with differing levels of skill and complexity. The discussions to follow will begin by describing the basics of each strategy and will then discuss each in depth.

# Covered 2
# Call Writing

## THE IMPORTANCE OF COVERED CALL WRITING

*Covered call writing* is the name given to the strategy by which one sells a call option while simultaneously owning the obligated number of shares of underlying stock. The writer should be mildly bullish, or at least neutral, toward the underlying stock. By writing a call option against stock, one always decreases the risk of owning the stock. It may even be possible to profit from a covered write if the stock declines somewhat. However, the covered call writer does limit his profit potential and therefore may not fully participate in a strong upward move in the price of the underlying stock. Use of this strategy is becoming so common that the strategist must understand it thoroughly. It will therefore be discussed at length.

### Covered Call Writing for Downside Protection

*Example:* An investor owns 100 shares of XYZ common stock, which is currently selling at $48 per share. If this investor sells an XYZ July 50 call option while still holding his stock, he establishes a covered write. Suppose the investor receives $300 from the sale of the July 50 call. If XYZ is below 50 at July expiration, the call option that was sold expires worthless and the investor earns the $300 that he originally received for writing the call. Thus he receives $300, or 3 points, of *downside protection*. That is, he can afford to have the XYZ stock drop by 3 points and still break even on the total transaction. At that time he can write another call option if he so desires.

Note that if the underlying stock should fall by more than 3 points, there will be a loss on the overall position. *Thus, the risk in the covered writing strategy materializes if the stock falls by a distance greater than the call option premium that was originally taken in.*

### The Benefits of an Increase in Stock Price

If XYZ increases in price moderately, he may be able to have the best of both worlds.

*Example:* If XYZ is at or just below 50 at July expiration, the call still expires worthless, and the investor makes the $300 from the option in addition to having a small profit from his stock purchase. Again, he still owns the stock.

Should XYZ increase in price by expiration to levels above 50, the covered writer has a choice of alternatives. As one alternative, he could do nothing, in which case the option would be exercised and his stock would be called away at the striking price of 50. In that case, his profits would be equal to the $300 received from selling the call plus the profit on the increase of his stock from the purchase price of 48 to the sale price of 50. In this case, however, he would no longer own the stock. If as another alternative he desires to retain his stock ownership, he can elect to buy back (or cover) the written call in the open market. This decision might involve taking a loss on the option part of the covered writing transaction, but he would have a correspondingly larger profit, albeit unrealized, from his stock purchase. Using some specific numbers, one can see how this second alternative works out.

*Example:* XYZ rises to a price of 60 by July expiration. The call option then sells near its intrinsic value of 10. If the investor covers the call at 10, he loses $700 on the option portion of his covered write. (Recall that he originally received $300 from the sale of the option, and now he is buying it back for $1,000.) However, he relieves the obligation to sell his stock at 50 (the striking price) by buying back the call, so he has an unrealized gain of 12 points in the stock, which was purchased at 48. His total profit, including both realized and unrealized gains, is $500.

This profit is exactly the same as he would have made if he had let his stock be called from him. If called, he would keep the $300 from the sale of the call, and he would have made 2 points ($200) from buying the stock at 48 and selling it, via exercise, at 50. This profit, again, is a total of $500. The major difference between the two cases is that the investor no longer owns his stock after letting it be called away, whereas he retains stock ownership if he buys back the written call. Which of the two alternatives is the better one in a given situation is not always clear.

No matter how high the stock climbs in price, the profit from a covered write is limited because the writer has obligated himself to sell stock at the striking price. The covered writer still profits when the stock climbs, but possibly not by as much as he might have had he not written the call. On the other hand, he is receiving $300 of immediate cash inflow, because the writer may take the premium immediately and do with it as he pleases. That income can represent a substantial increase in the income currently provided by the dividends on the underlying stock, or it can act to offset part of the loss in case the stock declines.

For readers who prefer formulae, the profit potential and break-even point of a covered write can be summarized as follows:

Maximum profit potential = strike price − stock price + call price

Downside breakeven point = stock price − call price

### Quantification of the Covered Write

Table 2-1 and Figure 2-1 depict the *profit graph* for the example involving the XYZ covered write of the July 50 call. The table makes the assumption that the call is bought back at parity. If the stock is called away, the same total profit of $500 results; but the price involved on the stock sale is always 50, and the option profit is always $300.

Several conclusions can be drawn. The break-even point is 45 (zero total profit) with risk below 45; the maximum profit attainable is $500 if the position is held until expiration; and the *profit if the stock price is unchanged* is $300, that is, the covered writer makes $300 even if his stock goes absolutely nowhere.

The profit graph for a covered write always has the *shape* shown in Figure 2-1. Note that the maximum profit always occurs at all stock prices equal to or greater than the striking price, if the position is held

**TABLE 2-1.** *The XYZ July 50 call.*

| XYZ Price at Expiration | Stock Profit | July 50 Call at Expiration | Call Profit | Total Profit |
|---|---|---|---|---|
| 40 | −$  800 | 0 | +$300 | −$500 |
| 45 | −    300 | 0 | +  300 | 0 |
| 48 | 0 | 0 | +  300 | +  300 |
| 50 | +    200 | 0 | +  300 | +  500 |
| 55 | +    700 | 5 | −  200 | +  500 |
| 60 | +  1,200 | 10 | −  700 | +  500 |

**FIGURE 2-1.** *XYZ covered write.*

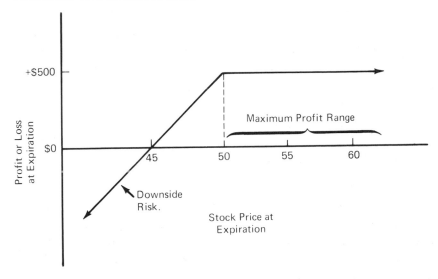

until expiration. However, there is downside risk. If the stock declines in price by too great an amount, the option premium cannot possibly compensate for the entire loss. Downside protective strategies, which will be discussed later, attempt to deal with the limitation of this downside risk.

## COVERED WRITING PHILOSOPHY

The primary objective of covered writing, for most investors, is increased income through stock ownership. An ever-increasing number of private and institutional investors are writing call options against the stocks that they own. The fact that the option premium acts as a partial compensation for a decline in price by the underlying stock, and that the premium represents an increase in income to the stockholder, are evident. *The strategy of owning the stock and writing the call will outperform outright stock ownership if the stock falls, remains the same, or even rises slightly.* In fact, the only time that the outright owner of the stock will outperform a covered writer is if the stock increases in price by a relatively substantial amount during the life of the call. Moreover, if one consistently writes call options against his stock, *his portfolio will show less variability of results from quarter to quarter.* The total position—long stock and short option—has less volatility than the stock alone, so on a quarter-by-quarter basis, results will be closer to average than they would be with normal stock ownership. This is an attractive feature, especially for portfolio managers.

### *Physical Location of the Stock*

Before getting more involved in the details of covered writing strategy, it may be useful to review exactly what stock holdings may be written against. Recall that this discussion applies to listed options. If one has deposited stock with his broker in either a cash or a margin account, he may write an option for each 100 shares that he owns without any additional requirement. However, it is possible to write covered options without actually depositing stock with a brokerage firm. There are several ways in which to do this, all involving the deposit of stock with a bank.

Once the stock is deposited with the bank, the investor may have the bank issue an *escrow receipt* or letter of guarantee to the brokerage firm at which the investor does his option business. The bank must be an "approved" bank in order for the brokerage firm to accept a *letter of guarantee,* and not all firms accept letters of guarantee. These items cost money, and as a new receipt or letter is required for each new option written, the costs may become prohibitive to the customer if only 100 or 200 shares of stock are involved. The cost of an escrow receipt can range from as low as $15 to upwards of $40, depending on the bank involved.

There is another alternative open to the customer who wishes to write options without depositing his stock at the brokerage firm. He may deposit his stock with a bank that is a member of the *Depository Trust Corporation* (DTC). The DTC guarantees the Options Clearing Corporation that it will, in fact, deliver stock should an assignment notice be given to the call writer. This is the most convenient method for the investor to use, and is the one used by most of the institutional covered writing investors. There is usually no additional charge for this service by the bank to institutional accounts. However, since there are only a limited number of banks who are members of DTC, and these banks are generally the larger banks located in metropolitan centers, it may be somewhat difficult for many individual investors to take advantage of the DTC opportunity.

### Types of Covered Writes

While all covered writes involve selling a call against stock that is owned, there are different terms used to describe various categories of covered writing. The two broadest terms, under which all covered writes can be classified, are the *out-of-the-money covered write* and the *in-the-money covered write.* These refer, obviously, to whether the option itself was in-the-money or out-of-the-money when the write was first established. Sometimes one may see covered writes classified by the nature of the stock involved (low-priced covered write, high-yield covered write, etc.), but these are only subcases of the two broad categories.

In general, out-of-the-money covered writes offer higher potential rewards but have less risk protection than do in-the-money covered writes. One can establish an aggressive or defensive covered writing position, depending on how far the call option is in- or out-of-the-money when the write is established. In-the-money writes are more defensive covered writing positions.

Some examples may help to illustrate how one covered write can be considerably more conservative, from a strategy viewpoint, than another.

*Example:* XYZ common stock is selling at 45 and two options are being considered for writing: an XYZ July 40 selling for 8, and an XYZ July 50 selling for 1. Table 2-2 depicts the profitability of utilizing the July 40 or the July 50 for the covered writing. The in-the-money covered write of the July 40 afford 8 points, or nearly 18% protection down to a price of 37 (the break-even point) at expiration. The out-of-the-money covered write of the July 50 offers only 1 point of downside protection at expiration. Hence, *the in-the-money covered write offers greater downside protection than does the out-of-the-money covered write.* This statement is true in general—not merely for this example.

In the balance of the financial world, it is normally true that

**TABLE 2-2.** *Profit or loss of the July 40 and July 50 calls.*

| In-the-Money Write of July 40 | | Out-of-the-Money Write of July 50 | |
|---|---|---|---|
| Stock at Expiration | Total Profit | Stock at Expiration | Total Profit |
| 35 | −$200 | 35 | −$900 |
| 37 | 0 | 40 | − 400 |
| 40 | + 300 | 44 | 0 |
| 45 | + 300 | 45 | + 100 |
| 50 | + 300 | 50 | + 600 |
| 60 | + 300 | 60 | + 600 |

investment positions offering less risk also have lower reward potential. The covered writing example just given is no exception. The in-the-money covered write of the July 40 has a maximum potential profit of $300 at any point above 40 at the time of expiration. However, the out-of-the-money covered write of the July 50 has a maximum potential of $600 at any point above 50 at expiration. *The maximum potential profit of an out-of-the-money covered write is generally greater than that of an in-the-money write.*

To make a true comparison between the two covered writes, one must look at what happens with the stock between 40 and 50 at expiration. The in-the-money write attains its maximum profit anywhere within that range. Even a 5-point *decline* by the underlying stock at expiration would still leave the in-the-money writer with his maximum profit. However, *for the maximum profit potential to be realized with an out-of-the-money covered write always requires a rise in price by the underlying stock.* This further illustrates the more conservative nature of the in-the-money write. It should be noted that in-the-money writes, although having a smaller profit potential, can still be attractive on a percentage return basis, especially if the write is done in a margin account.

One can construct a more aggressive position by writing an out-of-the-money call. One's outlook for the underlying stock should be bullish in that case. If one is neutral or moderately bearish on the stock, an in-the-money covered write is more appropriate. If one is truly bearish on a stock he owns, he should sell the stock instead of establishing a covered write.

# THE TOTAL RETURN CONCEPT OF COVERED WRITING

When one writes an out-of-the-money option, the overall position tends to reflect more of the result of the stock price movement and less of the benefits of writing the call. Since the premium on an out-of-the-money call is relatively small, the total position will be quite susceptible to loss if the stock declines. If the stock rises, the position will make money regardless of the result in the option at expiration. On the other hand, an in-the-money write is more of a "total" position—taking advantage of the benefit of the relatively large option premium. If the stock declines, the position can still make a profit—in fact, it can even make the maximum profit. Of course an in-the-money write will also make money if the stock rises in price, but the profit is not generally as great in percentage terms as is that of an out-of-the-money write.

Those who believe in the *total return concept of covered writing* consider both downside protection and maximum potential return as important factors and are willing to have the stock called away, if necessary, to meet their objectives. When premiums are moderate or small, only in-the-money writes satisfy the total return philosophy.

Some covered writers prefer never to lose their stock through exercise, and as a result will often write options quite far out-of-the-money to minimize the chances of being called by expiration. These writers receive little downside protection and, to make money, must depend almost entirely on the results of the stock itself. Such a philosophy is more like being a stockholder and *trading* options against one's stock position than actually operating a covered writing *strategy*. In fact, some covered writers will attempt to buy back written options for quick profits if such profits materialize during the life of the covered write. This, too, is a stock ownership philosophy, not a covered writing strategy. The total return concept represents the true strategy in covered writing, whereby one views the entire position as a single entity and is not predominantly concerned with the results of his stock ownership.

## The Conservative Covered Write

Covered writing is generally accepted to be a conservative strategy. This is because the covered writer always has less risk than a stockholder, provided that he holds the covered write until expiration of the written call. For, if the underlying stock declines, the covered writer will always offset part of his loss by the amount of the option premium received, no matter how small.

As was demonstrated in previous sections, however, some covered writes are clearly more conservative than others. Not all option writers agree on what is meant by a conservative covered write. Some feel that it involves writing an option (probably out-of-the-money) on a conservative stock, generally one with high yield and low volatility. It *is* true that the stock itself in such a position is conservative, but the position is more aptly termed a *covered write on a conservative stock.* This is distinctly different from a conservative covered write.

A true *conservative covered write* is one in which the *total* position is conservative—offering reduced risk and a good probability of making a profit. An in-the-money write, even on a stock that itself is not conservative, can become a conservative total position when the option itself is properly chosen. Clearly, one cannot write calls that are too deeply in-the-money. If he did, he would get large amounts of downside protection, but his returns would be severely limited. If all that one desired was maximum protection of his money at a nominal rate of profit, he could leave the money in a bank. Instead, the conservative covered writer strives to make a potentially acceptable return while still receiving an above-average amount of protection.

> *Example:* Again assume XYZ common stock is selling at 45 and an XYZ July 40 call is selling at 8. A covered write of the XYZ July 40 would require, in a cash account, an investment of $3,700—$4,500 to purchase 100 shares of XYZ, less the $800 received in option premiums. The write has a maximum profit potential of $300. The potential return from this position is therefore $300/$3,700, just over 8% for the period during which the write must be held. Since this period can be at most 9 months (listed options have a maximum life of 9 months), this return would be well in excess of 10% on a per annum basis. If the write were done in a margin account, the return would be considerably higher.
>
> Note that we have ignored dividends paid by the underlying stock and commission charges, factors that will be discussed in detail in the next section. Also, one should be aware that if he is looking at an *annualized return* from a covered write, there is no guarantee that such a return could actually be obtained. All that is certain is that the writer could make 8% in 9 months. There is no guarantee that 9 months from now, when the call expires, there will be an equivalent position to establish that will extend the same return for the remainder of the annualization period. Annual returns should only be used for comparative purposes between covered writes.

The writer has a position that has an annualized return (for comparative purposes) of over 10% and the position has 8 points of downside protection. Thus the *total position* is an investment that will not lose money unless XYZ common stock falls by more than 8 points, or about 18%, and is an investment that could return the equivalent of 10% annually should XYZ common stock rise, remain the same, or fall by 5 points (to 40). This is a conservative position. Even if XYZ itself is not a conservative stock, the action of writing this option has made the *total position* a conservative one. The only factor that might detract from the conservative nature of the total position would be if XYZ were so volatile that it could easily fall more than 8 points in 9 months.

In a strategic sense, the total position described above is better and more conservative than one in which a writer buys a conservative stock—yielding perhaps 6 or 7%—and writes an out-of-the-money call for a minimal premium. If this conservative stock were to fall in price, the writer would be in danger of being in a loss situation, because here the option is not providing anything more than the most minimal downside protection. As was described earlier, a high-yielding, low-volatility stock will not have much time premium in its in-the-money options, so that one cannot effectively establish an in-the-money write on such a "conservative" stock.

## COMPUTING RETURN ON INVESTMENT

Now that the reader has some general feeling for covered call writing, it is time to discuss the specifics of computing return on investment. One should always know exactly what his potential returns are, including all costs, when he establishes a covered writing position. Once the procedure for computing returns is clear, one can more logically decide which covered writes are the most attractive.

There are three basic elements of a covered write that should be computed before entering into the position. The first is the *return if exercised*. This is the return on investment that one would achieve if the stock were called away. For an out-of-the-money covered write, it is necessary for the stock to rise in price in order for the return if exercised to be achieved. However, for an in-the-money covered write, the return if exercised would be attained even if the stock were unchanged in price at option expiration. Thus it is often advantageous to compute the *return if unchanged*—that is, the return that would be realized if the underlying stock were unchanged when the option expired. One can more fairly compare out-of-the-money and in-the-money covered writes by using the return if unchanged, since no assumption is made concerning stock price movement. The third important statistic that the covered writer should consider is the exact *downside break-even point* after all costs are included. Once this downside break-even point is known, one can readily compute the percentage of *downside protection* that he would receive from selling the call.

*Example 1:* An investor is considering the following covered write of a 6-month call: buy 500 XYZ common at 43, sell 5 XYZ July 45 calls at 3. One must first compute the net investment required (Table 2-3). In a cash account, this investment consists of paying for the stock in full, less the net proceeds from the sale of the options. Note that this net investment figure includes all commissions necessary to establish the position. (The commissions used here are approximations, as they vary from firm to firm.) Of course, if the investor withdraws the option premium, as he is free to do, his net investment will consist of the stock cost plus commissions.

**TABLE 2-3.** *Net investment required—cash account.*

| | |
|---|---|
| Stock cost (500 shares at 43) | $21,500 |
| Plus stock purchase commissions | +    320 |
| Less option premiums received | −  1,500 |
| Plus option sale commissions | +      60 |
| Net cash investment | $20,380 |

Once the necessary investment is known, the writer can compute the return if exercised. Table 2-4 illustrates the computation.

**TABLE 2-4.** *Return if exercised—cash account.*

| | |
|---|---|
| Stock sale proceeds (500 shares at 45) | $22,500 |
| Less stock sale commissions | −    330 |
| Plus dividends earned until expiration | +    500 |
| Less net investment | − 20,380 |
| Net profit if exercised | $ 2,290 |

$$\text{Return if exercised} = \frac{\$2,290}{\$20,389} = 11.2\%$$

One first computes the profit if exercised and then divides that quantity by the net investment to obtain the return if exercised. Note that dividends are included in this computation; it is assumed that XYZ stock will pay $500 in dividends on the 500 shares during the life of the call. Moreover, all commissions are included as well—the net investment includes the original stock purchase and option sale commissions, and the stock sale commission is explicitly listed.

For the return computed above to be realized, XYZ stock would have to rise in price from its current price of 43 to any price above 45 by expiration. As noted earlier, it may be more useful to know what return could be made by the writer if the stock did not move anywhere at all. Table 2-5 illustrates the method of computing the *return if unchanged*—also called the *static return* and sometimes *incorrectly* referred to as the "expected return."

**TABLE 2-5.** *Return if unchanged—cash account.*

| | |
|---|---:|
| Unchanged stock value (500 shares at 43) | $21,500 |
| Plus dividends | + 500 |
| Less net investment | − 20,380 |
| Profit if unchanged | $ 1,620 |

$$\text{Return if unchanged} = \frac{\$1,620}{\$20,380} = 7.9\%$$

Again, one first calculates the profit and then calculates the return by dividing the profit by the net investment. An important point should be made here. There is no stock sale commission included in Table 2-5. This is the most common way of calculating the return if unchanged, and is done this way because in a majority of cases, one would continue to hold the stock if it were unchanged and would write another call option against the same stock. Recall again, though, that *if the written call is in-the-money, the return if unchanged is the same as the return if exercised*—stock sale commissions must therefore be included in that case.

Once the necessary returns have been computed and the writer has a feeling for how much money he could make in the covered write, he next computes the exact *downside break-even point* to determine what kind of *downside protection* the written call provides (Table 2-6). The total return concept of covered writing necessitates viewing both potential income *and* downside protection as important criteria for selecting a writing position. If the stock were held to expiration and the $500 in dividends received, the writer would break even at a price of 39¾ when rounded to the nearest eighth. Most computer printouts will express the break-even price in tenths. Again, a stock sale commission is not generally included in the break-even point computation, because the written call would expire totally worthless and the writer might then

**TABLE 2-6.** *Downside break-even point—cash account.*

| | |
|---|---|
| Net investment | $20,380 |
| Less dividends | − 500 |
| Total stock cost to expiration | $19,880 |
| Divide by shares held | ÷ 500 |
| Break-even price | 39.8 |

write another call on the same stock. Later, we will discuss the subject of continuing to write against stocks already owned. It will be seen that in many cases it is advantageous to continue to hold a stock and write against it again rather than to sell it and establish a covered write in a new stock.

Next, we translate the break-even price into *percent downside protection* (Table 2-7), which is a convenient way of comparing the levels of downside protection among variously priced stocks. We will see later that it is actually better to compare the downside protection with the *volatility* of the underlying stock. However, since percent downside protection is a common and widely accepted method that is more readily calculated, it is necessary to be familiar with it as well.

**TABLE 2-7.** *Percent downside protection—cash account.*

| | |
|---|---|
| Initial stock price | 43 |
| Less break-even price | −39.8 |
| Points of protection | 3.2 |
| Divide by original stock price | ÷43 |
| Equals percent downside protection | 7.4% |

Before moving on to discuss what kinds of returns one should attempt to strive for in which situations, the same example will be worked through again for a covered write in a margin account. The use of margin will provide higher potential returns since the net investment will be smaller. However, the margin interest charge incurred on the debit balance (the amount of money borrowed from the brokerage firm) will cause the break-even point to be higher, thus slightly reducing the amount of downside protection available from writing the call. Again, all commissions to establish the position are included in the net investment computation.

*Example 2:* Recall that the net investment for the cash write was $20,380. A margin covered write requires less than half of the investment of a cash write when the margin rate (set by the Federal Reserve) is 50%. In a margin account, if one desires to remove the premium from the account, he may do so immediately provided that he has enough reserve equity in the account to cover the purchase of the stock. If he does so, his net investment would be equal to the debit balance calculation shown on the right in Table 2-8.

**TABLE 2-8.** *Net investment required—margin account.*

| | | | |
|---|---|---|---|
| Stock cost | $21,500 | | |
| Plus stock commissions | +    320 | Debit balance calculation: | |
| Net stock cost | $21,820 | Net stock cost | $21,820 |
| Times margin rate | ×    50% | Less equity | −  10,910 |
| Equity required | $10,910 | Debit balance | $10,910 |
| Less premiums received | −  1,500 | (at 50% margin) | |
| Plus option commissions | +    60 | | |
| Net margin investment | $ 9,470 | | |

Tables 2-9 to 2-12 illustrate the computation of returns from writing on margin. If one has already computed the cash returns, he can use method 2 most easily. Method 1 involves no prior profit calculations.

**TABLE 2-9.** *Return if exercised—margin account.*

| Method 1 | | Method 2 | |
|---|---|---|---|
| Stock sale proceeds | $22,500 | Net profit if exercised—cash | $2,290 |
| Less stock commissions | −    330 | Less margin interest charges | −   545 |
| Plus dividends | +    500 | Net profit if exercised— | $1,745 |
| Less margin interest charges | | margin | |
| (10% on $10,910 for 6 | | | |
| months) | −    545 | | |
| Less debit balance | −  10,910 | | |
| Less net margin investment | −   9,470 | | |
| Net profit—margin | $1,745 | | |

$$\text{Return if exercised} = \frac{\$1,745}{\$9,470} = 18.4\%$$

The return if exercised is 18.4% for the covered write using margin. In Example 1 the return if exercised for a cash write was computed as 11.2%. Thus the return if exercised from a margin write is considerably higher. In fact, unless a fairly deep in-the-money write is being considered, the return on margin will always be higher than the return from cash. The farther out-of-the-money that the written call is, the bigger the discrepancy between cash and margin returns will be when the return if exercised is computed.

As with the computation for return if exercised for a write on margin, the return if unchanged calculation is similar for cash and margin also. The only difference is the subtraction of the margin interest charges from the profit. The return if unchanged is also higher for a margin write, provided that there is enough option premium to compensate for

**TABLE 2-10.** *Return if unchanged—margin account.*

| Method 1 | | Method 2 | |
|---|---|---|---|
| Unchanged stock value (500 shares at 43) | $21,500 | Profit if unchanged—cash | $1,620 |
| | | Less margin interest charges | − 545 |
| Plus dividends | + 500 | Net profit unchanged— margin | $1,075 |
| Less margin interest charges (10% on $10,910 debit for 6 months | − 545 | | |
| Less debit balance | − 10,910 | | |
| Less net investment (margin) | − 9,470 | | |
| Net profit unchanged— margin | $ 1,075 | | |

$$\text{Return if unchanged} = \frac{\$1,075}{\$9,470} = 11.4\%$$

the margin interest charges. The return if unchanged in the cash example was 7.9% versus 11.4% for the margin write. In general, the farther from the strike in either direction—out-of-the-money or in-the-money—the less return if unchanged on margin will exceed the cash return if unchanged. In fact, for deeply out-of-the-money or deeply in-the-money calls, the return if unchanged will be higher on cash than on margin. Table 2-11 shows that the break-even point on margin, 40⅞, is

**TABLE 2-11.** *Break-even point—margin write.*

| | |
|---|---|
| Net margin investment | $ 9,470 |
| Plus debit balance | + 10,910 |
| Less dividends | − 500 |
| Plus margin interest charges | + 545 |
| Total stock cost to expiration | $20,425 |
| Divide by shares held | ÷ 500 |
| Break-even point—margin | 40.9 |

higher than the break-even point from a cash write, 39¾, because of the margin interest charges. Again, the percent downside protection can be computed as shown in Table 2-12. Obviously, since the break-even

**TABLE 2-12.** *Percent downside protection—margin write.*

| | |
|---|---|
| Initial stock price | 43 |
| Less break-even price—margin | 40.9 |
| Points of protection | 2.1 |
| Divide by original stock price | ÷43 |
| Equals percent downside protection— margin | 4.9% |

point on margin is higher than that on cash, there is less percent downside protection in a margin covered write.

### Compound Interest

The astute reader will have noticed that our computations of margin interest have been overly simplistic; the compounding effect of interest rates has been ignored. That is, since interest charges are normally applied to an account monthly, the investor will be paying interest in the later stages of a covered writing position on not only the original debit, but on all previous monthly interest charges. This effect is described in detail in a later chapter on arbitrage techniques. Briefly stated, rather than computing the interest charge as the debit times the interest rate multiplied by the time to expiration, one should technically use:

$$\textit{Margin interest charges} = \text{debit} \left[ (1 + r)^t - 1 \right]$$

where $r$ is the interest rate per month and $t$ the number of months to expiration (it would be incorrect to use days to expiration since brokerage firms compute interest monthly, not daily).

In Example 2 of the preceding section, the debit was $10,910, the time was 6 months, and the annual interest rate was 10%. Using this more complex formula, the margin interest charges would be $557, as opposed to the $545 charge computed with the simpler formula. Thus the difference is usually small, in terms of percentage, and *it is therefore common practice to use the simpler method.*

### Size of the Position

So far it has been assumed that the writer was purchasing 500 shares of XYZ and selling 5 calls. This requires a relatively considerable investment for one position for the individual investor. However, one should be aware that buying too few shares for covered writing purposes can lower his returns considerably.

*Example:* If an investor were to buy 100 shares of XYZ at 43 and sell 1 July 45 call for 3, his return if exercised would drop from the 11.2% return (cash) that was computed earlier to a return of 9.9% in a cash account. Table 2-13 verifies this statement.

Since commissions are less, on a per-share basis, when one buys

**TABLE 2-13.** *Cash investment vs. return.*

| Net Investment—Cash (100 shares) | | Return if Exercised—Cash (100 shares) | |
|---|---|---|---|
| Stock cost | $4,300 | Stock sale price | $4,500 |
| Plus commissions | 85 | Stock commissions | − 85 |
| Less option premium | − 300 | Plus dividend | + 100 |
| Plus option commissions | + 25 | Less net investment | − 4,110 |
| Net Investment | $4,110 | Net profit if exercised | $ 405 |

$$\text{Return if exercised} = \frac{\$405}{\$4,110} = 9.9\%$$

more stock and sells more calls, the returns will naturally be higher with a 500- or 1,000-share position than with a 100- or 200-share position. This difference can be rather dramatic, as Tables 2-14 and 2-15 point out. Several interesting and worthwhile conclusions can be

**TABLE 2-14.** *Cash covered writes (costs included).*

| | Shares Written Against | | | | | | |
|---|---|---|---|---|---|---|---|
| | 100 | 200 | 300 | 400 | 500 | 1,000 | 2,000 |
| Return if exercised (%) | 9.9 | 10.0 | 10.4 | 10.8 | 11.2 | 12.1 | 12.7 |
| Return if unchanged (%) | 7.1 | 7.2 | 7.5 | 7.7 | 7.9 | 8.4 | 8.7 |
| Break-even point | 40.1 | 40.0 | 39.9 | 39.9 | 39.8 | 39.6 | 39.5 |

**TABLE 2-15.** *Margin covered write (costs included).*

| | Shares Written Against | | | | | | |
|---|---|---|---|---|---|---|---|
| | 100 | 200 | 300 | 400 | 500 | 1,000 | 2,000 |
| Return if exercised (%) | 10.4 | 15.8 | 16.6 | 17.4 | 18.4 | 20.4 | 21.6 |
| Return if unchanged (%) | 4.4 | 9.8 | 10.3 | 10.8 | 11.4 | 12.3 | 13.0 |
| Break-even point | 41.2 | 41.1 | 41.0 | 41.0 | 40.9 | 40.7 | 40.6 |

drawn from these tables. The first and most obvious conclusion is that *the more shares one writes against, the higher his returns and the lower his break-even point will be.* This is true for both cash and margin and is a direct result of the way commissions are figured— larger trades involve smaller *percentage* commission charges. While the percentage returns increase as the number of shares increases for both cash or margin covered writing, the increase is much more dramatic in the case of margin. Note that in the first table, which depicts cash transactions, the return from writing against 100 shares is 9.9% and increases to 12.7% if 2,000 shares are written against. This is an increase, but not a particularly dramatic one. However, in the margin table, the return if exercised more than doubles (21.6 vs. 10.4) and the return if unchanged nearly triples (13.0 vs. 4.4) when the 100-share write is compared to the 2,000-share write. This effect is more dramatic for margin writes due to two factors—the lower investment required and the more burdensome effect of margin interest charges on the profits of smaller positions. This effect is so dramatic that a 100-share write in a cash account in our example actually offers a higher return if unchanged than does the margin write—7.1% vs. 4.4%. This implies that *one should carefully compute his potential returns if he is writing against a small number of shares on margin.*

### What a Difference an Eighth Makes

Another aspect of covered writing that can be important as far as potential returns are concerned is, of course, the prices of the stock and option involved in the write. It may seem insignificant that one has to pay an extra eighth for the stock or possibly receives an eighth or quarter less for the call, but even a relatively small fraction can alter the potential returns by a surprising amount. This is especially true for in-the-money writes, although any write will be affected. Let us use the previous 500-share covered writing example, again including all costs.

As before, the results are more dramatic for the margin write than for the cash write. In neither case does the break-even point change by much. However, the potential returns are altered significantly. Notice that if one pays an extra eighth for the stock and receives an eighth less for the call—the far right-hand column in Table 2-16—he may greatly negate the effect of writing against a larger number of shares. From Tables 2-14 and 2-15, one can see that writing against *300 shares* at those prices (43 for the stock and 3 for the call) is approximately the same return as writing against *500 shares* where the stock costs 43⅛ and the option brings in 2⅞.

**TABLE 2-16.** *Effect of stock and option prices on writing returns.*

|  | Buy stock at 43<br>Sell Call at 3 | Buy Stock at 43⅛<br>Sell Call at 3 | Buy Stock at 43⅛<br>Sell Call at 2⅞ |
|---|---|---|---|
| Return if exercised | 11.2% cash<br>18.4% margin | 10.9% cash<br>17.7% margin | 10.6% cash<br>16.9% margin |
| Return if unchanged | 7.9% cash<br>11.4% margin | 7.6 cash<br>10.7% margin | 7.3% cash<br>9.9% margin |
| Break-even point | 39.8 cash<br>40.9 margin | 39.9 cash<br>41.0 margin | 40.0 cash<br>41.1 margin |

Table 2-16 should clearly demonstrate that entering a covered writing order *at the market* may not be a prudent thing to do, especially if one's calculations for the potential returns are based on last sales or on closing prices in the newspaper. The next section discusses, in depth, the proper procedure for entering a covered writing order.

## EXECUTION OF THE COVERED WRITE ORDER

When establishing a covered writing position, the question often arises: Which should be done first—buy the stock or sell the option? The correct answer is that neither should be done first! In fact, a *simultaneous transaction of buying the stock and selling the option is the only way of assuring that both sides of the covered write are established at desired price levels.*

If one "*legs*" into the position—that is, buys the stock first and then attempts to sell the option, or vice versa—he is subjecting himself to a risk.

> *Example:* An investor wants to buy XYZ at 43 and sell the July 45 call at 3. If he first sells the option at 3 and *then* tries to buy the stock, he may find that he has to pay more than 43 for the stock. On the other hand, if he tries to buy the stock first and *then* sell the option, he may find that the option price has moved down. In either case the writer will be accepting a lower return on his covered write. Table 2-16 demonstrated how one's returns might be affected if he has to give up an eighth by "legging" into the position.

### Establishing a Net Position

What the covered writer really wants to do is ensure that his net price is obtained. If he wants to buy stock at 43 and sell an option at 3, he is attempting to establish the position at 40 *net*. He normally would not mind paying 43⅛ for the stock if he can sell the call at 3⅛, thereby still obtaining 40 net.

A *"net" covered writing order* must be placed with a brokerage firm because it is essential for the person actually executing the order to have full access to both the stock exchange and the option exchange. This is also referred to as a *contingent order*. Most major brokerage firms offer this service to their clients, although some place a minimum number of shares on the order. That is, one must write against at least 500 or 1,000 shares in order to avail himself of the service. There are, however, brokerage firms that will take net orders even for 100-share covered writes. Since the chances of giving away an eighth of a point are relatively great if one attempts to execute his own order by placing separate orders on two exchanges—stock and option—he should avail himself of the broker's service. Moreover, if his orders are for a small number of shares, he should deal with a broker who will take net orders for small positions.

The reader must understand that *there is no guarantee that a net order will be filled.* The net order is always a "not held" order—meaning that the customer is not guaranteed an execution even if it appears that the order could be filled at prevailing market bids and offers. Of course, the broker will attempt to fill the order if it can reasonably be accomplished since that is his livelihood. However, if the net order is slightly away from current market prices, the broker may have to "leg" into the position to fill the order. The risk in this is the broker's responsibility, not the customer's. Therefore, the broker may elect not to take risk and to report "nothing done"—the order is not filled.

If one buys stock at 43 and sells the call at 3, is the return really the same as buying the stock at 43⅛ and selling the call at 3⅛? The answer is, yes, the returns are very similar when the prices differ by small amounts. This can be seen without the use of a table. If one pays an eighth more for the stock, his investment increases by $12.50 per 100 shares, or $62.50 total. However, the fact that he has received an eighth extra for the call means that the investment is reduced by $62.50. Thus there is no effect on the net investment except for commissions. The commission on 500 shares at 43⅛ are slightly higher than the commission for 500 shares at 43. Similarly, the commissions on 5 calls at 3⅛ are slightly higher than those on 5 calls at 3. Even so, these increased commissions would be so small that they would not affect the return by more than one-tenth of 1%. Of course, should the covered write at 40 net be executed with stock at 42⅞ and the call at 2⅞, the net investment will still remain essentially the same, but the commissions will go *down* slightly. Again, the effect is miniscule.

To carry this concept to extremes may prove somewhat misleading. If one were to buy stock at 40½ and sell the call at ½, he would still be receiving 40 net, but several aspects would have changed considerably. The return if exercised remains amazingly constant, but the return if unchanged and the percentage downside protection are reduced dramatically. If one were to buy stock at 48 and sell the call at 8—again for 40 net—he would improve the return if unchanged and the percentage downside protection. In reality, when one places a "net" order with a brokerage firm, he normally gets an execution with prices quite close to the ones at the time the order was first entered. It would be a rare case, indeed, when either upside or downside extremes such as those mentioned here would result in the same trading day.

"*Side-by-side*" *trading* of stock and options has been proposed by the option exchanges: that is, both the options and their underlying stocks would trade in close physical proximity. If this were approved, the covered call writer would benefit. In a side-by-side market, a single net order could be given to *one* exchange and the floor broker on that exchange could then buy stock and sell the call at the stated net price.

## SELECTING A COVERED WRITING POSITION

The preceding sections, in describing types of covered writes and how to compute returns and break-even points, have laid the groundwork for the ultimate decision that every covered writer must make—choosing which stock to buy and which option to write. This is not necessarily an easy task, because there are large numbers of stocks, striking prices, and expiration dates to choose from.

Since the primary objective of covered writing for most investors is increased income through stock ownership, the return on investment is an important consideration in determining which write to choose. However, the decision must not be made on the basis of return alone. More volatile stocks will offer higher returns, but they may also involve more risk because of their ability to fall in price quickly. Thus the amount of downside protection is the other important objective of covered writing. Finally, the quality and technical or fundamental outlook of the underlying stock itself are of importance as well. The following section will help to quantify how these factors should be viewed by the covered writer.

### Projected Returns

The return that one strives for is somewhat a matter of personal preference. In general, *the annualized return if unchanged should be used as the comparative measure between various covered writes.* In using this return as the measuring criterion, one does not make any assumptions about the stock moving up in price in order to attain the potential return. A general rule used in deciding what is a minimally acceptable return is to consider a covered writing position only if the return unchanged is at least 1% per month. That is, a 3-month write would have to offer a return of at least 3% and a 6-month write would have to have a return if unchanged of at least 6%. During periods of expanded option premiums, there may be so many writes that satisfy this criterion that one would want to raise his sights somewhat—say to 1½% and 2% per month. Also, one must feel personally comfortable that his minimum return criterion—whether it be 1% per month or 2% per month—is large enough to compensate for the risks he is taking. That is, the downside risk of owning stock, should it fall far enough to outdistance the premium received, should be adequately compensated for by the potential return. It should be pointed out that 1% per month is not a return to be taken lightly, especially if there is a reasonable assurance that it can be attained. However, if less risky investments, such as bonds, were yielding 12% annually, the covered writer must set his sights higher.

Normally, the returns from various covered writing situations are compared by annualizing the returns. One should not, however, be deluded into believing that he can always attain the projected annual return. A 6-month write that offers a 6% return annualizes to 12%. But if one establishes such a position, all that he can achieve is 6% in 6 months. One does not really know for sure that 6 months from now there will be another position available that will provide 6% over the next 6 months.

The deeper that the written option is in-the-money, the higher the probability that the return if unchanged will actually be attained. In an in-the-money situation, recall that the return if unchanged is the same as the return if exercised. Both would be attained unless the stock fell below the striking price by expiration. Thus, for an in-the-money write, the projected return is attained if the stock rises, remains unchanged, or even falls slightly by the time the option expires. Higher potential returns are available for out-of-the-money writes if the stock rises. However, should the stock remain the same or decline in price, the out-of-the-money write will generally underperform the in-the-money write. This is why the return if unchanged is a good comparison.

### Downside Protection

Downside protection is more difficult to quantify than projected returns are. As mentioned earlier, the percentage of downside protection is often used as a measure. This is somewhat misleading, however, since the more volatile stocks will always offer a large percentage of downside protection (their premiums are higher). The difficulty arises in trying to decide if 10% protection on a volatile stock is better than or worse than, say, 6% protection on a less volatile stock. There are mathematical ways to quantify this, but because of the relatively advanced nature of the computations involved, they will not be discussed until later in the text.

Rather than go into involved mathematical calculations, many covered writers use the percentage of downside protection and will only consider writes that offer a certain minimum level of protection—say 10%. Although this is not exact, it does strive to ensure that one has minimal downside protection in a covered write as well as an acceptable return. A standard figure that is often used is the 10% level of protection. Alternatively, one may also require that the write be a certain percent in-the-money, say 5%. This is just another way of arriving at the same concept.

### The Importance of Strategy

In a conservative option writing strategy, one should be looking for minimum returns if unchanged of 1% per month, with downside protection of at least 10% as general guidelines. Employing such criteria automatically forces one to write in-the-money options, in line with the total return concept. The overall position constructed by using such guidelines as these will be a relatively conservative position—regardless of the volatility of the underlying stock—since the levels of protection will be large but a reasonable return can still be attained. There is a danger, however, in using fixed guidelines because market conditions change. In the early days of listed options, premiums were so large that virtually every at- or in-the-money covered write satisfied the foregoing criteria. However, now one should work with a ranked list of covered writing positions, or perhaps two lists. A daily computer ranking of either or both of the following categories would help establish the most attractive types of conservative covered writes. One list would rank, by annualized return, the writes that afford, as a minimum, the desired downside protection level, say 10%. The other list would rank, by percentage downside protection, all the writes that meet at least the minimum acceptable return if unchanged, say 12%. If premium levels shrink and the lists become quite small on a daily basis, one might consider expanding the criteria to view more potential situations. On the other hand, if premiums expand dramatically, one might consider using more restrictive criteria, to reduce the number of potential writing candidates.

A different group of covered writers may favor a more aggressive strategy of out-of-the-money writes. *There is some mathematical basis to believe, in the long run, that moderately out-of-the-money covered writes will perform better than in-the-money writes.* In falling or static markets, any covered writer—even the more aggressive one—will outperform the stockowner who does not write calls. The out-of-the-money covered writer has more risk in such a market than the in-the-money writer does. But in a rising market, the out-of-the-money covered writer will not limit his returns as much as the in-the-money writer will. As stated earlier, the out-of-the-money writer's performance will more closely follow the performance of the underlying stock—that is, it will be more volatile on a quarter-by-quarter basis.

There is merit in either philosophy. The in-the-money writes appeal to those investors looking to earn a relatively consistent, moderate rate of return. This is the *total return concept.* These investors are generally concerned with preservation of capital, thus striving for the greater levels of downside protection available from in-the-money writes. On the other hand, some investors prefer to strive for higher potential returns through writing out-of-the-money calls. These more aggressive investors are willing to accept more downside risk in their covered writing positions in exchange for the possibility of higher returns should the underlying stock rise in price. These investors will often rely on a bullish research opinion on a stock in order to select out-of-the-money writes.

Although the type of covered writing strategy pursued is a matter of personal philosophy, it would seem that the benefits of in-the-money strategy—more consistent returns and lessened risk than stock ownership will normally provide—would lead the portfolio manager or less aggressive investor toward this strategy. If the investor is interested in achieving higher returns, some of the strategies to be presented later in the book may be able to provide higher returns with less risk than can out-of-the-money covered writing.

The final important consideration in selecting a covered write is the underlying stock itself. One does not necessarily have to be bullish on the underlying stock to take a covered writing position. As long as one does not foresee a potential decline in the underlying stock, he can feel free to establish the covered writing position. It is generally best if one is neutral or slightly bullish on the underlying stock. *If one is bearish, he should not take a covered writing position on that stock,* regardless of the levels of protection that can be obtained. An even broader statement would be that one should not establish a covered write on a stock that he does not want to own. Some individual investors may have qualms about buying stock they feel is too volatile for them. Impartially, if the return and protection are adequate, the characteristics of the total position are different from those of the underlying stock. However, it is still true that one should not invest in positions that he considers too risky for his portfolio—nor should one establish a covered write just because he likes a particular stock. If the potential return if unchanged or levels of downside protection do not meet one's criteria, the write should not be established.

The covered writing *strategist* strives for a balance between acceptable returns and downside protection. He rejects situations that do not meet his criteria in either category and rejects stocks on which he is bearish. The resulting situations will probably fulfill the objectives of a conservative covered writing program—increased income, protection, and less variability of results on a less volatile investment portfolio.

## WRITING AGAINST STOCK ALREADY OWNED

Establishing covered writing positions involves other factors. It is often the case that an investor owns stock that has listed options trading, but feels that the returns from writing are too low in comparison to other covered writes that simultaneously exist in the marketplace. This opinion may be valid, but often arises from the fact that the investor has seen a computer-generated list showing returns on his stock as being low in comparison to similarly priced stocks. One should note that such lists generally assume that stock is bought in order to establish the covered write; the returns are usually not computed and published for writing against stock already held. It may be the case that the commission costs for selling one stock and investing in another may alter the returns so substantially that one would be better off to write against the shares of stock initially held.

*Example:* An investor owns XYZ stock and is comparing it against AAA stock for writing purposes. If AAA is more volatile than XYZ, the current prices might appear as follows:

| Stock | Oct 50 Call |
|---|---|
| XYZ: 50 | 4 |
| AAA: 50 | 6 |

Table 2-17 summarizes the computation of the return if exercised as one might see it listed on a daily or weekly summary of available covered writing returns. Assume that 500 shares are being written against, that XYZ will pay 50 cents per share in dividends while AAA pays none during the life of the call, and that the October 50 is a 6-month call.

**TABLE 2-17.** *Summary of covered writing returns, XYZ and AAA.*

|  | XYZ | AAA |
|---|---|---|
| Buy 500 shares at 50 | $25,000 | $25,000 |
| Plus stock commissions | + 345 | + 345 |
| Less option premiums received | − 2,000 | − 3,000 |
| Plus option sale commissions | + 77 | + 91 |
| Net investment—cash | $23,422 | $22,436 |
| Sell 500 shares at 50 | $25,000 | $25,000 |
| Less stock sale commissions | − 345 | − 345 |
| Dividend received | + 250 | 0 |
| Less net investment | − 23,422 | − 22,436 |
| Net profit | $ 1,483 | $ 2,219 |
| Return if exercised—cash | 6.3% | 9.9% |

Without going into as much detail, the other significant aspects of these two writes are:

|  | XYZ | AAA |
|---|---|---|
| Return if exercised—margin | 7.9% | 16.2% |
| Downside break-even point—cash | 46.3 | 44.9 |
| Downside break-even point—margin | 47.6 | 46.1 |

Seeing these calculations, the XYZ stockholder may feel that it is not advisable to write against his stock, or he may even be tempted to sell XYZ and buy AAA in order to establish a covered write. Either of these actions could be a mistake.

First, he should compute what his returns would be, at current prices, from writing against the XYZ *he already owns.* Since the stock is already held, no stock buy commissions would be involved. This would reduce the net investment shown above by the stock purchase commissions, or $345, giving a total net investment (cash) of $23,077. In theory, the stockholder does not really make an investment per se— after all, he already owns the stock. However, for the purposes of computing returns, an investment figure is necessary. This reduction in the net investment will then increase his profit by the same amount— $345—thus bringing the profit up to $1,828. Consequently, the return if exercised (cash) would be 7.9% on XYZ stock already held. On margin, the return would increase to 11.3% after eliminating purchase commissions. This return, assumed to be for a 6-month period, is well in excess of 1% per month—the level nominally used for acceptable covered writes. Thus the investor who already owns stock may inadvertently be overlooking a potentially attractive covered write because he has not computed the returns excluding the stock purchase commission on his current stock holding.

It could conceivably be an even more extreme oversight for the investor to switch from XYZ to AAA for writing purposes. The investor may consider making this switch because he thinks that he could substantially increase his return from 6.3% to 9.9% for the 6-month period, as shown in Table 2-17 comparing the two writes.

However, returns are not truly comparable because the investor already owns XYZ. To make the switch, he would first have to spend $345 in stock commissions to sell his XYZ—thereby reducing his profits on AAA by $345. Referring again to the preceding detailed breakdown of the return if exercised, the profit on AAA would then decline to $1,874 on the investment of $22,436, a return if exercised (cash) of 8.4%. On margin, the comparable return from switching stocks would drop to 14.8%.

The real comparison in returns from writing against these two stocks should be made in the following manner. The return from writing against XYZ *that is already held* should be compared with the return from writing AAA *after switching from XYZ*:

|  | XYZ Already Held | Switch from XYZ to AAA |
|---|---|---|
| Return if exercised—cash | 7.9% | 8.4% |
| Return if exercised—margin | 11.3% | 14.8% |

Each investor must decide for himself whether it is worth this much *smaller increase* in return to switch to a more volatile stock that pays a smaller dividend. He can, of course, only make this decision by making the true comparison shown immediately above as opposed to the first comparison, which assumed that both stocks had to be purchased in order to establish the covered write.

The same logic applies in situations where an investor has *been* doing covered writing. If he owns stock on which an option has expired, he will have to decide whether to write against the same stock again or to sell that stock and buy a new stock for covered writing purposes. Generally, the investor should write against the stock already held. This justifies the method of computation of return if unchanged for out-of-the-money writes and also the computation of downside break-even points in which a stock sale commission was not charged. That is, the writer would not normally sell his stock after an option has expired worthless, but would instead write another option against the same stock. It is thus acceptable to make these computations without including a stock sales commission.

### A Word of Caution

The stockholder who owns stock from a previous purchase and later contemplates writing calls against that stock must be aware of his sitution. He must realize and accept the fact that he might lose his stock via assignment. If he is determined to retain ownership of the stock, he may have to buy back the written option at a loss should the underlying stock increase in price. In essence, he is limiting the stock's upside potential. If a stockholder is going to be frustrated and disappointed when he is not fully participating during a rally in his stock, he should not write a call in the first place. Perhaps he could utilize the incremental return concept of covered writing—a topic to be covered later in this chapter.

As stressed earlier, a covered writing strategy involves viewing the stock and option as a *total* position—*it is not a strategy wherein the investor is a stockholder who also trades options against his stock position.* If the stockholder is selling the calls because he thinks the stock is going to decline in price and the call trade itself will be profitable, he may be putting himself in a tenuous position. Thinking this way, he will probably only be satisfied if he makes a profit on the call trade, regardless of the unrealized result in the underlying stock. This sort of philosophy is contrary to a covered writing strategy philosophy. Such an investor—he is really becoming a trader—should carefully review his motives for writing the call and anticipate his reaction if the stock rises substantially in price after the call has been written.

## DIVERSIFYING RETURN AND PROTECTION IN A COVERED WRITE

### Fundamental Diversification Techniques

Quite clearly, the covered writing strategist would like to have as much of a combination of high potential returns and adequate downside protection as he can obtain. Writing an out-of-the-money call will offer higher returns if exercised, but it usually affords only a modest amount of downside protection. On the other hand, writing an in-the-money call will provide more downside cushion but offers a lower return if exercised. For some strategists, this diversification is realized in practice by writing out-of-the-money calls on some stocks and in-the-moneys on other stocks. There is no guarantee that writing in this manner on a list of diversified stocks will produce superior results— one is still forced to pick the stocks that he expects will perform better (for out-of-the-money writing) and that is difficult to do. Moreover, the individual investor may not have enough funds available to diversify into many such situations. There is, however, another alternative to obtaining diversification of both returns and downside protection in a covered writing situation.

*The writer may often do best by writing half of his position against in-the-moneys and half against out-of-the-moneys on the same stock.* This is especially attractive for a stock whose out-of-the-money calls do not appear to provide enough downside protection, and at the same time, the in-the-money calls do not provide quite enough return. By writing *both* options, the writer may be able to acquire the return and protection diversification that he is seeking.

**TABLE 2-18.** *Attributes of various writes.*

|  | *In-the-Money Write* | *Out-of-the-Money Write* | *Write Both Calls* |
|---|---|---|---|
| Buy 1,000 XYZ and sell | 10 April 40's | 10 April 45's | 5 April 40's and 5 April 45's |
| Return if exercised | 5.1% | 12.2% | 8.4% |
| Return if unchanged | 5.1% | 6.0% | 5.4% |
| Percent protection | 10.5% | 5.7% | 8.1% |

*Example:* The following prices exist for 6-month calls:

    XYZ common stock, 42;

    XYZ April 40 call, 4; and

    XYZ April 45 call, 2.

The writer wishing to establish a covered write against XYZ common stock may like the protection afforded by the April 40 call, but may not find the return particularly attractive. He may be able to improve his return by writing April 45's against part of his position. Assume the writer is considering buying 1,000 shares of XYZ. Table 2-18 compares the attributes of writing the out-of-the-money (April 40) only, or of writing only the in-the-money (April 45), or of writing 5 of each. The table is based on a cash covered write, but returns and protection would be similar for a margin write. Commissions are included in the figures.

It is easily seen that the *"combined" write*—half of the position against the April 40's and the other half against the April 45's—offers the best balance of return and protection. The in-the-money call, by itself, provides over 10% downside protection, but the 5% return if exercised is less than 1% per month. Thus one might not want to write April 40's against his entire position because the potential return is small. At the same time, the April 45's, if written against the entire stock position, would provide for an attractive return if exercised (over 2% per month) but offer only 5% downside protection. The combined write, which has the better features of both options, offers over 8% return if exercised (1⅓% per month) and affords over 8% downside protection. By writing both calls, the writer has potentially solved the problems inherent in writing entirely out-of-the-moneys or entirely in-the-moneys. The "combined" write frees the covered writer from having to initially take a bearish (in-the-money write) or bullish (out-of-the-money write) posture on the stock if he does not want to. This is often necessary on a low-volatility stock trading between striking prices.

**FIGURE 2-2.** *Comparison: combined write vs. in-the-money write and out-of-the-money write.*

For those who prefer a graphic representation, the profit graph shown in Figure 2.2 compares the combined write of both calls with either the in-the-money write or the out-of-the-money write (dashed lines). It can be observed that all three choices are equal if XYZ is near 42 at expiration—all three lines intersect there.

Since this technique can be useful in providing diversifications between protection and return, not only for an individual position but for a large part of a portfolio, it may be useful to see how to exactly compute the potential returns and break-even points. Tables 2-19 and 2-20 calculate the return if exercised and the return if unchanged using the prices from the previous example. Assume XYZ will pay $1 per share in dividends before April expiration.

**TABLE 2-19.** *Net investment—cash account.*

| | |
|---|---|
| Buy 1,000 XYZ at 42 | $42,000 |
| Plus stock commissions | +     460 |
| Less options premiums: | |
|    Sell 5 April 40's at 4 | −   2,000 |
|    Sell 5 April 45's at 2 | −   1,000 |
| Plus total option commissions | +     140 |
| Net investment | $39,600 |

**TABLE 2-20.** *Net return—cash account.*

| *Return if Exercised* | | *Return if Unchanged* | |
|---|---|---|---|
| Sell 500 XYZ at 45 | $22,500 | Unchanged stock value | |
| | | (500 shares at 42) | $21,000 |
| Sell 500 XYZ at 40 | 20,000 | Sell 500 at 40 | + 20,000 |
| Less total stock sale | | | |
|   commissions | −     560 | Commissions on sale at 40 | −     280 |
| Plus dividends ($1/share) | +   1,000 | Plus dividends ($1/share) | +   1,000 |
| Less net investment | − 39,600 | Less net investment | − 39,600 |
| Net profit if exercised | $ 3,340 | Net profit if unchanged | $ 2,120 |

$$\text{Return if exercised (cash)} = \frac{3,340}{39,600} = 8.4\% \qquad \text{Return if unchanged (cash)} = \frac{2,120}{39,600} = 5.4\%$$

     Note that the profit calculations are similar to those described in earlier sections, except that now there are two prices for stock sales since there are two options involved. In the "return if exercised" section, half of the stock is sold at 45 and half is sold at 40. The "return if unchanged" calculation is somewhat more complicated now because half of the stock will be called away if it remains unchanged (the in-the-money portion) whereas the other half will not. Stock sale commissions are included only for the stock called away. This is consistent with the method of calculating the return if unchanged that was introduced previously.

     The break-even point is calculated as before. The "total stock cost to expiration" would be the net investment of $39,600 less the $1,000 received in dividends. This is a total of $38,600. On a per-share basis, then, the break-even point of 38.6 is 8.1% below the current stock price of 42, and this is thus the amount of percentage downside protection.

The foregoing calculations clearly demonstrate that the returns on the "combined" write are *not* exactly the averages of the in-the-money and out-of-the-money returns, because of the different commission calculations at various stock prices. However, if one is working with a computer-generated list and does not want to bother to calculate exactly the return on the combined write, he can arrive at a relatively close approximation by averaging the returns for the in-the-money write and the out-of-the-money write.

### *Other Diversification Techniques*

Holders of large positions in a particular stock may want even more diversification than can be provided by writing against two different striking prices. Institutions, pension funds, and large individual stockholders may fall into this category. It is often advisable for such large stockholders to *diversify* their writing *over time* as well as over at least two striking prices. By diversifying over time—for example, writing one-third of the position against near-term calls, writing one-third against the middle-term calls, and the remaining third against long-term calls—one can gain several benefits. First, all of one's positions need not be adjusted at the same time. This includes either having the stock called away, or buying back one written call and selling another. Moreover, one is not subject to the level of option premiums that exist only at the time one series of calls expire. For example, if one only writes 9-month calls and then rolls them over when they expire, he may unnecessarily be subjecting himself to the potential of lower returns. If option premium levels happen to be low when it is time for this 9-month call writer to sell more calls, he will be establishing a less-than-optimum write for up to 9 months. By spreading his writing out over time, he would, at worst, be subjecting only one-third of his holding to the low-premium write. Hopefully, premiums would expand before the next expiration 3 months later, and he would then be getting a relatively better premium on the next third of his portfolio. There is an important aside here. The individual or relatively small investor who only owns enough stock to write one series of options should generally not write the longest-term calls for this very reason. He may not be obtaining a particularly attractive level of premiums but may feel he is forced to retain the position until expiration. Thus he could be in a relatively poor write for as long as 9 months. Finally, this type of diversification may also lead to having calls at various striking prices as the market fluctuates cyclically. All of one's stock is not necessarily committed at one price if this diversification technique is employed.

This concludes the discussion of how to establish a covered writing position against stock. Covered writes against other types of securities will be described later.

## FOLLOW-UP ACTION

Establishing a covered write—or any option position for that matter—is only part of the strategist's job. Once the position has been taken, it must be monitored closely so that adjustments may be made should the stock drop too far in price. Moreover, even if the stock remains relatively unchanged, adjustments will need to be made as the written call approaches expiration.

Some writers take no follow-up action at all, preferring to let a stock be called away if it rises above the striking price at the expiration of the option, or preferring to let the original expire worthless if the stock is below the strike. These are not always optimum actions; there may be much more decision making involved.

Follow-up action can be divided into three general categories:

1. protective action to take if the stock drops,
2. aggressive action to take when the stock rises, or
3. action to avoid assignment if the time premium disappears from an in-the-money call.

There may be times when one decides to close the entire position before expiration or to let the stock be called away. These cases will be discussed as well.

### Protective Action If the Underlying Stock Declines in Price

The covered writer who does not take protective action in the face of a relatively substantial drop in price by the underlying stock may be risking the possibility of large losses. Since covered writing is a strategy with limited profit potential, one should also take care to limit losses. Otherwise, one losing position can negate several winning positions. The simplest form of follow-up action in a decline is to merely close out the position. This might be done if the stock declines by a certain percentage, or if the stock falls below a technical support level. Unfortunately, this method of defensive action may prove to be an inferior one. The investor will often do better to continue to sell more time value in the form of additional option premiums.

Follow-up action is generally taken by buying back the call that was originally written and then writing another call—with a different striking price and/or expiration date—in its place. Any adjustment of this sort is referred to as a *"rolling" action.* When the underlying stock drops in price, one generally buys back the original call—presumably at a profit since the underlying stock has declined—and then sells a call with a *lower* striking price. This is known as *rolling down*, since the new option has a lower striking price.

> *Example:* The covered writing position described as "buy XYZ at 51, sell the XYZ January 50 call at 6" would have a maximum profit potential at expiration of 5 points. Downside protection is 6 points down to a stock price of 45 at expiration. These figures do not include commissions, but for the purposes of an elementary example the commissions will be ignored.
>
> If the stock begins to decline in price, taking perhaps two months to fall to 45, the following option prices might exist:
>
> XYZ common, 45;
>
> XYZ January 50 call, 1; and
>
> XYZ January 45 call, 4.

The covered writer of the January 50 would, at this time, have a small unrealized loss of one point in his overall position—his loss on the common stock is 6 points, but he has a 5-point gain in the January 50 call (this demonstrates that *prior to expiration*, a loss occurs at the "break-even" point). If the stock should continue to fall from these levels, he could have a larger loss at expiration. The call, selling for one point, only affords one more point of downside protection. If a further stock price drop is anticipated, *additional downside protection can be obtained by rolling down.* In this example, if one were to buy back the January 50 call at 1 and sell the January 45 at 4, he would be rolling down. This would increase his protection by another three points—the credit generated by buying the 50 call at 1 and selling the 45 call at 4. Hence, his downside break-even point would be 42 after rolling down.

Moreover, if the stock were to remain unchanged—that is, if XYZ were exactly 45 at January expiration—the writer would make an *additional* $300. If he had not rolled down, the most *additional* income that he could make, if XYZ remained unchanged, would be the remaining $100 from the January 50 call. So *rolling down gives more downside protection against a further drop in stock price and may also produce additional income if the stock price stabilizes.*

In order to more exactly evaluate the overall effect that was obtained by rolling down in this example, one can either compute a profit table (Table 2-21) or draw a net profit graph (Figure 2-3) that compares the original covered write with the rolled-down position.

**TABLE 2-21.** *Profit table.*

| XYZ Price at Expiration | Profit from January 50 Write | Profit from Rolled Position |
|---|---|---|
| 40 | −$500 | −$200 |
| 42 | − 300 | 0 |
| 45 | 0 | + 300 |
| 48 | + 300 | + 300 |
| 50 | + 500 | + 300 |
| 60 | + 500 | + 300 |

**FIGURE 2-3.** *Comparison: original covered write vs. rolled-down write.*

Note that the rolled-down position has a smaller maximum profit potential than the original position did. This is because, by rolling down to a January 45 call, the writer limits his profits anywhere above 45 at expiration. He has committed himself to sell stock 5 points lower than the original position, which utilized a January 50 call and thus had limited profits above 50. *Rolling down generally reduces the*

*maximum profit potential of the covered write.* Limiting the maximum profit may be a secondary consideration, however, when a stock is breaking downward. Additional downside protection is often a more pressing criterion in that case.

Anywhere below 45 at expiration, the rolled-down position does $300 better than the original position, because of the $300 credit generated from rolling down. In fact, the rolled-down position will outperform the original position even if the stock rallies back to, but not above, a price of 48. At 48 at expiration, the two positions are equal, both producing a $300 profit. If the stock should reverse direction and rally back above 48 by expiration, the writer would have been better off not to have rolled down. All these facts are clear from Table 2-21 and Figure 2-3.

Consequently, the only case in which it does *not* pay to roll down is the one in which the stock experiences a reversal—a rise in price after the initial drop. The selection of where to roll down is important because rolling down too early or at an inappropriate price could limit the returns. Technical support levels of the stock are often useful in selecting prices at which to roll down. If one rolls down after technical support has been broken, the chances of being caught in a stock-price-reversal situation would normally be reduced.

The above example is rather simplistic; in actual practice, more complicated situations may arise, such as a sudden and fairly steep decline in price by the underlying stock. This may present the writer with what is called a *"locked-in-loss."* This means, simply, that there is no option to which the writer can roll down that will provide him with enough premium to realize any profit if the stock were then called away at expiration. These situations arise more commonly on lower-priced stocks, where the striking prices are relatively far apart in percentage terms. Out-of-the-money writes are more susceptible to this problem than are in-the-money writes. Although it is not emotionally satisfying to be in an investment position that cannot produce a profit—at least for a limited period of time—it may still be beneficial to roll down to protect as much of the stock price decline as is possible.

*Example:* For the covered write described as "buy XYZ at 20, sell the January 20 call at 2," the stock unexpectedly drops very quickly to 16, and the following prices exist:

XYZ common, 16;

XYZ January 20 call, ½; and

XYZ January 15 call, 2½.

The covered writer is faced with a difficult choice. He currently has an unrealized loss of 2½ points—a 4-point loss on the stock which is partially offset by a 1½-point gain on the January 20 call. This represents a fairly substantial percentage loss on his investment in a short period of time. He could do nothing, hoping for the stock to recover its loss. Unfortunately, this may prove to be wishful thinking.

If he considers rolling down, he will not be excited by what he sees. Suppose that the writer wants to roll down from the January 20 to the January 15. He would thus buy the January 20 at ½ and sell the January 15 at 2½, for a net credit of 2 points. By rolling down, he is obligating himself to sell his stock at 15—the striking price of the January 15 call. Suppose XYZ were above 15 in January and were called away. How would the writer do? He would lose 5 points on his stock, since he originally bought it at 20 and is selling it at 15. This 5-point loss is substantially offset by his option profits, which amount to 4 points: 1½ points of profit on the January 20—sold at 2 and bought back at ½—plus the 2½ points received from the sale of the January 15. However, his net result is a 1-point loss, since he lost 5 points on the stock and only made 4 points on the options. Moreover, this 1-point loss is the best that he can hope for! This is true because, as has been demonstrated several times, a covered writing position makes its maximum profit anywhere above the striking price. Thus, by rolling down to the 15 strike, he has limited the position severely, to the extent of "locking in a loss."

Even considering what has been shown about this loss, *it is still correct for this writer to roll down to the January 15.* Once the stock has fallen to 16, there is nothing anybody can do about the unrealized losses. However, if the writer rolls down, he *can* prevent the losses from accumulating at a faster rate. In fact, he will do better by rolling down if the stock drops further, remains unchanged, or even rises slightly. Table 2-22 and Figure 2-4 compare the original write with the rolled-down position. It is clear from the figure that the rolled-down position is locked into a loss. However, the rolled-down position still outperforms the original position unless the stock rallies back above 17 by expiration. Thus, if the stock continues to fall, if it remains unchanged, or

**TABLE 2-22.** *Profits of original write and rolled position.*

| Stock Price at Expiration | Profit from January 20 Write | Profit from Rolled Position |
|:---:|:---:|:---:|
| 10 | −$800 | −$600 |
| 15 | − 300 | − 100 |
| 18 | 0 | − 100 |
| 20 | + 200 | − 100 |
| 25 | + 200 | − 100 |

FIGURE 2-4. *Comparison: original write vs. "locked in loss".*

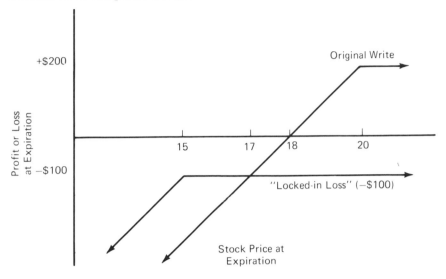

even if it rallies less than 1 point, the rolled-down position actually outperforms the original write. It is for this reason that the writer is taking the most logical action by rolling down, even though to do so locks in a loss.

Technical analysis may be able to provide a little help for the writer faced with the dilemma of rolling down to lock in a loss or else holding onto a position that has no further downside protection. If XYZ has broken a support level or important trend line, it is added evidence for rolling down. In our example, it is difficult to imagine the case where a $20 stock suddenly drops to become a $16 stock without substantial harm to its technical picture. Nevertheless, if the charts should show that there is support at 15½ or 16, it may be worth the writer's while to wait and see if that support level can hold before rolling down.

Perhaps the best way to avoid having to lock in losses would be to establish positions that are less likely to become such a problem. In-the-money covered writes on higher-priced stocks that have a moderate amount of volatility will rarely force the writer to lock in a loss by rolling down. Of course, any stock, should it fall far enough and fast enough, could force the writer to lock in a loss if he has to roll down two or three times in a fairly short time span. However, the higher-priced stock has striking prices that are much closer together (in percentages) and thus presents the writer with the opportunity to utilize a new option with a lower striking price much sooner in the decline of the stock. Also, higher volatility should help in generating large enough premiums that substantial portions of the stock's decline can be hedged by rolling down. Conversely, low-priced stocks, especially nonvolatile ones, often present the most severe problems for the covered writer when they decline in price.

A related point concerning order entry can be inserted here. When one simultaneously buys one call and sells another, he is executing a *spread*. Spreads, in general, will be discussed at length later. However, the covered writer should be aware that whenever he rolls his position, the order can be placed as a spread order. This will normally help the writer to obtain a better price execution.

### An Alternative Method of Rolling Down

There is another alternative that the covered writer can use to attempt to gain some additional downside protection without necessarily having to lock in a loss. Basically, the writer only rolls down part of his covered writing position.

*Example:* One thousand shares of XYZ were bought at 20 and 10 January 20 calls were sold at 2 points each. As before, the stock falls to 16, with the following prices: XYZ January 20 call, ½; and XYZ January 15 call, 2½. As was demonstrated in the last section, if the writer were to roll all 10 calls down from the January 20 to the January 15, he would be locking in a loss. Although there may be some justification for this action, the writer would naturally rather not have to place himself in such a position.

One can attempt to achieve some balance between added downside protection and upward profit potential by only rolling down part of the calls. In this example, the writer would buy back only 5 of the January 20's and sell 5 January 15 calls. He would then have this position:

long 1,000 XYZ at 20;

short 5 XYZ January 20's at 2;

short 5 XYZ January 15's at 2½; and

realized gain, $750 from 5 January 20's.

This strategy is generally referred to as a *partial roll-down*, in which only a portion of the original calls are rolled, as opposed to the more conventional complete roll-down. By analyzing the partially rolled position, it will be clear that the writer no longer locks in a loss.

If XYZ rallies back above 20, the writer would, at expiration, sell 500 XYZ at 20 (breaking even) and 500 at 15 losing $2,500 on this portion). He would make $1,000 from the five January 20's held until expiration, plus $1,250 from the five January 15's, plus the $750 of realized gain from the January 20's that were rolled down. This amounts to $3,000 worth of option profits and $2,500 worth of stock losses, or an overall net gain of $500, less commissions. Thus, the partial roll-down offers the writer a chance to make *some* profit if the stock rebounds. Obviously, the partial roll-down will not provide as much downside protection as the complete roll-down does, but it does give more protection than not rolling down at all. To see this, compare the results given in Table 2-23 if XYZ is at 15 at expiration.

**TABLE 2-23.** *Stock at 15 at expiration.*

| Strategy | Stock Loss | Option Profit | Total Loss |
|---|---|---|---|
| Original position | −$5,000 | +$2,000 | −$3,000 |
| Partial roll-down | − 5,000 | + 3,000 | − 2,000 |
| Complete roll-down | − 5,000 | + 4,000 | − 1,000 |

In summary, the covered writer who would like to roll down, but who does not want to lock in a loss or who feels the stock may rebound somewhat before expiration, should consider rolling down only part of his position. If the stock should continue to drop—making it evident that there is little hope of a strong rebound back to the original strike—the rest of the position can then be rolled down as well.

### *Utilizing Different Expiration Series When Rolling Down*

In the examples thus far, the same expiration month has been used whenever rolling-down action was taken. In actual practice, the writer may often want to use a more distant expiration month when rolling down and, in some cases, he may even want to use a nearer expiration month.

The advantage of rolling down into a more distant expiration series is that more actual points of protection are received. This is a common action to take when the underlying stock has become somewhat worrisome on a technical or fundamental basis. However, since rolling down reduces the maximum profit potential—a fact that has been demonstrated several times—every roll-down should not be made to a more distant expiration series. By utilizing a longer-term call when rolling down, one is reducing his maximum profit potential for a longer period of time. Thus the longer-term call should be used only if the writer has grown concerned over the stock's capability to hold current price levels. The partial-roll-down strategy is particularly amenable to rolling down to a longer-term call since, by rolling down only part of the position, one has already left the door open for profits if the stock should rebound. Therefore, he can feel free to avail himself of the maximum protection possible in the part of his position that is rolled down.

The writer who must roll down to lock in a loss, possibly because of circumstances beyond his control, such as a sudden fall in the price of the underlying stock, may actually want to roll down to a *near-term* option. This allows him to make back the available time premium in the short-term call in the least time possible.

*Example:* A writer buys XYZ at 19 and sells a 6-month call for 2 points. Shortly thereafter, however, bad news appears concerning the common stock and XYZ falls quickly to 14. At that time, the following prices exist for the calls with the striking price 15:

XYZ common, 14;

near-term call, 1;

middle-term call, 1½; and

far-term call, 2.

If the writer rolls down into any of these three calls, he will be locking in a loss. Therefore, the best strategy may be to roll down into the near-term call, planning to capture one point of time premium in 3 months. In this way, he will be beginning to work himself out of the loss situation by availing himself of the most potential time premium decay in the shortest period of time. When the near-term call expires—3 months from now—he can reassess the situation to see if he wants to write another near-term call to continue taking in short-term premiums or perhaps write a long-term call at that time.

When rolling down into the near-term call, one is attempting to return to a potentially profitable situation in the shortest period of time. By writing short-term calls one or two times, the writer will eventually be able to reduce his stock cost nearer to 15 in the shortest time period. Once his stock cost approaches 15, he can then write a long-term call with striking price 15 and return again to a potentially profitable situation—he will no longer be locked into a loss.

### Action to Take If the Stock Rises

A more pleasant situation for the covered writer to encounter is the one in which the underlying stock rises in price after the covered writing position has been established. There are generally several choices available if this happens. The writer may decide to do nothing and to let his stock be called away, thereby making the return that he had hoped for when he established the position. On the other hand, if the underlying stock rises fairly quickly and the written call comes to parity, the writer may either close the position early or roll the call up. Each case will be discussed.

**TABLE 2-24.** *Comparison of original and current prices.*

| Original Position | Current Prices | |
|---|---|---|
| Buy XYZ at 50 | XYZ common | 60 |
| Sell XYZ July 50 call at 6 | XYZ July 50 | 11 |
| | XYZ July 60 | 7 |

*Example:* Someone establishes a covered writing position by buying a stock at 50 and selling a 6-month call for 6 points. His maximum profit potential is 6 points anywhere above 50 at expiration, and his downside break-even point is 44. Furthermore, suppose that the stock experiences a substantial rally and that it climbs to a price of 60 in a short period of time. With the stock at 60, the July 50 might be selling for 11 points and a July 60 might sell for as much as 7 points. Thus, the writer may consider buying back the call that was originally written and rolling up to the call with a higher striking price. Table 2-24 summarizes the situation.

If the writer were to *roll up*—that is, buy back the July 50 and sell the July 60—he would be increasing his profit potential. For, if XYZ were above 60 in July and were called away, he would make his option credits—6 points from the July 50 plus 7 points from the July 60—less the 11 points he paid to buy back the July 50. Thus his option profits would amount to 2 points, which, added to the stock profit of 10 points, increases his maximum profit potential to 12 points anywhere above 60 at July expiration.

To increase his profit potential by such a large amount, the covered writer has given up some of his downside protection. *The downside break-even point is always raised by the amount of the debit requied to roll up.* The debit required to roll up in this example is 4 points—buy the July 50 at 11 and sell the July 60 at 7. Thus the break-even point is increased from the original 44 level to 48 after rolling up. There is another method of calculating the new profit potential and break-even point. In essence, the writer has raised his net stock cost to 55 by taking the realized 5-point loss on the July 50 call. Hence he is essentially in a covered write where he has bought stock at 55 and has sold a July 60 call for 7. When expressed in this manner, it may be easier to see that the break-even point is 48 and the maximum profit potential, above 60, is 12 points.

Note that *when one rolls up, there is a debit incurred.* That is, the investor must deposit additional cash into the covered writing position. This was not the case in rolling down, where credits were generated. Debits are considered by many investors to be a seriously negative aspect of rolling up, and they therefore prefer never to roll up for debits. Although the debit required to roll up may not be a negative aspect to every investor, it does translate directly into the fact that the break-even point is raised and the writer is subjecting himself to a potential loss if the stock should pull back. It is often advantageous to roll to a more distant expiration when rolling up. This will reduce the debit required.

The rolled-up position has a break-even point of 48. Thus, if XYZ falls back to 48, the writer who rolled up will be left with no profit. However, if he had not rolled up, he would have made 4 points with XYZ at 48 at expiration in the original position. A further comparison can be made between the original position and the rolled-up position. The two are equal at July expiration at a stock price of 54—both have a profit of 6 points with XYZ at 54 at July expiration. Thus, although it may appear attractive to roll up, one should determine the point where the rolled-up position and the original position will be equal at expiration. If the writer believes XYZ could be subject to a 10% correction by expiration from 60 to 54—certainly not out of the question for any stock—he should stay with his original position.

Figure 2-5 compares the original position with the rolled-up position. Note that the break-even point has moved up from 44 to 48, that the maximum profit potential has increased from 6 points to 12 points, and that at expiration the two writes are equal, at 54.

In summary, it can be said that rolling up increases one's profit potential but also exposes one to risk of loss if a stock price reversal should occur. Therefore, an element of risk is introduced as well as the possibility of increased rewards. Generally, it is not advisable to roll up if at least a 10% correction in the stock price cannot be withstood. One's initial goals for the covered write were set when the position was established. If the stock advances and these goals are being met, the writer should be very cautious about risking that profit.

The discussion to this point has been directed at rolling up *before* expiration. At or near expiration, when the time value premium has disappeared from the written call, one may have no choice but to write the next-higher striking price if he wants to retain his stock. This will be discussed soon, when we analyze action to take at or near expiration.

If the underlying stock rises, one's choices are not necessarily limited to rolling up or doing nothing. As the stock increases in price, the written call will lose its time premium and may begin to trade near parity. The writer may decide to close the position himself—perhaps

**FIGURE 2-5.** *Comparison: original write vs. rolled-up position.*

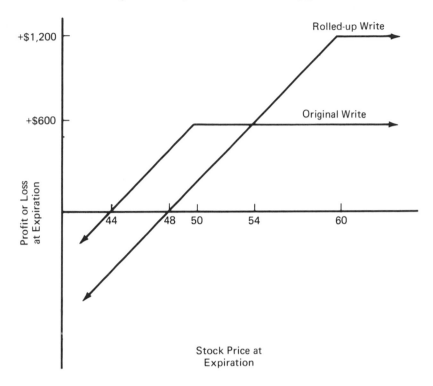

well in advance of expiration—by buying back the written call and selling the stock out, hopefully near parity.

> *Example:* A customer originally bought XYZ at 25 and sold the 6-month July 25 for 3 points—a net of 22. Now, three months later, XYZ has risen to 33 and the call is trading at 8 (parity) because it is so deeply in-the-money. At this point, the writer may want to sell the stock at 33 and buy back the call at 8, thereby realizing an effective net of 25 for the covered write which is his maximum profit potential. This is certainly preferable to remaining in the position for 3 more months with no more profit potential available. The advantage of closing a parity covered write early is that one is realizing the maximum return in a shorter period than anticipated. He is thereby increasing his annualized return on the position. Although it is generally to the cash writer's advantage (margin writers read on) to take such action, there are a few additional costs involved that he would not experience if he held the position until the call expired. First, the commission for the option purchase (buy-back) is an additional expense. Second, he will be selling his stock at a higher price than the striking price, so he will pay a

slightly higher commission on that trade as well. If there is a dividend left until expiration, he will not be receiving that dividend if he closes the write early. Of course, if the trade was done in a margin account, the writer will be reducing the margin interest that he had planned to pay in the position because the debit will be erased earlier. In most cases, the increased commissions are very small and the lost dividend is not significant compared to the increase in annualized return that one can achieve by closing the position early. However, this is not always true and one should be aware of exactly what his costs are for closing the position early.

Obviously, getting out of a covered writing position can be as difficult as establishing it. Therefore, one should place the order to close the position with his brokerage firm's option desk, to be executed as a "net" order. The same traders who facilitate establishing covered writing positions at net prices will also facilitate getting out of the position. One would normally place the order by saying that he wanted to sell his stock and buy the option "at parity" or, in the example, at "25 net." Just as it is often necessary to be in contact with both the option and stock exchanges to *establish* a position, so is it necessary to maintain the same contacts to *remove* a position at parity.

### Margin Considerations

It is extremely important for covered writers using margin to be aware of a *potential reduction of buying power when an in-the-money write is closed.* The amount of excess value (also called SMA) that is released, when the current margin rate is 50%, would be one-half of the value of the stock sale less the full cost of the options that are bought back. If the options are deeply in-the-money, the margin writer may lose nearly all of his SMA—a fact that would cause him to reject the idea of closing the write in advance of expiration.

*Example:* A covered writer on margin finds the stock at 40 and the July 25 call at 15. If he has a 1,000-share position, his SMA after closing the position would be:

| | |
|---|---:|
| 50% of stock value = .50 × $40,000 = | $20,000 |
| Less option cost (10 calls at 15) | − 15,000 |
| Net SMA release for substitution | $ 5,000 |

This $5,000 figure should be compared to the SMA that would be released for substitution if the write were held to expiration and the stock were called away at 25. Upon assignment, the stock would be sold at 25, the striking price, and the option would be gone, thus releasing SMA of 50% of $25,000, or $12,500.

This example demonstrates a pitfall the margin writer must avoid. If the call is too deeply in-the-money, he may lose a good deal of buying power by closing the write in the market. It may be more feasible for him to wait until the call is assigned. In either case, *a covered writer on margin can use same-day substitution privileges* to reinvest those funds that are released in another covered write, provided that he establishes the new position on the same day that he closed the previous position (or on the same day that he receives an assignment notice).

### *Action to Take at or Near Expiration*

As expiration nears and the time value premium disappears from a written call, the covered writer may often want to *roll forward*, that is, buy back the currently written call and sell a longer-term call with the same striking price. For an in-the-money call, the optimum time to roll forward is generally when the time value premium has completely disappeared from the call. For an out-of-the-money call, the correct time to move into the more distant option series is when the return offered by the near-term option is less than the return offered by the longer-term call.

The in-the-money case is quite simple to analyze. As long as there is time premium left in the call, there is little risk of assignment, and therefore the writer is earning time premium by remaining with the original call. However, when the option begins to trade at parity or a discount, there becomes a significant probability of exercise by arbitrageurs. It is at this time that the writer should roll the in-the-money call forward. For example, if XYZ were offered at 51 and the July 50 call were bid at 1, the writer should be rolling forward into the October 50 or January 50 call.

The out-of-the-money case is a little more difficult to handle, but there is a relatively straightforward analysis that can be applied to facilitate the writer's decision. One can compute the return per day remaining in the written call and compare it to the net return per day from the longer-term call. If the longer-term call has a higher return, one should roll forward.

*Example:* An investor previously entered a covered writing situation in which he wrote five January 30 calls against 500 XYZ common. The following prices exist currently, 1 month before expiration:

XYZ common, 29½;

January 30 call, ½; and

April 30 call, 2½.

The writer can only make ½ of a point more of time premium on this covered write for the time remaining until expiration. It is possible that his money could be put to better use by rolling forward to the April 30 call. Commissions for rolling forward must be subtracted from the April 30's premium to present a true comparison.

By remaining in the January 30, the writer could make, at most, $250 for the 30 days remaining until January expiration. This is a return of $8.33 per day. The commissions for rolling forward would be approximately $100—including both the buy-back and the new sale. Since the current time premium in the April 30 call is $250 per option, this would mean that the writer would stand to make 5 times $250 less the $100 in commissions during the 120-day period until April expiration. $1,150 divided by 120 days is $9.58 per day. Thus the per-day return is higher from the April 30 than from the January 30, after commissions are included. The writer should roll forward to the April 30 at this time.

Rolling forward, since it involves a positive cash flow (that is, it is a credit transaction) simultaneously increases the writer's maximum profit potential and lowers the break-even point. In the example above, the credit for rolling forward is 2 points, so the break-even point will be lowered by 2 points and the maximum profit potential is also increased by the 2-point credit.

A simple calculator can provide one with the return-per-day calculation necessary to make the decision concerning rolling forward. The preceding analysis is only directly applicable to rolling forward at the *same striking price*. Rolling-up or rolling-down decisions at expiration, since they involve different striking prices, cannot be based solely on the differential returns in time premium values offered by the options in question.

In the earlier discussion concerning rolling up, it was mentioned that at or near expiration, one may have no choice but to write the next higher striking price if he wants to retain his stock. This does not necessarily involve a debit transaction, however. If the stock is volatile enough, one might even be able to *roll up* for even money or a slight credit at expiration. Should this occur, it would be a desirable situation and should always be taken advantage of.

*Example:* The following prices exist at January expiration:

XYZ, 50;

XYZ January 45 call, 5; and

XYZ July 50 call, 7.

In this case, if one had originally written the January 45 call, he could now roll up to the July 50 at expiration for a *credit* of 2 points. This action is quite prudent, since the break-even point and the maximum profit potential are enhanced. The break-even point is lowered by the 2 points of credit received from rolling up. The maximum profit potential is increased substantially—by 7 points—since the striking price is raised by 5 points and an additional 2 points of credit are taken in from the roll up. Consequently, whenever one can roll up for a credit, a situation that would normally arise only on more volatile stocks, he should do so.

Another choice that may occur at or near expiration is that of *rolling down.* The case may arise where one has allowed a written call to expire worthless with the stock more than a small distance below the striking price. The writer is then faced with the decision of either writing a small premium out-of-the-money call or a larger premium in-the-money call. Again an example may prove to be useful.

*Example:* Just after the January 25 call has expired worthless,

XYZ is at 22,

XYZ July 25 call at ¾, and

XYZ July 20 call at 3½.

If the investor were now to write the July 25 call, he would be receiving only ¾ of a point of downside protection. However, his maximum profit potential would be quite large if XYZ could rally to 25 by expiration. On the other hand, the October 20 at 3½ is an attractive write that affords substantial downside protection and its 1½ points of time value premium are twice that offered by the July 25 call. In a purely analytic sense, one should not base his decision on what his performance has been to date, but that is a difficult axiom to supply in practice. If this investor owns XYZ at a higher price, he will almost surely opt for the July 25 call. If, however, he owns XYZ at approximately the same price, he will have no qualms about writing the July 20 call. There is no absolute rule that can be applied to all such situations, but one is usually better off writing the call that provides the best balance between return and downside protection at all times. Only if one is bullish on the underlying stock should he write the July 25 call.

### Avoiding the Uncovered Position

There is a margin rule that the covered writer must be aware of if he is considering taking any sort of follow-up action on the day that the written call ceases trading. If another call is sold on that day—even though the written call is obviously going to expire worthless—the writer will be considered uncovered, for margin purposes, over the weekend and will be obligated to put forth the collateral for an uncovered option. This is usually not what the writer intends to do, and being aware of this rule will eliminate unwanted margin calls. Furthermore, uncovered options may be considered unsuitable for many covered writers.

> *Example:* A customer owns XYZ and has January 20 calls outstanding on the last day of trading of the January series (the third Friday of January; the calls actually do not expire until the following day, Saturday). If XYZ is at 15 on the last day of trading, the January 20 call will almost certainly expire worthless. However, should the writer decide to sell a longer-term call on that day without buying back the January 20, he will be considered uncovered over the weekend. Thus *if one plans to wait for an option to expire totally worthless before writing another call, he must wait until the Monday after expiration before writing again, assuming that he wants to remain covered.* The writer should also realize that it *is* possible for some sort of news item to be announced between the end of trading in an option series and the actual expiration of the series. Thus call holders might exercise because they believe the stock will jump sufficiently in price to make the exercise profitable. This has happened in the past, two of the most notable cases being IBM in January 1975 and Carrier Corp. in September 1978.

### When to Let Stock Be Called Away

Another alternative that is open to the writer, as the written call approaches expiration, is to let the stock be called away if it is above the striking price. In most cases, it is to the advantage of the writer to keep rolling options forward before he is called, thereby retaining his stock ownership. However, in certain cases, it may be advisable to allow the stock to be called away. It should be emphasized that the writer often has a definite choice in this matter, since he can generally tell when the call is about to be exercised—when the time value premium disappears.

The reason that it is *normally* desirable to roll forward is that, over time, the covered writer will realize a higher return by rolling instead of being called. The option commissions for rolling forward every three or six months are smaller than the commissions for buying and selling the underlying stock every three or six months, and therefore the eventual return will be higher. However, if by rolling forward, an inferior return has to be accepted or the break-even point raised significantly, one must consider the alternative of letting the stock be called away.

> *Example:* A covered write is established by buying XYZ at 49 and selling an April 50 call for 3 points. The original break-even point was thus 46. Near expiration, suppose XYZ has risen to 56 and the April 50 is trading at 6. If the investor wants to roll forward, now is the time to do so, because the call is at parity. However, he notes that the choices are somewhat limited. Suppose the following prices exist with XYZ at 56: XYZ October 50 call, 7; and XYZ October 60 call, 2. It seems apparent that the premium levels have declined since the original writing position was established, but that is an occurrence beyond the control of the writer, who must work in the current market environment.
>
> If the writer attempts to roll forward to the October 50, he could make at most 1 additional point of profit until October (the time premium in the call). This represents an extremely low rate of return and the writer should reject this alternative since there are surely better returns available in covered writes on other securities.
>
> On the other hand, if the writer tries to roll up and forward, it will cost 4 points to do so—6 points to buy back the April 50 less 2 points received for the October 60. This debit transaction means that his break-even point would move up from the original level of 46 to a new level of 50. If the common declines below 54, he would be eating into profits already at hand, since the October 60 only provides 2 points of protection from the current stock price of 56. If the writer is not confidently bullish on the outlook for XYZ, he should not roll up and forward.
>
> At this point, the writer has exhausted his alternatives for rolling. His remaining choice is to let the stock be called away and to use the proceeds to establish a covered write in a new stock—one that offers a more attractive rate of return with reasonable downside protection. This choice of allowing the stock to be called away is generally the wisest strategy if both of the following *criteria* are met:
>
> 1. Rolling forward offers only a minimal return.
> 2. Rolling up and forward significantly raises the break-even point and leaves the position relatively unprotected should the stock drop in price.

## SPECIAL WRITING SITUATIONS

Our discussions have pertained directly to writing against common stock. However, one may also write covered call options against convertible securities or warrants. In addition, a different type of covered writing strategy will be described that has a large amount of appeal to large stockholders, both individuals and institutions.

### Covered Writing Against a Convertible Security

It may be more advantageous to buy a security that is convertible into common stock than to buy the stock itself, for covered call writing purposes. Convertible bonds and convertible preferred stocks are securities commonly used for this purpose. One advantage of using the convertible security is that it often has a higher yield than does the common stock itself.

Before describing the covered write, it may be beneficial to review the basics of convertible securities. Suppose XYZ common stock has an XYZ convertible Preferred A stock that is convertible into 1.5 shares of common. The number of shares of common that the convertible security converts into is an important piece of information that the writer *must* know. It can be found in a Standard & Poor's Stock Guide (or Bond Guide, in the case of convertible bonds).

The writer also needs to determine how many shares of the convertible security must be owned in order to equal 100 shares of the common stock. This is quickly determined by dividing 100 by the *conversion ratio*—1.5 in our XYZ example. Since 100 divided by 1.5 equals 66.666, one must own 67 shares of XYZ cv Pfd A to cover the sale of one XYZ option for 100 shares of common. Note that the market prices of neither XYZ common nor the convertible security are necessary for this computation.

When using a convertible bond, the conversion information is usually stated in a form such as "converts into 50 shares at a price of 20." The price is irrelevant. What *is* important is the number of shares that the bond converts into—50 in this case. Thus if one were using these bonds for covered writing of 1 call, he would need two (2,000) bonds to own the equivalent of 100 shares of stock.

Once one knows how much of the convertible security must be purchased, he can use the actual prices of the securities, and their yields, to determine whether a covered write against the common or the convertible is more attractive.

*Example:* The following information is known:

XYZ common, 50;

XYZ cv Pfd A, 80;

XYZ July 50 call, 5;

XYZ dividend, 1.00 per share annually; and

XYZ cv Pfd A dividend, 5.00 per share annually.

Note that, in either case, the same call—the July 50—would be written. *The use of the convertible as the underlying security does not alter the choice of which option to use.* To make the comparison of returns easier, commissions will be ignored in the calculations given in Table 2-25. In reality, the commissions for the stock purchase—either common or preferred—would be very similar. Thus, from a numerical point of view, it appears to be more advantageous to write against the convertible than against the common.

**TABLE 2-25.** *Comparison of common and convertible writes.*

|  | *Write against Common* | *Write against Convertible* |
|---|---|---|
| Buy underlying security | $5,000 (100 XYZ) | $5,360 (67 XYZ cv Pfd A) |
| Sell one July 50 call | − 500 | − 500 |
| Net cash investment | $4,500 | $4,860 |
| Premium collected | $ 500 | $ 500 |
| Dividends until July | 50 | 250 |
| Maximum profit potential | $ 550 | $ 750 |
| Return (profit divided by investment) | 12.2% | 15.4% |

When writing against a convertible security, there are additional considerations that should be looked at. The first is the *premium of the convertible security.* In the example, with XYZ selling at 50, the XYZ cv Pfd A has a true value of 1.5 times 50, or $75 per share. However, it is selling at 80, which represents a premium of 5 points above its computed value of 75. *Normally, one would not want to buy a convertible security if the premium is too large.* In this example, the premium appears quite reasonable. Any convertible premium greater than 15% above computed value might be considered to be too large.

Another consideration when writing against convertible securities is the *handling* of *assignment.* If the writer is assigned, he may either (1) convert his preferred stock into common and deliver that, or (2) sell the *preferred* in the market and use the proceeds to buy 100

shares of common stock in the market for delivery against the assignment notice. The second choice is usually preferable if the convertible
security has any premium at all, since converting the preferred into
common causes the *loss* of any premium in the convertible, as well as
the loss of accrued interest in the case of a convertible bond.

The writer should also be aware of whether or not the convertible
is *callable,* and, if so, what the exact terms are. Once the convertible
has been called by the company, it will no longer trade in relation to
the underlying stock, but will instead trade at the call price. Thus, if
the stock should climb sharply, the writer could be incurring losses on
his written option without any corresponding benefit from his convertible security. Consequently, if the convertible is called, the entire
position should normally be closed immediately by selling the convertible and buying the option back.

Other aspects of covered writing, such as rolling down or forward, do not change even if the option is written against a convertible
security—one would take action based on the relationship of the
option price and the common stock price, as usual.

### Writing Against Warrants

It is also possible to write covered call options against warrants.
Again, one must own enough warrants to convert into 100 shares of
the underlying stock—generally, this would be 100 warrants. The
transaction must be a cash transaction—the warrants must be paid for
in full, and they have no loan value. Technically, listed warrants may
be marginable but many brokerage houses still require payment in full.
There may also be an *additional investment requirement.* Warrants
also have an exercise price. If the exercise price of the warrant is
*higher* than the striking price of the call, the covered writer must also
deposit the difference between the two as part of his investment.

The advantage of using warrants is that, if they are deeply in-the-
money they may provide the cash covered writer with a higher return
since less of an investment is involved.

> *Example:* XYZ is at 50 and there are XYZ warrants to buy the
> common at 25. Since the warrant is so deeply in-the-money, it will be
> selling for approximately 25 dollars per warrant. XYZ pays no divi-
> dend. Thus if the writer were considering a covered write of the XYZ
> July 50, he might choose to use the warrant instead of the common,
> since his investment, per 100 shares of common, would only be $2,500

instead of the $5,000 required to buy 100 XYZ. The potential profit would be the same in either case because no dividend is involved.

Even if the stock does pay a dividend (warrants themselves have no dividend), the writer may still be able to earn a higher return by writing against the warrant than the common because of the smaller investment involved. This would depend, of course, on the exact size of the dividend and on how deeply the warrant is in-the-money.

Covered writing against warrants is not a frequent practice because of the small number of warrants on optionable stocks and the problems inherent in checking available returns. However, in certain circumstances, the writer may actually have a decided advantage by writing against a deep in-the-money warrant. It is often not advisable to write against a warrant that is at- or out-of-the-money, since it can decline by a large percentage if the underlying stock drops in price—producing a high-risk position. Also, the writer's investment may increase in this case if he rolls down to an option with a striking price lower than the warrant's exercise price.

### *The Incremental Return Concept of Covered Writing*

The incremental return concept of covered call writing is a way in which *the covered writer can earn the full value of stock appreciation between today's stock price and a target sale price, which may be substantially higher.* At the same time, the writer can earn an incremental, positive return from writing options.

Many institutional investors are somewhat apprehensive about covered call writing because of the upside limit that is placed on profit potential. If a call is written against a stock that subsequently declines in price, most institutional managers would *not* view this as an unfavorable situation, since they would be outperforming all managers who owned the stock and who did not write a call. However, if the stock rises substantially after the call is written, many institutional managers do not like having their profits limited by the written call. This strategy is not only for institutional money managers, although one should have a relatively substantial holding in an underlying stock to attempt the strategy—at least 500 shares, and preferably, 1,000 shares or more. *The incremental return concept can be used by anyone who is planning to hold his stock, even if it should temporarily decline in price, until it reaches a predetermined, higher price at which he is willing to sell the stock.*

The basic strategy involves, as an initial step, selecting the target price at which the writer is willing to sell his stock.

*Example:* A customer owns 1,000 shares of XYZ, which is currently at 60, and is willing to sell the stock at 80. In the meantime, he would like to realize a *positive cash flow* from writing options against his stock. This positive cash flow does not necessarily result in a realized option gain until the stock is called away. Most likely, with the stock at 60, there would not be options available with a striking price of 80, so one could not write 10 July 80's, for example. This would not be an optimum strategy even if the July 80's existed, for the investor would be receiving so little in option premiums—perhaps ⅛ of a point per call— that writing might not be worthwhile. The incremental return strategy allows this investor to achieve his objectives regardless of the existence of options with a higher striking price.

The foundation of the incremental return strategy is to write against only a *part* of the entire stock holding initially, and to write these calls at the striking price nearest the current stock price. Then, should the stock move up to the next higher striking price, one rolls up for a *credit* by adding to the number of calls written. Rolling for a credit is mandatory and is the key to the strategy. Eventually, the stock reaches the target price and the stock is called away, the investor sells all his stock at the target price and, in addition, earns the total *credits* from all the option transactions.

*Example:* XYZ is 60, the investor owns 1,000 shares, and his target price is 80. One might begin by selling three of the longest-term calls at 60 for 7 points apiece. Table 2-26 shows how a poor case—one in which the stock climbs directly to the target price—might work. As Table 2-26 shows, if XYZ rose to 70 in one month, the three original calls would be bought back and enough calls at 70 would be sold to produce a credit—five XYZ October 70's. If the stock continued

**TABLE 2-26.** *Two months of incremental return strategy.*

| | |
|---|---|
| Day 1:  XYZ = 60 | |
|     Sell 3 XYZ October 60's at 7 | +$2,100 credit |
| One month later: XYZ = 70 | |
|     Buy back the 3 XYZ Oct 60's at 11 and | −$3,300 debit |
|     sell 5 XYZ Oct 70's at 7 | +$3,500 credit |
| Two months later: XYZ = 80 | |
|     Buy back the 5 Oct 70's at 11 and | −$5,500 debit |
|     sell 10 XYZ Oct 80's at 6 | +$6,000 credit |
| | +$2,800 credit |

upward to 80 in another month, the 5 calls would be bought back and the entire position—10 calls—would be written against at the target price.

If XYZ remains above 80, the stock will be called away and *all 1,000 shares will be sold at the target price of 80*. In addition, the investor will earn all the option credits generated along the way. These amount to $2,800. Thus the writer obtained the full appreciation of his stock to the target price plus an *incremental*, positive return from option writing.

In a flat market, the strategy is relatively easy to monitor. If a written call loses its time value premium, and therefore might be subject to assignment, the writer can roll forward to a more distant expiration series, keeping the quantity of written calls constant. This transaction would generate additional credits as well.

## COVERED CALL WRITING SUMMARY

This concludes the chapter on covered call writing. The strategy will be referred to later, when compared to other strategies. The following items are a brief summary of the more important points that were discussed.

Covered call writing is a viable strategy because it reduces the risk of stock ownership and will make one's portfolio less volatile to short-term market movements. The choice of which call to write can make for a more aggressive or more conservative write—writing in-the-money calls is strategically more conservative than writing out-of-the-money calls, because of the larger amount of downside protection received. The total return concept of covered call writing attempts to achieve the maximum balance between income from all sources—option premiums, stock ownership, and dividend income—and downside protection. This balance is usually realized by writing calls when the stock is near the striking price—either slightly in- or out-of-the-money.

The writer should compute various returns before entering into the position—the return if exercised, the return if the stock is unchanged at expiration, and the break-even point. To truly compare various writes, returns should be annualized, and all commissions and dividends should be included in these calculations. Returns will be increased by taking larger positions in the underlying stock—500 or 1,000 shares. Also, by utilizing a brokerage firm's capability to produce "net" executions, buying the stock and selling the call at a specified net price differential, one will receive better executions and realize higher returns in the long run.

The selection of which call to write should be made on a comparison of available returns and downside protection. One can sometimes write part of his position out-of-the-money and the other part in-the-money to force a balance between return and protection that might not otherwise exist. Finally, one should not write against an underlying stock if he is bearish on the stock. The writer should be slightly bullish, or at least neutral, on the underlying stock.

Follow-up action can be as important as the selection of the initial position itself. By rolling down if the underlying stock drops, the investor can add downside protection and current income. If one is unwilling to limit his upside potential too severely, he may consider rolling down only part of his call writing position. As the written call expires, the writer should roll forward into a more distant expiration month if the stock is relatively close to the original striking price. Higher consistent returns are achieved in this manner, because one is not spending additional stock commissions by letting the stock be called away. An aggressive follow-up action can also be taken when the underlying stock rises in price—the writer can roll up to a higher striking price. This action increases the maximum profit potential but also exposes the position to loss if the stock should subsequently decline. One would want to take no follow-up action and let his stock be called if it is above the striking price and if there are better returns available elsewhere in other securities.

Covered call writing can also be done against convertible securities—bonds or preferred stocks. These convertibles sometimes offer higher dividend yields and therefore increase the overall return from covered writing. Also, the use of warrants in place of the underlying stock may be advantageous in certain circumstances because the net investment is lowered while the profit potential remains the same. Therefore, the overall return could be higher.

Finally, the larger individual stockholder or institutional investor who wants to achieve a certain price for his stock holdings should operate his covered writing strategy under the incremental return concept. This will allow him to realize the full profit potential of his underlying stock, up to the target sale price, and to earn additional positive income from option writing.

# *Call Buying*

The success of a call buying strategy depends primarily on one's ability to select stocks that will go up and to time the selection reasonably well. Thus call buying is not a strategy in the same sense of the word as most of the other strategies discussed in this text. Most other strategies are designed to remove some of the exactness of stock picking—allowing one to be neutral or at least to have some room for error and still make a profit. Techniques of call buying are important, though, because it is necessary to understand the long side of calls in order to understand more complex strategies correctly.

Call buying is the simplest form of option investment, and therefore is the most frequently used option "strategy" by the public investor. The following section will outline the basic facts that one needs to know to implement an intelligent call buying program.

## *WHY BUY?*

*The main attraction in buying calls is that they provide the speculator with a great deal of leverage.* One could potentially realize large percentage profits from only a modest rise in price by the underlying stock. Moreover, even though they may be large percentagewise, the risks cannot exceed a fixed dollar amount—the price originally paid for the call. Calls must be paid for in full—they have no margin value and do not constitute equity for margin purposes. The following simple example illustrates how a call purchase might work.

> *Example:* Assume that XYZ is at 48 and the 6-month call, the July 50, is selling for 3. Thus, with an investment of $300, the call buyer may participate, for 6 months, in a move upward in the price of XYZ common. If XYZ should rise in price by 10 points (just over 20%), the July 50 call will be worth at least $800 and the call buyer would have a 167% profit on a move in the stock of just over 20%. This is the leverage that attracts speculators to call buying. At expiration, if XYZ is below 50, the buyer's loss is total, but is limited to his initial $300 investment, even if XYZ declines in price substantially. Although this risk is equal to 100% of his initial investment, it is still small dollar-wise. *One should normally not invest more than 15% of his risk capital in call buying,* because of the relatively large percentage risks involved.

Some investors participate in call buying on a limited basis to add some upside potential to their portfolios while keeping the risk to a fixed amount. For example, if an investor normally only purchased low-volatility, conservative, stocks because he wanted to limit his downside risk, he might consider putting a small percentage of his cash into calls on more volatile stocks. In this manner, he could "trade" higher risk stocks than he might normally do. If these volatile stocks increase in price, the investor will profit handsomely. However, if they decline substantially—as well they might, being volatile—the investor has limited his dollar risk by owning the calls rather than the stock.

Another reason some investors buy calls is to be able to buy stock at a reasonable price without missing a market.

> *Example:* With XYZ at 75, this investor might buy a call on XYZ at 80. He would like to own XYZ at 80 if it can prove itself capable of rallying and be in-the-money at expiration. He would exercise the call in that case. On the other hand, if XYZ declines in price instead, he has not tied up money in the stock and can only lose an amount equal to the call premium that he paid, an amount that is generally much less than the price of the stock itself.

Another approach to call buying is sometimes utilized, also by an investor who does not want to "miss the market." Suppose an investor knows that, in the near future, he will have an amount of money large enough to purchase a particular stock—perhaps he is closing the sale of his house or a Certificate of Deposit is maturing. However, he would like to buy the stock now, for he feels a rally is imminent. He might buy calls at the present time if he had a small amount of cash available. The call purchases would require an investment much smaller than the stock purchase. Then, when he receives the cash that he knew was forthcoming, he could exercise the calls and buy the stock. In this way, he might have participated in a rally by the stock before he actually had the money available to pay for the stock in full.

## RISK/REWARD FOR THE CALL BUYER

The most important fact for the call buyer to realize is that he will only win if the stock rises in price. All the worthwhile analysis in the world spent in selecting which call to buy will not produce profits if the underlying stock declines. However, this fact should not dissuade one from making reasonable analyses in his call buying selections. Too often, the call buyer feels that a stock will move up—and is correct in that part of his projection—but still loses money on his call purchase because he failed to analyze the risk and rewards involved with the various calls available for purchase at the time. He bought the wrong call on the right stock.

Since the only ally that the call buyer has is upward movement in the underlying stock, the selection of the underlying stock is the most important choice the call buyer has to make. Since timing is so important when buying calls, the technical factors of stock selection probably outweigh the fundamentals, because even if positive fundamentals do exist, one does not know how long it will take in order for them to be reflected in the price of the stock. One must be bullish on the underlying stock in order to consider buying calls on that stock. Once the stock selection has been made, only then can the call buyer begin to consider other factors, such as which striking price to use and which expiration to buy.

The purchase of an out-of-the-money call generally offers both larger potential risk and larger potential reward than does the purchase of an in-the-money call. Many call buyers tend to select the out-of-the-money call merely because it is cheaper in price. *Absolute dollar price should in no way be a deciding factor for the call buyer.* If one's funds are so limited that he can only afford to buy the cheapest calls, he should not be speculating in this strategy. If the underlying stock increases in price substantially, the out-of-the-money call will naturally provide the largest rewards. However, if the stock only advances moderately in price, the in-the-money call may actually perform better.

*Example:* XYZ is at 65 and the July 60 sells for 7 while the July 70 sells for 3. If the stock moves up to 68 relatively slowly, the buyer of the July 70—the out-of-the-money call—may actually experience a loss, even if the call has not yet expired. However, the holder of the in-the-money July 60 will definitely have a profit because the call will sell for at least 8 points—its intrinsic value. The point is that, percentagewise, *an in-the-money call will offer better rewards for a modest stock gain and the out-of-the-money call is better for larger stock gains.*

When risk is considered, the in-the-money call clearly has less probability of risk. In the example, the in-the-money call buyer would not lose his entire investment unless XYZ fell by at least 5 points. However, the buyer of the out-of-the-money July 70 would lose all of his investment unless the stock *advanced* by more than 5 points by expiration. Obviously, the probability that the in-the-money call will expire worthless is much smaller than that for the out-of-the-money call.

The time remaining to expiration is also relevant to the call buyer. If the stock is fairly close to the striking price, the near-term call will most closely follow the price movement of the underlying stock, so it has the greatest rewards and also the greatest risks. The far-term call, because it has a large amount of time remaining, offers the least risk and least percentage reward. *The intermediate-term call offers a moderate amount of each, and is therefore often the most attractive one to buy.* Many times an investor will buy the longer-term call because it only costs a point or a point and a half more than the intermediate-term call. He feels that the extra price is a bargain to pay for three extra months of time. This line of thought may prove somewhat misleading, however, because most call buyers don't hold calls for more than 60 or 90 days. Thus, even though it looks attractive to pay the extra point for the long-term call, it may prove to be an unnecessary expense if, as is usually the case, one will be selling the call in two or three months.

### Certainty of Timing

The certainty with which one expects the underlying stock to advance may also help to play a part in his selection of which call to buy. If one is fairly sure that the underlying stock is about to rise immediately, he should strive for more reward and not be as concerned about risk. This would mean buying short-term, slightly out-of-the money calls. Of course, this is only a general rule—one would not normally buy an out-of-the-money call that only has one week remaining until expiration in any case. At the opposite end of the spectrum, if one is very uncertain about his timing, he should buy the longest-term call, to moderate his risk in case his timing is wrong by a wide margin. This situation could easily result, for example, if one feels that a positive fundamental aspect concerning the company will assert itself and cause the stock to increase in price at an unknown time in the future. Since the buyer does not know whether this positive fundamental will come to light in the next month or 6 months from now, he should buy the longer-term call to allow room for error in timing.

In many cases, one is not intending to hold the purchased call for any significant period of time—he is just looking to capitalize on a quick, short-term movement by the underlying stock. In this case, he would want to buy a relatively short-term in-the-money call. Although such a call may be more expensive than an out-of-the-money call on the same underlying stock, it will most surely move up on any increase in price by the underlying stock. Thus the short-term trader would profit. Also, commissions are generally smaller, percentage-wise, on the more expensive calls. The short-term trader, who naturally accumulates relatively large commission costs, thus has another reason for preferring to utilize in-the-money calls.

### The Delta

The reader should by now be familiar with basic facts concerning call options: the time premium is highest when the stock is at the striking price of the call; it is lowest deep in- or out-of-the-money; option prices do not decay at a linear rate—the time premium disappears more rapidly as the option approaches expiration. As a further means of review, the *option pricing curve* introduced in Chapter 1 is reprinted here. Notice that all the facts listed above can be observed from Figure 3-1. The curves are much nearer the "intrinsic value" line at the ends than they are in the middle, implying that the time value premium is greatest when the stock is at the strike and is least when the stock moves away from the strike—either in-to or out-of-the-money. Furthermore, the fact that the curve for the three-month option lies only about half-way between the intrinsic value line and the curve of the nine-month option implies that the rate of decay of an option is not linear. The reader may also want to refer back to the graph of time value premium decay in Chapter 1.

There is another property of call options that the buyer should be

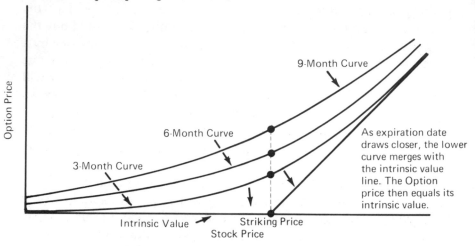

**FIGURE 3-1.** *Option pricing curve: 3-, 6-, and 9-month calls.*

9-Month Curve

6-Month Curve

3-Month Curve

As expiration date draws closer, the lower curve merges with the intrinsic value line. The Option price then equals its intrinsic value.

Intrinsic Value

Striking Price

Stock Price

Option Price

familiar with, the delta of the option (also called the hedge ratio). Simply stated, *the delta of an option is the amount by which the call will increase or decrease in price if the underlying stock moves by 1 point.*

> *Example:* The delta of a call option is close to 1 when the underlying stock is well above the striking price of the call. If XYZ were 60 and XYZ July 50 call were 10⅛, the call would change in price by nearly 1 point if XYZ moved by 1 point, either up or down. A deeply out-of-the-money call has a delta of nearly zero. If XYZ were 40, the July 50 call might be selling at ¼ of a point. The call would change very little in price if XYZ moved by one point—either to 41 or 39. When the stock is *at* the striking price, the delta is usually between one-half of a point and five-eighths of a point. Thus, if XYZ were 50 and the XYZ July 50 call were 5, the call might increase to 5½ if XYZ rose to 51 or would decrease to 4½ if XYZ dropped to 49.

Actually, the delta changes each time the underlying stock changes even fractionally in price—it is an exact mathematical derivation that will be presented in a later chapter. This is most easily seen by the fact that a deep in-the-money option has a delta of 1. However, if the stock should undergo a series of 1-point drops down to the striking price, the delta will be more like ½—certainly not 1 any longer. In reality, the delta changed instantaneously all during the price decline by the stock. For those who are geometrically inclined, the preceding option price curve is useful in determining a graphic representation of the delta. The delta is the *slope* of the tangent line to the price curve. Notice that a deeply in-the-money option lies to the upper right side of the curve, very nearly on the intrinsic value line, which has a slope of 1 above the strike. Similarly, a deeply out-of-the-money call lies to the left on the price curve, again near the intrinsic value line, which has a slope of zero below the strike.

Since it is more common to relate the option's price change to a full point change in the underlying stock (rather than to deal in "instantaneous" price changes), the concepts of *"up delta"* and *"down delta"* arise. That is, if the underlying stock moves up by 1 full point, a call with a delta of .50 might increase by ⅝. However, should the stock fall by one full point, the call might only decrease by ⅜. There is a different net price change in the call when the stock moves up by 1 full point as opposed to when it falls by a point—the up delta is observed to be ⅝ while the down delta is ⅜. In the true mathematical sense, there is only one delta and it measures "instantaneous" price change. The concepts of up delta and down delta are practical, rather than theoretical, concepts which merely illustrate the fact that the true delta changes whenever the stock price changes, even by as little as 1 point. In the following examples and in later chapters, only one delta will be referred to.

The delta is an important piece of information for the call buyer because it can tell him how much of an increase or decrease he can expect for short-term moves by the underlying stock. This piece of information may help the buyer decide which call to buy.

*Example:* If XYZ is 47½ and the call buyer expects a quick, but possibly limited, rise in price in the underlying stock, should he buy the 45 call or the 50 call? The delta may help him decide. He has the following information:

| | | | |
|---|---|---|---|
| XYZ: 47½ | XYZ July 45 call: | price = 3½, | delta = ⅝ |
| | XYZ July 50 call: | price = 1, | delta = ¼ |

It will make matters easier to make a slightly incorrect, but simplifying, assumption that the deltas remain constant over the short term. Which call is the better buy if the buyer expects the stock to quickly rise to 49? This would represent a 1½-point increase in XYZ, which would translate into a 15/16 increase in the July 45 (1½ times ⅝) or a ⅜ increase in the July 50 (1½ times ¼). Consequently, the July 45—if it increased in price by 15/16—would appreciate by 27%. The July 50—if it increased by ⅜—would appreciate by over 37%. Thus the July 50 appears to be the better buy in this simple example. Commissions should, of course, be included when making an analysis for actual investment.

The investor does not have to bother with computing deltas for himself. Any good call-buying data service will supply the information, and some brokerage houses provide this information free of charge.

More advanced applications of deltas will be described in many of the succeeding chapters, as they apply to a variety of strategies.

## ADVANCED SELECTION CRITERIA

The criteria presented above are elementary techniques for selecting which call to buy. In actual practice, one is not usually bullish on just one stock at a time. In fact, he would like to have a list of the "best" calls to buy at any given time. Then, using some method of stock selection, either technical or fundamental, he can select three or four calls that appear to offer the best rewards. This list should be ranked in order of the best potential rewards available, but the construction of the list itself is important.

*Call option rankings for buying purposes must be based on the volatilities of the underlying stocks.* This is not easy to do, mathematically, and as a result many published rankings of calls are based strictly on percentage change in the underlying stock. Such a list is quite misleading and can lead one to the wrong conclusions.

*Example:* There are two stocks with listed calls—NVS, which is not volatile, and VVS, which is quite volatile. Since a call on the volatile stock will be higher-priced than a call on the nonvolatile stock, the following prices might exist:

| | | | |
|---|---|---|---|
| NVS: | 40 | VVS: | 40 |
| NVS July 40 call: | 2 | VVS July 40 call: | 4 |

If these two calls are ranked, for buying purposes, based strictly on a percentage change in the underlying stock, the NVS call will appear to be the better buy. For example, one might see a list such as "best call buys if the underlying stock advances by 10%." In this example, if each stock advanced 10% by expiration, both NVS and VVS would be at 44. Thus the NVS July 40 would be worth 4, having doubled in price, for a 100% potential profit. Meanwhile, the VVS July 40 would be worth 4 also, for a 0% profit to the call buyer. This analysis would lead one to believe that the NVS July 40 is the better buy. Such a conclusion may be wrong, because an incorrect assumption was made in the ranking of the potentials of the two stocks—it is not right to assume that both stocks have the same probability of moving 10% by expiration. Certainly, the volatile stock has a much better chance of advancing by 10% (or more) than the nonvolatile stock does. *Any ranking based on equal percentage changes in the underlying stock, regardless of their volatilities, is useless and should be avoided.*

The correct method of comparing these two July 40 calls is to utilize the actual volatilities of the underlying stocks. Suppose that it is known that the volatile stock, VVS, could expect to move 15% in the time to July expiration. The nonvolatile stock, NVS, however, could only expect a move of 5% in the same period. Using this information, the call buyer can arrive at the conclusion that VVS July 40 is the best call to buy:

| Stock Price in July | Call Price |
|---|---|
| VVS: 46 (up 15%) | VVS July 40: 6 (up 50%) |
| NVS: 42 (up 5%) | NVS July 40: 2 (unchanged) |

By assuming that each stock can rise in accordance with its volatility, the VVS July 40 has the better reward potential, despite the fact that it was twice as expensive to begin with. This method of analysis is much more realistic.

One more refinement needs to be made in this ranking process. Since most call purchases are made for holding periods of from 30 to 90 days, it is not correct to assume that the calls are held to expiration. That is, even if one buys a 6-month call, he will normally liquidate it— to take profits or cut losses—in 1 to 3 months. *The call buyer's list should thus be based on how the call will perform if held for a realistic time period, such as 90 days.*

Suppose the volatile stock in our example, VVS, has the potential to rise by 12% in 90 days while the less-volatile stock, NVS, only has the potential of rising 4% in 90 days. In 90 days, the July 40 calls will not be at parity because there would be some time remaining until July expiration. Thus it is necessary to attempt to predict what their prices would be at the end of the 90-day holding period. Assume that the following prices are accurate estimates of what the July 40 calls would be selling for in 90 days, if the underlying stocks advanced in relation to their volatilities:

| Stock Price in 90 Days | Call Price |
|---|---|
| VVS: 44.8 (up 12%) | VVS July 40: 6 (up 50%) |
| NVS: 41.6 (up 4%) | NVS July 40: 2½ (up 25%) |

With some time remaining in the calls, they would both have time value premium at the end of 90 days. The bigger time premium would be in the VVS call, since the underlying stock is more volatile. Under this method of analysis, the VVS call is still the best one to buy.

The correct method of ranking potential reward situations for call buyers is as follows:

1. Assume each underlying stock can advance in accordance with its volatility over a fixed period (30, 60, or 90 days).
2. Estimate the call prices after the advance.
3. Rank all potential call purchases by highest percentage reward opportunity for aggressive purchases.
4. Assume each stock can *decline* in accordance with its volatility.
5. Estimate the call prices after the decline.
6. Rank all purchases by reward/risk ratio (percentage gain from item 2 divided by percentage loss from item 2).

The list from item 3 will generate more aggressive purchases because it incorporates potential rewards only. The list from item 6 would be a less speculative one. This method of analysis automatically incorporates the criteria set forth earlier, such as buying short-term out-of-the-money calls for aggressive purchases and buying longer-term in-the-money calls for a more conservative purchase. The delta is also incorporated as part of the volatility.

It is virtually impossible to perform this sort of analysis without a computer. The call buyer can generally obtain such a list from a brokerage firm or from a data service. For those individuals who have access to a computer and would like to generate such an analysis for themselves, the details of computing a stock's volatility and for predicting the call prices will be provided later in a section on mathematical techniques.

### Overpriced or Underpriced Calls

There are formulae available that are capable of predicting what a call should be selling for, based on the relationship of the stock price and the striking price, the time remaining to expiration, and the volatility of the underlying stock. These are useful, for example, in performing the second step in the foregoing analysis—estimating the call price after an advance in the underlying stock. In reality, a call's actual price may deviate somewhat from the price computed by the formula. If the call is actually selling for more than the "fair" (computed) price, the call is said to be *overvalued*. An *undervalued* call would be one that is actually trading at a price that is less than the "fair" price.

Generally, the amount by which a call is overvalued or under-valued may be only a small fraction of a point—such as an eighth or a quarter. In theory, the call buyer who purchases an undervalued call has gained a slight advantage in that the call should return to its *"fair" value*. However, in practice, this information is most useful only to market-makers or firm traders who pay little or no commissions for trading options. The general public cannot benefit directly from the knowledge that such a small discrepancy exists, because of commis-sion costs.

One should not base his call buying decisions merely on the fact that a call is underpriced. It is small solace to the call buyer to find that he bought a "cheap" call which subsequently declined in price. The method of ranking calls for purchase that have been described does, in fact, give some slight benefit to underpriced calls. However, under the recommended method of analysis, a call will not automatically appear as an attractive purchase just because it is slightly undervalued.

## FOLLOW-UP ACTION

The simplest follow-up action that the call buyer can implement when the underlying stock drops is to sell his call and cut his losses. There is often a natural tendency to hold out hope that the stock can rally back to or above the striking price. Most of the time, the buyer does best by cutting his losses in situations where the stock is per-forming poorly. He might use a "mental" stop price, or could actually place a sell stop order, depending on the rules of the exchange where the call is traded.

If the stock should rise, the buyer should be willing to take profits as well. Most buyers will quite readily take a profit if, for example, a call that was bought for 5 points had advanced to be worth 10 points. However, the same investor is often reluctant to sell a call at 2 that he had previously bought for 1 point, because "I've only made a point." The similarity is clear—both cases resulted in approximately a 100% profit—and the investor should be as willing to accept the one as he is the other. This is not to imply that all calls that are bought at 1 should be sold when and if they get to 2, but the same factors that induce one to sell the 10-point call after doubling his money should apply to the 2-point call as well.

It is rarely to the call buyer's benefit to exercise the call if he has to pay commissions. When one exercises a call, he pays a stock commission to buy the stock at the striking price. Then when the stock is sold, a stock sale commission must also be paid. Since option commissions are much smaller, dollarwise, than stock commissions are, the call holder will usually realize more net dollars by selling the call in the option market than by exercising it.

### Locking in Profits

When the call buyer is fortunate enough to see the underlying stock advance relatively quickly, there are a number of strategies that he can implement to enhance his position. These strategies are often useful to the call buyer who has an unrealized profit but is torn between taking the profit or holding on in an attempt to generate more profits if the underlying stock should continue to rise.

*Example:* A call buyer bought an XYZ October 50 call for 3 points when the stock was at 48. Then the stock rises to 58. The buyer might consider selling his October 50 (which would probably be worth about 9 points) and possibly taking one of several actions—some of which might involve the October 60 call, which may be selling for 3 points. Table 3-1 summarizes the situation. At this point, the call buyer might take one of four basic actions:

**TABLE 3-1.** *Present situation on XYZ October calls.*

| Original Trade | Current Prices |
|---|---|
| XYZ common: 48 | XYZ common: 58 |
| Bought XYZ October 50 at 3 | XYZ October 50: 9 |
| | XYZ October 60: 3 |

1. Liquidate the position by selling the long call for a profit.
2. Sell the October 50 that he is currently long and use part of the proceeds to purchase October 60's.
3. Create a spread by selling the October 60 call against his long October 50.
4. Do nothing and continue to remain long the October 50 call.

Each of these actions would produce different levels of risk and reward from this point forward in time. If the holder sells the October 50 call, he makes a 6 point profit, less commissions, and terminates the position. He can realize no further appreciation from the call, nor can he lose any of his current profits—he has realized a 6-point gain. *This is the least aggressive tactic of the four.* If the underlying stock continues to advance and rises above 63, any of the other three strategies will outperform the complete liquidation of the call. However, if the underlying stock should instead decline below 50 by expiration, this action would have provided the most profit of the four strategies.

The other simple tactic—the fourth one listed above—would be to do nothing. If the call is then held to expiration, *this tactic would be the riskiest of the four.* It is the only one that could produce a loss at expiration if XYZ fell back below 50. However, if the underlying stock continues to rise in price, more profits would accrue on the call. Every call buyer realizes the ramifications of these two tactics—liquidating or doing nothing—and is generally looking for an alternative that might allow him to reduce some of his risk without cutting off his profit potential completely. The remaining two tactics are geared to this purpose—limiting the total risk while providing the opportunity for further profits of an amount greater than those that could be realized by liquidating.

The strategy in which the holder sells the call that he is currently holding—the October 50—and uses part of the proceeds to buy the call at the next higher strike will be called *rolling up.* In this example, he could sell the October 50 at 9, pocket his initial 3-point investment, and use the remaining proceeds to buy two October 60 calls at 3 points each. Thus it is sometimes possible for the speculator to recoup his entire original investment and still increase the number of calls outstanding by rolling up. Once this has been done, the October 60 calls will represent pure profits, whatever their price. *The buyer who "rolls up" in this manner is essentially speculating with someone else's money*—he has put his own money back in his pocket and is using accrued profits to attempt to realize further gains. At expiration, this tactic would perform best if XYZ were to continue to experience a substantial rise in price. Since the call buyer is long two October 60's as opposed to one October 50 (the original position), profits would accrue twice as fast if XYZ rose above 60 by a substantial amount. This tactic turns out to be the worst of the four at expiration if XYZ remains near its current price—staying above 53 but not rising above 63 in this example.

The final alternative of the four is to continue to hold the October 50 call but to sell the October 60 call against it. This would create what is known as a bull spread, and the tactic can *only* be used by traders who have a margin account and can meet their firm's minimum equity requirement for spreading (generally $2,000). This spread position has no risk, for the long side of the spread—the October 50—cost 3 points and the short side of the spread—the October 60—brought in 3 points via its sale. Even if the underlying stock drops below 50 by expiration and all the calls expire worthless, the trader cannot lose anything except commissions. On the other hand, the maximum potential of this spread is 10 points, the difference between the striking prices of 50 and 60.

This maximum potential would be realized if XYZ were anywhere above 60 at expiration, for at that time the October 50 call would be worth 10 points more than the October 60 call, regardless of how far above 60 the underlying stock had risen. *This strategy will be the best performer of the four if XYZ remains relatively unchanged,* above the lower strike but not much above the higher strike by expiration. It is interesting to note that this tactic is *never the worst performer of the four tactics,* no matter where the stock is at expiration. For example, if XYZ drops below 50, this strategy has no risk and is therefore better than the "do nothing" strategy. If XYZ rises substantially, this spread produces a profit of 10 points, which is better than the 6 points of profit offered by the "liquidate" strategy.

There is no definite answer as to which of the four tactics is the best one to apply in a given situation. However, if a call can be sold against the currently long call to produce a bull spread which has little or no risk, it may often be an attractive thing to do. It can never turn out to be the worst decision, and it would produce the largest profits if XYZ does not rise substantially or fall substantially from its current levels. Tables 3-2 and 3-3 summarize the four alternative tactics, when a call holder has an unrealized profit. The four tactics, again, are:

**TABLE 3-2.** *Comparison of the four alternative strategies.*

| If the underlying stock then . . . | The best tactic was . . . | And the worst tactic was . . . |
| --- | --- | --- |
| continues to rise dramatically. . . | "roll up" | liquidate |
| rises moderately above the next strike | "do nothing" | liquidate or "roll up" |
| remains relatively unchanged | "spread" | "roll up" |
| falls back below the original strike | liquidate | "do nothing" |

1. "Do nothing"—continue to hold the currently long call.

2. "Liquidate"—sell the long call to take profits and do not reinvest.

3. "Roll up"—sell the long call, pocket the original investment, and use the remaining proceeds to purchase as many out-of-the-money calls as possible.

4. "Spread"—create a bull spread by selling the out-of-the-money call against the currently profitable long call, preferably taking in at least the original cost of the long call.

**TABLE 3-3.** *Results at expiration.*

| XYZ Price at Expiration | "Roll-up" Profit | "Do Nothing" Profit | "Spread" Profit | Liquidating Profit |
|---|---|---|---|---|
| 50 or below | $   0 | −$   300 (W) | $     0 | +$600 (B) |
| 53 | 0 (W) | 0 (W) | +    300 | +  600 (B) |
| 56 | 0 (W) | +    300 | +    600 (B) | +  600 (B) |
| 60 | 0 (W) | +    700 | +  1,000 (B) | +  600 |
| 63 | +   600 (W) | +  1,000 (B) | +  1,000 (B) | +  600 (W) |
| 67 | + 1,400 (B) | +  1,400 (B) | +  1,000 | +  600 (W) |
| 70 | + 2,000 (B) | +  1,700 | +  1,000 | +  600 (W) |

*Note that each of the four tactics proves to be the best tactic in one case or another, but that the spread tactic is never the worst one.* Tables 3-2 and 3-3 represent the results from holding until expiration. For those who prefer to see the actual numbers involved in making these comparisons between the four tactics, Table 3-3 summarizes the potential profits and losses of each of the four tactics using the prices from the example above. "W" indicates that the tactic is the worst one at that price, and "B" indicates that it is the best one.

There are, of course, modifications that one might make to any of these tactics. For example, he might decide to sell out half of his long call position—recovering a major part of his original cost—and continue to hold the remainder of the long calls. This still leaves room for further appreciation.

### Defensive Action

There are two follow-up strategies that are sometimes employed by the call buyer when the underlying stock declines in price. Both involve spread strategies—that is being long and short two different calls on the same underlying stock simultaneously. Spreads are discussed in detail in a later chapter. This discussion of spreads applies only to their use by the call buyer.

*"Rolling Down."* If an option holder owns an option at a currently unrealized loss, it may be possible to greatly increase the chances of making a limited profit on a relatively small rebound in the stock price. In certain cases, the investor may be able to implement such a strategy at little or no increase in risk.

Many call buyers have encountered a situation such as this: an XYZ October 35 call was originally bought for 3 points in hopes of a quick risk in the stock price. However, because of downward movements in the stock—to 32, say—the call is now at 1½ with October

103

expiration nearer. If the call buyer still expects a mild rally in the stock before expiration, he might either hold the call or possibly "average down" (buy more calls at 1½). In either case he will need a rally to nearly 38 by expiration in order to break even. Since this would necessitate at least a 15% upward move by the stock before expiration, it cannot be considered too likely. Instead, the buyer should consider implementing the following strategy, which will be explained through the use of an example.

>*Example:* The investor is long the October 35 call at this time:
>
>XYZ, 32;
>
>XYZ October 35 call, 1½; and
>
>XYZ October 30 call, 3.

One could sell two October 35's and, at the same time, buy one October 30 for no additional investment before commissions. That is, the sale of 2 October 35's at $150 each would bring in $300, exactly the cost, before commissions, of buying the October 30 call. *This is the key to implementing the roll-down strategy—that one be able to buy the lower strike call and sell two of the higher strike calls for nearly even money.*

Note that the investor is now *short* the call that he previously owned—the October 35. Where he previously owned one October 35, he has now sold two of them. He is also now long one October 30 call. Thus his position is:

>long 1 XYZ October 30 call,
>short 1 XYZ October 35 call.

This is technically known as a *bull spread,* but the terminology is not important. Table 3-4 summarizes the transactions that the buyer has made to acquire this spread. The trader now "owns" the spread at a cost of $300, plus commissions. By making this trade, he has lowered his break-even point significantly without increasing his risk. However, the maximum profit potential has also been limited—he can no longer capitalize on a strong rebound by the underlying stock.

**TABLE 3-4.** *Transactions in bull spread.*

|  | Trade | Cost before Commissions |
|---|---|---|
| Original trade | Buy 1 October 35 call at 3 | $300 debit |
| Later trade | Sell 2 October 35 calls at 1½<br>Buy 1 October 30 call at 3 | $300 credit<br>$300 debit |
| Net position | Long 1 October 30 call<br>Short 1 October 35 call | $300 debit |

In order to see that the break-even point has been lowered, consider what the results are if XYZ is at 33 at October expiration. The October 30 call would be worth 3 points and the October 35 would expire worthless with XYZ at 33. Thus the October 30 call could be sold to bring in $300 at that time and there would not be any expense to buy back the October 35. Consequently, the spread could be liquidated for $300— exactly the amount for which it was "bought." The spread then breaks even at 33 at expiration. If the call buyer had not rolled down, his break-even point would be 38 at expiration, for he paid 3 points for the original October 35 call and he would thus need XYZ to be at 38 in order to be able to liquidate the call for 3 points. Clearly, the stock has a better chance of recovering to 33 than to 38. *Thus the call buyer significantly lowers his break-even point by utilizing this strategy.*

Lowering the break-even point is not the investor's only concern. He must also be aware of what has happened to his profit and loss opportunities. The risk remains essentially the same—the $300 in debits, plus commissions that have been paid out. The risk has actually increased slightly, by the amount of the commissions spent in "rolling down." However, the stock price at which this maximum loss would be realized has been lowered. With the original long call, the October 35, the buyer would lose the entire $300 investment anywhere below 35 at October expiration. The spread strategy, however, would result in a total loss of $300 only if XYZ were below *30* at October expiration. With XYZ above 30 in October, the long side of the spread could be liquidated for some value, thereby avoiding a total loss. *The investor has reduced the chance of realizing the maximum loss,* since the stock price at which that loss would occur has been lowered by 5 points.

As with most investments, the improvement of risk exposure— lowering the break-even point and lowering the maximum loss price— necessitates that some potential reward be sacrificed. In the original long call position (the October 35), the maximum profit potential was unlimited. In the new position, the potential profit is limited to 2 points if XYZ should rally back to, *or anywhere above,* 35 by October expiration. To see this, assume XYZ is 35 at expiration. Then the long October 30 call would be worth 5 points, while the October 35 would expire worthless. Thus the spread could be liquidated for 5 points, a 2-point profit over the 3 points paid for the spread. This is the limit of profit for the spread, however, since if XYZ is above 35 at expiration, any further profits in the long October 30 call would be offset by a corresponding loss on the short October 35 call. *Thus, if XYZ were to rally heavily by expiration, the "rolled-down" position would not realize as large a profit as the original long call position would have realized.*

**TABLE 3-5.** *Original and spread positions compared.*

| Stock Price at Expiration | Long Call Result | Spread Result |
|---|---|---|
| 25 | −$300 | −$300 |
| 30 | − 300 | − 300 |
| 33 | − 300 | 0 |
| 35 | − 300 | + 200 |
| 38 | 0 | + 200 |
| 40 | + 200 | + 200 |
| 45 | + 700 | + 200 |

**FIGURE 3-2.** *Comparison: original call purchase vs. spread.*

Table 3-5 and Figure 3-2 summarize the original and new positions. Note that the new position is better for stock prices between 30 and 40. Below 30, the two positions are equal, except for the additional commissions spent. If the stock should rally back above 40, the original position would have worked out better. *The new position is an improvement, provided that XYZ does not rally back above 40 by expiration.* The chances that XYZ could rally 8 points, or 25%, from 32 to 40 would have to be considered relatively remote. Rolling the long call down into the spread would thus appear to be the correct thing to do in this case.

This example is particularly attractive, because no additional money was required to establish the spread. In many cases, however, one may find that the long call cannot be rolled into the spread at even money. Some debit may be required. This fact should not necessarily preclude making the change, since a small additional investment may still significantly increase the chance of breaking even or making a profit on a rebound.

> *Example:* The following prices now exist, rather than the ones used earlier. Only the October 30 call price has been altered:
>
> XYZ, 32;
>
> XYZ October 35 call, 1½; and
>
> XYZ October 30 call, 4.
>
> With these prices, a 1-point debit would be required to roll down. That is, selling 2 October 35 calls would bring in $300 ($150 each), but the cost of buying the October 30 call is $400. Thus the transaction would have to be done at a cost of $100, plus commissions. With these prices, the break-even point after rolling down would be 34—still well below the original break-even price of 38. The risk has now been increased by the additional 1 point spent to roll down. If XYZ should drop below 30 at October expiration, the investor would have a total loss of 4 points plus commissions. The maximum loss with the original long October 35 call was limited to 3 points plus a smaller amount of commissions. Finally, the maximum amount of money that the spread could make is now $100, less commissions. The alternative in this example is not nearly as attractive as the previous one, but it might still be worthwhile for the call buyer to invoke such a spread if he feels that XYZ has limited rally potential up to October expiration.

One should not automatically discard the use of this strategy merely because a debit is required to convert the long call to a spread. Note that to *"average down"* by buying an additional October 35 call at 1½ would require an additional investment of $150. This is more than the $100 required to convert into the spread position in the immediately preceding example. The break-even point on the position that was "averaged down" would be over 37 at expiration, whereas the break-even point on the spread is 34. Admittedly, the averaged-down position has much more profit potential than the spread does, but the conversion to the spread is less expensive than "averaging down" and also provides a lower break-even price.

In summary, then, if the call buyer finds himself with an unrealized loss because the stock has declined, and yet is unwilling to sell, he may be able to improve his chances of breaking even by "rolling down" into a spread. That is, he would sell 2 of the calls that he is currently long—the one that he owns plus another one—and simultaneously buy one call at the next lower striking price. If this transaction of selling 2 calls and buying 1 call can be done for approximately even money, it could definitely be to the buyer's benefit to implement this strategy because the break-even point would be lowered considerably and the buyer would have a much better chance of getting out even or making a small profit should the underlying stock have a small rebound.

*Creating a Calendar Spread.* A different type of defensive spread strategy is sometimes used by the call buyer who finds that the underlying stock has declined. In this strategy, the holder of an inter- mediate- or long-term call sells a near-term call, with the same striking price as the call he already owns. This creates what is known as a *calendar spread.* The idea behind doing this is that if the short-term call expires worthless, the overall cost of the long call will be reduced to the buyer. Then, if the stock should rally, the call buyer has a better chance of making a profit.

> *Example:* Suppose that an investor bought an XYZ October 35 call for 3 points sometime in April. By June the stock has fallen to 32, and it appears that the stock might remain depressed for a while longer. The holder of the October 35 call might consider selling a July 35 call— perhaps for a price of 1 point. Should XYZ remain below 35 until *July* expiration, the short call would expire worthless, earning a small, "1-" point profit. The investor would still own the October 35 call and would then hope for a rally by XYZ before October in order to make profits on that call. Even if XYZ does not rally by October, he has decreased his overall loss by the amount received for the sale of the July 35 call.
>
> This strategy is not as attractive to use as the previous one. If XYZ should rally before July expiration, the investor might find himself with two losing positions. For example, suppose that XYZ rallied back to 36 in the next week. His short call that he sold for 1 point would be selling for something more than that, so he would have an unrealized loss on the short July 35. In addition, the October 35 would probably not have appreciated back to its original price of 3 and he would therefore have an unrealized loss on that side of the spread as well.

Consequently, this strategy should be used with great caution, for if the underlying stock rallies quickly before the near-term expiration, the spread could be at a loss on both sides. Note that in the former spread strategy, this could not happen. Even if XYZ rallied quickly, some profit would be made on the rebound.

## *A FURTHER COMMENT ON SPREADS*

Anyone not familiar with the margin requirements for spreads—both under the federal margin rules and the rules of the brokerage firm he is dealing with—should not attempt to utilize a spread transaction. Later chapters on spreads outline the more common requirements for spread transactions. In general, one must have a margin account to establish a spread and he must have a minimum amount of equity in the account. Thus the call buyer who operates in a cash account cannot necessarily use these spread strategies. To do so might incur a margin call and possible restriction of one's trading account. Therefore, check on specific requirements necessary before utilizing a spread strategy. Do not assume that a long call can automatically be "rolled" into any sort of a spread.

CHAPTER

# Other Call *4*
# Buying
# Strategies

In this chapter, two additional strategies that utilize the purchase of call options will be described. Both of these strategies involve buying calls against the short sale of the underlying stock. Where listed puts are traded on the underlying stock, these strategies become passé—they are better implemented with the use of put options. However, since some stocks have listed calls without listed puts, these strategies are applicable in those cases. Another well-known call buying strategy—the simultaneous purchase of options and fixed-income securities—will be described in Chapter 25.

## THE PROTECTED SHORT SALE (OR SYNTHETIC PUT)

*Purchasing a call at the same time that one is short the underlying stock is a means of limiting the risk of the short sale to a fixed amount.* Since the risk is theoretically unlimited in a short sale, many investors are reluctant to use the strategy. Even for those investors who *do* sell stock short, it can be rather upsetting if the stock rises in price. One may be forced into an emotional—and perhaps incorrect—decision to cover the short sale in order to relieve the psychological pressure. By owning a call at the same time one is short, the risk is limited to a fixed and generally small amount.

*Example:* An investor sells XYZ short at 40 and simultaneously purchases an XYZ July 40 call for 3 points. If XYZ falls in price, the short
seller will make his profit on the short sale, less the 3 points paid for the
call, which will expire worthless. *Thus, by buying the call for protection, a small amount of profit potential is sacrificed.* However, the
advantage of owning the call is demonstrated when the results are
examined for a stock rise. If XYZ should rise to any price above 40 by
July expiration, the short seller can cover his short by exercising the
long call and buying stock at 40. Thus the maximum risk that the short
seller can incur in this example is the 3 points paid for the call. Table
4-1 and Figure 4-1 depict the results at expiration from utilizing this

**TABLE 4-1.** *Results at expiration—protected short sale.*

| XYZ Price at Expiration | Profit on XYZ | Call Price at Expiration | Profit on Call | Total Profit |
|---|---|---|---|---|
| 20 | +$2,000 | 0 | −$ 300 | +$1,700 |
| 30 | + 1,000 | 0 | − 300 | + 700 |
| 37 | + 300 | 0 | − 300 | 0 |
| 40 | 0 | 0 | − 300 | − 300 |
| 50 | − 1,000 | 10 | + 700 | − 300 |
| 60 | − 2,000 | 20 | + 1,700 | − 300 |

**FIGURE 4-1.** *Protected short sale.*

strategy. Commissions are not included. Note that the break-even point is 37 in this example. That is, if the stock drops 3 points, the protected short sale position will break even because of the 3-point loss on the stock. The short seller who did not spend the extra money for the long call would, of course, have a 3-point profit at 37. To the upside, however, the protected short sale outperforms a regular short sale if the stock climbs anywhere above 43. At 43, both types of short sales have $300 losses. But above that level, the loss would continue to grow for a regular short sale, while it is fixed for the short seller who also bought a call. In either case, the short seller's risk is increased slightly by the fact that he is obligated to pay out the dividends on the underlying stock, if any are declared.

A simple formula is available for determining the maximum amount of risk when one protects a short sale by buying a call option:

$$Risk = \text{Striking price of purchased call} + \text{Call price} - \text{Stock price}$$

Depending on how much risk the short seller is willing to absorb, he might want to buy an out-of-the-money call as protection rather than an at-the-money call as was shown in the example above. A smaller dollar amount is spent for the protection when one buys an out-of-the-money call, so that the short seller does not give away as much of his profit potential. However, his risk is larger because the call does not start its protective qualities until the stock goes above the striking price.

> *Example:* With XYZ at 40, the short seller of XYZ buys the July 45 call at ½ for protection. His maximum possible loss, if XYZ is above 45 at July expiration, would be 5½ points—the five points between the current stock price of 40 and the striking price of 45, plus the amount paid for the call. On the other hand, if XYZ declines, the protected short seller will make nearly as much as the short seller who did not protect, since he only spent ½ point for the long call.

If one buys an *in-the-money* call as protection for the short sale, his risk will be quite minimal. However, his profit potential will be severely limited. As an example, with XYZ at 40, if one had purchased a July 35 call at 5½, his risk would be limited to ½ point anywhere above 35 at July expiration. Unfortunately, he would not realize any profit on the position until the stock went below 34½, a drop of 5½ points. This is too much protection, for it limits the profit so severely that there is only a small hope of making a profit.

*Generally, it is best to buy a call that is at-the-money or only slightly out-of-the-money as the protection for the short sale.* It is not of much use to buy a deeply out-of-the-money call as protection, since it does very little to moderate risk unless the stock climbs quite dramatically. Normally, one would cover a short sale before it went heavily against him. Thus the money spent for such a deeply out-of-the-money call is wasted.

### Margin Requirements

Even though one has limited risk in this position, there is no benefit as far as margin requirements are concerned. A short seller has his position marked to the market daily—that is, the amount of profit or loss is added to, or subtracted from, his excess collateral (called SMA) on a daily basis. Consequently, if a stock that one has sold short should rise dramatically, one could receive a margin call because of the buildup of unrealized losses. Even if one has purchased a call as protection for the short sale, this same margin procedure is followed. It is illogical to mark the short seller to market even when his risk is limited. However, the federal margin rules have not been altered to cover this strategy. Should one receive such a margin call while he owns the long call for protection, he can easily satisfy the margin requirement by exercising the call option and closing out the position. This action would return a positive collateral balance to his margin account.

### Follow-up Action

There is little that the protected short seller needs to perform in the way of follow-up action in this strategy, other than closing out the position. If the underlying stock moves down quickly and it appears that it might rebound, the short sale could be covered without selling the long call. In this manner, one could potentially profit on the call side as well if the stock came back above the original striking price. If the underlying stock *rises* in price, a similar strategy of taking off only the profitable side of the transaction is *not* recommended. That is, if XYZ climbed from 40 to 50 and the July 40 call also rose from 3 to 10, it is *not* advisable to take the 7-point profit in the call, hoping for a drop in the stock price. The reason for this is that one is entering into a highly risk oriented situation by removing his protection when the call is in-the-money. Thus when the stock *drops,* it is all right—perhaps even desirable—to take the profit because there is little or no additional risk if the stock continues to drop. However, when the stock *rises,* it is *not* an equivalent situation. In that case, if the short seller sells his call for a profit and the stock subsequently rises even further, large losses could result.

It may often be advisable to close the position if the call is at or near parity, in-the-money, by exercising the call. In most strategies, the option holder has no advantage in exercising the call because of the large dollar difference between stock commissions and option commissions. However, in the protected short sale strategy, the short seller is eventually going to have to cover the short stock in any case and incur the stock commission by so doing. It may be to his advantage to exercise the call and buy his stock at the striking price, thereby buying stock at a lower price and thus paying a slightly lower commission amount.

> *Example:* XYZ rises to 50 from the original short sale price of 40 and the XYZ July 40 call is selling at 10 somewhere close to expiration. The position could be liquidated by either (1) buying the stock back at 50 and selling the call at 10, or (2) exercising the call to buy stock at 40. In the first case, one would pay a stock commission at a price of $50 per share plus an option commission on a $10 option. In the second case, the only commission would be a stock commission at the price of $40 per share. Since both actions accomplish the same end result—closing the position entirely for 40 points plus commissions—clearly the second choice is least costly and therefore more desirable. Of course, if the call has time value premium in it of an amount greater than the commission savings, the first alternative should be used.

## THE REVERSE HEDGE (SIMULATED STRADDLE)

There is another strategy involving the purchase of long calls against the short sale of stock. In this strategy, one purchases calls on more shares than he has sold short. The strategist can profit if the underlying stock rises far enough or falls far enough during the life of the calls. This strategy is generally referred to as a *reverse hedge* or a *simulated straddle.* On stocks where listed puts are traded, this strategy is outmoded—the same results can be better achieved by buying a straddle (a call and a put). Hence the name "simulated straddle" is also applied to the reverse hedge strategy.

*This strategy has limited loss potential,* usually amounting to a moderate percentage of the initial investment, *and theoretically unlimited profit potential.* The frequency of loss can be high (that is, a large percentage of the trades may result in losses), but the unlimited profit potential feature means that one or two large profits can over-come the losses incurred. These features make this an attractive strategy, especially when call premiums are low in comparison to the volatility of the underlying stock.

*Example:* XYZ is at 40 and an investor feels that the stock has the potential of moving by a relatively large distance, but he is not sure of the direction the stock will take. This investor could short XYZ at 40 and buy 2 XYZ July 40 calls at 3 each to set up a reverse hedge. If XYZ moves up by a large distance, he will incur a loss on his short stock, but the fact that he owns *two* calls means that the call profits will outdistance the stock loss. If, on the other hand, XYZ drops far enough, the short sale profit will be larger than the loss on the calls, which is limited to 6 points. Table 4-2 and Figure 4-2 show the possible

**TABLE 4-2.** *Reverse hedge at July expiration.*

| XYZ Price at Expiration | Stock Profit | Profit on 2 Calls | Total Profit |
|---|---|---|---|
| 20 | +$2,000 | −$ 600 | +$1,400 |
| 25 | + 1,500 | − 600 | + 900 |
| 30 | + 1,000 | − 600 | + 400 |
| 34 | + 600 | − 600 | 0 |
| 40 | 0 | − 600 | − 600 |
| 46 | − 600 | + 600 | 0 |
| 50 | − 1,000 | + 1,400 | + 400 |
| 55 | − 1,500 | + 2,400 | + 900 |
| 60 | − 2,000 | + 3,400 | + 1,400 |

**FIGURE 4-2.** *Reverse hedge (simulated straddle).*

Profit or Loss at Expiration

−$600

34    40    46

Stock Price at Expiration

outcomes for various stock prices at July expiration. If XYZ falls, the stock profits on the short sale will accumulate, but the loss on the two calls is limited to $600 (3 points each) so that, below 34, the reverse hedge can make ever-increasing profits. To the upside, even though the short sale is incurring losses, the call profits grow faster because there are two long calls. For example, at 60 at expiration, there will be a 20-point ($2,000) loss on the short stock, but each XYZ July 40 call will be worth 20 points with the stock at 60. Thus the two calls are worth $4,000, representing a profit of $3,400 over the initial cost of $600 for the calls.

Table 4-2 and Figure 4-2 illustrate another important point—*the maximum loss would occur if the stock were exactly at the striking price at expiration of the calls.* This maximum loss would occur if XYZ were at 40 at expiration and would amount to $600. In actual practice, since the short seller must pay out any dividends paid by the underlying stock, the risk in this strategy is increased by the amount of such dividends.

The net margin required for this strategy is 50% of the underlying stock plus the full purchase price of the calls. In the example above, this would be an initial investment of $2,000 (50% of the stock price) plus $600 for the calls, or $2,600 total plus commissions. The short sale is marked to market so the collateral requirement would grow if the stock rose. Since the maximum risk, before commissions, is $600, this means that the net percentage risk in this transaction is $600/$2,600, about 23%. This is a relatively small percentage risk in a position that could have profits which are potentially very large. There is also very little chance that the entire maximum loss would ever be realized since it occurs only at one specific stock price. One should not be deluded into thinking that this strategy is a sure money maker. In general, stocks do not move very far in a 3- or 6-month period. Thus the probability of loss is high in this strategy. This is balanced out by the fact that significant gains can be realized.

It is obvious from the information above that profits are made if the stock moves far enough in either direction. In fact, one can exactly determine the prices beyond which the stock would have to move by expiration in order for profits to result. These prices are 34 and 46 in the foregoing example. The downside break-even point is 34 and the upside break-even point is 46. These break-even points can be easily computed. First the maximum risk is computed. Then the break-even points are determined.

Maximum risk = Striking price + 2 × Call price − Stock price

Upside break-even point = Striking price + Maximum risk

Downside break-even point = Striking price − Maximum risk

In the preceding example, the striking price was 40, the stock price was also 40, and the call price was 3. Thus the maximum risk = $40 + 2 \times 3 - 40 = 6$. This confirms that the maximum risk in the position is 6 points, or $600. The upside break-even point is then $40 + 6$, or 46, and the downside break-even point is $40 - 6$, or 34. These also agree with Table 4-2 and Figure 4-2.

*Before expiration, profits can be made even closer to the striking price, because there will be some time value premium left in the purchased calls.*

> *Example:* If XYZ moved to 45 in one month, each call might be worth 6. If this happened, the investor would have a 5-point loss on the stock, but would also have a 3-point gain on each of the two options, for a net overall gain of 1 point, or $100. Before expiration, the break-even point is clearly somewhere below 46, because the position is at a profit at 45.

Ideally, one would like to find relatively underpriced calls on a fairly volatile stock in order to implement this strategy most effectively. Unfortunately, this combination occurs mostly in books and not very often in the actual marketplace. Normally, call premiums quite accurately reflect the volatility of the underlying stock. Still, this strategy can be quite viable, because nearly every stock, regardless of its volatility, occasionally experiences a straight-line, fairly large, move. It is during these times that the investor can profit from this strategy.

Generally, the underlying stock selected for the reverse hedge should be volatile. Even though option premiums are larger on these stocks, they can still be outdistanced by a straight-line move in a volatile situation. Another advantage of utilizing volatile stocks is that they generally pay little or no dividends. This is desirable for the reverse hedge, because the short seller will not be required to pay out as much.

The technical pattern of the underlying stock can also be useful when selecting the position. One generally would like to have little or no technical support and resistance within the loss area. This pattern would facilitate the stock's ability to make a fairly quick move either up or down. It is sometimes possible to find a stock that is in a wide trading range, frequently swinging from one side of the range to the other. If a reverse hedge can be set up that has its loss area well within this trading range, the position may also be attractive.

*Example:* The XYZ stock in the previous example is trading in the range 30 to 50, perhaps swinging to one end and then the other rather frequently. Now the reverse hedge example position, which would make profits above 46 or below 34, would appear more attractive.

## Follow-up Action

Since the reverse hedge has a built-in limited loss feature, it is not necessary to take any follow-up action to avoid losses. The investor could quite easily put the position on and take no action at all until expiration. This is often the best method of follow-up action in this strategy.

There is a follow-up strategy that can be applied, although it has some disadvantages associated with it. This follow-up strategy is sometimes known as *"trading against the straddle."* When the stock moves far enough in either direction, the profit on that side can be taken. Then if the stock swings back in the opposite direction, a profit can also be made on the other side. Two examples will show how this type of follow-up strategy works.

*Example 1:* The XYZ stock in the previous example quickly moves down to 32. At that time, an 8-point profit could be taken on the short sale. This would leave two long calls. Even if they expired worthless, a 6-point loss would be all that would be incurred on the calls. Thus the entire strategy would still have produced a profit of 2 points. However, if the stock should rally above 40, profits could be made on the calls as well. A slight variation would be to sell *one* of the calls at the same time the stock profit is taken. This would result in a slightly larger realized profit, but, if the stock rallied back above 40, the resulting profits there would be smaller because the investor would only be long one call instead of two.

*Example 2:* XYZ has moved up to a price where the calls are each worth 8 points. *One* of the calls could then be sold, realizing a 5-point profit. The resulting position would be short 100 shares of stock and long one call, a protected short sale. The protected short sale has a limited risk, above 40, of 3 points (the stock was sold short at 40 and the call was purchased for 3 points). Even if XYZ remains above 40 and the maximum 3-point loss has to be taken, the overall reverse hedge would still have made a profit of 2 points because of the 5-point profit taken on the one call. Conversely, if XYZ drops below 40, the protected short sale position could add to the profits already taken on the call.

There is a variation of this upside protective action.

*Example 3:* Instead of selling the one call, one could instead short an additional 100 shares of stock at 48. If this was done, the overall position would be short 200 shares of stock (100 at 40 and the other 100 at 48) and long two calls—again a protected short sale. If XYZ remained above 40, there would again be an overall gain of 2 points. To see this, suppose that XYZ was above 40 at expiration and the two calls were exercised to buy 200 shares of stock at 40. This would result in an 8-point profit on the 100 shares sold short at 48 and no gain or loss on the 100 shares sold short at 40. The initial call cost of 6 points would be lost. Thus the overall position would profit by 2 points. This means of follow-up action to the upside is more costly in commissions, but would provide bigger profits if XYZ fell back below 40, because there are 200 shares of XYZ short.

In theory, if any of the foregoing types of follow-up action were taken and the underlying stock did indeed reverse direction and cross back through the striking price, the original position could again be established. Suppose that, after covering the short stock at 32, XYZ rallied back to 40. Then XYZ could be sold short again, reestablishing the original position. If the stock moved outside the break-even points again, further follow-up action could be taken. This process could theoretically be repeated a number of times. If the stock continued to whipsaw back and forth in a trading range, the repeated follow-up actions could produce potentially large profits on a small net change in the stock price. In actual practice, it is unlikely that one would be fortunate to find a stock that moved that far that quickly.

The disadvantage of applying these follow-up strategies is obvious—*one can never make a large profit if he continually cuts his profits off at a small, limited amount.* When XYZ falls to 32, the stock can be covered to ensure an overall profit of 2 points on the transaction. However, if XYZ continued to fall to 20, the investor who took no follow-up action would make 14 points while the one who did take follow-up action would only make 2 points. Recall that it was stated earlier that there is a high probability of realizing limited losses in the reverse hedge strategy, but that this was balanced by the potentially large profits available in the remaining cases. If one takes follow-up action and cuts off these potentially large profits, he is operating at a distinct disadvantage unless he is an extremely adept trader.

Proponents of using the follow-up strategy often counter with the argument that it is frustrating to see the stock fall to 32 and then return back nearly 40 again. If no follow-up action were taken, the unrealized profit would have dissolved into a loss when the stock rallied. This is true as far as it goes, but it is not an effective enough argument to counterbalance the negative effects of cutting off one's profits.

## ALTERING THE RATIO OF LONG CALLS TO SHORT STOCK

There is another aspect of this strategy that should be discussed. One does not have to buy exactly two calls against 100 shares of short stock. More bullish positions could be constructed by buying three or four calls against 100 shares short. More bearish positions could be constructed by buying three calls and shorting 200 shares of stock. One might adopt a ratio other than 2:1 because he is more bullish or bearish. He also might use a different ratio if the stock is between two striking prices, but he still wants to create that a position that has break-even points spaced equidistant from the current stock price. A few examples will illustrate these points.

> *Example:* XYZ is at 40 and the investor is slightly bullish on the stock but still wants to employ the reverse hedge strategy because he feels there is a chance the stock could drop sharply. He might then short 100 shares of XYZ at 40 and buy 3 July 40 calls for 3 points apiece. Since he paid 9 points for the calls, his maximum risk is that 9 points if XYZ were to be at 40 at expiration. This means his downside break-even price is 31, for at 31 he would have a 9-point profit on the short sale to offset the 9-point loss on the calls. To the upside, his break-even is now 44½. If XYZ were at 44½ and the calls at 4½ each at expiration, he would lose 4½ points on the short sale, but would make 1½ on each of the three calls, for a total call profit of 4½.

A more bearish investor might short 200 XYZ at 40 and buy 3 July 40 calls at 3. His break-even points would be 35½ on the downside and 49 on the upside, and his maximum risk would be 9 points. There is a general formula that one can always apply to calculate the maximum risk and the break-even points, regardless of the ratios involved.

Maximum risk = (striking price − stock price) × round lots shorted
+ number of calls bought × call price

Upside break-even = striking price + $\dfrac{\text{maximum risk}}{\begin{array}{c}\text{(number of calls bought}\\ -\text{ number of round lots short)}\end{array}}$

$$\text{Downside break-even} = \text{striking price} - \frac{\text{maximum risk}}{\text{number of round lots short}}$$

To verify this, use the numbers from the example where 100 XYZ was shorted at 40 and three July 40 calls were purchased for 3 each.

Maximum risk $= (40 - 40) \times 1 + 3 \times 3 = 9$

Upside break-even $= 40 + 9/(3 - 1) = 40 + 4\frac{1}{2} = 44\frac{1}{2}$

Downside break-even $= 40 - 9/1 = 31$

It was stated earlier that *one might use an adjusted ratio in order to space the break-even points evenly around the current stock price.*

*Example:* Suppose XYZ is at 38 and the XYZ July 40 call is at 2. If one wanted to set up a reverse hedge that would profit if XYZ moved either up or down by the same distance, he could not use the 2:1 ratio. The 2:1 ratio would have break-even points of 34 and 46. Thus the stock would start out much closer to the downside break-even point— only 4 points away—than to the upside break-even point, which is 8 points away. By altering the ratio, the investor can set up a reverse hedge that is more neutral on the underlying stock. Suppose that the investor shorted 100 shares of XYZ at 38 and bought *three* July 40 calls at 2 each. Then his break-even points would be 32 on the downside and 44 on the upside. This is a more neutral situation, with the downside break-even point being 6 points below the current stock price and the upside break-even point being 6 points away. The formulae above can be used to verify that, in fact, the break-evens are 32 and 44. Note that the 3:1 ratio has a maximum risk of 8 points, while the 2:1 ratio only had 6 points maximum risk.

A final adjustment that can be applied to this strategy is to short the stock and buy two calls, but with the calls having *different striking prices.* If XYZ were at 37½ to start with, one would have to use a ratio other than 2:1 to set up a position with break-even points spaced equidistant from the current stock price. When these higher ratios are used, the maximum risk is increased and the investor has to adopt a bullish or bearish stance. One may be able to create a position with equidistant break-even points and a smaller maximum risk by utilizing two different striking prices.

*Example:* The following prices exist:

XYZ, 37½;
XYZ July 40 call, 2; and
XYZ July 35 call, 4.

If one were to short 100 XYZ at 37½ and to buy one July 40 call for 2 and one July 35 call for 4, he would have a position that is similar to a reverse hedge except that *the maximum risk would be realized anywhere between 35 and 40 at expiration.* Although this risk is over a much wider range than in the normal reverse hedge, it is now much smaller in dimension. Table 4-3 and Figure 4-3 show the results from this type of position at expiration. The maximum loss is 3½ points ($350), which is a smaller amount than could be realized using any ratio with strictly the July 35 or the July 40 call. However, this maximum loss is realizable over the entire range 35 to 40. Again, large

**TABLE 4-3.** *Reverse hedge using two strikes.*

| XYZ Price at Expiration | Stock Profit | July 40 Call Profit | July 35 Call Profit | Total Profit |
|---|---|---|---|---|
| 25 | +$1,250 | −$200 | −$ 400 | +$650 |
| 30 | + 750 | − 200 | − 400 | + 150 |
| 31½ | + 600 | − 200 | − 400 | 0 |
| 35 | + 250 | − 200 | − 400 | − 350 |
| 37½ | 0 | − 200 | − 150 | − 350 |
| 40 | − 250 | − 200 | + 100 | − 350 |
| 43½ | − 600 | + 150 | + 450 | 0 |
| 45 | − 750 | + 300 | + 600 | + 150 |
| 50 | − 1,250 | + 800 | + 1,100 | + 650 |

**FIGURE 4-3.** *Reverse hedge using two strikes (simulated combination purchase).*

Stock Price at
Expiration

potential profits are available if the stock moves far enough either to the upside or to the downside.

This form of the strategy should only be used when the stock is nearly centered between two strikes and the strategist wants a neutral positioning of the break-even points. Similar types of follow-up action to those described earlier can be applied to this form of the reverse hedge strategy as well.

## SUMMARY

The strategies described in this chapter would not normally be used if the underlying stock has listed put options. However, if no puts exist, and the strategist feels that a volatile stock could move a relatively large distance in either direction during the life of a call option, he should consider using one of the forms of the reverse hedge strategy—shorting a quantity of stock and buying calls on more shares than he is short. If the desired movement does develop, potentially large profits could result. In any case, the loss is limited to a fixed amount, generally around 20 to 30% of the initial investment. Although it is possible to take follow-up action to lock in small profits and attempt to gain on a reversal by the stock, it is wiser to let the position run its course to capitalize on those occasions when the profits become large. Normally a 2:1 ratio (long 2 calls, short 100 shares of stock) is used in this strategy, but this ratio can be adjusted if the investor wants to be more bullish or more bearish. If the stock is initially between two striking prices, a neutral profit range can be set up by shorting the stock and buying calls at both the next higher strike and the next lower strike.

CHAPTER 5

# Naked
# Call Writing

The next two chapters will concentrate on various aspects of writing uncovered call options. These strategies have risk of loss if the underlying stock should rise in price, but they offer profits if the underlying stock declines in price. This chapter—on naked, or uncovered, call writing—demonstrates some of the risks and rewards inherent in this aggressive strategy.

## THE UNCOVERED (NAKED) CALL OPTION

When one sells a call option without owning the underlying stock or any equivalent security (convertible stock or bond or another call option), he is considered to have written an *uncovered call option*. This strategy has limited profit potential and theoretically unlimited loss. For this reason, this strategy is unsuitable for some investors. This fact is not particularly attractive, but since there is no actual cash investment required to write a naked call—the position can be financed with collateral loan value of marginable securities—the strategy can be operated as an adjunct to many other investment strategies.

A simple example will outline the basic profit and loss potential from naked writing.

*Example:* XYZ is selling at 50 and a July 50 call is selling for 5. If one were to sell the July 50 call naked—that is, without owning XYZ stock, or any security convertible into XYZ, or another call option on XYZ— he could make, at most, 5 points of profit. This profit would accrue if XYZ were at, or anywhere below, 50 at July expiration as the call would then expire worthless. If XYZ were to rise, however, the naked writer could lose potentially large sums of money. Should the stock climb to 100, say, the call would be at a price of 50. If the writer then covered (bought back) the call for a price of 50, he would have a loss of 45 points on the transaction. In theory, this loss is unlimited, although *in practice the loss is limited by time.* The stock cannot rise an infinite amount during the life of the call. Clearly, defensive strategies are important in this strategy, as one would never want to let a loss run as far as the one here. Table 5-1 and Figure 5-1 (solid line) depict the results of this position at July expiration. Note that the break-even point

**TABLE 5-1.** *Position at July expiration.*

| XYZ Price at Expiration | Call Price at Expiration | Profit on Naked Write |
|---|---|---|
| 30 | 0 | +$  500 |
| 40 | 0 | +     500 |
| 50 | 0 | +     500 |
| 55 | 5 | 0 |
| 60 | 10 | −     500 |
| 70 | 20 | −  1,500 |
| 80 | 30 | −  2,500 |

in this example is 55. That is, if XYZ rose 10%, or 5 points, at expiration, the naked writer would break even. He could buy the call back at parity, 5 points, which is exactly what he sold it for. There is some room for error to the upside. *A naked write will not necessarily lose money if the stock moves up.* It will only lose if the stock advances by more than the amount of the time value premium that was in the call when it was originally written.

Naked writing is not the same as a short sale of the underlying stock. While both strategies have large potential risk, the short sale has much higher reward potential, but the naked write will do better if the underlying stock remains relatively unchanged. It is possible for the naked writer to make money in situations where the short seller would have lost money. For example, in the example above, suppose one investor had written the July 50 call naked for 5 points while another investor sold the stock short at 50. If XYZ were at 52 at expiration,

**FIGURE 5-1.** *Uncovered (naked) call write.*

the naked writer could buy the call back at parity, 2 points, for a 3-point profit. The short seller would have a 2-point *loss*. Moreover, the short seller pays out the dividends on the underlying stock, whereas the naked call writer does not. The naked call will expire, of course, but the short sale does not. This is a situation in which the naked write outperforms the short sale. However, if XYZ were to fall sharply—to 20, say—the naked writer could only make 5 points while the short seller would make 30 points. The dashed line in Figure 5-1 shows how the short sale of XYZ at 50 would compare with the naked write of the July 50 call. Notice that the two strategies are equal at 45 at expiration—they both make a 5-point profit there. Above 45, the naked write does better; it has larger profits and smaller losses. Below 45, the short sale does better, and the farther the stock falls, the better the short sale becomes in comparison. As will be seen later, one can more closely simulate a short sale by writing an in-the-money naked call.

## *INVESTMENT REQUIRED*

The *margin requirements* for writing a naked call are 30% of the stock price plus the amount by which the stock is above the striking price. If the stock is below the striking price, the differential is subtracted from the requirement. However, a minimum of $250 is required for each call, even if the computation results in a smaller number. Table 5-2 gives four examples of how the initial margin requirement would be computed for four different stock prices. The 30% collateral figure is the minimum exchange requirement and may vary somewhat among different brokerage houses. *The call premium may be applied against the requirement.* In the first line of Table 5-2, if the XYZ July 50 call was selling for 7 points, the $700 call premium could be applied against the $2,150 margin requirement, reducing the actual amount that the investor would have to put up as collateral to $1,450.

**TABLE 5-2.** *Initial collateral requirements for four stock prices.*

| Call Written | Stock Price When Call Written | 30% of Stock Price | Differ- ential | Total Margin Requirement |
|---|---|---|---|---|
| XYZ July 50 | 55 | $1,650 | +$ 500 | $2,150 |
| XYZ July 50 | 50 | 1,500 | 0 | 1,500 |
| XYZ July 50 | 45 | 1,350 | − 500 | 850 |
| XYZ July 50 | 40 | 1,200 | − 1,000 | 250* |

*Requirement cannot be less than $250.

In addition to the basic requirements, a brokerage firm may require that for a customer to participate in uncovered writing, he have a minimum equity in his account. This equity requirement may range from as low as $2,000 to as high as $10,000. In addition, some brokers require that a *maintenance* requirement be applied against each option written naked. This requirement, sometimes called a *"kicker,"* is usually less than $250 per call and is generally used by the broker to ensure that, should the customer fail to respond to an assignment notice against his naked call, the commissions costs for buying and selling the underlying stock would be defrayed.

*Naked option positions are marked to the market daily.* This means that the collateral requirement for the position is recomputed daily, just as in the short sale of stock. The same margin formula that was described above is applied and, if the stock has risen far enough, the customer will be required to deposit additional collateral or close the position. The need for such a mark to market is obvious. If the underlying stock should rise, the brokerage firm must ensure that the customer has enough collateral to cover the eventuality of buying the stock in the open market and selling it at the striking price if an assignment notice should be received against the naked call. The mark to market works to the customer's favor if the stock falls in price.

Excess collateral is then released back into the customer's margin account, and may then be used for other purposes.

It is important to realize that, *in order to write a naked call, collateral is all that is required. No cash need be "invested"* if one owns securities with sufficient collateral loan value.

> *Example:* An investor owns 100 shares of a stock selling at $60 per share. This stock is worth $6,000. If the loan rate on stock is 50% of $6,000, this investor has a collateral loan value equal to 50% of $6,000, or $3,000. This investor could write any of the naked calls in Table 5-2 without adding cash or securities to his account. Moreover, he would have satisfied a minimum equity requirement of at least $6,000, since his stock is equity.

This aspect of naked call writing—using collateral value to finance the writing—is attractive to many investors, since one is able to write calls and bring in premiums without disturbing his existing portfolio. Of course, if the stock underlying the naked call should rise too far in price, additional collateral may be called for by the broker because of the mark to market. Moreover, there is risk whether cash or collateral is used. If one buys in a naked call at a loss, he will then be spending cash, creating a debit in his account.

## RISK AND REWARD

One can adjust the apparent risks and rewards from naked call writing by his selection of an in-the-money or out-of-the-money call. Writing an out-of-the-money call naked, especially one quite deeply out-of-the-money, offers a high probability of achieving a small profit. Writing an in-the-money call naked has the most profit potential, but it also has higher risks.

> *Example:* XYZ is selling at 40 and the July 50 call is selling for ½.
> This call could be sold naked. The probability that XYZ could rise to 50 by expiration has to be considered small, especially if there is not a large amount of time remaining in the life of the call. In fact, the stock could rise 25%, or 10 points, by expiration to a price of 50 and the call would still expire worthless. Thus this naked writer has a good chance of realizing a $50 profit, less commissions. There could, of course, be substantial risk in terms of

potential profit versus potential loss if the stock rises substantially in price by expiration. Still, this apparent possibility of achieving additional limited income with a high probability of success has led many investors to use the collateral value of their portfolios to sell deeply out-of-the-money naked calls.

For those employing this technique, a favored position is to have a stock at or just above 15 and then sell the near-term option with striking price 20 naked. This option would sell for one-eighth or one-quarter, perhaps, although at times there might not be any bid at all. At this price, the stock would have to rally nearly one-third, or 33%, for the writer to lose money. Although there are not usually many optionable stocks selling at or just above $10 per share, these same out-of-the-money writers would also be attracted to selling a call with striking price 15 when the stock is at 10, because a 50% upward move by the stock would be required for a loss to be realized.

This strategy of selling deeply out-of-the-money calls has its apparent attraction in that the writer is assured of a profit unless the underlying stock can rally rather substantially before the call expires. The danger in this strategy is that one or two losses—perhaps only amounting to a couple of points each—could wipe out many periods of profits. The stock market does occasionally rally heavily in a short period, as witnessed by both the January 1976 and April 1978 markets. Thus the writer who is adopting this strategy cannot regard it as a "sure thing" and certainly cannot afford to establish the writes and forget them. Close monitoring is required if the market begins to rally and by no means should losses by allowed to accumulate. Even with monitoring, *this is not an attractive strategy and should generally be avoided.*

The opposite end of the spectrum in naked call writing is the writing of fairly deeply in-the-money calls. Since an in-the-money call would not have much time value premium in it, this writer does not have much leeway to the upside. If the stock rallies at all, the writer of the deeply in-the-money naked call will normally experience a loss. However, should the stock drop in price, this writer will make larger dollar profits than will the writer of the out-of-the-money call. The sale of the deeply in-the-money call simulates the profits that a short seller could make, at least until the stock drops close to the striking price, since the delta of a deeply in-the-money call is close to 1.

*Example:* XYZ is selling at 60 and the July 50 call is selling for 10½. If XYZ rises, the naked writer will lose money, because there is only ½ of a point of time value premium in the call. If XYZ falls, the writer will make profits on a point-for-point basis until the stock falls much closer to 50. That is, if XYZ dropped from 60 to 57, the call price would fall by almost 3 points as well. Thus for quick declines by the stock, the deeply in-the-money write can provide profits nearly equal to those that the short seller could accumulate. Notice that if XYZ falls all the way to 50, the profits on the written call will be large, but will be accumulating at a slower rate as the time value premium builds up with the stock near the striking price.

*If one is looking to trade a stock on the short side for just a few points of movement, he might use a deeply in-the-money naked write instead of shorting the stock.* His investment will be smaller—30% of the stock price for the write as compared to 50% of the stock price for the short sale—and his return will thus be larger (the requirement for the in-the-money amount is offset by applying the call's premium). The writer should take great caution in ascertaining that the call does have *some* time premium in it. He does not want to receive an assignment notice on the written call. It is easiest to find time premium in the more distant expiration series, so the writer would normally be safest from assignment by writing the longest-term deep in-the-money call if he wants to make a bearish trade in the stock.

*Example:* An investor thinks that XYZ could fall 3 or 4 points from its current price of 60 in a quick downward move and wants to capitalize on that move by writing a naked call. If the April 50 was the near-term call, he might have the choice of selling the April 50 at 10, the July 50 at 10¼, or the October 50 at 10½. Since all three calls will drop nearly point for point with the stock in a move to 56 or 57, he should write the October 50, as it has the least risk of being assigned. A trader utilizing this strategy should limit his losses in much the same way a short seller would, by covering if the stock rallies, perhaps breaking through overhead technical resistance.

### Rolling for Credits

Most writers of naked calls prefer to use one of the two strategies described above. The strategy of writing *at-the-money* calls, where the stock price is initially close to the striking price of the written call, is not widely utilized. This is because the writer who wants to limit risk will write an out-of-the-money call, whereas the writer who wants to make larger, quick trading profits will write an in-the-money call. There is, however, a strategy that is designed to utilize the at-the-money call. This strategy offers a high degree of eventual success, although there may be an accumulation of losses before the success point is reached. It is a strategy that requires large collateral backing, and is therefore only for the largest investors. We will call this strategy "rolling for credits."

In essence, *the writer sells the most time premium that he can at any point in time.* This would generally be the longest-term, at-the-money call. If the stock declines, the writer makes the time premium that he sold. However, if the stock rises in price, the writer rolls up for a *credit*. That is, when the stock reaches the next higher striking price, the writer buys back the calls that were originally sold and sells *enough* long-term calls at the higher strike to generate a credit. In this way, no debits are incurred, although a realized loss is taken on the rolling up. If the stock persists and rises to the next striking price, the process is repeated. Eventually, the stock will stop rising—they always do—and the last set of written options will expire worthless. At that time, the writer would make an overall profit consisting of an amount equal to all the credits that he had taken in so far.

There are really only two requirements for success in this strategy. The first is that the underlying stock eventually fall back—that it does not rise indefinitely. This is hardly a requirement; it is axiomatic that all stocks will eventually undergo a correction, so this is a simple requirement to satisfy. The second requirement is that the investor have enough collateral backing to stay with the strategy even if the stock runs up heavily against him. This is the harder requirement to satisfy and definitely makes the strategy only applicable to the largest investors. For those investors who do have the collateral available to participate in such a strategy, this is an excellent way of adding additional income to an overall portfolio. Recall that the collateral required for naked call writing may be in the form of cash or securities. Thus a large stock portfolio may be used to finance such a strategy through its loan value. There would be no margin interest charges incurred, because all transactions are credit transactions (no debits are created) and the securities portfolio would remain untouched unless the strategy was terminated before being allowed to reach completion.

> *Example:* The basic strategy in the case of rising stock is shown in Table 5-3. Note that each transaction is a credit and that all (except the last) involve taking a realized loss.

This example assumes that the stock rose so quickly that a longer-term call was never available to roll into. That is, the October calls were always utilized. If there were a longer-term call available

**TABLE 5-3.** *Rolling for credits when stock is rising.*

| | |
|---|---:|
| Initially:  XYZ = 50 | |
| Sell 5 XYZ October 50's at 7 | +$3,500 credit |
| Later:  XYZ rises to 60 | |
| Buy 5 XYZ October 50's at 11 and | − 5,500 debit |
| sell 8 XYZ October 60's at 7 | + 5,600 credit |
| Later:  XYZ rises further to 70 | |
| Buy 8 XYZ October 60's at 11 and | − 8,800 debit |
| sell 15 XYZ October 70's at 6 | + 9,000 credit |
| Finally, XYZ falls and the October 70's expire worthless | |
| Net gain = | +$3,800 |

(the January series, for example), the writer should roll up and out as well. In this way, larger credits could be generated. The number of calls written increased from 5 to 15 and the collateral required as backing for the writing of the naked calls also increased heavily. Recall that the collateral requirement is equal to 30% of the stock price plus the amount by which the call is in-the-money or less the amount by which it is out-of-the-money. The premium may be used against the collateral requirements. Using the stock and call prices of the example above, the investment is computed in Table 5-4. While the number

**TABLE 5-4.** *Increase in collateral requirement.*

| | |
|---|---|
| Initially:  XYZ = 50 | |
| Sell 5 XYZ October 50's at 7 | $4,000 collateral required |
| ($3,500 net credit) | |
| Later:  XYZ = 60 | |
| Sell 8 XYZ October 60's at 7 | |
| Buy 5 October 50's at 11 | |
| ($3,600 net credit to date) | $10,800 collateral required |
| Later:  XYZ = 70 | |
| Sell 15 XYZ October 70's at 6 | |
| Buy 8 XYZ October 60's at 11 | |
| ($3,800 net credit to date) | $27,700 collateral required |

of written calls has tripled from 5 to 15, the collateral requirement has multiplied almost sevenfold, from $4,000 to nearly $28,000. This is why the investor must have ample collateral backing to utilize this strategy. The general philosophy of the large investors who do apply this strategy is that they hope to eventually make a profit and, since they are using the collateral value of large security positions already held, they are not really investing any more money. The strategy does not really "cost" these investors anything. *All profits represent additional income and do not in any way disturb the underlying security portfolio.* Unfortunately, losses taken due to aborting the strategy could seriously affect the portfolio. This is why the investor *must* have sufficient collateral to carry through to completion.

The sophisticated strategist who implements this strategy will generally do more rolling than that discussed in the simple example above. First, if the stock drops, the calls will be rolled down to the next strike—for a credit—in order to constantly be selling the most time premium, which is always found in the longest-term at-the-money call. Furthermore, the strategist may want to roll out to a more distant expiration series whenever the opportunity presents itself. This rolling out, or forward, action is only taken when the stock is relatively unchanged from the initial price and there is no need to roll up or down.

This strategy is very attractive as long as one has enough collateral backing. Should one use up all of his available collateral, the strategy could collapse, causing substantial losses. It may not necessarily generate large rates of return in rising markets, but in stable or declining markets the generation of additional income can be quite substantial. Since the investor is not putting up any additional cash but is utilizing the collateral power of his present securities, his "investment" is actually zero. Any profits represent additional income. The investor must be aware of one other factor that can upset the strategy. If a stock should rise so far as to require the number of calls to exceed the position limits set by the OCC, the strategy is ruined. The position limit is currently 1,000 short calls. In the example above, XYZ would probably have to rise to about a price of over 200, without a correction, before the sale of 1,000 calls would be required. If the strategist originally started with too many naked calls, he could potentially exceed the limit in a short time period. Rather than attempting to sell too many calls initially in any one security, the strategist should diversify several moderately sized positions throughout a variety of underlying stocks. In this way, he will probably never have to exceed the position limit of 1,000 contracts short in any one security.

## SUMMARY

In a majority of cases, naked call writing is applied as a deeply out-of-the-money strategy in which the investor uses the collateral value of his security holdings to participate in a strategy that offers a large probability of making a very limited profit. It is a poor strategy because one loss may wipe out many profits. The trader who desires an alternative to a short sale may use the sale of an in-the-money naked call in order to attempt to make a quick profit on a smaller investment than the short seller would have to make. Both of these strategies could have large risk if one does not have sufficient capital backing.

A better strategy, but one that is only available to very large investors, is to sell at-the-money calls naked, rolling up and forward for credits if the underlying stock rises in price. This strategy will eventually generate a profit if the underlying stock declines and is therefore a probable way of adding additional income to a large portfolio. However, it is essential that the investor have sufficient collateral backing.

CHAPTER 6

# *Ratio* 6
# *Call Writing*

Two basic types of call writing have been described in the previous chapters: covered call writing, in which one owns the underlying stock and sells a call, and naked call writing. Ratio writing is a combination of these two types of positions.

## *THE RATIO WRITE*

Simply stated, *ratio call writing* is the strategy in which one owns a certain number of shares of the underlying stock and sells calls against more shares than he owns. Thus there is a ratio of calls written to stock owned. The most common ratio is the 2:1 ratio, where one owns 100 shares of the underlying stock and sells 2 calls. Note that this type of position involves writing a number of naked call options as well as a number of covered options. This resulting position has both downside risk, as does a covered write, and unlimited upside risk, as does a naked write. The ratio write generally will provide much larger profits than either covered writing or naked writing if the underlying stock remains relatively unchanged during the life of the calls. However, the ratio write has two-sided risk, a quality absent from either covered or naked writing.

Generally, when an investor establishes a ratio write, he attempts to be neutral in outlook regarding the underlying stock. This means that he writes the calls with striking price closest to the current stock price.

> *Example:* A ratio write is established by buying 100 shares of XYZ at 49 and selling two XYZ October 50 calls at 6 points each. If XYZ should decline in price and be anywhere below 50 at October expiration, the calls will expire worthless and the writer will make 12 points from the sale of the calls. Thus, even if XYZ drops 12 points to a price of 37, the ratio writer will break even. The stock loss of 12 points would be offset by a 12-point gain on the calls. As with any strategy in which calls are sold, the maximum profit occurs at the striking price of the written calls at expiration. In this example, if XYZ were at 50 at expiration, the calls would still expire worthless for a 12-point gain and the writer would have a 1-point profit on his stock, which has moved up from 49 to 50, for a total gain of 13 points. This position therefore has ample downside protection and a relatively large potential profit. Should XYZ rise above 50 by expiration, the profit will decrease and eventually become a loss if the stock rises too far. To see this, suppose XYZ is at 63 at October expiration. The calls will be at 13 points each, representing a 7-point loss on each call, because they were originally sold for 6 points apiece. However, there would be a 14-point gain on the stock, which has risen from 49 to 63. The overall net is a break-even situation at 63—a 14-point gain on the stock offset by 14 points of loss on the options (7 points each). Table 6-1 and Figure 6-1 summarize the profit

**TABLE 6.1** *Profit and Loss at October expiration.*

| XYZ Price at Expiration | Stock Profit | Call Price | Profit on Calls | Total Profit |
|---|---|---|---|---|
| 30 | −$1,900 | 0 | +$1,200 | −$ 700 |
| 37 | − 1,200 | 0 | + 1,200 | 0 |
| 45 | − 400 | 0 | + 1,200 | + 800 |
| 50 | + 100 | 0 | + 1,200 | + 1,300 |
| 55 | + 600 | 5 | + 200 | + 800 |
| 63 | + 1,400 | 13 | − 1,400 | 0 |
| 70 | + 2,100 | 20 | − 2,800 | − 700 |

and loss potential of this example at October expiration. The shape of the graph resembles a roof with its peak located at the striking price of the written calls—50. It is obvious that the position has both large upside risk above 63 and large downside risk below 37. Therefore, it is imperative that the ratio writer plan to take follow-up action if the stock should move outside these prices. Follow-up action will be discussed later. If the stock remains within the range 37 to 63, some profit will result before commission charges. This range between the downside

**FIGURE 6-1.** *Ratio write (2:1).*

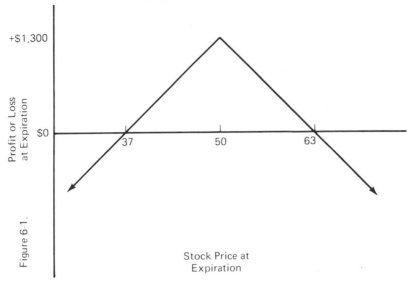

break-even point and the upside break-even point is called the *profit range.*

This example represents essentially a neutral position, because the ratio writer will make some profit unless the stock falls by more than 12 points or rises by more than 14 points before the expiration of the calls in October. This is frequently an attractive type of strategy to adopt because, normally, stocks do not move very far in a 3- or 6- month time period. Consequently, this strategy has a rather high probability of making a limited profit. The profit in this example would, of course, be reduced by commission costs and margin interest charges if the stock is bought on margin.

Before discussing the specifics of ratio writing, such as investment required, selection criteria, and follow-up action, it may be beneficial to counter two fairly common objections to this strategy. The first objection, although not heard as frequently today as when listed options first began trading, is "why bother to buy 100 shares of stock and sell 2 calls? You will be naked one call. Why not just sell one naked call?" The ratio writing strategy and the naked writing strategy have very little in common except that both have upside risk. The profit graph for naked writing (Figure 5-1) bears no resemblance to the roof-shaped profit graph for a ratio write (Figure 6-1). Clearly, the two strategies are quite different in profit potential and in many other respects as well.

137

The second objection to ratio writing for the conservative investor is slightly more valid. The conservative investor may not feel comfortable with a position that has risk if the underlying stock moves up in price. This can be a psychological detriment to ratio writing—when stock prices are rising and everyone who owns stocks is happy making profits, the ratio writer is in danger of losing money. However, in a purely strategic sense, one should be willing to assume some upside risk in exchange for larger profits if the underlying stock does not rise heavily in price. The covered writer has upside protection all the way to infinity; that is, he has no upside risk at all. This cannot be the mathematically optimum situation, because stocks never rise to infinity. Rather, the ratio writer is engaged in a strategy that makes its profits in a price range more in line with the way stocks actually behave. In fact, if one were to try to set up the optimum strategy, he would want it to make its most profits in line with the most probable outcomes for a stock's movement. Ratio writing is such a strategy.

Figure 6-2 shows a simple probability curve for a stock's movement. It is most likely that a stock will remain relatively unchanged and there is very little chance that it will rise or fall a great distance. Now compare the results of the ratio writing strategy with the graph of probable stock outcomes. Notice that the ratio write and the probability curve have their "peaks" in the same area—that is, the ratio write makes its profits in the range of most likely stock prices, because

**FIGURE 6-2.** *Stock price probability curve overlaid on profit graph of ratio write.*

there is only a small chance that any stock will increase or decrease by a large amount in a fixed period of time. The large losses are at the edges of the graph, where the probability curve gets very low, approaching zero probability.

## INVESTMENT REQUIRED

The ratio writer has a combination of covered writes and naked writes. The margin requirements for each of these strategies have been described previously and the ratio writing strategy is just the sum of the requirements for a naked write and a covered write. Ratio writing is normally done in a margin account, although one could technically keep the stock in a cash account.

*Example:* Ignoring commissions, the investment required can be computed as follows: buy 100 XYZ at 49 on 50% margin and sell 2 XYZ October 50 calls at 6 points each (Table 6-2). The commissions for buying the stock and selling the calls would be added to these requirements. A shorter formula (Table 6-3) is actually more desirable to use. It is merely a combination of the investment requirements listed in Table 6-2.

**TABLE 6-2.** *Investment required.*

Covered writing portion (buy 100 XYZ and sell 1 call)

| | |
|---|---|
| 50% of stock price | $2,450 |
| Less premium received | − 600 |
| Requirement for covered portion | $1,850 |

Naked writing portion (sell 1 XYZ call)

| | |
|---|---|
| 30% of stock price | $1,470 |
| Less out-of-money amount | − 100 |
| Less premium received | − 600 |
| Requirement for naked portion | $ 770 |

| | |
|---|---|
| Total requirement for ratio write | $2,620 |

**TABLE 6-3.** *Initial investment required for a ratio write.*

| | |
|---|---|
| 80% of stock cost (XYZ = 49) | $3,920 |
| Less total premiums received | − 1,200 |
| Plus or minus striking price differential on naked calls | − 100 |
| Total requirement | $2,620 (plus commissions) |

In addition to the basic requirement, there may be minimum equity requirements and maintenance requirements since there are naked calls involved. As these vary from one brokerage firm to another, it is best for the ratio writer to check with his broker to determine the equity and maintenance requirements. Again, since there are naked calls involved in ratio writing, there will be a mark to market of the position. If the stock should rise in price, the investor will have to put up more collateral. Generally, since one would normally take follow-up action at the upside break-even point, he should allow enough collateral for the position in case the stock rises to the upside break-even point. In the example that is being used, the upside break-even point is 63. Thus the requirements for the position with XYZ at 63 should be computed (Table 6-4). In this case, it is necessary to separate the covered writing requirement from the naked call requirement—the covered writing requirement does not change as the stock moves up, but the naked call requirement does.

TABLE 6-4. *Collateral required with stock at upside break-even point of 63.*

| | |
|---|---|
| Covered writing requirement | $1,850 (see above) |
| 30% of stock price (XYZ = 63) | 1,890 |
| Plus in-the-money amount | 1,300 |
| Less initial call premium received | − 600 |
| Total requirement with XYZ at 63 | $4,440 |

It is conceivable that the ratio writer would want to stay with his original position as long as the stock did not penetrate the upside break-even point of 63. Therefore, he should allow for enough collateral to cover the eventuality of a move to 63. In this case, he would need $4,440. This is the requirement that the ratio writer should be concerned with—not the initial collateral requirement—and he should therefore plan to invest $4,440 in this position, not $2,620 (the initial requirement). Obviously, he only has to put up $2,620, but from a strategic point of view, he should allow $4,440 for the position. If the ratio writer does this with all his positions, he would not receive a margin call even if all the stocks in his portfolio climbed to their upside break-even points.

There is a quick way to figure the collateral requirement at the upside break-even point, if one has already computed the *initial* collateral requirement. As the stock rises in price, the requirement increases by $130 per uncovered call for each 1-point rise by the common stock. Thus the following formula could be used:

$$\text{Collateral requirement at upside break-even} = \begin{aligned}&\$130 \times \text{(upside break-even price}\\&- \text{current price)} + \text{initial requirement}\end{aligned}$$

$$= \$130 \times (63 - 49) + \$2,620$$

$$= \$4,440$$

## SELECTION CRITERIA

To decide whether a ratio write is a desirable position, the writer must first determine the break-even points of the position. Once the break-even points are known, the writer can then decide if the position has a wide-enough profit range to allow for defensive action if it should become necessary. One simple way of determining if the profit range is wide enough is to require that the next higher and lower striking prices be within the profit range.

*Example:* The writer is buying 100 XYZ at 49 and selling 2 October 50 calls at 6 points apiece. It was seen, by inspection, that the break-even points in the position are 37 on the downside and 63 on the upside. There is a mathematical formula that allows one to quickly compute the break-even points for a 2:1 ratio write.

| Points of maximum profit | = strike price − stock price + 2 × call price |
|---|---|
| Downside break-even point | = strike price − points of maximum profit |
| | = stock price − 2 × call price |
| Upside break-even point | = strike price + points of maximum profit |

In this example, the points of maximum profit are $50 - 49 + 2 \times 6$, or 13. Thus the downside break-even point would be 37 $(50 - 13)$ and the upside break-even point would be 63 $(50 + 13)$. These numbers agree with the figures determined earlier by analyzing the position.

This profit range is quite clearly wide enough to allow for defensive action should the underlying stock rise to the next strike of 60 or fall to the next two lower strikes, at 45 and 40. In practice, a ratio write is not automatically a good position only because the profit range extends far enough. Theoretically, one would want the profit range to be wide in relation to the volatility of the underlying stock. If the range is wide in relation to the volatility and the break-even points encompass the next higher and lower striking prices, a desirable position is available. Volatile stocks are the best candidates for ratio writing since their premiums will more easily satisfy both these conditions. A nonvolatile stock may, at times, have relatively large premiums in its calls, but the resulting profit range may still not be wide enough numerically to ensure that follow-up action could be taken. Specific measures for determining volatility may be obtained from many data services and brokerage firms. Moreover, methods of computing volatility will be presented later in a chapter on mathematical applications.

Technical support and resistance levels are also important in establishing the position. If both support and resistance lie within the profit range, there is a better chance that the stock will remain within the range. A position should not necessarily be rejected if there is not support and resistance within the profit range, but the writer is then subjecting himself to a possible undeterred move by the stock in one direction or the other.

The ratio writer is generally a neutral strategist. He tries to take in the most time premium that he can to earn the premium erosion while the stock remains relatively unchanged. If one is more bullish on a particular stock, he can set up a 2:1 ratio write with out-of-the-money calls. This will allow more room to the upside than to the downside, and therefore makes the position slightly more bullish. Conversely, if one is more bearish on the underlying stock, he can write in-the-money calls in a 2:1 ratio.

There is another way to produce a slightly more bullish or bearish ratio write. This is to *change the ratio of calls written* to stock purchased. This method is also used to construct a neutral profit range when the stock is not close to a striking price.

> *Example:* An investor is slightly bearishly inclined in his outlook for the underlying stock, so he might write more than two calls for each 100 shares of stock purchased. His position might be buy 100 XYZ at 49 and sell 3 XYZ October 50 calls at 6 points each. This position breaks even at 31 on the downside because if the stock dropped by 18 points at expiration, the call profits would amount to 18 points and would produce a break-even situation. To the upside, the break-even point lies at 59½ for the stock at expiration. Each call would be at 9½ at expiration there and would thus be at a loss of 3½ points, for a total loss of 10½ points on the three calls. However, XYZ would have risen from 49 to 59½—a 10½-point gain—therefore producing a break-even situation. Again, a formula is available to aid in determining the break-even point for any ratio.

Maximum profit = (striking price − stock price) × round lots purchased
                              + number of calls written × call price

Downside break-even $=$ striking price $-\dfrac{\text{maximum profit}}{\text{number of round lots purchased}}$

Upside break-even $=$ striking price $+\dfrac{\text{maximum profit}}{\text{(calls written} - \text{round lots purchased)}}$

Note that in the case of a 2:1 ratio write, where the number of round lots purchased equals 1 and the number of calls written equals 2, these formulae reduce to the ones given earlier for the more common 2:1 ratio write. To verify that the formulae above are correct, insert the numbers from the most recent example.

> *Example:* Three XYZ October 50 calls at a price of 6 were sold against the purchase of 100 XYZ at 49. The number of round lots purchased is 1.
>
> Maximum profit $= (50 - 49) \times 1 + 3 \times 6 = 19$
>
> Downside break-even $= 50 - 19/1 = 31$
>
> Upside break-even $= 50 + 19/(3 - 1) = 59\frac{1}{2}$

In the 2:1 ratio writing example given earlier, the break-even points were 37 and 63. The 3:1 write has lower break-even points of 31 and 59½, reflecting the more bearish posture on the underlying stock.

A more bullish write is constructed by buying 200 shares of the underlying stock and writing three calls. To quickly verify that this ratio (3:2) is more bullish, again use 49 for the stock price, 6 for the call price, and now assume that two round lots were purchased.

> Maximum profit $= (50 - 49) \times 2 + 3 \times 6 = 20$
>
> Downside break-even $= 50 - 20/2 = 40$
>
> Upside break-even $= 50 + 20/(3 - 2) = 70$

Thus this ratio of 3 calls against 200 shares of stock has break-even points of 40 and 70, reflecting a more bullish posture on the underlying stock.

A 2:1 ratio may not necessarily be neutral. There is, in fact, a mathematically correct way of determining exactly what a neutral ratio should be. *The neutral ratio is determined by dividing the delta of the written call into 1.* Assume that the delta of the XYZ October 50 call in the previous example is .60. Then the neutral ratio is 1.0/.60, or 1.666:1. This means that one might buy 300 shares and sell 5 calls. Using the formulae above, the details of this position can be observed:

Maximum profit $= (50 - 49) \times 3 + 5 \times 6 = 33$

Downside break-even $= 50 - 33/3 = 39$

Upside break-even $= 50 + 33/(5 - 3) = 66\frac{1}{2}$

According to the mathematics of the situation, then, this would be a neutral position initially. It is often the case that a 5:3 ratio is approximately neutral for an at-the-money call.

By now, the reader should have recognized a similarity between the ratio writing strategy and the reverse hedge (or simulated straddle) strategy presented in Chapter 4. The two strategies are the reverse of each other—in fact, this is where the reverse hedge strategy acquires its name. The ratio write has a profit graph that looks like a roof, while the reverse hedge has a profit graph that looks like a trough—the roof upside down. In one strategy the investor buys stock and sells calls while the other strategy is just the opposite—the investor shorts stock and buys calls. Which one is better? Normally, the ratio writing strategy is the better strategy in terms of expected results. Even though ratio writing has limited profits and potentially large losses, the strategy will result in a profit in a large majority of cases. The reverse hedge strategy, with its limited losses and potentially large profits, only provides profits on large stock moves—a nonfrequent event. Thus in normal markets, the ratio writing strategy is generally superior. However, in times of depressed option premiums, the reverse hedge strategy gains a distinct advantage. If calls are underpriced, the advantage lies with the buyer of calls, and that is inherent in the reverse hedge strategy.

## THE VARIABLE RATIO WRITE

In ratio writing, one generally likes to establish the position when the stock is trading relatively close to the striking price of the written calls. However, it is sometimes the case that the stock is nearly exactly between two striking prices and neither the in-the-money nor the out-of-the-money call offers a neutral profit range. If this is the case, and one still wants to be in a 2:1 ratio of calls written to stock owned, he can sometimes write one in-the-money call *and* one out-of-the-money call against each 100 shares of common. This strategy, often termed a variable ratio write or trapezoidal hedge, serves to establish a more neutral profit range.

> *Example:* Given the following prices: XYZ common, 65; XYZ October 60 call, 8; and XYZ October 70 call, 3
>
> If one were to establish a 2:1 ratio write with only the October 60's, he would have a somewhat bearish position. His profit range would be 49

to 71 at expiration. Since the stock is already at 65, this means that he would be allowing room for 16 points of downside movement and only 6 points on the upside. This is certainly not neutral. On the other hand, if he were to attempt to utilize only the October 70 calls in his ratio write, he would have a bullish position. This profit range for the October 70 ratio write would be 59 to 81 at expiration. In this case, the stock at 65 is too close to the downside break-even point in comparison to its distance from the upside break-even point.

A more neutral position can be established by buying 100 XYZ and selling one October 60 and one October 70. This position has a profit range that is centered about the current stock price. Moreover, the new position has both an upside and a downside risk, as does a more normal ratio write. However, now *the maximum profit can be obtained anywhere between the two strikes at expiration.* To see this, note that if XYZ is anywhere between 60 and 70 at expiration, the stock will be called away at 60 against the sale of the October 60 call and the October 70 call will expire worthless. It makes no difference whether the stock is at 61 or at 69—the same result will occur. Table 6-5 and Figure 6-3 depict the results from this variable hedge at expiration. In the table, it is assumed that the option is bought back at parity to close the position, but if the stock were called away, the results would be the same.

**TABLE 6-5.** *Results at expiration of variable hedge.*

| XYZ Price at Expiration | XYZ Profit | October 60 Profit | October 70 Profit | Total Profit |
|---|---|---|---|---|
| 45 | −$2,000 | +$ 800 | +$ 300 | −$900 |
| 50 | − 1,500 | + 800 | + 300 | − 400 |
| 54 | − 1,100 | + 800 | + 300 | 0 |
| 60 | − 500 | + 800 | + 300 | + 600 |
| 65 | 0 | + 300 | + 300 | + 600 |
| 70 | + 500 | − 200 | + 300 | + 600 |
| 76 | + 1,100 | − 800 | − 300 | 0 |
| 80 | + 1,500 | −$1,200 | − 700 | − 400 |
| 85 | + 2,000 | − 1,700 | − 1,200 | − 900 |

Note that the shape of Figure 6-3 is something like a trapezoid. This is the source of the name "trapezoidal hedge," although the strategy is more commonly known as a variable hedge or variable ratio write. The reader should observe that the maximum profit is indeed obtained if the stock is anywhere between the two strikes at expiration. The maximum profit potential in this position, $600, is smaller than the maximum profit potential available from writing only the October 60's or only the October 70's. However, there is a vastly greater probability of realizing the maximum profit in a variable ratio write than there is of realizing the maximum profit in a normal ratio write.

FIGURE 6-3. *Variable ratio write (trapezoidal hedge).*

The break-even points for a variable ratio write can be computed most quickly by first computing the maximum profit potential, which is equal to the time value that the writer takes in. The break-even points are then computed directly by subtracting the points of maximum profit from the lower striking price to get the downside break-even point and adding the points of maximum profit to the upper striking price to arrive at the upside break-even point. This is a similar procedure to that followed for a normal ratio write.

Points of maximum profit = total option premiums + lower striking price − stock price

Downside break-even point = lower striking price − points of maximum profit

Upside break-even point = higher striking price + points of maximum profit

Substituting the numbers from the example above will help to verify the formula. The total points of option premium brought in were 11 (8 for the October 60 and 3 for the October 70). The stock price was 65, and the striking prices involved were 60 and 70.

$$\text{Points of maximum profit} = 11 + 60 - 65 = 6$$
$$\text{Downside break-even point} = 60 - 6 = 54$$
$$\text{Upside break-even point} = 70 + 6 = 76$$

Thus the break-even points as computed by the formula agree with Table 6-5 and Figure 6-3. Note that the formula applies only if the stock is initially between the two striking prices and the ratio is 2:1. If the stock is above both striking prices, the formula is not correct. However, the writer should not be attempting to establish a variable ratio write with two in-the-money calls.

## FOLLOW-UP ACTION

Aside from closing the position completely, there are three reasonable approaches to follow-up action in a ratio writing situation. The first, and most popular, is to roll the written calls up if the stock rises too far or to roll down if the stock drops too far. The second method uses the delta of the written calls. The third follow-up method is to utilize stops on the underlying stock to alter the ratio of the position as the stock moves either up or down. In addition to these types of defensive follow-up action, the investor must also have a plan in mind for taking profits as the written calls approach expiration. These types of follow-up action will be discussed separately.

### Rolling Up or Down as a Defensive Action

The reader should already be familiar with the definition of a rolling action—the currently written calls are bought back and calls at a different striking price are written. The ratio writer can use rolling actions to his advantage to readjust his position if the underlying stock moves to the edges of his profit range.

The reason one of the selection criteria for a ratio write was to encompass both the next higher and lower striking prices was to facilitate the rolling actions that might become necessary as a follow-up measure. Since an option has its greatest time premium when the stock price and the striking price are the same, one would normally want to roll exactly at a striking price.

*Example:* A ratio writer bought 100 XYZ at 49 and sold two October 50 calls at 6 points each. Subsequently, the stock drops in price and the following prices exist: XYZ, 40; XYZ October 50, 1; and XYZ October 40, 4.

One would roll down to the October 40 calls by buying back the 2 October 50's that he is short and selling 2 October 40's. In so doing, he would reestablish a somewhat neutral position. His profit on the buy back of the October 50 calls would be 5 points each—they were originally sold for 6—and he would realize a 10-point gain on the two calls. This 10-point gain effectively reduces his stock cost from 49 to 39, so that he now has the equivalent of the following position: long 100 XYZ at 39 and short 2 XYZ October 40 calls at 4. This adjusted ratio write has a profit range of 31 to 49 and is thus a new, neutral position with the stock currently at 40. He is now in a position where he can make profits if XYZ remains near this level or he could take further defensive action if the stock experiences a relatively large change in price again.

Defensive action to the upside—rolling up—works in much the same manner.

*Example:* The initial position again consists of buying 100 XYZ at 49 and selling two October 50 calls at 6. If XYZ then rose to 60, the following prices might exist: XYZ, 60; XYZ October 50, 11; and XYZ October 60, 6.

The ratio writer could thus roll this position up to reestablish a neutral profit range. If he bought back the two October 50 calls, he would take a 5-point loss on each one for a net loss on the calls of 10 points. This would effectively raise his stock cost by 10 points to a price of 59. The rolled-up position would then be long 100 XYZ at 59 and short 2 October 60 calls at 6. This new, neutral position has a profit range of 47 to 73 at October expiration.

In both of the examples above, the writer could have closed out the ratio write at a very small profit of about 1 point before commissions. This would not be advisable, because of the relatively large stock commissions, unless he expects the stock to continue to move dramatically. Either rolling up or rolling down gives the writer a fairly wide new profit range to work with and he could easily expect to make more than 1 point of profit if the underlying stock stabilizes at all.

*Having to take rolling defensive action immediately after the position is established is the most detrimental case.* If the stock moves very quickly after having set up the position, there will not be much time for time value premium erosion in the written calls, and this will make for smaller profit ranges after the roll is done. It may be useful to use technical support and resistance levels as keys for when to take rolling action if these levels are near the break-even points and/or striking prices.

It should be noted that this method of defensive action—rolling at or near striking prices—automatically means that one is buying back little or no time premium and is selling the greatest amount of time premium currently available. That is, if the stock rises, the call's premium will consist mostly of intrinsic value and very little of time premium value since it is substantially in-the-money. Thus the writer who rolls up by buying back this in-the-money call is buying back mostly intrinsic value and is selling a call at the next strike. This newly sold call consists mostly of time value. By continually buying back "real" or intrinsic value and by selling "thin air" or time value, the writer is taking the optimum neutral action at any given time.

If a stock undergoes a dramatic move in one direction or the other, the ratio writer will not be able to keep pace with the dramatic movement by remaining in the same ratio.

*Example:* If XYZ was originally at 49, but then undergoes a fairly straight-line move to 80 or 90, the ratio writer who maintains a 2:1 ratio will find himself in a deplorable situation. He will have accumulated rather substantial losses on the calls and will not be able to compensate for these losses by the gain in the underlying stock. A similar situation could arise to the downside. If XYZ were to plunge from 49 to 20, the ratio writer would make a good deal of profit from the calls by rolling down, but may still have a larger loss in the stock itself than the call profits can compensate for.

Many ratio writers who are large enough to diversify their positions into a number of stocks will continue to maintain 2:1 ratios on all their positions and will just close out a position which has gotten out of hand by running dramatically to the upside or to the downside. They feel that the chances of such a dramatic move occurring are small, and that they will take the infrequent losses in such cases in order to be basically neutral on the other stocks in their portfolio.

There is, however, a way to combat this sort of dramatic move. This is done by *altering the ratio* of the covered write as the stock moves either up or down. For example, as the underlying stock moves up dramatically in price, the ratio writer can decrease the number of calls outstanding against his long stock each time that he rolls. Eventually, the ratio might decrease as far as 1:1—which is nothing more than a covered writing situation. As long as the stock continues to move in the same upward direction, the ratio writer who is decreasing his ratio of calls outstanding will be giving more and more weight to the stock gains in the ratio write and less and less weight to the call losses. It is interesting to note that this decreasing ratio effect can also be produced by buying extra shares of stock at each new striking price as the stock moves up and simultaneously keeping the number of outstanding calls written constant. In either case, the ratio of calls outstanding to stock owned is reduced.

When the stock moves down dramatically, a similar action can be taken to increase the number of calls written to stock owned. Normally, as the stock falls, one would sell out some of his long stock and roll the calls down. Eventually, after the stock falls far enough, he would be in a naked writing position. The idea is the same here—as the stock falls, more weight is given to the call profits and less weight is given to the stock losses that are accumulating.

This sort of strategy is more oriented to extremely large investors or to firm traders, market-makers, and the like. Commissions will be exorbitant if frequent rolls are to be made and only those investors who pay very small commissions or who have such a large holding that their commissions are quite small on a percentage basis will be able to profit substantially from such a strategy.

### Adjusting with the Delta

*The delta of the written calls can be used to determine the correct ratio to be used in this ratio-adjusting defensive strategy.* The basic idea is to use the call's delta to remain as neutral as possible at all times.

> *Example:* An investor initially sets up a neutral 5:3 ratio of XYZ October 50 calls to XYZ stock, as was determined previously. The stock is at 49 and the delta is .60. Furthermore, suppose the stock rises to 57 and the call now has a delta of .80. The neutral ratio would currently be 1/.80 (= 1.20) or 5:4. The ratio writer could thus buy another 100 shares of the underlying stock. Alternatively, he might buy in one of the short calls.

In this particular example, buying in one call would produce a 4:3 ratio, which is not absolutely correct. If he had had a larger position initially, it would be easier to adjust to fractional ratios. When the stock declines, it is necessary to increase the ratio. This can be accomplished by either selling more calls or selling out some of the long stock. In theory, these adjustments could be made constantly to keep the position neutral. In practice, one would allow for a few points of movement by the underlying stock before adjusting. If the underlying stock rises too far, it may be logical for the neutral strategist to adjust by rolling up. Similarly, he would also roll down if the stock fell to or below the next lower strike. The neutral ratio in that case is determined by using the delta of the option into which he is rolling.

> *Example:* With XYZ at 57, an investor is contemplating rolling up to the October 60's from his present position of long 300 shares and short 5 XYZ October 50's. If the October 60 has a delta of .40, the neutral ratio for the October 60's is 2.5:1 (1 divided by .40). Since he is already long 300 shares of stock, he should now be short 7.5 calls (3 times 2.5). Obviously, he would sell 7 or 8, probably depending on his short-term outlook for the stock.

If one prefers to adopt an even more sophisticated approach, he can make adjustments between striking prices by altering his stock position, and can make adjustments if the stock reaches a new striking price by rolling up or down. For those who prefer formulae, the following ones summarize this information:

1. When establishing a new position or when rolling up or down, at the next strike:

$$\text{Number of calls to sell} = \frac{\text{round lots held long}}{\text{delta of call to be sold}}$$

> *Note:* When establishing a new position, one must first decide how many shares of the underlying stock he can buy before utilizing the formula; 1,000 shares would be a workable amount.

2. When adjusting between strikes by buying or selling stock:

$$\text{Number of round lots to buy} = \text{current delta} \times \text{number of short calls} - \text{round lots held long}$$

> *Note:* If a negative number results, stock should be sold, not bought.

These formulae can be verified by using the numbers from the examples above. For example, when the delta of the October 50 was .80 with the stock at 57, it was seen that buying 100 shares of stock would reestablish a neutral ratio.

$$\text{Number of round lots to buy} = .80 \times 5 - 3 = 4 - 3 = 1$$

Also, if the position was to be rolled up to the October 60 (delta = .40), it was seen that 7.5 October 60's would theoretically be sold:

$$\text{Number of calls to sell} = \frac{3}{.40} = 7.5$$

For investors who do not have the funds or are not in a position to utilize such a ratio adjusting strategy, there is a less time-consuming method of taking defensive action in a ratio write.

### Using Stop Orders as a Defensive Strategy

A ratio writer can use buy or sell stops on his stock position in order to automatically and unemotionally adjust the ratio of his position. This type of defensive strategy is not an aggressive one and will provide some profits unless a whipsaw occurs in the underlying stock.

As an example of how the use of stop orders can aid the ratio writer, let us again assume that the same basic position was established by buying XYZ at 49 and selling two October 50 calls at 6 points each. This produces a profit range of 37 to 63 at expiration. If the stock begins to move up too far or to fall too far, the ratio writer can adjust the ratio of calls short to stock long automatically through the use of stop orders on his stock.

*Example:* An investor places a stop order to buy 100 shares of XYZ at 57 at the same time that he establishes the original position. If XYZ should get to 57, the stop would be set off and he would then own 200 shares of XYZ and be short 2 calls. That is, he would have a 200-share covered write of XYZ October 50 calls.

To see how such an action affects his overall profit picture, note that his average stock cost is now 53—he paid 49 for the first 100 shares and then paid 57 for the second 100 shares bought via the stop order. Since he sold the calls at 6 each, he essentially has a covered write in which he bought stock at 53 and sold calls for 6 points. This does not represent a lot of profit potential, but it will ensure some profit unless the stock falls back below the new break-even point. This new break-even point is 47—the stock cost, 53, less the 6 points received for the call. He will realize the maximum profit potential from the covered write as long as the stock remains above 50 until expiration. Since the stock is already at 57, the probabilities are relatively strong that it will remain above 50 and even stronger that it will remain above 47 until the expiration date. If the buy stop order was placed just above a technical resistance area, this probability is even better.

Hence *the use of a buy stop order on the upside allows the ratio writer to automatically convert the ratio write into a covered write* if the stock moves up too far. Once the stop goes off, he has a position that will make some profit as long as the stock does not experience a fairly substantial price reversal.

Downside protective action using a sell stop order works in a similar manner.

*Example:* The investor placed a sell stop for 100 shares of stock after establishing the original position. If this sell stop were placed at 41, for example, the position would become a naked call writer's position if the stock fell to 41. At that time, the 100 shares of stock that he owned would be sold, at an 8-point loss, but he would have the capability of making 12 points from the sale of his two calls as long as the stock remained below 50 until expiration. In fact, his break-even point after converting into the naked write would actually be 52 at expiration, since at that price, the calls could be bought back for 2 points each, or 8 points total profit, to offset the 8-point loss on the stock. This action limits his profit potential but will allow him to make some profit as long as the stock does not experience a strong price reversal and climb back above 52 by expiration.

There are several advantages to using this method of protection for inexperienced ratio writers. First, the implementation of the protective strategies—buying an extra 100 shares of stock if the stock moves up, or selling out the 100 shares that are long if the stock moves down—is unemotional *if the stop orders are placed at the same time that the original position is established.* This prevents the writer from attempting to impose his own market judgment "in the heat of battle." That is, if XYZ has moved up to 57, the writer who has not placed a buy stop order may be tempted to wait just a little longer, hoping for the stock to fall in price. If the stop orders are placed as soon as the position is established, a great deal of emotion is removed. Second, *this strategy will produce some profit*—assuming that the stops are properly placed—*as long as the stock does not whipsaw,* or experience a price reversal and go back through the striking price in the other direction. Most follow-up actions in *any* writing strategy, whether they involve rolling actions or the use of stops, are subject to losses if the stock whipsaws back and forth.

The disadvantage to using this type of protective action is that the writer may be tying up relatively large amounts of capital in order to make only a small profit after the stop order is set off. However, in a diversified portfolio, only a small percentage of the stocks may go through their stop points, thereby still allowing the ratio writer plenty of profit potential on his other positions.

Once either the buy stop or the sell stop is set off, the writer still needs to watch the position. His first action *after one stop is touched should be to cancel the other stop order,* because the stops are good orders until they are canceled. From that time on, the writer need do nothing if the stock does not experience a price reversal. In fact, he would just as soon have the stock experience a greater move in the same direction to minimize the chances of a price reversal.

If a price reversal does occur, the most conservative action is to close out the position just after the stock crosses back through the striking price. This will normally result in a small loss, but, again, it should happen in only a relatively small number of his positions. Recall that in a limited profit strategy such as ratio writing, it is important to limit losses as well. If the stock does indeed whipsaw and the position is closed, the writer will still have most of his original equity and can then reestablish a new position in another underlying stock.

*Placement of Stops.* The writer would ideally like to place his stops at prices that allow a reasonable rate of return to be made, while also having the stops far enough away from the original striking price to reduce the chances of a whipsaw occurring. It is a fairly simple matter to calculate the returns that could be made, after commissions are included, if one or the other of the stops goes off. Dividends should be included as well, since they will accrue to the writer. If the writer is willing to accept returns as low as 5% annually for those positions that go through their stop points, he will be able to place his stops farther from the original striking price. If he feels that he needs a higher return when the stops go off, the stops must be placed closer in. As with any stock or option investment, the writer who operates in large size will experience less of a commission charge, percentagewise. That is, the writer who is buying 500 shares of stock and selling 10 calls to start with, will be able to place his stop points farther out than the writer who is buying 100 shares of stock and selling 2 calls.

Technical analysis can be helpful in selecting the stop points as well. If there is resistance overhead, the buy stop should be placed above that resistance. Similarly, if there is support, the sell stop should be placed beneath the support point. Later, when straddles are discussed, it will be seen that this type of strategy can be operated at less of a net commission charge since the purchase and sale of stock will not be involved.

### Closing Out the Write

The methods of follow-up action discussed above deal with the eventuality of preventing losses. However, if all goes well, the ratio write will begin to accrue profits as the stock remains relatively close to the original striking price. *To retain these paper profits that have accrued, it is necessary to move the protective action points closer together.*

> *Example:* XYZ is at 51 after some time has passed and the calls are at 3 points each. The writer would, at this time, have an unrealized profit of $800—$200 from the stock purchase at 49 and $300 each on the two calls, which were originally sold at 6 points each. Recall that the maximum potential profit from the position—if XYZ were exactly at 50 at expiration—is $1,300. The writer would like to adjust the protective points so that nearly all of the $800 paper profit might be retained while still allowing for the profit to grow to the $1,300 maximum.
>
> At expiration, $800 profit would be realized if XYZ were at 45 or at 55. This can be verified by referring again to Table 6-1 and Figure 6-1. The 45 to 55 range is now the area that the writer must be concerned with. The original profit range of 39 to 61 has become meaningless, since the position has performed well to this point in time. If the writer is using the rolling method of protection, he would roll forward to the next expiration series if the stock were to reach 45 or 55. If he is using the stop-out method of protection, he could either merely close the position

at 45 or 55 or he could also roll to the next expiration series and readjust his stop points. The neutral strategist using deltas would determine the number of calls to roll forward to by using the delta of the longer-term call.

By moving the protective action points closer together, the ratio writer can then adjust his position while he still has a profit; he is attempting to "lock in" his profit. As even more time passes and expiration draws nearer, it may be possible to move the protective points even closer together. Thus, as the position continues to improve over time, the writer should be constantly "telescoping" his action points and finally roll out to the next expiration series. This is generally the more prudent move, because the commissions to sell stock to close the position and then buy another stock to establish yet another position may prove to be prohibitive. In summary, then, as a ratio write nears expiration, the writer should be concerned with an ever-narrowing range within which his profits can grow but outside of which his profits could dissipate if he does not take action.

## RATIO WRITING SUMMARY

Ratio writing is a viable, neutral strategy that can be employed with differing levels of sophistication. The initial ratio of short calls to long stock can be selected simplistically by comparing one's opinion for the underlying stock with projected break-even points from the position. In a more sophisticated manner, the delta of the written calls can be used to determine the ratio.

Since the strategy has potential large losses either to the upside or the downside, follow-up action is mandatory. This action can be taken by simple methods such as rolling up or down in a constant ratio, or by placing stop orders on the underlying stock. A more sophisticated technique involves using the delta of the option to either adjust the stock position or to roll to another call. By using the delta, a theoretically neutral position can be maintained at all times.

Ratio writing is a relatively sophisticated strategy that involves selling naked calls. It is therefore not suitable for all investors. Its attractiveness lies in the fact that vast quantities of time value premium are sold and the strategy is profitable for the most probable price outcomes of the underlying stock. It has a relatively large probability of making a limited profit.

# An Introduction to Call Spread Strategies

A *spread* is a transaction in which one simultaneously buys one option and sells another option, with different terms, on the same underlying security. In a call spread, the options are all calls. The basic idea behind spreading is that the strategist is using the sale of one call to reduce the risk of buying another call. The short call in a spread is considered covered, for margin purposes, only if the long call has an expiration date equal to or longer than the short call. Before delving into the individual types of spreads, it may be beneficial to cover some general facts that pertain to most spread situations.

All spreads fall into three broad categories: *vertical, horizontal,* or *diagonal.* A *vertical spread* is one in which the calls involved have the same expiration date but different striking prices. An example might be to buy the XYZ October 30 and sell the October 35 simultaneously. A *horizontal spread* is one in which the calls have the same striking price but different expiration dates. This would be a horizontal spread: sell the XYZ January 35 and buy the XYZ April 35. A *diagonal spread* is any combination of vertical and horizontal and may involve calls that have different expiration dates as well as different striking prices. These three names that classify the spreads can be related to the way option prices are listed in any newspaper summary of closing option prices. A vertical spread would involve two options from the same column in a newspaper listing. Newspaper columns run vertically. A horizontal spread would involve two calls whose prices are listed in the same row in a newspaper listing—rows are horizontal. This relationship to the listing format in newspapers is not important, but it is an easy way to remember what vertical spreads and horizontal spreads are. There are several types of vertical and horizontal spreads, and many of them will be discussed in detail in the following chapters.

## Spread Order

The term "spread" designates not only a type of strategy, but a type of order as well. *All spread transactions in which both sides of the spread are opening (initial) transactions must be done in a margin account.* This means that the customer must generally maintain a minimum equity in the account—normally $2,000. Some brokerage houses may also have a maintenance requirement, or "kicker."

It *is* possible to transact a spread in a cash account, but one of the sides must be a closing transaction. In fact, many of the follow-up actions taken in the covered writing strategy are actually spread transactions. Suppose that a covered writer is currently short one XYZ April call against 100 shares of the underlying stock. If he wants to roll forward to the July 35 call, he will be buying back the April 35 and selling the July 35 simultaneously. This is a spread transaction, technically, since one call is being bought and the other is being sold. However, in this transaction the buy side is a closing transaction and the sell side is an opening transaction. This type of spread could be done in a cash account. Whenever a covered writer is rolling—up, down, or forward—he should place the order as a spread order to facilitate a better price execution.

The spreads to be discussed in the following chapters are predominantly spread strategies, ones in which both sides of the spread are opening transactions. These are designed to have their own profit and risk potentials, and are not merely follow-up actions to some previously discussed strategy.

When a spread order is entered, the options being bought and sold must be specified. Two other items must be specified as well—the price at which the spread is to be executed and whether that price is a credit or a debit. If the total price of the spread results in a cash inflow to the spread strategist, the spread is a *credit spread*. This merely means that the sell side of the spread brings in a higher price than is paid for the buy side of the spread. If the reverse is true—that is, there is a cash outflow from the spread transaction—the spread is said to be a *debit spread*. This means that the buy side of the spread costs more than is received from the sell side. It is also common to refer to the purchased side of the spread as the *"long side"* and to refer to the written side of the spread as the *"short side."*

The price at which a certain spread can be executed is generally *not* the difference between the last sale prices of the two options involved in the spread.

*Example:* An investor wants to buy an XYZ October 30 and simultaneously sell an XYZ October 35 call. If the last sale price of the October 30 was 4 points and the last sale price of the October 35 was 2 points, it does not necessarily mean that the spread could be done for a 2-point debit (the difference in the last sale prices). In fact, *the only way to determine the market price for a spread transaction is to know what the bid and asked prices of the options involved are.* Suppose the following quotes are available on these two calls:

|                 | Bid | Asked | Last Sale |
|-----------------|-----|-------|-----------|
| October 30 call | 3⅞  | 4⅛    | 4         |
| October 35 call | 1⅞  | 2     | 2         |

Since the spread in question involves buying the October 30 call and selling the October 35, the spreader will, at market, have to pay 4⅛ for the October 30 (the asked or offering quote) and will only receive 1⅞ (the bid quote) for the October 35. This results in a debit of 2¼ points, significantly more than the 2-point difference in the last sale prices. Of course, one is free to specify any price he wants for any type of transaction. One might enter this spread order at a 2⅛-point debit and could have a reasonable chance of having the order filled if the floor broker can do better than the bid side on the October 35 or better than the offering side on the October 30.

The point to be learned here is that *one cannot assume that last sale prices are indicative of the price at which a spread transaction can be executed.* This makes computer analysis of spread transactions via closing price data somewhat difficult. Some computer data services offer—generally at a higher cost—closing bid and asked prices as well as closing sale prices. If a strategist is forced to operate with closing prices only, however, he should attempt to build some screens into his output to allow for the fact that last sale prices might not be indicative of the price at which the spread can be executed. One simple method for screening is to only look at relatively liquid options—that is, those that have traded a substantial number of contracts during the previous trading day. If an option is experiencing a great deal of trading activity, there is a much better chance that the current quote is "tight"—that is, the bid and offering prices are quite close to the last sale price.

In the early days of listed options, it was somewhat common practice to *"leg"* into a spread. That is, the strategist would place separate buy and sell orders for the two transactions comprising his spread. As the listed markets have developed—adding depth and liquidity—*it is generally a poor idea to leg into a spread.* If the floor broker handling the transaction knows the entire transaction, he has a much better chance of "splitting a quote," buying on the bid, or selling on the offering. *"Splitting a quote"* merely means executing at a price that is between the current bid and asked prices. For example, if the bid is 3⅞ and the offering is 4⅛, a transaction at a price of 4 would be "splitting the quote."

The public customer must be aware that spread transactions may involve substantially higher commission costs, because there are twice as many calls involved in any one transaction. Some brokers offer slightly lower rates for spread transactions, but these are not nearly as low as spreads in commodity trading, for example.

The *bull spread* is one of the most popular forms of spreading. In this type of spread one buys a call at a certain striking price and sells a call at a higher striking price. Generally, both options have the same expiration date. This is a vertical spread. *A bull spread tends to be profitable if the underlying stock moves up in price—hence it is a bullish position.* The spread has both limited profit potential and limited risk. Although both can be substantial percentagewise, the risk can never exceed the net investment. In fact, a bull spread requires a smaller dollar investment and therefore has a smaller maximum dollar loss potential than does an outright call purchase of a similar call.

*Example:* The following prices exist:

XYZ common, 32;

XYZ October 30 call, 3; and

XYZ October 35 call, 1.

A bull spread would be established by buying the October 30 call and simultaneously selling the October 35 call. Assume that this could be done at the indicated 2-point debit. *A bull spread is always a debit transaction,* since the call with the lower striking price must always trade for more than a call with a higher price, if both have the same expiration date. Table 7-1 and Figure 7-1 depict the results of this

**TABLE 7-1.** *Results at expiration of bull spread.*

| XYZ Price at Expiration | October 30 Profit | October 35 Profit | Total Profit |
|---|---|---|---|
| 25 | −$ 300 | +$100 | −$200 |
| 30 | −  300 | + 100 | − 200 |
| 32 | −  100 | + 100 | 0 |
| 35 | +  200 | + 100 | + 300 |
| 40 | +  700 | − 400 | + 300 |
| 45 | + 1,200 | − 900 | + 300 |

transaction at expiration. The indicated call profits or losses would be realized if the calls were liquidated at parity at expiration. Note that *the spread has a maximum profit and that this profit is realized if the stock is anywhere above the higher striking price at expiration.* The maximum loss is realized if the stock is anywhere below the lower strike at expiration and is equal to the net investment, 2 points in this example. Moreover, there is a break-even point which always lies between the two striking prices at expiration. In this example, the break-even point is 32. All bull spreads have profit graphs with the same shape as the one shown above when the expiration dates are the same for both calls.

**FIGURE 7.1.** *Bull spread.*

The investor who establishes this position is bullish on the underlying stock, but is generally looking for a way to hedge himself. If he were rampantly bullish, he would merely buy the October 30 call outright. However, the sale of the October 35 call against the purchase of the October 30 allows him to have a position that will outperform the outright purchase of the October 30—dollarwise—as long as the stock does not rise above 36 by expiration. This fact is demonstrated by the dashed line on Figure 7-1. Therefore, *the strategist establishing the bull spread is bullish, but not overly so.* To verify that this comparison is correct, note that if one bought the October 30 call outright for 3 points, he would have a 3-point profit at expiration if XYZ were at 36. Both strategies have a 3-point profit at 36 at expiration. Below 36, the bull spread does better because the sale of the October 35 call brings in the extra point of premium. Above 36 at expiration, the outright purchase outperforms the bull spread, because there is no limit on the profits that can occur in an outright purchase situation.

The net investment required for a bull spread is the net debit plus commissions. Since the spread must be transacted in a margin account, there will generally be a minimum equity requirement imposed by the brokerage firm. In addition, there may be a maintenance requirement by some brokers. Suppose that one was establishing 10 spreads at the prices given in the example above. His investment, before commissions, would be $2,000 ($200 per spread), plus commissions. It is a simple matter to compute the break-even point and the maximum profit potential of a bull spread:

Break-even point = lower striking price + net debit of spread

Maximum profit potential = higher striking price − lower striking price − net debit of spread

In the example above, the net debit was 2 points. Therefore, the break-even point would be 30 + 2, or 32. The maximum profit potential would be 35 − 30 − 2, or 3 points. These figures agree with Table 7-1 and Figure 7-1. *Commissions may represent a significant percentage of the profit and net investment,* and should therefore be calculated *before* establishing the position. If these commissions are included in the net debit to establish the spread, they conveniently fit into the preceding formulae. Commission charges can be reduced, percentagewise, by spreading a larger quantity of calls. For this reason, it is generally advisable to spread at least 5 options at a time.

## DEGREES OF AGGRESSIVENESS

### Aggressive Bull Spread

Depending on how the bull spread is constructed, it may be an extremely aggressive or more conservative position. The most commonly used bull spread is of the *aggressive* type—the stock is generally well below the higher striking price when the spread is established. This aggressive bull spread generally has the ability to generate substantial percentage returns if the underlying stock should rise in price far enough by expiration. *Aggressive bull spreads are most attractive when the underlying common stock is relatively close to the lower striking price at the time the spread is established.* A bull spread established under these conditions will generally be a low-cost spread with substantial profit potential, even after commissions are included.

### Extremely Aggressive Bull Spread

An extremely aggressive type of bull spread is the "out-of-the-money" spread. In such a spread, *both* calls are out-of-the-money when the spread is established. These spreads are extremely inexpensive to establish and have large potential profits if the stock should climb to the higher striking price by expiration. However, they are usually quite deceptive in nature—the underlying stock has only a relatively remote chance of advancing such a great deal by expiration and the spreader could realize a 100% loss of his investment even if the underlying stock advances moderately, since both calls are out-of-the-money. This spread is akin to buying a deeply out-of-the-money call as an outright speculation. It is not recommended that such a strategy be pursued with more than a very small percentage of one's speculative funds.

### Least Aggressive Bull Spread

Another type of bull spread can be found occasionally—the "in-the-money" spread. In this situation, both calls are in-the-money. This is a much less aggressive position, since it offers a large probability of realizing the maximum profit potential, although that profit potential will be substantially smaller than the profit potentials offered by the more aggressive bull spread.

*Example:* XYZ is at 37 some time before expiration, and the October 30 call is at 7 while the October 35 call is at 4. Both calls are in-the-money and the spread would cost 3 points (debit) to establish. The maximum profit potential is 2 points, but it would be realized as long as XYZ were above 35 at expiration. That is, XYZ could *fall* by 2 points and the spreader would still make his maximum profit. This is certainly a more conservative position than the aggressive spread described above. The commission cost in this spread would be substantially larger than those in the spreads above, which involve less expensive options initially, and they should therefore be figured into one's profit calculations before entering into the spread transaction. Since this stock would have to decline 7 points to fall below 30 and cause a loss of the entire investment, it would have to be considered a rather low probability event. This fact adds to the less aggressive nature of this type of spread.

## RANKING BULL SPREADS

To accurately compare the risk/reward potentials of the many bull spreads that are available in a given day, one has to use a computer to perform the mass calculations. It is possible to use a strictly arithmetic method of ranking bull spread, but such a list will not be as accurate as the correct method of analysis. In reality, it is necessary to incorporate the volatility of the underlying stock, and possibly the expected return from the spread as well, into one's calculations. The concept of expected return is described in detail in Chapter 28, where a bull spread is used as an example.

The exact method for using volatility and predicting an option's price after an upward movement are presented later. Many data services offer such information. However, if the reader wants to attempt a simpler method of analysis, the following one may suffice. In any ranking of bull spreads, *it is important not to rank the spreads by their maximum potential profits at expiration.* Such a ranking will always give the most weight to deeply out-of-the-money spreads which can rarely achieve their maximum profit potential. It would be better to screen out any spreads whose maximum profit prices are too far away from the current stock price. A simple method of allowing for a stock's movement might be to assume that the stock could, at expiration, advance by an amount equal to twice the time value premium in an at-the-money call. Since more volatile stocks have options with greater time value premium, this is a simple attempt to incorporate volatility into the analysis. Also, since longer-term options have more time value premium than do short-term options, this will allow for larger movements during a longer time period. Percentage returns should include commission costs. This simple analysis is not completely correct, but it may prove useful to those traders looking for a simple, arithmetic method of analysis that can be quickly computed.

The bull spreads described in previous examples utilize the same expiration date for both the short call and the long call. It is sometimes useful to buy a call with a longer time to maturity than the short call has. Such a position is known as a diagonal bull spread and will be discussed in a later chapter.

With most types of spreads, it is necessary for some time to pass for the spread to become significantly profitable, even if the underlying stock moves in favor of the spreader. For this reason, *bull spreads are not for traders.* If a speculator is bullishly oriented for a short-term upward move in an underlying stock, it is generally better for him to buy a call outright than to establish a bull spread. Since the spread differential changes mainly as a function of time, small movements in price by the underlying stock will not cause much of a short-term change in the price of the spread. However, the bull spread has a distinct advantage over the purchase of a call if the underlying stock advances moderately by *expiration.*

In the previous example, a bull spread was established by buying the XYZ October 30 call for 3 points and simultaneously selling the XYZ October 35 call for 1 point. This spread can be compared to the outright purchase of the XYZ October 30 alone. There is a short-term advantage in using the outright purchase.

*Example:* The underlying stock jumps from 32 to 35 in one day's time. The October 30 would be selling for approximately 5½ points if that happened, and the outright purchaser would be ahead by 2½ points, less one option commission. The long side of the bull spread would do as well, of course, since it utilizes the same option, but the short side—the October 35—would probably be selling for about 2½ points. Thus the bull spread would be worth 3 points in total (5½ points on the long side, less 2½ points loss on the short side). This represents a 1-point profit to the spreader, less two option commissions, since the spread was initially established at a debit of 2 points. Clearly, then, for the shortest time period—one day—the outright purchase outperforms the bull spread on a quick rise.

For a slightly longer time period, such as 30 days, the outright purchase still has the advantage if the underlying stock moves up quickly. Even if the stock should advance above 35 in 30 days, the bull spread will still have time premium in it and thus will not have yet reached its maximum spread potential of 5 points. Recall that the maximum potential of a bull spread is always equal to the difference between the striking prices. Clearly, the outright purchaser will do very well if the underlying stock should advance that far in 30 days' time.

When risk is considered, however, it must be pointed out that the bull spread has fewer dollars at risk and, if the underlying stock should drop rather than rise, the bull spread will often have a smaller loss than the outright call purchase would.

*The longer it takes for the underlying stock to advance, the more the advantage swings to the spread.* Suppose XYZ does not get to 35 until expiration. In this case, the October 30 call would be worth 5 points and the October 35 call would be worthless. The outright purchase of the October 30 call would make a 2-point profit less one commission, but the spread would now have a 3-point profit, less two commissions. Even with the increased commissions, the spreader will make more of a profit—both dollarwise and percentagewise.

The conclusion that can be drawn from these examples is that, in general, the outright purchase is a better strategy if one is looking for a quick rise by the underlying stock. Overall, the bull spread is a less aggressive strategy than the outright purchase of a call. The spread will not produce as much of a profit on a short-term move, or on a sustained large upward move. It will, however, outperform the outright purchase of a call if the stock advances slowly and moderately by expiration. Also, the spread always involves fewer actual dollars of risk, because it requires a smaller debit to establish initially. Table 7-2 summarizes which strategy has the upper hand for various stock movements over differing time periods.

**TABLE 7-2.** *Bull spread and outright purchase compared.*

| | | *If the underlying stock . . .* | | |
|---|---|---|---|---|
| | *Declines* | *Remains Relatively Unchanged* | *Advances Moderately* | *Advances Substantially* |
| in . . . | | | | |
| 1 week | Bull spread | Equal | Outright purchase | Outright purchase |
| 1 month | Bull spread | Bull spread | Outright purchase | Outright purchase |
| At expiration | Bull spread | Bull spread | Bull spread | Outright purchase |

## FOLLOW-UP ACTION

Since the strategy has both limited profit and limited risk, it is not mandatory for the spreader to take any follow-up action prior to expiration. If the underlying stock advances substantially, the spreader should watch the time value premium in the short call closely in order to close the spread if it appears that there is a possibility of assignment. This possibility would increase substantially if the time value premium disappeared from the short call. If the stock falls, the trader may want to close the spread in order to limit his losses even further.

When the spread is closed, the order should also be entered as a spread transaction. If the underlying stock has moved up in price, the order to liquidate would be a *credit* spread involving two closing transactions. *The maximum credit that can be recovered from a bull spread is an amount equal to the difference between the striking prices.* In the previous example, if XYZ were above 35 at expiration, one might enter an order to liquidate the spread as follows. Buy the October 35 (it is common practice to specify the buy side of a spread first when placing an order); sell the October 30 at a 5-point credit. In reality, because of the difference between bids and offers, it is quite difficult to obtain the entire 5-point credit even if expiration is quite near. Generally, one might ask for a 4¾ or 4⅞ credit. It *is* possible to close the spread via exercise, although this method is normally advisable only to traders who pay little or no commissions. If the short side of a spread is assigned, the spreader may satisfy the assignment notice by exercising the long side of his spread. There is no margin required to do so, but there are stock commissions involved. Since these stock commissions—to a public customer—would be substantially larger than the option commissions involved in closing the spread by liquidating the options, *it is recommended that the public customer attempt to liquidate rather than exercise.*

A minor point should be made here. Since the amount of commissions paid to liquidate the spread would be larger if higher call prices are involved, the actual net maximum profit point for a bull spread is for the stock to be exactly at the higher striking price at expiration. If the stock exceeds the higher striking price by a great deal, the gross profit will be the same (it was demonstrated earlier that this gross profit is the same anywhere above the higher strike at expiration), but the net profit will be slightly smaller since the investor will pay more in commissions to liquidate the spread.

Some spreaders prefer to buy back the short call if the underlying stock drops in price in order to lock in the profit on the short side. They will then hold the long call in hopes of a rise in price by the underlying stock in order to make the long side of the spread profitable as well. This amounts to "legging" out of the spread, although the overall increase in risk is small—the amount paid to repurchase the short call. If he attempts to "leg" out of the spread in such a manner, the spreader should not attempt to buy back the short call at too high a price. If it can be repurchased at 1/8 or 1/16, the spreader will be giving away virtually nothing by buying back the short call. However, he should not be quick to repurchase it if it still has much more value than that unless he is closing out the entire spread. At no time should one attempt to "leg" out after a stock price increase—taking the profit on the long side and hoping for a stock price decline to make the short side profitable as well. The risk is too great.

## OTHER USES OF BULL SPREADS

Superficially, the bull spread is one of the simplest forms of spreading. However, it can be an extremely useful tool in a wide variety of situations. Two such situations were described in Chapter 3. If the outright purchaser of a call finds himself with an unrealized loss, he may be able to substantially improve his chances of getting out even by "rolling down" into a bull spread. If, however, he has an unrealized profit, he may be able to sell a call at the next higher strike—creating a bull spread—in an attempt to lock in some of his profit.

In a somewhat similar manner, a common stockholder who is faced with an unrealized loss may be able to utilize a bull spread to lower the price at which he can break even. He may often have a significantly better chance of breaking even or making a profit by using options. The following example illustrates the stockholder's strategy.

*Example:* An investor buys 100 shares of XYZ at 48, and later finds himself with an unrealized loss with the stock at 42. A 6-point rally in the stock would be necessary in order to break even. However, if XYZ has listed options trading, he may be able to significantly reduce his break-even price. The prices are:

XYZ common, 42;

XYZ October 40, 4; and

XYZ October 45, 2.

The stock owner could enhance his overall position by buying *one* October 40 call and selling *two* October 45 calls. Note that no extra money, except commissions, is required for this transaction, because the credit received from selling two October 45's is $400 and is equal to the cost of buying the October 40 call. However, maintenance and equity requirements still apply because a spread has been established.

The resulting position does *not* have an uncovered, or naked, option in it. One of the October 45 calls that was sold is covered by the underlying stock itself. The other is part of a bull spread with the October 40 call. It is not particularly important that the resulting position is a combination of both a bull spread and a covered write. What is important is the profit characteristic of this new total position.

If XYZ should continue to decline in price and be below 40 at October expiration, all the calls will expire worthless, and the resulting loss to the stock owner will be the same (except for the option commissions spent) as if he had merely held onto his stock without having done any option trading.

Since both a covered write and a bull spread are strategies with a limited profit potential, *this new position obviously must have a limited profit.* If XYZ is anywhere above 45 at October expiration, the maximum profit will be realized. To determine the size of the maximum profit, assume that XYZ is at exactly 45 at expiration. In that case, the two short October 45's would expire worthless and the long October 40 call would be worth 5 points. The option trades would have resulted in a $400 profit on the short side ($200 from each October 45 call) plus a $100 profit on the long side, for a total profit of $500 from the option trades. Since the stock was originally bought at 48 in this example, the stock portion of the position is a $300 loss with XYZ at 45 at expiration. The overall profit of the position is thus $500 less $300, or $200.

For stock prices between 40 and 45 at expiration, the results are shown in Table 7-3 and Figure 7-2. Figure 7-2 depicts the two columns from the table labeled "Profit on Stock" and "Total Profit" so that one can visualize how the new total position compares with the original stockholder's profit. There are several points that should be noted from either the graph or the table. First, the break-even point is lowered from 48 to 44. The new total position breaks even at 44, so that only a 2-point rally by the stock by expiration is necessary in order to break even. The two strategies are equal at 50 at expiration. That is, the stock would have to rally more than 8 points from 42 to 50 by expiration for the original stockholder's position to outperform the new position. Below 40, the two strategies produce the same result. Finally, between

**TABLE 7-3.** *Lowering the Break-Even Price on Common Stock.*

| XYZ Price at Expiration | Profit on Stock | Profit on Short October 45's | Profit on Long October 40 | Total Profit |
|---|---|---|---|---|
| 35 | −$1,300 | +$400 | −$400 | −$1,300 |
| 38 | − 1,000 | + 400 | − 400 | − 1,000 |
| 40 | − 800 | + 400 | − 400 | − 800 |
| 42 | − 600 | + 400 | − 200 | − 400 |
| 43 | − 500 | + 400 | − 100 | 200 |
| 44 | − 400 | + 400 | 0 | 0 |
| 45 | − 300 | + 400 | + 100 | + 200 |
| 48 | 0 | − 200 | + 400 | + 200 |
| 50 | + 200 | − 600 | + 600 | + 200 |

**FIGURE 7-2.** *Lowering the Break-even Price on Common Stock*

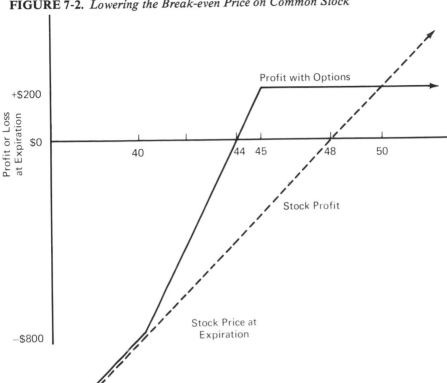

40 and 50, the new position outperforms the original stockholder's position.

In summary, then, the stockholder stands to gain much and gives away very little by adding the indicated options to his stock position. If the stock stabilizes at all—anywhere between 40 and 50 in the example above—the new position would be an improvement. Moreover, the investor can break even or make profits on a small rally. If the stock continues to drop heavily, nothing additional will be lost except for option commissions. Only if the stock rallies very sharply will the stock position outperform the total position.

This strategy—combining a covered write and a bull spread—is sometimes used as an initial (opening) trade as well. That is, an investor who is considering buying XYZ at 42 might decide to buy the October 40 and sell two October 45's (for even money) at the outset. The resulting position would not be inferior to the outright purchase of XYZ stock, in terms of profit potential, unless XYZ rose above 50 by October expiration.

Bull spreads may also be used as a "substitute" for covered writing. Recall from Chapter 2 that writing against *warrants* can be useful because of the smaller investment required, especially if the warrant was in-the-money and was not selling at much of a premium. The same thinking applies to call options. *If there is an in-the-money call with little or no time premium remaining in it, its purchase may be used as a substitute for buying the stock itself.* Of course the call will expire, whereas the stock will not, but the profit potential of owning a deeply in-the-money call can be very similar to owning the stock. Since such a call costs less to purchase than the stock itself would, the buyer is getting essentially the same profit or loss potential with a smaller investment. It is natural, then, to think that one might write another call—one closer to the money—against the deeply in-the-money purchased call. This position would have profit characteristics much like a covered write since the long call "simulates" the purchase of stock. This position really is, of course, a *bull spread,* where the purchased call is well in-the-money and the written call is closer to the money. Clearly, one would not want to put all of his money into such a strategy and forsake covered writing, since, with bull spreads, he could be entirely wiped out in a moderate market decline. In a covered writing strategy, one still owns the stocks even after a severe market decline. However, one may achieve something of a compromise by investing a much smaller amount of money in bull spreads than he might have invested in covered writes. He can still retain the same profit potential. The balance of the investor's funds could then be placed in interest-bearing securities.

> *Example:* The following prices exist:
>
>     XYZ common, 49;
>
>     XYZ April 50 call, 3; and
>
>     XYZ April 35 call, 14.

Since the deeply in-the-money call has no time premium, its purchase will perform much like the purchase of the stock until April expiration. Table 7-4 summarizes the profit potential from the covered write or the bull spread. The profit potentials are the same from a cash covered write or the bull spread. Both would yield a $400 profit before commissions if XYZ were above 50 at April expiration. However, since the bull spread requires a much smaller investment, the spreader could put $3,500 into interest-bearing securities. This interest could be considered as the equivalent of receiving the dividends on the stock. In any case, the spreader can only lose $1,100 even if the stock declines substantially. The covered writer could have a larger unrealized loss than

**TABLE 7-4.** *Results for covered write and bull spread compared.*

|  | Covered Write: Buy XYZ and Sell April 50 Call | Bull Spread: Buy XYZ April 35 Call and Sell April 50 Call |
|---|---|---|
| Maximum profit potential (stock over 50 in April) | $ 400 | $ 400 |
| Break-even point | 46 | 46 |
| Investment | $4,600 | $1,100 |

that if XYZ were below 35 at expiration. Also, in the bull spread situation, the writer can "roll down" the April 50 call if the stock declines in price, just as he might do in a covered writing situation.

Thus the bull spread offers the same dollar rewards, the same break-even point, smaller commission costs, less potential risk, and interest income from the fixed income portion of the investment. While it is not always possible to find a deeply in-the-money call to use as a "substitute" for buying the stock, when one does exist, the strategist should consider using the bull spread instead of the covered write.

## SUMMARY

The bull spread is one of the simplest and most popular forms of spreading. It will generally perform best in a moderately bullish environment. The bull spread can also be applied for more sophisticated purposes in a far wider range of situations than merely wanting to attempt to capitalize on a moderate advance by the underlying stock. Both call buyers and the stock buyers may be able to use bull spreads to "roll down" and produce lower break-even points for their positions. The covered writer may also be able to use bull spreads as a substitute for covered writes in certain situations where a deeply in-the-money call exists.

# CHAPTER 8

# Bear Spreads Using Call Options

Options are a versatile investment vehicle. For every type of bullish position that can be established, there is normally a corresponding bearish type of strategy. For every neutral strategy there is an aggressive strategy for the investor with an opposite opinion. One such case has already been explored in some detail—the ratio write is a neutral strategy with a relatively large probability of making a limited profit. The reverse hedge strategy was the opposite side of the spectrum. Many of the strategies to be described from this point on will have a correspondingly similar strategy, designed for the strategist with the opposite point of view. In this vein, the bear spread is the opposite of a bull spread.

## THE BEAR SPREAD

*In a bear spread, one buys a call at a certain striking price and sells a call at a lower striking price.* This is a vertical spread, as was the bull spread. The bear spread tends to be profitable if the underlying stock declines in price. Like the bull spread, it has limited profit and loss potential. However, unlike the bull spread, the bear spread is a *credit* spread when the spread is set up with call options. Since one is selling the option with the lower strike, and a call at a lower strike always trades at a higher price than a call at a higher strike with the same expiration, the bear spread must be a credit position. It should be pointed out that most bearish strategies that can be established with call options may be more advantageously constructed using put options. Many of these same strategies will therefore be discussed again in Part III.

*Example:* An investor is bearish on XYZ. Using the same prices that were used for the examples in Chapter 7, an example of a bear spread can be constructed:

XYZ common, 32;

XYZ October 30 call, 3; and

XYZ October 35 call, 1.

A bear spread would be established by buying the October 35 call and selling the October 30 call. This would be done for a 2-point credit, before commissions. *In a bear spread situation, the strategist is hoping that the stock will drop in price and that both options will expire worthless.* If this happens, he will not have to pay anything to close his spread—he will profit by the entire amount of the original credit taken in. In this example, then, the maximum profit potential is 2 points, since that is the amount of the initial credit. This profit would be realized if XYZ were anywhere below 30 at expiration, because both options would expire worthless in that case.

If the spread expands in price, rather than contracts, the bear spreader will be losing money. This expansion would occur in a rising market. The maximum amount that this spread could expand to is 5 points—the difference between the striking prices. Hence the most that the bear spreader would have to pay to buy back this spread would be 5 points, resulting in a maximum potential loss of 3 points. This loss would be realized if XYZ were anywhere above 35 at October expiration. Table 8-1 and Figure 8-1 depict the actual profit and loss potential of this example at expiration (commissions are not included). The astute reader will note that the figures in the table are exactly the reverse of those shown for the bull spread example in Chapter 7. Also,

**TABLE 8-1.** *Bear spread.*

| XYZ Price at Expiration | October 30 Profit | October 35 Profit | Total Profit |
|---|---|---|---|
| 25 | +$300 | −$100 | +$200 |
| 30 | + 300 | − 100 | + 200 |
| 32 | + 100 | − 100 | 0 |
| 35 | − 200 | − 100 | − 300 |
| 40 | − 700 | + 400 | − 300 |

**FIGURE 8-1.** *Bear spread.*

the profit graph of the bull spread looks like a bull spread profit graph that has been turned upside down. All bear spreads have a profit graph with the same shape as the graph shown above, at expiration.

The break-even point, maximum profit potential, and investment required are all quite simple computations for a bear spread.

Maximum profit potential = net credit received

Break-even point = lower striking price + amount of credit

Maximum risk = collateral investment required = difference in striking prices − credit received + commissions

In the example above, the net credit received from the sale of the October 30 call at 3 and the purchase of the October 35 call at 1 was two points. This is the maximum profit potential. The break-even point is then easily computed as the lower striking price, 30, plus the amount of the credit, 2, or 32. The risk is equal to the investment, and the difference between the striking prices—5 points—less the net credit received—2 points—for a total investment of 3 points plus commissions. Since this spread involves a call that is not "covered" by a long call with a striking price equal to or lower than that of the short call, some brokerage firms may require a higher maintenance requirement per spread than would be required for a bull spread. Again, since a spread must be done in a margin account, most brokerage firms will require that a minimum amount of equity be in the account as well.

Since this is a credit spread, the investor does not really "spend" any dollars to establish the spread. The investment is really a reduction in the buying power of the customer's margin account, but it does not actually require dollars to be spent when the transaction is initiated.

## SELECTING A BEAR SPREAD

Depending on where the underlying stock is trading with respect to the two striking prices, the bear spread may be very aggressive, with a high profit potential, or it may be less aggressive, with a low profit potential. If a large credit is initially taken in, there is obviously the potential for a good deal of profit. However, for the spread to take in a large credit, the underlying stock must be well above the lower striking price. This means that a relatively substantial downward move would be necessary in order for the maximum profit potential to be realized. Thus *a large credit bear spread is usually an aggressive position*—the spreader needs a substantial move by the underlying stock in order to make his maximum profit. The probabilities of this occurring cannot be considered large.

A less aggressive type of bear spread is one in which the underlying stock is actually *below* the lower striking price when the spread is established. The credit received from establishing a bear spread in such a situation would be small, but the spreader would realize his maximum profit even if the underlying stock remained unchanged or actually rose slightly in price by expiration.

> *Example:* XYZ is at a price of 29. The October 30 call might be sold for 1½ points and the October 35 call bought for ½ point with the stock at 29. While the net credit, and hence the maximum profit potential, is a small dollar amount—1 point—it will be realized even if XYZ rises slightly by expiration, as long as it does not rise above 30.

It is not always clear which type of spread is better—the large credit bear spread or the small credit bear spread. One has a small probability of making a large profit and the other has a much larger probability of making a much smaller profit. In general, *bear spreads established when the underlying stock is closer to the lower striking price will be the best ones.* To see this, note that if a bear spread is initiated when the stock is at the higher striking price, the spreader is selling a call that has mostly intrinsic value and little time value premium (since it is in the money) and is buying a call that is nearly all time value. This is just the opposite of what the option strategist should be attempting to do. *The basic philosophy of option strategy is to sell time value and buy intrinsic value.* For this reason, the larger credit bear spread is not an optimum strategy. It will be interesting to observe later that bear spreads with puts are more attractive when the underlying stock is at the *higher* striking price!

## FOLLOW-UP ACTION

Follow-up strategies are not difficult, in general, for bear spreads. The major thing that the strategist must be aware of is impending assignment of the short call. If the short side of the spread is in-the-money and has no time premium remaining, the spread should be closed regardless of how much time remains until expiration. This disappearance of time value premium could be caused either by the stock being significantly above the striking price of the short call, or by an impending dividend payment. In either case, the spread should be closed to avoid assignment and the resultant large commission costs on stock transactions. Note that the large credit bear spread—one established with the stock well above the lower striking price—is dangerous from the viewpoint of early assignment, since the time value premium in the call will be small to begin with.

## SUMMARY

The call bear spread is a bearishly oriented strategy. Since the spread is a credit spread—requiring only a reduction in buying power, but no actual layout of cash to establish—it is a moderately popular strategy. Since the strategy requires selling a call with a lower striking price than the one that is purchased, the strategist may be buying more time value than he is selling. For this reason, the bear spread using calls is not the optimum type of bearish spread that is available—a bear spread using put options is. However, in cases where the underlying stock does not have listed puts trading, the call bear spread may be an attractive way of capitalizing on a downward move by the underlying stock.

CHAPTER

# *Calendar Spreads* 9

A *calendar spread,* also frequently called a *time spread,* involves the sale of one option and the simultaneous purchase of a more distant option, both with the same striking price. In the broad definition, the calendar spread is a horizontal spread. The neutral philosophy for using calendar spreads is that time will erode the value of the near-term option at a faster rate than it will the far-term option. If this happens, the spread will widen and a profit may result at near-term expiration. With call options, one may construct a more aggressive, bullish calendar spread. Both types of spread will be discussed.

*Example:* The following prices exist sometime in late January:

|         | April 50 Call (3-month call) | July 50 Call (6-month call) | October 50 Call (9-month call) |
|---------|------------------------------|-----------------------------|--------------------------------|
| XYZ: 50 | 5                            | 8                           | 10                             |

If one sells the April 50 call and buys the July 50 at the same time, he will pay a debit of 3 points—the difference in the call prices—plus commissions. That is, *his investment is the net debit of the spread plus commissions.* Furthermore, suppose that in three months, at April expiration, XYZ is unchanged at 50. Then the three-month call should be worth 5 points, and the six-month call should be worth 8 points, as they were previously.

|           | April 50 Call (Expiring) | July 50 Call (3-month call) | October 50 Call (6-month call) |
|-----------|--------------------------|-----------------------------|--------------------------------|
| XYZ: 50   | 0                        | 5                           | 8                              |

The spread between the April 50 and the July 50 has now widened to 5 points. Since the spread cost 3 points originally, this widening effect has produced a 2-point profit. The spread could be closed at this time in order to realize the profit, or the spreader may decide to continue to hold the July 50 call which he is long. By continuing to hold the July 50 call, he is risking the profits that have accrued to date, but he could profit handsomely if the underlying stock rises in price over the next three months before July expiration.

It is not necessary for the underlying stock to be exactly at the striking price of the options at near-term expiration for a profit to result. In fact, some profit can be made in a range that extends both below and above the striking price. The risk in this type of position is that the stock will drop a great deal or rise a great deal, in which case the spread between the two options will shrink and the spreader will lose money. Since the spread between two calls at the same strike cannot shrink to less than zero, however, *the risk is limited to the amount of the original debit spent to establish the spread, plus commissions.*

## THE NEUTRAL CALENDAR SPREAD

As mentioned earlier, the calendar spreader can either have a neutral outlook on the stock or he can construct the spread for an aggressively bullish outlook. The neutral outlook will be described first. The calendar spread that is established when the underlying stock is at or near the striking price of the options used is a neutral spread. The strategist is interested in selling time and not in predicting the direction of the underlying stock. If the stock remains relatively unchanged until the near-term option expires, the neutral spread will make a profit. *In a neutral spread, one should initially have the intent of closing the spread by the time the near-term option expires.*

Let us again turn to our example calendar spread described earlier in order to more accurately demonstrate the potential risks and

**FIGURE 9-1.** *Calendar spread at near-term expiration.*

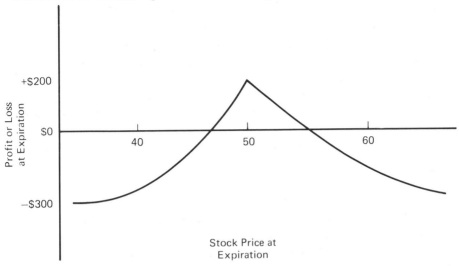

rewards from that spread when the near-term, April, call expires. To do this, it is necessary to estimate the price of the July 50 call at that time. Notice that, with XYZ at 50 at expiration, the results agree with the less detailed example presented earlier. The graph shown in Figure 9-1 is the "total profit" from Table 9-1. The graph is a curved, rather than straight, line since the July 50 call still has time premium. There is a slightly bullish bias to this graph: the profit range extends slightly farther above the striking price than it does below the striking price. This is due to the fact that the spread is a call spread. If puts had been used, the profit range would have a bearish bias. The total width of the profit range is a function of the volatility of the underlying stock, as well as a function of the time remaining to near-term expiration.

Table 9-1 and Figure 9-1 clearly depict several of the more significant aspects of the calendar spread. *There is a range within which*

**TABLE 9-1.** *Estimated profit or losses at April expiration.*

| XYZ Stock Price | April 50 Price | April 50 Profit | July 50 Price | July 50 Profit | Total Profit |
|---|---|---|---|---|---|
| 40 | 0 | +$500 | ½ | −$750 | −$250 |
| 45 | 0 | + 500 | 2½ | − 550 | − 50 |
| 48 | 0 | + 500 | 4 | − 400 | + 100 |
| 50 | 0 | + 500 | 5 | − 300 | + 200 |
| 52 | 2 | + 300 | 6 | − 200 | + 100 |
| 55 | 5 | 0 | 8 | 0 | 0 |
| 60 | 10 | − 500 | 10½ | + 250 | − 250 |

*the spread is profitable at near-term expiration.* That range would appear to be about 46 to 55 in the example. Outside that range, losses can occur, but they are limited to the amount of the initial debit. Notice in the example that the stock would have to be well below 40 or well above 60 for the maximum loss to occur. Even if the stock is at 40 or 60, there is some time premium left in the longer-term option and the loss is not quite as large as the maximum possible loss of $300.

This type of calendar spread has limited profits and relatively large commission costs. It is generally best to establish such a spread 8 to 12 weeks before the near-term option expires. If this is done, one is capitalizing on the maximum rate of decay of the near-term option with respect to the longer-term option. That is, when a call has less than 8 weeks of life, the rate of decay of its time value premium increases substantially with respect to the longer-term options on the same stock.

## FOLLOWING-UP ON THE NEUTRAL CALENDAR SPREAD

Ideally, the spreader would like to have the stock be just below the striking price when the near-term call expires. If this happens, he can close the spread with only one commission cost—that of selling out the long call. If the calls are in-the-money at the expiration date, he will, of course, have to pay two commissions to close the spread. As with all spread positions, the order to close the spread should be placed as a single order. "Legging" out of a spread is highly risky and is not recommended.

Prior to expiration, the spreader should close the spread if the near-term, short call is trading at parity. He does this to avoid assignment. Being called out of spread position is devastating from the viewpoint of the stock commissions involved for the public customer. The near-term call would not normally be trading at parity until quite close to the last day of trading, unless the stock has undergone a substantial rise in price.

In the case of an early *downside* breakout by the underlying stock, the spreader has several choices. He could immediately close the spread and take a small loss on the position. Another choice he has is to leave the spread alone until the near-term call expires and then to hope for a partial recovery from the stock in order to be able to recover some value from the long side of the spread. Such a holding action is often better than the immediate close-out, because the expense of buying back the short call can be quite large percentagewise. A riskier downside defensive action is to sell out the long call if the stock begins to break down heavily. In this way, the spreader recovers something from the long side of his spread immediately, and then looks for the stock to remain depressed so that the short side of the spread will expire worthless. This action requires that one have enough collateral available to margin the naked call—often an amount substantially in excess of the original debit paid for the spread. Moreover, if the underlying stock should reverse direction and rally back to or above the striking price, the short side of the spread is naked and could produce substantial losses. The risk assumed by such a follow-up violates the initial neutral premise of the spread, and should therefore be avoided. Of these three types of downside defensive action, *the easiest and most conservative one is to do nothing at all*—letting the short call expire worthless and then hoping for a recovery by the underlying stock. If this tack is taken, the risk still remains fixed at the original debit paid for the spread, and occasionally a rally may produce large profits on the long call. Although this rally is a nonfrequent event, it generally costs the spreader very little to allow himself the opportunity to take advantage of such a rally if it should occur.

In fact, the strategist can employ a slight modification of this sort of action, even if the spread is not at a large loss. If the underlying stock is moderately below the striking price at near-term expiration, the short option will expire worthless and the spreader will be left holding the long option. He could sell the long side immediately and perhaps take a small gain or loss. However, it is often a reasonable strategy to sell out a portion of the long side—recovering all, or a substantial portion, of the initial investment—and hold the remainder. If the stock rises, the remaining long position may appreciate substantially. Although this sort of action deviates from the true nature of the time spread, it is not overly risky.

An early breakout to the upside by the underlying stock is generally handled in much the same way as downside breakout. Doing nothing is often the best course of action. If the underlying stock rallies shortly after the spread is established, the spread will shrink by a small amount, but not substantially, because both options will hold premium in a rally. If the spreader were to rush in to close the position, he would be paying commissions on two rather expensive options. He will usually do better by waiting and giving himself as much of a chance for a reversal as possible. In fact, even at near-term expiration, there will normally be some time premium left in the long option so that the maximum loss would not have to be realized. A highly risk-oriented upside defensive action is to cover the short call on a technical breakout and continue to hold the long call. This can become disastrous if the breakout fails and the stock drops, possibly resulting in losses far in excess of the original debit. Therefore this action cannot be considered anything but extremely aggressive and illogical for the neutral strategist.

If a breakout does not occur, the spreader will normally be making unrealized profits as time passes. Should this be the case, he may want to set some mental stop-out points for himself. For example, if the underlying stock is quite close to the striking price with only 2 weeks to go, there will be some more profit potential left in the spread, but the spreader should be ready to close the position quickly if the stock begins to get too far away from the striking price. In this manner, he can leave room for more profits to accrue, but he is also attempting to protect the profits that have already built up. This is somewhat similar to the action that the ratio writer takes when he narrows the range of his action points as more and more time passes.

## THE BULLISH CALENDAR SPREAD

A less neutral and more bullish type of calendar spread is pre-ferred by the more aggressive investor. In a bullish calendar spread, one sells the near-term call and buys a longer-term call, but *he does this when the underlying stock is some distance below the striking price of the calls.* This type of position has the attractive features of low dollar investment and large potential profits. Of course, there is risk involved as well.

> *Example:* One might set up a bullish calendar spread in the following manner:
>
> XYZ common, 45;
>
> sell the XYZ April 50 for 1; and
>
> buy the XYZ July 50 for 1½.
>
> This investor ideally wants two things to happen. *First, he would like the near-term call to expire worthless.* That is why the bullish calendar spread is established with out-of-the-money calls—to increase the chances of the short call expiring worthless. If this happens, the investor will then own the longer-term call at a net cost of his original debit. In this example, his original debit was only ½ of a point to create the spread. If the April 50 call expires worthless, the investor will own the July 50 call at a net cost of ½ point, plus commissions.
>
> *The investor now needs a second criterion to be fulfilled—the*

*stock must rise in price by the time the July 50 call expires.* In this example, even if XYZ were to rally to only 52 between April and July, the July 50 call could be sold for at least 2 points. This represents a substantial percentage gain because the cost of the call has been reduced to ½ point. Thus there is the potential for large profits in bullish calendar spreads if the underlying stock rallies above the striking price before the longer-term call expires, provided that the short-term call has already expired worthless.

What chance does the investor have that both ideal conditions will occur? There is a reasonably good chance that the written call will expire worthless since it is a short-term call and the stock is below the striking price to start with. If the stock falls, or even rises a little—up to, but not above, the striking price—the first condition will have been met. It is the second condition—a rally above the striking price by the underlying stock before the longer-term expiration date—that normally presents the biggest problem. The chances of this happening are usually small, but the rewards can be large when it does happen. Thus *this strategy offers a small probability of making a large profit.* In fact, one large profit can easily offset several losses, because the losses are small, dollarwise. Even if the stock remains depressed and the July 50 call in the example expires worthless, the loss is limited to the initial debit of ½ a point. Of course, this loss represents 100% of the initial investment, so one cannot put all his money into bullish calendar spreads.

This strategy is a reasonable way to speculate, provided that the spreader adheres to the following criteria when establishing the spread:

1. *Select underlying stocks that are volatile enough to move above the striking price within the allotted time.* Bullish calendar spreads may appear to be very "cheap" on nonvolatile stocks that are well below the striking price. But if a large stock move—say 20%—is required in only a few months, the spread is not worthwhile for a nonvolatile stock.

2. *Do not use options more than one striking price above the current market.* For example, if XYZ were 26, use the 30 strike, not the 35 strike, since the chances of a rally to 30 are many times greater than the chances of a rally to 35.

3. *Do not invest a large percentage of available trading capital in bullish calendar spreads.* Since these are such low-cost spreads, one should be able to follow this rule easily and still diversify into several positions.

## FOLLOW-UP ACTION

If the underlying stock should rally before the near-term call expires, the bullish calendar spreader must *never* consider "legging" out of the spread, or consider covering the short call at a loss and attempting to ride the long call. Either action could turn the initial small limited loss into a disastrous loss. Since the strategy hinges on the fact that all the losses will be small and the infrequent large profits will be able to overcome these small losses, one should do nothing to jeopardize the strategy and possibly generate a large loss.

The only reasonable sort of follow-up action that the bullish calendar spreader can take in advance of expiration is to close the spread if the underlying stock has moved up in price and the spread has widened to become profitable. This might occur if the stock moves up to the striking price after some time has passed. In the example above, if XYZ moved up to 50 with a month or so of life left in the April 50 call, the call might be selling for 1½ while the July 50 call might be selling for 3 points. Thus the spread could be closed at 1½ points, representing a 1-point gain over the initial debit of ½ point. Two commissions would have to be paid to close the spread, of course, but there would still be a net profit in the spread.

## USING ALL THREE EXPIRATION SERIES

In either the neutral calendar spread or the bullish calendar spread, the investor has three choices of which months to use. He could sell the nearest-term call and buy the intermediate-term call. This is usually the most common way to set up these spreads. However, there is no rule that prevents him from selling the intermediate-term and buying the longest-term, or possibly selling the near-term and buying the long-term. Any of these situations would still be a calendar spread.

Some proponents of calendar spreads prefer to initially sell the near-term and buy the long-term call. Then, if the near-term call expires worthless, they have an opportunity to sell the intermediate-term call if they so desire.

*Example:* An investor establishes a calendar spread by selling the April 50 call and buying the October 50 call. The April call would have less than 3 months remaining and the October call would be the long-term call. At April expiration, if XYZ is below 50, the April call will expire worthless. At that time, the July 50 call could be sold against the

October 50 which is held long, thereby creating another calendar spread with no additional commission cost on the long side.

The advantage of this type of strategy is that it is possible for the two sales (April 50 and July 50 in this example) to actually bring in more credits than were spent for the one purchase (October 50). Thus the spreader might be able to create a position where he has a guaranteed profit. That is, if the sum of his transactions is actually a credit, he cannot lose money in the spread (provided that he does not attempt to "leg" out of the spread). The disadvantage of using the long-term call in the calendar spread is that the initial debit is larger, and therefore more dollars are initially at risk. If the underlying stock moves substantially up or down in the first three months, the spreader could realize a larger dollar loss with the April/October spread because his loss will approach the initial debit.

The remaining combination of the expiration series is to initially buy the longest-term call and sell the intermediate-term call against it. This combination will generally require the smallest initial debit, but there is not much profit potential in the spread until the intermediate-term expiration date draws near. Thus there is a lot of time for the underlying stock to move some distance away from the initial striking price. For this reason, this is generally an inferior approach to calendar spreading.

## SUMMARY

Calendar spreading is a low-dollar-cost strategy that is a non-aggressive approach, provided that the spreader does not invest a large percentage of his trading capital in the strategy, and provided that he does not attempt to "leg" into or out of the spreads. The neutral calendar spread is one in which the strategist is mainly selling time— he is attempting to capitalize on the known fact that the near-term call will lose time premium more rapidly than will a longer-term call. A more aggressive approach is the bullish calendar spread, in which the speculator is essentially trying to reduce the net cost of a longer-term call by the amount of credits taken in from the sale of a nearer-term call. This bullish strategy requires that the near-term call expire worthless and then that the underlying stock rises in price. In either strategy, the most common approach is to sell the nearest-term call and buy the intermediate-term call. However, it may sometimes prove advantageous to sell the near-term and buy the longest-term initially, with the intention of letting the near-term expire and then possibly writing against the longer-term call a second time.

# *The Butterfly* **10** *Spread*

The recipient of one of the more exotic names given to spread positions, *the butterfly spread is a neutral position that is a combination of both a bull spread and a bear spread.* This spread is for the neutral strategist—one who thinks the underlying stock will not experience much of a net rise or decline by expiration. It generally requires only a small investment and has limited risk. Although profits are limited as well, they are larger than the potential risk. For this reason, the butterfly spread is a viable strategy. However, it is costly in terms of commissions. In this chapter, the strategy will be explained using only calls. The strategy can also be implemented using a combination of puts and calls, as will be demonstrated later.

*There are three striking prices involved in a butterfly spread.* Using only calls, the butterfly spread consists of buying one call at the lowest striking price, selling two calls at the middle striking price and buying one call at the highest striking price. The following example will demonstrate how the butterfly spread works.

*Example:* The spread requires a relatively low debit of $300 (Table 10-1), although there are four option commissions involved and these may represent a substantial percentage of the net investment. As usual, *the maximum amount of profit is realized at the striking price of the written calls.* With most types of spreads, this is a useful fact to

**TABLE 10-1.** *Butterfly spread example.*

Current prices:

| | |
|---|---|
| XYZ common: | 60 |
| XYZ July 50 call: | 12 |
| XYZ July 60 call: | 6 |
| XYZ July 70 call: | 3 |

Butterfly spread:

| | |
|---|---|
| Buy 1 July 50 call | $1,200 debit |
| Sell 2 July 60 calls | $1,200 credit |
| Buy 1 July 70 call | $300 debit |
| Net debit | $300 (plus commissions) |

remember, for it can aid in quick computation of the potential of the spread. In this example, if the stock were at the striking price of the written options at expiration—60—the two July 60's which are short would expire worthless for a $1,200 gain. The long July 70 call would expire worthless—a $300 loss—and the long July 50 call would be worth 10 points, for a $200 loss on that call. The sum of the gains and losses would thus be a $700 gain, less commissions. This is the maximum profit potential of the spread.

*The risk is limited in a butterfly spread—both to the upside and to the downside—and is equal to the amount of the net debit required to establish the spread.* In the example above, the risk is limited to $300 plus commissions.

Table 10-2 and Figure 10-1 depict the results of this butterfly spread at various prices at expiration. The profit graph resembles that of a ratio write except that the loss is limited on both the upside and the downside. There is a profit range within which the butterfly spread makes money—53 to 67 in the example, before commissions are included. Outside this profit range, losses will occur at expiration, but

**TABLE 10-2.** *Results of butterfly spread at expiration.*

| XYZ Price at Expiration | July 50 Profit | July 60 Profit | July 70 Profit | Total Profit |
|---|---|---|---|---|
| 40 | −$1,200 | +$1,200 | −$300 | −$300 |
| 50 | − 1,200 | + 1,200 | − 300 | − 300 |
| 53 | − 900 | + 1,200 | − 300 | 0 |
| 56 | − 600 | + 1,200 | − 300 | + 300 |
| 60 | − 200 | + 1,200 | − 300 | + 700 |
| 64 | + 200 | + 400 | − 300 | + 300 |
| 67 | + 500 | − 200 | − 300 | 0 |
| 70 | + 800 | − 800 | − 300 | − 300 |
| 80 | + 1,800 | − 2,800 | + 700 | − 300 |

**FIGURE 10-1.** *Butterfly spread.*

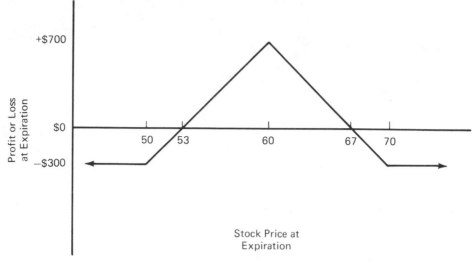

these losses are limited to the amount of the original debit plus commissions.

The *collateral investment* required for the butterfly spread is *not* equal to the net debit expended. Since the spread consists of both a bull spread and a bear spread, the collateral requirement for the butterfly spread is the sum of the requirements for the bull spread and the bear spread. The bull spread—buying the July 50 and selling the July 60 in the example above—has a requirement of the net debit, or $600 (the July 50 cost 12 and the July 60 was sold for 6). The bear spread—buying the July 70 and selling the July 60—has a margin requirement of $700 (the 10-point difference between the strikes plus the 3 points paid for the July 70 less the 6 points received from the sale of the July 60). The butterfly spread, then, has a requirement of $1,300, even though the strategist only directly pays out the $300 debit plus commissions required to establish the spread. The rest of the requirement represents a reduction in the excess buying power in the spreader's margin account. When the striking prices are evenly spaced—the spacing is 10 points in this example—the following formulae can be used to quickly compute the important details of this spread.

Net collateral investment = distance between strikes + net debit

Maximum profit = distance between strikes − net debit

Downside break-even = lowest strike + net debit

Upside break-even = highest strike − net debit

In the example, the distance between strikes is 10 points, the net debit is 3 points (before commissions), the lowest strike used is 50, and the highest strike is 70. These formulae would then yield the following results for this example spread.

$$\text{Net investment} = 10 + 3 = \$1,300$$

$$\text{Maximum profit} = 10 - 3 = \$700$$

$$\text{Downside break-even} = 50 + 3 = 53$$

$$\text{Upside break-even} = 70 - 3 = 67$$

Note that all of these answers agree with the results that were previously obtained by analyzing the example spread in detail.

In this example, the maximum profit potential is $700, the maximum risk is $300, and the investment required is $1,300. In percentage terms, this means that the butterfly spread has a loss limited to about 22% and could make profits of nearly 54% in this case. These represent an attractive risk/reward relationship. This is, however, just an example, and two factors that exist in the actual marketplace may greatly affect these numbers. First, commissions are large—it is possible that eight commissions might have to be paid to establish and liquidate the spread. Second, depending on the level of premiums to be found in the market at any point in time, it may not be possible to establish a spread for a debit as low as 3 points when the strikes are 10 points apart.

## SELECTING THE SPREAD

Ideally, one would want to establish a butterfly spread at as small of a debit as possible in order to limit his risk to a small amount, both dollarwise and percentagewise. One would also like to have the stock be near the middle striking price to begin with, because he will then be in his maximum profit area if the stock remains relatively unchanged. Unfortunately, it is difficult to satisfy both conditions simultaneously.

*The smallest-debit butterfly spreads are those where the stock is some distance away from the middle striking price.* To see this, note that if the stock were well above the middle strike and all the options were at parity, the net debit would be zero. Although no one would attempt to establish a butterfly spread with parity options because of the risk of early assignment, it may be somewhat useful to try to obtain a small debit by taking an opinion on the underlying stock. For example, if the stock is close to the higher striking price, the debit would be small normally, but the investor would have to be somewhat bearish on the underlying stock in order to maximize his profit—that is, the stock would have to decline in price from the upper striking price to the middle striking price for the maximum profit to be realized. An analogous situation exists when the underlying stock is originally close to the lower striking price. The investor could establish the spread for a small debit in this case also, but he would now have to be somewhat bullish on the underlying stock in order to attempt to realize his maximum profit.

> *Example:* XYZ is at 70. One may be able to establish a low-debit butterfly spread with the 50's, 60's, and 70's if the following prices exist:
>
> XYZ common, 70;
>
> XYZ July 50, 20;
>
> XYZ July 60, 12; and
>
> XYZ July 70, 5.
>
> The butterfly spread would require a debit of only $100 plus commissions to establish because the cost of the calls at the higher and lower strike cost 25 points, and a 24-point credit would be obtained by selling two calls at the middle strike. This is indeed a low-cost butterfly spread, but the stock will have to move down in price for much of a profit to be realized. The maximum profit of $900 less commissions would be realized at 60 at expiration. The strategist would have to be bearish on XYZ for him to want to establish such a spread.

Without the aid of an example, the reader should be able to determine that if XYZ were originally at 50, a low-cost butterfly spread could be established by buying the 50, selling two 60's, and buying a 70. In this case, however, the investor would have to be bullish on the stock because he would want it to move up to 60 by expiration in order for the maximum profit to be realized.

In general, then, if the butterfly spread is to be established at an extremely low debit, the spreader will have to make a decision as to whether he wants to be bullish or bearish on the underlying stock. Many strategists prefer to remain as neutral as possible on the underlying stock at all times in any strategy. This philosophy would lead to slightly higher debits, such as the $300 debit in the example at the beginning of this chapter, but would theoretically have a better chance of making money because there would be a profit if the stock remained relatively unchanged—the most probable occurrence.

In either philosophy, there are other considerations for the butterfly spread. *The best butterfly spreads are generally found on the more expensive and/or more volatile stocks which have striking prices spaced 10 or 20 points apart.* In these situations, the maximum profit is large enough to overcome the weight of the commission costs involved in the butterfly spread. When one establishes butterfly spreads on lower-priced stocks where the striking prices are only 5 points apart, he is normally putting himself at a disadvantage unless the debit is extremely small. One exception to this rule is that attractive situations are often found on higher-priced stocks with striking prices 5 points apart (50, 55, and 60, for example). They do exist from time to time.

In analyzing butterfly spreads, one commonly works with closing prices. It was mentioned earlier that using closing prices for analysis can prove somewhat misleading since the actual execution will have to be done at bid and asked prices, and these may differ somewhat from closing prices. Normally, this difference is small, but since there are three different calls involved in a butterfly spread, the difference could be substantial. Therefore, it is usually necessary to check the appropriate bid and asked price for each call before entering the spread in order to be able to place a reasonable debit on the order. As with other types of spreads, the butterfly spread order can be placed as one order.

Before moving on to discuss follow-up action, it may be worthwhile to describe a tactic for stocks with five points between striking prices. For example, the butterfly spreader might work with strikes of 45, 50, and 60. If he sets up the usual type of butterfly spread, he would end up with a position that has too much risk near 60 and very little or none at all near 45. If this is what he wants, fine, but if he wants to remain neutral, the standard type of butterfly spread will have to be modified slightly.

*Example:* The following prices exist:
   XYZ common, 50;
   July 45 call, 7;
   July 50 call, 5; and
   July 60 call, 2.

The normal type of butterfly spread—buying one 45, selling two 50's, and buying one 60—can actually be done for a credit of 1 point. However, the profitability is no longer symmetric about the middle striking price. In this example, the investor cannot lose to the downside, because, even if the stock collapses and all the calls expire worthless, he will still make his 1-point credit. However, to the upside, there is risk: if XYZ is anywhere above 60 at expiration, the risk is 4 points. This is no longer a neutral position—the fact that the lower strike is only 5 points from the middle strike while the higher strike is 10 points away has made this a somewhat bearish position. If the spreader wants to be neutral and still use these striking prices, he will have to put on *two* bull spreads and only one bear spread. That is, he should:

|                    |                |
| ------------------ | -------------- |
| Buy 2 July 45's:   | $1,400 debit   |
| Sell 3 July 50's:  | $1,500 credit  |
| Buy 1 July 60:     | $  200 debit   |

This position now has a net debit of $100 but has a better balance of risk at either end. If XYZ drops and is below 45 at expiration, the spreader will lose his $100 initial debit. But now, if XYZ is at or above 60 at expiration, he will lose $100 in that range also. Thus by establishing two bull spreads with a 5-point difference between the strikes versus one bear spread with a 10-point difference between strikes, the risk has been balanced at both ends.

The same analysis obviously applies anywhere that 5-point striking price intervals exist. There are numerous combinations that could be worked out for lower-priced stocks by merely skipping over a striking price (using the 25's, 30's, and 40's, for example). Although there are not normally many stocks trading over $100 per share, the same analysis is applicable by using 130's, 140's, and 160's for example.

## FOLLOW-UP ACTION

Since the butterfly spread has limited risk by its construction, there is usually little that the spreader has to do in the way of follow-up action other than avoiding early exercise or possibly closing out the position early to take profits or limit losses even further. The only part of the spread that is subject to assignment is the call at the middle strike. If this call trades at or near parity, in-the-money, the spread should be closed. This may happen before expiration if the underlying stock is about to go ex-dividend.

If the stock is near the middle strike after a reasonable amount of time has passed, an unrealized profit will begin to accrue to the spreader. If one feels that the underlying stock is about to move away from the middle striking price and thereby jeopardize these profits, it may be advantageous to close the spread to take the available profit. Be certain to include commission costs when determining if an unrealized profit exists. As a general rule of thumb, if one is doing 10 spreads at a time, he can estimate that the commission cost for each option is about ⅛ point. That is, if one has 10 butterfly spreads and the spread is currently at 6 points, he could figure that he would net about 5½ points after commissions to close the spread. This ⅛ estimate is only valid if the spreader has at least 10 options at each strike involved in a spread.

Normally, one would not close the spread early to limit losses since these losses are limited to the original net debit in any case. However, if that original debit was large and the stock is beginning to break out above the higher strike or to break down below the lower strike, the spreader may want to close the spread to limit losses even further.

It has been repeatedly stated that one should not attempt to "leg" out of a spread because of the risk that is incurred if one is wrong. However, there is a method of legging out of a butterfly spread that is acceptable and may even be prudent. Since the spread consists of both a bull spread and a bear spread, it may often be the case that the stock experiences a relatively substantial move in one direction or the other during the life of the butterfly spread and that the bull spread portion or the bear spread portion could be closed out near their maximum profit potentials. If this situation arises, the spreader may want to take advantage of it in order to be able to profit more if the underlying stock reverses direction and comes back into the profit range.

*Example:* This strategy can be explained by using the initial example from this chapter and then assuming that the stock falls from 60 to 45. Recall that this spread was initially established with a 3-point debit and a maximum profit potential of 7 points. The profit range was 53 to 67 at July expiration. However, a rather unpleasant situation has occurred: the stock has fallen quickly and is below the profit range. If the spreader does nothing and keeps the spread on, he will lose at most 3 points if the stock remains below 50 until July expiration. However, by increasing his risk slightly, he may be able to improve his position. Notice in Table 10-3 that the bear spread portion of the overall spread—short July 60, long July 70—has very nearly reached its maximum potential. The bear spread could be bought back for ½ of a point total (pay 1 point to buy back the July 60 and receive ½ point from selling out the July 70). Thus the spreader could convert the butterfly spread to a bull

**TABLE 10-3.** *Initial spread and current prices.*

| Initial Spread | | Current Prices | |
|---|---|---|---|
| XYZ Common: | 60 | XYZ Common: | 45 |
| July 50 call: | 12 | July 50 call: | 2 |
| July 60 call: | 6 | July 60 call: | 1 |
| July 70 call: | 3 | July 70 call: | ½ |

spread by spending ½ of a point. What would such an action do to his overall position? First, his risk would be increased by the ½ point spent to close the bear spread. That is, if XYZ continues to remain below 50 until July expiration, he would now lose 3½ rather than 3 points, plus commissions in either case. He has, however, potentially helped his chances of realizing something close to the maximum profit available from the original butterfly spread.

After buying back the bear spread, he is left with the following bull spread:

> Long July 50 call
> Short July 60 call    —    net debit 3½ points

He has a bull spread at the total cost paid to date—3½ points. From the earlier discussion of bull spreads, the reader should know that the break-even point for this position is 53½ at expiration, and it could make a 6½-point profit if XYZ is anywhere over 60 at July expiration. Hence the break-even point for the position was raised from 53 to 53½ by the expense of the ½ point to buy back the bear spread. However, if the stock should rally back above 60, the strategist will be making a profit nearly equal to the original maximum profit that he was aiming for (7 points). Moreover, this profit is now available anywhere over 60, not just exactly at 60 as it was in the original position. Although the chances of such a rally cannot be considered great, it does not cost the spreader much to restructure himself into a position with a much broader maximum profit area.

A similar situation is available if the underlying stock moves up in price. In that case, the bull spread may be able to be removed at nearly its maximum profit potential, thereby leaving a bear spread. Again, suppose that the same initial spread was established but that XYZ has risen to 75. When the underlying stock advances substantially, the bull spread portion of the butterfly spread may expand to near its maximum potential. Since the strikes are 10 points apart in this bull spread, the widest that it can grow to is 10 points. At the prices shown in Table 10-4, the bull spread—long July 50 and short July 60—has grown to 9½ points. Thus the bull spread position could be removed within ½ point of its maximum profit potential and the original butterfly spread would

**TABLE 10-4.** *Initial spread and new current prices.*

| Initial Spread | | Current Prices | |
|---|---|---|---|
| XYZ common: | 60 | XYZ common: | 75 |
| XYZ July 50 call: | 12 | July 50 call: | 25½ |
| July 60 call: | 6 | July 60 call: | 16 |
| July 70 call: | 3 | July 70 call: | 7 |

become a bear spread. Note that the closing of the bull spread portion generates a 9½-point *credit*—the July 50 is sold at 25½ and the July 60 is bought back at 16. The original butterfly spread was established at a 3-point debit, so the net position is the remaining position:

> Long July 70 call
> Short July 60 call — net credit 6½ points

This bear spread has a maximum profit potential of 6½ points anywhere below 60 at July expiration. The maximum risk is 3½ points anywhere above 70 at expiration. Thus the original butterfly spread was again converted into a position where a stock price reversal to any price below 60 could produce something close to the maximum profit. Moreover, the risk was only increased by an additional ½ point.

## SUMMARY

*The butterfly spread is a viable, low-cost strategy with both limited profit potential and limited risk.* It is actually a combination of a bull spread and a bear spread, and involves using three striking prices. The risk is limited should the underlying stock fall below the lowest strike or rise above the highest strike. The maximum profit is obtained at the middle strike. One can keep his initial debits to a minimum by initially assuming a bullish or bearish posture on the underlying stock. If he would rather remain neutral, he will normally have to pay a slightly larger debit to establish the spread, but may have a better chance of making money. If the underlying stock experiences a large move in one direction or the other prior to expiration, the spreader may want to close the profitable side of his butterfly spread near its maximum profit potential in order to be able to capitalize on a stock price reversal, should one occur.

# Ratio Call Spreads *11*

A *ratio call spread* is a neutral strategy in which one buys a number of calls at a lower strike and sells more calls at a higher strike. It is somewhat similar to a ratio write in concept, although the spread has less downside risk and normally requires a smaller investment than does a ratio write. The ratio spread and ratio write are similar in that both involve uncovered calls, and both have profit ranges within which a profit can be made at expiration. Other comparisons will be demonstrated throughout the chapter.

> *Example:* The following prices exist:
>     XYZ common, 44;
>     XYZ April 40 call, 5; and
>     XYZ April 45 call, 3.

A 2:1 ratio call spread could be established by buying one April 40 call and simultaneously selling two April 45's. This spread would be done for a credit of 1 point—the sale of the two April 45's bringing in 6 points and the purchase of the April 40 costing 5 points. This spread can be entered as one spread order, specifying the net credit or debit for the position. In this case, the spread would be entered at a net credit of 1 point.

*Ratio spreads, unlike ratio writes, have a relatively small, limited downside risk.* In fact, if the spread is established at an initial credit, there is no downside risk at all. In a ratio spread, *the profit or loss at expiration is constant below the lower striking price,* because both options would be worthless in that area. In the example above, if XYZ is below 40 at April expiration, all the options would expire worthless and the spreader would have made a profit of his initial 1-point credit, less commissions. This 1-point gain would occur anywhere below 40 at expiration—it is a constant.

The maximum profit at expiration for a ratio spread occurs if the stock is exactly at the striking price of the written options. This is true for nearly all types of strategies involving written options. In the example, if XYZ were at 45 at April expiration, the April 45 calls would expire worthless for a gain of $600 on the two of them, and the April 40 call would be worth 5 points, resulting in no gain or loss on that call. Thus the total profit would be $600 less commissions.

*The greatest risk is a ratio spread lies to the upside,* where the loss may theoretically be unlimited. The upside break-even point in this example is 51, as shown in Table 11-1. The table and Figure 11-1 illustrate the statements made in the preceding paragraphs.

**TABLE 11-1.** *Ratio call spread.*

| XYZ Price at Expiration | April 40 Call Profits | April 45 Call Profits | Total Profits |
|---|---|---|---|
| 35 | −$ 500 | +$ 600 | +$100 |
| 40 | − 500 | + 600 | + 100 |
| 42 | − 300 | + 600 | + 300 |
| 45 | 0 | + 600 | + 600 |
| 48 | + 300 | 0 | + 300 |
| 51 | + 600 | − 600 | 0 |
| 55 | + 1,000 | − 1,400 | − 400 |
| 60 | + 1,500 | − 2,400 | − 900 |

In a 2:1 ratio spread two calls are sold for each one purchased. The maximum profit amount and the upside break-even point can be easily computed by using the following formulae:

Points of maximum profit=initial credit + difference between strikes or

= difference between strikes − initial debit

Upside break-even point = higher strike price + points of maximum profit

In the preceding example, the initial credit was 1 point, so the

FIGURE 11-1. *Ratio call spread (2:1).*

points of maximum profit = 1 + 5 = 6, or $600. The upside break-even point is then 45 + 6, or 51. This agrees with the results determined earlier. Note that if the spread is established at a debit rather than a credit, the debit is subtracted from the striking price differential to determine the points of maximum profit.

Many neutral investors prefer ratio spreads over ratio writes for two reasons:

1. The downside risk or gain is predetermined in the ratio spread at expiration, and therefore the position does not require much monitoring on the downside.

2. The margin investment required for a ratio spread is normally smaller than that required for a ratio write, since on the long side one is buying a call rather than buying the common stock itself.

For margin purposes, a ratio spread is really the combination of a bull spread and a naked call write. There is no margin requirement for a bull spread other than the net debit to establish the bull spread. The net investment for the ratio spread is thus equal to the collateral required for the naked calls in the spread plus or minus the net debit or credit of the spread. In the example above, there is one naked call. The requirement for the naked call is 30% of the stock price plus the difference between the stock price and the striking price. So the requirement in the example would be 30% of 44, or $1,320, less the one point that the stock is below the striking price—a $1,220 requirement for the naked call. Since the spread was established at a credit of one point, this credit can also be applied against the initial requirement, thereby reducing that requirement to $1,120. Since there is a naked call in this spread, there will be a *mark to market* if the stock moves up. Just as was recommended for the ratio write, *it is recommended that the ratio spreader allow at least enough collateral to reach the upside break-even point.* Since the upside break-even point is 51 in this example, the spreader should allow 30% of 51, or $1,530, plus the 6 points that the stock would be above the strike less the 1-point initial net credit—a total of $2,030 for this spread ($1,530 + $600 − $100).

## DIFFERING PHILOSOPHIES

As in many strategies, there is more than one philosophy of how to implement the strategy. Ratio spreads are no exception, with three philosophies being predominant. One philosophy holds that ratio spreading is quite similar to ratio writing—that one should be looking for opportunities to purchase an in-the-money call with little or no time premium in it so that the ratio spread simulates the profit opportunities from the ratio write as closely as possible with a smaller investment. The ratio spreads established under this philosophy may have rather large debits if the purchased call is substantially in-the-money. Another philosophy of ratio spreading is that spreads should be established for credits so that there is no chance of losing money on the downside. Both philosophies have merit and both will be described. A third philosophy, called the "delta spread," is more concerned with neutrality, regardless of the initial debit or credit.

### Ratio Spread As Ratio Write

There are several spread strategies similar to strategies that involve common stock. In this case, the ratio spread is similar to the ratio write. Whenever such a similarity exists, it may be possible for the strategist to buy an in-the-money call with little or no time premium as a substitute for buying the common stock. This was seen earlier in the covered call writing strategy, where it was shown that the purchase of in-the-money calls or warrants might be a viable substitute for the purchase of stock. *If one is able to buy an in-the-money call as a substitute for the stock, he will not affect his profit potential substantially.* When comparing a ratio spread to a ratio write, the maximum profit potential and the profit range are reduced by the time value premium paid for the long call. If this call is at parity (the time value premium is thus zero), the ratio spread and the ratio write have exactly the same profit potential. Moreover, the net investment is reduced and there is less downside risk should the stock fall in price below the striking price of the purchased call. The spread also involves smaller commission costs than does the ratio write, which involves a stock purchase. The ratio writer does receive stock dividends, if any are paid, whereas the spreader does not.

*Example:* XYZ is at 50, and an XYZ July 40 call is selling for 11 while an XYZ July 50 call is selling for 5. Table 11-2 compares the important points between the ratio write and the ratio spread.

**TABLE 11-2.** *Ratio write and ratio spread compared.*

|  | Ratio Write: Buy XYZ at 50 and Sell 2 July 50's at 5 | Ratio Spread: Buy 1 July 40 at 11 and Sell 2 July 50's at 5 |
|---|---|---|
| Profit range | 40 to 60 | 41 to 59 |
| Maximum profit | 10 points | 9 points |
| Downside risk | Unlimited | 1 point |
| Upside risk | Unlimited | Unlimited |
| Initial investment | $3,000 | $1,600 |

In Chapter 6, it was pointed out that ratio writing was one of the better strategies from a probability of profit viewpoint. That is, the profit potential conforms well to the expected movement of the underlying stock. The same statement holds true for ratio spreads as substitutes for ratio writes. In fact, the ratio spread may often be a better position than the ratio write itself when the long call can be purchased with little or no time value premium in it.

### Ratio Spread for Credits

*The second philosophy of ratio spreads is to establish them only for credits.* Strategists who follow this philosophy generally want a second criterion fulfilled also—that the underlying stock be below the striking price of the written calls when the spread is established. In fact, the farther the stock is below the strike, the more attractive the spread would be. This type of ratio spread has no downside risk, because, even if the stock collapses, the spreader will still make a profit equal to the initial credit received. This application of the ratio spread strategy is actually a subcase of the application discussed above. That is, it may be possible to both buy a long call for little or no time premium, thereby simulating a ratio write, and also to be able to set up the position for a credit as well.

Since the underlying stock is generally below the maximum profit point when one establishes a ratio spread for a credit, *this is actually a mildly bullish position.* The investor would want the stock to move up slightly in order for his maximum profit potential to be realized. Of course, the position does have unlimited upside risk, so it is not an overly bullish strategy. The ratio spread strategy is sometimes referred to as a ratio bear spread. This is obviously a misnomer since the investor does not really want the underlying stock to decline in price.

These two philosophies are not mutually exclusive. The strategist who uses ratio spreads without regard to whether they are debit or credit spreads will generally have a broader array of spreads to choose from and will also be able to assume a more neutral posture on the stock. The spreader who insists on generating credits only will be forced to establish spreads where his return will be slightly smaller if the underlying stock remains relatively unchanged. However, he will not have to worry about downside defensive action since he has no risk to the downside. The third philosophy—the "delta spread"—will be described after the next section, in which the uses of ratios other than 2:1 are described.

### *Altering the Ratio*

Under either of the two philosophies discussed above, the strategist may find that a 3:1 ratio or a 3:2 ratio better suits his purposes than the 2:1 ratio. It is not common to write in a ratio of greater than 4:1 because of the large increase in upside risk at such high ratios. The higher the ratio that is used, the higher will be the credits of the spread. This means that the profits to the downside will be greater if the stock collapses. The lower the ratio that is used, the higher the upside break-even point will be, thereby reducing upside risk.

*Example:* If the same prices are used as in the initial example in this chapter, it will be possible to demonstrate these facts using three different ratios (Table 11-3):

XYZ common, 44;

XYZ April 40 call, 5; and

XYZ April 45 call, 3.

**TABLE 11-3.** *Comparison of three ratios.*

|  | *3:2 Ratio:* <br> *Buy 2 April 40's* <br> *Sell 3 April 45's* | *2:1 Ratio:* <br> *Buy 1 April 40* <br> *Sell 2 April 45's* | *3:1 Ratio:* <br> *Buy 1 April 40* <br> *Sell 3 April 45's* |
|---|---|---|---|
| Price of spread <br> (downside risk) | 1 debit | 1 credit | 4 credit |
| Upside break-even | 54 | 51 | 49½ |
| Downside break-even | 40½ | None | None |
| Maximum profit | 9 | 6 | 9 |

In Chapter 6, on ratio writing, it was seen that it was possible to alter the ratio to adjust the position to one's outlook for the underlying stock. The altering of the ratio in a ratio spread accomplishes the same objective. In fact, as will be pointed out later in the chapter, the ratio may be adjusted continuously to achieve what is considered to be a "neutral spread." A similar tactic, using the option's delta, was described for ratio writes.

The following formulae allow one to determine the maximum profit potential and upside break-even point for any ratio:

Points of maximum profit = net credit + number of long calls × difference in striking prices    *or*

= number of long calls × difference in striking prices − net debit

$$\text{Upside break-even point} = \frac{\text{points of maximum profit}}{\text{number of naked calls}} + \text{higher striking price}$$

These formulae can easily be verified by checking the numbers in Table 11-3.

### The "Delta Spread"

The third philosophy of ratio spreading is a more sophisticated approach that is often referred to as the *"delta spread,"* because the deltas of the options are used to establish and monitor the spread. Recall that the delta of a call option is the amount by which the option is expected to increase in price if the underlying stock should rise by one point. *Delta spreads are neutral spreads* in that one uses the deltas of the two calls to set up a position that is initially neutral.

*Example:* The deltas of the two calls that appeared in the previous examples were .80 and .50 for the April 40 and April 45, respectively. If one were to buy 5 of the April 40's and simultaneously sell 8 of the April 45's, he would have a delta neutral spread. That is, if XYZ moved up by one point, the 5 April 40 calls would appreciate by .80 point each, for a net gain of 4 points. Similarly, his 8 April 45 calls that he is short would each appreciate by .50 point each, for a net loss of 4 points on the short side. Thus the spread is initially neutral—the long side and the short side will offset each other. *The idea of setting up this type of neutral spread is to be able to capture the time value premium decay in the preponderance of short calls without subjecting the spread to an inordinate amount of market risk.* The actual credit or debit of the spread is not a determining factor.

It is a fairly simple matter to determine the correct ratio to use in the delta spread—merely *divide the delta of the purchased call by the delta of the written call.* In the example, this implies that the neutral ratio is .80 divided by .50, or 1.6:1. Obviously, one cannot sell 1.6 calls, so it is common practice to express that ratio as 16:10. Thus the neutral spread would consist of buying 10 April 40's and selling 16 April 45's. This is the same as an 8:5 ratio. Notice that this calculation does not include anything about debits or credits involved in the spread. In this example, an 8:5 ratio would involve a small debit of one point (5 April 40's cost 25 points and 8 April 45's bring in 24 points). Generally, reasonably selected delta spreads involve small debits.

Certain selection criteria can be offered to help the spreader eliminate some of the myriad possibilities of delta spreads on a day-to-day basis. First, one does not want the ratio of the spread to be too large. An absolute limit, such as 4:1, can be placed on all spread candidates. Also, if one eliminates any options selling for less than ½ point as candidates for the short side of the spread, the higher ratios will be eliminated. Second, one does not want the ratio to be too *small*. If the delta neutral ratio is less than 1.2:1 (6:5), the spread should probably be rejected. Finally, if one is concerned with downside risk, he might want to limit the total debit outlay. This might be done with a simple parameter, such as not paying a debit of more than 1 point per long option. Thus in a spread involving 10 long calls, the total debit must be 10 points or less. These screens are quickly applied, especially with the aid of a computer analysis. One merely uses the deltas to determine the neutral ratio. Then if it is too small or too large, or if it requires the outlay of too large of a debit, the spread is rejected from consideration. If not, it is a potential candidate for investment.

## FOLLOW-UP ACTION

Depending on the initial credit or debit of the spread, it may not be necessary to take any downside defensive action at all. *If the initial debit was large, the writer may roll down the written calls as in a ratio write.*

*Example:* An investor has established the ratio write by buying an XYZ July 40 call and selling two July 60 calls with the stock near 60. He might have done this because the July 40 was selling at parity. If the underlying stock declines, this spreader could roll down to the 50's and then to the 45's, in the same manner as he would with a ratio write. *On the other hand, if the spread was initially set up with continguous striking prices—the lower strike being just below the higher strike—no rolling-down action would be necessary.*

### Reducing the ratio

*Upside follow-up action does not normally consist of rolling up* as it does in a ratio write. Rather, *one should usually buy in some more long calls to reduce the ratio in the spread.* Eventually, he would want to reduce the spread to 1:1, or a normal bull spread. An example may help to illustrate this concept.

*Example:* In the initial example, one April 40 call was bought and two April 45's were sold, for a net credit of one point. Assume that the spreader is going to buy one more April 40 as a means of upside defensive action if he has to. When and if he buys this second long call, his total position will be a normal bull spread—long 2 April 40's and short 2 April 45's. The liquidating value of this bull spread would be 10 points if XYZ were above 45 at April expiration, since each of the two bull spreads would widen to its maximum potential—five points—with the stock above 45 in April. The ratio spreader originally brought in a one point credit for the 2:1 spread. If he were to later pay 11 points to buy the additional long April 40 call, his total outlay would have been 10 points. This would represent a break-even situation at April expiration if XYZ were above 45 at that time, since it was just shown that the spread could be liquidated for 10 points in that case. So the ratio spreader could wait to take defensive action until the April call was selling for 11 points. This is a dynamic type of follow-up action, one that is dependent on the options' price, not the stock price per se.

This outlay of 11 points for the April 40 would leave a break-even situation as long as the stock did not reverse and fall in price below 45 after the call was bought. The spreader may decide that he would rather leave some room for upside profit rather than merely trying to break even if the stock rallies too far. He might thus decide to buy in the long call at 9 or 10 points rather than waiting for it to get to 11. Of course, this might increase the chances of a whipsaw occurring, but it would leave some room for upside profits if the stock continues to rise.

Where ratios other than 2:1 are involved initially, the same thinking can be applied. In fact, the purchase of the additional long calls might take place in a two-step process.

*Example:* If the spread was initially long 5 calls and short 10 calls, the spreader would not necessarily have to wait until the April 40's were selling at 11 and then buy in all five of the ones needed to make the spread a normal bull spread. He might decide to buy 2 or 3 at a lower price, thereby reducing his ratio somewhat. Then, if the stock rallied even further, he could buy in the remaining long calls. By buying in a few at a cheaper price, the spreader gives himself the leeway to wait considerably longer to the upside. In essence, all five additional long calls in this spread would have to be bought at an average price of 11 or lower in order for the spread to break even. However, if the first two of them are bought for 8 points, the spreader would not have to buy in the remaining 3 until they were selling around 13. Thus he could wait longer to the upside before reducing the spread ratio to 1:1 (a bull spread). There is a formula that can be applied to determine the price one would have to pay for the additional long calls, to convert the ratio spread into a bull spread. If the calls are bought in, such a bull spread would break even with the stock above the higher striking price at expiration:

$$\text{Break-even cost of} \atop \text{long calls} = \frac{\text{number of short calls} \times \text{difference in strikes} - \text{total debit to date}}{\text{number of naked calls}}$$

In the simple 2:1 example, the number of short calls was 2, the difference in the strikes was 5, the total debit was minus one ($-1$) (since it was actually a 1-point credit), and the number of naked calls is 1. Thus the break-even cost of the additional long call is $[2 \times 5 - (-1)]/1 = 11$. As another verification of the formula, consider the 10:5 spread at the same prices. The initial credit of this spread would be 5 points and the break-even cost of the five additional long calls is 11 points each. Assume that the spreader bought in two additional April 40's for 8 points each (16 debit). This would make the total debit to date of the spread equal to 11 points, and reduce the number of naked calls to 3. The break-even cost of the remaining 3 long calls that would need to be purchased if the stock continued to rally would be $(10 \times 5 - 11)/3 = 13$. This agrees with the observation made earlier. This formula can be used before actual follow-up action is implemented. For example, in the 10:5 spread, if the April 40's were selling for 8, the spreader might ask: "To what would I raise the purchase price of the remaining long calls if I buy 2 April 40's for 8 right now?" By using the formula, he could easily see that the answer would be 13.

## Adjusting with the Delta

The theoretically oriented spreader can use the delta neutral ratio to monitor his spreads as well as establishing them. If the underlying stock moves up in price too far or down in price too far, the delta neutral ratio of the spread will change. The spreader can then readjust his spread to a neutral status by buying in some additional long calls on an upside movement by the stock, or by selling some additional short calls on a downward movement by the stock. Either action will serve to make the spread delta neutral again. The public customer who is employing the delta neutral adjustment method of follow-up action should be careful not to overadjust, because the commission costs would become prohibitive. A more detailed description of the use of the deltas as a means of follow-up action is contained in Chapter 28 under market-maker strategies, but the general concept is the same as that shown earlier for ratio writing. A brief example will explain the concept.

*Example:* Early in this chapter, when selection criteria were described, a neutral ratio was determined to be 16:10, with XYZ at 44. Suppose, after establishing the spread, that the common rallied to 48. One could use the current deltas to adjust. This information is summarized in Table 11-4. The current neutral ratio is approximately 14:10. Thus two of the short April 45's could be bought closing. In practice, one usually decreases his ratio by adding to the long side. Consequently, one would buy two April 40's, decreasing his overall ratio to 16:12, which is 1.33 and is close to the actual neutral ratio of 1.38. The position would therefore be delta neutral once more.

**TABLE 11-4.** *Original and current prices and deltas.*

|                | Original Situation | Current Situation |
|----------------|--------------------|--------------------|
| XYZ common     | 44                 | 47                 |
| April 40 call  | 5                  | 8                  |
| April 45 call  | 3                  | 5                  |
| April 40 delta | .80                | .90                |
| April 45 delta | .50                | .65                |
| Neutral ratio  | 16:10 (.80/.50)    | 14:10 (.90/.65 = 1.38) |

### Taking Profits

In addition to defensive action, the spreader may find that he can close the spread early to take a profit or to limit losses. If enough time has passed and the underlying stock is close to the maximum profit point—the higher striking price—the spreader may want to consider closing the spread and taking his profit. Similarly, if the underlying stock is somewhere between the two strikes as expiration draws near, the writer will normally find himself with a profit as the long call retains some intrinsic value and the short calls are nearly worthless. If at this time one feels that there is little to gain (a price decline might wipe out the long call value), he should close the spread and take his profit.

## SUMMARY

Ratio spreads can be an attractive strategy, similar in some ways to ratio writing. Both strategies offer a large probability of making a limited profit. The ratio spread has limited downside risk, or possibly no downside risk at all. In addition, if the long call(s) in the spread can be bought with little or no time value premium in them, the ratio spread becomes a superior strategy to the ratio write. One can adjust the ratio used to reflect his opinion on the underlying stock or to make a neutral profit range if desired. This ratio adjustment can be accomplished by using the deltas of the options. In a broad sense, this is one of the more attractive forms of spreading, since the strategist is buying mostly intrinsic value and is selling a relatively large amount of time value.

# *Combining* **12**
# *Calendar and*
# *Ratio Spreads*

The previous chapters on spreading have introduced the basic types of spreads. The simplest forms of bull spreads, bear spreads, or calendar spreads can often be combined to produce a position with a more attractive potential. The butterfly spread, which is a combination of a bull spread and a bear spread, is an example of such a combination. The next three chapters will be devoted to describing other combinations of spreads, wherein the strategist not only mixes basic strategies—bull, bear, and calendar—but also uses varying expiration dates as well. Although these may seem overly complicated at first glance, they are combinations that are often employed by professionals in the field.

## RATIO CALENDAR SPREAD

In this chapter, the *ratio calendar spread* will be described. It is a combination of the techniques used in the calendar and ratio spreads. Recall that one philosophy of the calendar spread strategy was to sell the near-term call and buy a longer term call, with both being out-of-the-money. This is a bullish calendar spread. If the underlying stock never advances, the spreader loses the entire amount of the relatively small debit that he paid for the spread. However, if the stock advances after the near-term call expires worthless, large profits are possible. It was stated that this bullish calendar spread philosophy had a small probability of attaining large profits, and that the few profits could easily exceed the preponderance of small losses.

The ratio calendar spread is an attempt to raise the probabilities while allowing for large potential profits. *In the ratio calendar spread, one sells a number of near-term calls while buying fewer of the intermediate-term or long-term calls.* Since more calls are being sold than are being bought, naked options are involved. It is often possible to set up a ratio calendar spread for a credit, meaning that if the underlying stock never rallies above the strike, the strategist will still make money. However, since there are naked calls involved, the collateral requirements for participating in this strategy may be large.

> *Example:* As in the bullish calendar spreads described in Chapter 9, the prices are:
>
> XYZ common, 45;
>
> XYZ April 50 call, 1; and
>
> XYZ July 50 call, 1½.
>
> In the bullish calendar spread strategy, one July 50 is bought for each April 50 sold. This means that the spread is established for a debit of ½ point and that the investment is $50 per spread, plus commissions. The strategist using the ratio calendar spread has essentially the same philosophy as the bullish calendar spreader—the stock will remain below 50 until April expiration and may then rally. The ratio calendar spread might be set up as follows:

| | |
|---|---|
| Buy 1 XYZ July 50 call at 1½ | 1½ debit |
| Sell 2 XYZ April 50 calls at 1 each | 2  credit |
| Net | ½ credit |

Although there is no cash involved in setting up the ratio spread since it is done for a credit, there is a collateral requirement for the naked April 50 call.

If the stock remains below 50 until April expiration, the long call—the July 50—will be owned free. After that, no matter what happens to the underlying stock, the spread cannot lose money. In fact, if the underlying stock advances dramatically after near-term expiration, large profits will accrue as the July 50 call increases in value. Of course, this is entirely dependent on the near-term call expiring worthless. If the underlying stock should rally above 50 *before* the April calls expire, the ratio calendar spread is in danger of losing a large amount of money because of the naked calls, and defensive action must be taken. Follow-up actions will be described later.

The collateral required for the ratio calendar spread is equal to the amount of collateral required for the naked calls less the credit taken in for the spread. Since naked calls will be marked to market as the stock moves up, *it is always best to allow enough collateral to get to a defensive action point*. In the example above, suppose that one felt he would definitely be taking defensive action if the stock rallied to 53 before April expiration. He should then figure his collateral requirement as if the stock were at 53, regardless of what the collateral requirement is at the current time. *This is a prudent tactic wherever naked options are involved, since the strategist will never be forced into an unwanted close-out before his defensive action point is reached.* The collateral required for this example would then be:

| | |
|---|---:|
| 30% of 53 | $1,590 |
| In-the-money amount | + 300 |
| Less initial credit | − 50 |
| Total collateral to set aside | $1,840 |

The strategist is not really "investing" anything in this strategy, because his requirement is in the form of collateral, not cash. That is, his current portfolio assets need not be disturbed to set up this spread, although losses would, of course, create debits in the account. Many naked option strategies are similar in this respect, and the strategist may earn additional money from the collateral value of his portfolio without disturbing the portfolio itself. However, he should take care to operate such strategies in a conservative manner since *any* income earned is "free," but losses may force him to disturb his portfolio. In light of this fact, it is always difficult to compute returns on investment in a strategy that requires only collateral to operate. One can, of course, compute the return on the collateral used, but that is not a completely correct computation because the collateral itself is making a return also. The large investor participating in such a strategy should be satisfied with any sort of positive return.

Returning to the example above, the strategist would make his $50 credit, less commissions, if the underlying stock remained below 50 until July expiration. It is not possible to determine the results to the upside so definitively. If the April 50 calls expire worthless and then the stock rallies, the potential profits are limited only by time. The case where the stock rallies before April expiration is of the most concern. If the stock rallies *immediately,* the spread will undoubtedly show a loss. If the stock rallies to 50 more slowly, but still before April expiration, it is possible that the spread will not have changed much.

Again using the same example, suppose that XYZ rallies to 50 with only a few weeks of life remaining in the April 50 calls. Then the April 50 calls might be selling at 1½ while the July 50 call might be selling at 3. The ratio spread could be closed for even money at that point—the cost of buying back the 2 April 50's would equal the credit received from selling the one July 50. He would thus make ½ point, less commissions, on the entire spread transaction. Finally, at the expiration date of the April 50 calls, one can estimate where he would break even. Suppose one estimated that the July 50 call would be selling for 5½ points if XYZ were at 53 at April expiration. Since the April 50 calls would be selling for 3 at that time (they would be at parity), there would be a debit of ½ point to close the ratio spread. The two April 50 calls would be bought for 6 points and the July 50 call sold for 5½—a ½ debit. The entire spread transaction would thus have broken even, less commissions, at 53 at April expiration since the spread was put on for a ½ credit and was taken off for a ½ debit. *The risk to the upside depends clearly, then, on how quickly the stock rallies above 50 before April expiration.*

## CHOOSING THE SPREAD

Some of the same criteria used in setting up a bullish calendar spread apply here as well. Select a stock that is volatile enough to move above the striking price in the allotted time—after the near-term expires, but before the long call expires. Do not use calls that are so far out-of-the-money that it would be virtually impossible for the stock to reach the striking price. Always set up the spread for a credit, commissions included. This will assure that a profit will be made even if the stock goes nowhere. However, if the credit has to be generated by using an extremely large ratio—greater than 3 short calls to every long one—one should be extremely selective in attempting to set up the spread, since the potential losses in an immediate rally would be large.

The *upside break-even point* prior to April expiration should be determined using a pricing model. Such a model, or the output from one, can generally be obtained from a data service or from some brokerage firms. It is useful to the strategist to know exactly how much room he has to the upside if the stock begins to rally. This will allow him to take defensive action in the form of closing out the spread before his break-even point is reached. Since a pricing model can estimate a call price for any length of time, the strategist can compute his break-even points at April expiration, one month before April expiration, 6 weeks before, and so on. When the long option in a spread expires at a different time than the short option, the break-even point is dynamic. That is, it changes with time. Table 12-1 shows how this information might be accumulated for the example spread used above. Since this example spread was established for a ½-point credit with the stock at 45, the break-even points would be at stock prices where the spread could be removed for a ½-point debit. Suppose the spread was initiated with 95 days remaining until April expiration. In each line of the table, the cost for buying 2 April 50's is ½ point more than the price of the July 50. That is, there would be a ½-point debit involved in closing the spread at those prices. Notice that *the break-even price increases as time passes.* Initially, the spread would show a loss if the stock moved up at all. This is to be expected, since an immediate move would not allow for any erosion in the time value premium of the near-term calls. As more and more time passes, time weighs more heavily on the near-term April calls than on the longer-term July call. Once the strategist has this information, he might then look at a chart of the underlying stock. If there is resistance for XYZ below 53, his eventual break-even point at April expiration, he could then feel more confident about this spread.

**TABLE 12-1.** *Break-even points changing over time.*

| *Days Remaining Until April Expiration* | *Break-even Point (Stock Price)* | *Estimated April 50 Price* | *Estimated July 50 Price* |
|---|---|---|---|
| 90 | 45 | 1 | 1½ |
| 60 | 48 | 1½ | 2½ |
| 30 | 51 | 2½ | 4½ |
| 0 | 53 | 3 | 5½ |

## FOLLOW-UP ACTION

The main purpose of defensive action in this strategy is to limit losses if the stock should rally before April expiration. The strategist should be quick to close out the spread before any serious losses accrue. The long call quite adequately compensates for the losses on the short calls up to a certain point, a fact demonstrated in Table 12-1. However, the stock cannot be allowed to run. A rule of thumb that is often useful is to close the spread if the stock breaks out above technical resistance or if it breaks above the eventual break-even point at expiration. In the example above, the strategist would close the spread if, at any time, XYZ rose above 53 (before April expiration, of course).

If a significant amount of time has passed, the strategist might act even more quickly in closing the spread. As was shown earlier, if the stock rallies to 50 with only a few weeks of time remaining, the spread may actually be at a slight profit at that time. It is often the best course of action to take the small profit, if the stock rises above the striking price.

### The Probabilities Are Good

This is a strategy with a rather large probability of profit, provided that the defensive action described above is adhered to. The spread will make money if the stock never rallies above the striking price, since the spread is established for a credit. This in itself is a rather high-probability event, because the stock is initially below the striking price. In addition, the spread can make large potential profits if the stock rallies after the near-term calls expire. Although this is a much less probable event, the profits that can accrue add to the expected return of the spread. The only time that the spread loses is when the stock rallies quickly, and the strategist should close out the spread in that case to limit losses.

Although Table 12-2 is not mathematically definitive, it can be seen that this strategy has a positive expected return. Small profits occur more frequently than small losses do, and sometimes large profits can occur. These expected outcomes, when coupled with the fact that the strategist may utilize collateral such as stocks, bonds, or government securities to set up these spreads, demonstrate that this is a viable strategy for the advanced investor.

**TABLE 12-2.** *Profitability of ratio calendar spreading.*

| Event | Outcome | Probability |
|---|---|---|
| Stock never rallies above strike | Small profit | Large probability |
| Stock rallies above strike in a short time | Small loss if defensive action employed | Small probability |
| Stock rallies above strike after near-term call expires | Large potential profit | Small probability |

# Reverse Spreads 13

In general, when a strategy has the term "reverse" in its name, the strategy is the opposite of a more commonly used strategy. The reader should be familiar with this nomenclature from the earlier discussions comparing ratio writing (buying stock and selling calls) with reverse hedging (shorting stock and buying calls). If the reverse strategy is sufficiently well-known, it usually acquires a name of its own. For example, the bear spread is really the reverse of the bull spread, but the bear spread is a popular enough strategy in its own right to have acquired a shorter, unique name.

## REVERSE CALENDAR SPREAD

One type of reverse spread that is infrequently used is the *reverse calendar spread*. This strategy is not particularly attractive, but it is being included in this discussion to point out why it should *not* generally be used. In a reverse calendar spread, one would buy the near-term call and sell a longer-term call at the same strike. Note that this is exactly the opposite of the calendar spread. The reverse calendar spread would be established for a credit and the strategist would like the spread to shrink in value. Again, this is opposite of the calendar spread, where the spread is initially put on for a debit and the strategist wants the spread to widen. For a calendar spread to shrink in value, the stock must move far away from the striking price before the near-term call expires. The spread cannot shrink to less than zero, however, so the reverse calendar spread has a limited profit potential equal to the net credit taken in initially. To demonstrate the profit potential of the reverse calendar spread, it is useful to look at the extreme cases. Suppose the stock falls dramatically in price. Then both options would be nearly worthless and the spread between the two would approach zero. On the other hand, if the stock rises dramatically in price, both options would trade at parity and again the spread would approach zero.

The risk would always be greater than the profit potential. The reverse calendar spread would have its greatest loss at near-term expiration if the underlying stock were exactly at the striking price. The near-term call, which is held long, would expire worthless, and the longer-term call, which is short, would have to be bought back. It has been demonstrated earlier that a calendar spread widens to its fullest extent if the stock is exactly at the striking price when the near-term call expires. Thus the reverse calendar spread would perform worst in that case. This would represent a limited loss, but it could possibly be two or three times the original credit.

*The long-term call in the reverse calendar spread is a naked call.* Recall that the margin definition of a spread requires that the long option have an expiration equal to or longer than the short option. This is not true in a reverse calendar spread, so the collateral requirement would be equal to the collateral required for the naked longer-term call, less the initial credit received, plus commission costs. Note that if the underlying stock advances substantially—representing a desirable event in the reverse calendar spread since the spread will be approaching zero differential—the collateral requirement will grow quite large as the naked call is marked to market. So even if the spread is shrinking, the increase in investment may become prohibitive.

*No serious strategist employs this strategy by itself as a profit-making vehicle.* For some reason, the strategy often appeals to the novice as "something to try," and is being included here to demonstrate that it is *not* something to try.

## REVERSE RATIO SPREAD (BACKSPREAD)

A more sensible reverse strategy, although also infrequently used, is the *reverse ratio spread. In this type of spread one would sell a call at one striking price and then would buy several calls at a higher striking price.* This is exactly the opposite of the ratio spread described in Chapter 11. This position is also known as a *backspread*. *As in most reverse spreading strategies, the spreader wants the stock to move dramatically.* He does not generally care whether it moves up or down. Recall that in the reverse hedge strategy described in Chapter 4, the strategist had the potential for large profits if the stock moved either up or down by a great deal. In the reverse ratio spread, large potential profits exist if the stock moves up dramatically, but there is a limited profit potential to the downside.

*Example:* XYZ is selling for 43 and the July 40 call is at 4, with the July 45 call at 1. A reverse ratio spread would be established as follows:

| | |
|---|---|
| Buy 2 July 45 calls at 1 each | 2 debit |
| Sell 1 July 40 call at 4 | 4 credit |
| Net | 2 credit |

These spreads are generally established for credits. In fact, *if the spread cannot be initiated at a credit, it is usually not attractive.* If the underlying stock drops in price and is below 40 at July expiration, all the calls will expire worthless and the strategist will make a profit equal to his initial credit. The maximum *downside* potential of the reverse ratio spread is equal to the initial credit received. On the other hand, if the stock rallies substantially, the potential *upside* profits are unlimited, since the spreader owns more calls than he is short. *Simplistically, the investor is bullish and is buying out-of-the-money calls but is simultaneously hedging himself by selling another call.* He can profit if the stock rises in price, as he thought it would, but he also profits if the stock collapses and all the calls expire worthless.

This strategy has limited risk. *With most spreads, the maximum loss is attained at expiration at the striking price of the purchased call.* This is a true statement for reverse ratio spreads.

*Example:* If XYZ is at exactly 45 at July expiration, the July 45 calls will expire worthless for a loss of $200 and the July 40 call will have to be bought back for 5 points, a $100 loss on that call. The total loss would thus be $300, and this is the most that can be lost in this example. If the underlying stock should rally dramatically, this strategy has unlimited profit potential, since there are two long calls for each short one. In fact, one can always compute the upside break-even point at expiration. That break-even point happens to be 48 in this example. At 48 at July expiration, each July 45 call would be worth 3 points, for a net gain of $400 on the two of them. The July 40 call would be worth 8 with the stock at 48 at expiration, representing a $400 loss on that call. Thus the gain and the loss are offsetting and the spread breaks even, except for commissions, at 48 at expiration. If the stock is higher than 48 at July expiration, profits will result.

Table 13-1 and Figure 13-1 depict the potential profits and losses from this example of a reverse ratio spread. Note that the profit graph is exactly like the profit graph of a ratio spread that has been rotated around the stock price axis. Refer to Figure 11-1 for a graph of the ratio spread. There is actually a range outside of which profits can be made—below 42 or above 48 in this example. The maximum loss occurs at the striking price of the purchased calls—45—at expiration.

There are no naked calls in this strategy, so *the investment is relatively small.* The strategy is actually a long call added to a bear

**TABLE 13-1.** *Profits and losses for reverse ratio spread.*

| XYZ Price at July Expiration | Profit on 1 July 40 | Profit on 2 July 45's | Total Profit |
|---|---|---|---|
| 35 | +$  400 | −$  200 | +$  200 |
| 40 | +    400 | −    200 | +    200 |
| 42 | +    200 | −    200 | 0 |
| 45 | −    100 | −    200 | −    300 |
| 48 | −    400 | +    400 | 0 |
| 55 | −  1,100 | +  1,800 | +    700 |
| 70 | −  2,600 | +  4,800 | +  2,200 |

**FIGURE 13-1.** *Reverse ratio spread (backspread).*

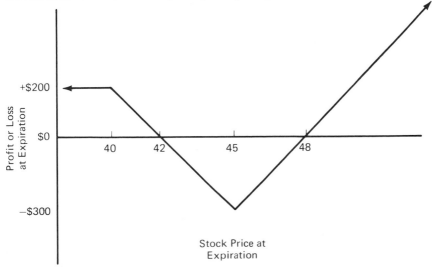

spread. In this example, the bear spread portion is long the July 45 and short the July 40. This requires a $500 collateral requirement, because there are 5 points difference in the striking prices. The credit of $200 received for the spread can be applied against the initial requirement, so that the total requirement would be $300 plus commissions. There is no increase or decrease in this requirement since there are no naked calls.

Notice that *the concept of a delta neutral spread can be utilized in this strategy,* in much the same way that it was used for the ratio call spread. The number of calls to buy and sell can be computed mathematically by using the deltas of the options involved.

*Example:* The neutral ratio is determined by dividing the delta of the July 45 into the delta of the July 40.

| Prices | | Delta |
| --- | --- | --- |
| XYZ common: | 43 | |
| XYZ July 40 call: | 4 | .60 |
| XYZ July 45 call: | 1 | .25 |

In this case, that would be a ratio of 2.4:1 (.60/.25). That is, if one sold five July 40's, he would buy 12 July 45's (or if he sold 10, he would then buy 24). By beginning with a neutral ratio, the spreader should be able to make money on a quick move by the stock in either direction.

The neutral ratio can also help the spreader to avoid being too bearish or too bullish to begin with. For example, a spreader would not be bullish enough if he merely used a 2:1 ratio for convenience, instead of using the 2.4:1 ratio. If anything, one might normally establish the spread with an extra bullish emphasis since the largest profits are to the upside. There is little reason for the spreader to have too little bullishness in this strategy. Thus, if the deltas are correct, the neutral ratio can aid the spreader in the determination of a more accurate initial ratio.

*The strategist must be alert to the possibility of early exercise* in this type of spread since he has sold a call that is in-the-money. Aside from watching for this possibility, there is little in the way of defensive follow-up action that needs to be implemented since the risk is limited by the nature of the position. He might take profits by closing the spread if the stock rallies before expiration.

This strategy presents a reasonable method of attempting to

capitalize on a large stock movement with little tie-up of collateral. *Generally, the strategist would seek out volatile stocks* for implementation of this strategy, because he would want as much potential movement as possible by the time the calls expire. In Chapter 14, it will be shown that this strategy can become more attractive by buying calls with a longer maturity than the calls sold.

# Diagonalizing *14*
# a Spread

*When one uses both different striking prices* and *different expiration dates in a spread, it is a diagonal spread.* Generally, the long side of the spread would expire later than the short side of the spread. Note that this is within the definition of a spread for margin purposes: the long side must have a maturity equal to or longer than the maturity of the short side. With the exception of calendar spreads, all the previous chapters on spreads have described ones in which the expiration dates of the short call and the long call were the same. However, any of these spreads can be diagonalized—one merely has to purchase a call with a longer expiration as opposed to one with the same expiration as the written side of the spread.

In general, *diagonalizing a spread makes it slightly more bearish at near-term expiration.* This can be seen by observing what would happen if the stock fell or rose substantially. If the stock falls, the long side of the spread will retain some value because of its longer maturity. Thus a diagonal spread will generally do better to the downside than will a regular spread. If the stock rises substantially, all calls will come to parity. Thus there is no advantage in the long-term call—it will be selling for approximately the same price as the purchased call in a normal spread. However, since the strategist had to originally pay more for the longer-term call, his upside profits would not be as great.

A diagonalized position has an advantage in that one can re-establish the position if the written calls expire worthless in the spread. Thus the increased cost of buying a longer-term call initially may prove to be a savings if one can write against it twice. These tactics will be described for various spread strategies.

## THE DIAGONAL BULL SPREAD

A normal bull spread consists of buying a call at a lower striking price and selling a call at a higher striking price, both with the same expiration date. *The diagonal bull spread would be similar except that one would buy a longer-term call at the lower strike and would sell a near-term call at the higher strike.* The number of calls long and short would still be the same. By diagonalizing the spread, the position is hedged somewhat on the downside in case the stock does not advance by near-term expiration. Moreover, once the near-term option expires, the spread can often be reestablished by selling the call with the next maturity.

*Example:* The following prices exist:

| | Strike | April | July | October | Stock Price |
|---|---|---|---|---|---|
| XYZ | 30 | 3 | 4 | 5 | 32 |
| XYZ | 35 | 1 | 1½ | 2 | 32 |

A regular bull spread could be established in any of the expiration series by buying the call at 30 and selling the call at 35. A diagonal bull spread would consist of buying the July 30 or October 30 and selling the April 35. To compare a normal bull spread with diagonal spread, the following two spreads will be used:

Normal bull spread: buy the April 30 call, sell the April 35—2 debit

Diagonal bull spread: buy the July 30 call, sell the April 35—3 debit

The normal bull spread has a 3-point potential profit if XYZ is above 35 at April expiration. The maximum risk in the normal bull spread is 2 points (the original debit) if XYZ is anywhere below 30 at April expiration. By diagonalizing the spread, the strategist lowers his potential profit slightly at April expiration, but also lowers the probability of losing 2 points in the position. Table 14-1 compares the two types of

**TABLE 14-1.** *Comparison of spreads at expiration.*

| XYZ Price at April Expiration | April 30 Price | April 35 Price | July 30 Price | Normal Bull Spread Profit | Diagonal Spread Profit |
|---|---|---|---|---|---|
| 20 | 0 | 0 | 0 | −$200 | −$300 |
| 24 | 0 | 0 | ½ | − 200 | − 250 |
| 27 | 0 | 0 | 1 | − 200 | − 200 |
| 30 | 0 | 0 | 2 | − 200 | − 100 |
| 32 | 2 | 0 | 3 | 0 | 0 |
| 35 | 5 | 0 | 5½ | + 300 | + 250 |
| 40 | 10 | 5 | 10 | + 300 | + 200 |
| 45 | 15 | 10 | 15 | + 300 | + 200 |

spreads at April expiration. The price of the July 30 call is estimated in order to derive the estimated profits or losses from the diagonal bull spread at that time. If the underlying stock drops too far—to 20, for example—both spreads will experience nearly a total loss at April expiration. However, the diagonal spread will not lose its entire value if XYZ is much above 24 at expiration, according to Table 14-1. The diagonal spread actually has a smaller dollar loss than the normal spread between 27 and 32 at expiration, despite the fact that the diagonal spread was more expensive to establish. On a percentage basis, the diagonal spread has an even larger advantage in this range. If the stock rallies above 35 by expiration, the normal spread will provide a larger profit. There is an interesting characteristic of the diagonal spread that is shown in Table 14-1. If the stock advances substantially and all the calls come to parity, the profit on the diagonal spread is limited to 2 points. However, if the stock is near 35 at April expiration, the long call will have some time premium in it and the spread will actually widen to more than 5 points. Thus *the maximum area of profit at April expiration for the diagonal spread is to have the stock near the higher strike.* The figures demonstrate that the diagonal spread gives up a small portion of potential upside profits to provide a hedge to the downside.

Once the April 35 call expires, the diagonal spread can be closed. However, if the stock is below 35 at that time, it may be more prudent to then sell the July 35 call against the July 30 call that is held long. This would establish a normal bull spread for the 3 months remaining until July expiration. Note that if XYZ were still at 32 at April expiration, the July 35 call might be sold for 1 point. This should be true since the April 35 call was worth 1 point with the stock at 32 three months before expiration. Consequently, the strategist who had pursued this course of action would end up with a normal July bull spread for a net debit of 2 points—he originally paid 4 for the July 30 call, but then sold the April 35 for 1 point and subsequently sold the July 35 for 1 point. By looking at the table of prices for the first example in this chapter, the reader can see that it would have cost 2½ points to set up the normal July bull spread originally. Thus, by diagonalizing and having the near-term call expire worthless, the strategist is able to acquire the normal July bull spread at a cheaper cost than he could have originally. This is a specific example of how *the diagonalizing effect can prove beneficial if the writer is able to write against the same long call two times*—or three times if he originally purchased the longest-term call. In this example, if XYZ were anywhere between 30 and 35 at April expiration, the spread would be converted to a normal July bull spread. If the stock were above 35, the spread should be closed to take the profit. Below 30, the July 30 call would probably be closed or left outright long.

In summary, the diagonal bull spread may often be an improvement over the normal bull spread. The diagonal spread is an improvement when the stock remains relatively unchanged or falls, up until the near-term written call expires. At that time, the spread can be converted to a normal bull spread if the stock is at a favorable price. Of course, if at any time the underlying stock rises above the higher striking price at an expiration date, the diagonal spread will be profitable.

## OWNING A CALL FOR "FREE"

Diagonalization can be used in other spread strategies to accomplish much the same purposes already described, but, in addition, it may also be possible for the spreader to wind up owning a long call at a substantially reduced cost, possibly even for free.

The easiest way to see this would be to consider a *diagonal bear spread.*

*Example:* XYZ is at 32 and the near-term April 30 call is selling for 3 points while the longer-term July 35 call is selling for 1½ points. A diagonal bear spread could be established by selling the April 30 and buying the July 35. This is still a bear spread, because a call with a lower striking price is being sold while a call at a higher strike is being purchased. However, since the purchased call has a longer maturity date than the written call, the spread is diagonalized.

This diagonal bear spread will make money if XYZ falls in price before the near-term, April call expires. For example, if XYZ is at 29 at expiration, the written call will expire worthless and the July 35 will still have some value, perhaps ½. Thus the profit would be 3 points on the April 30, less a 1-point loss on the July 35, for an overall profit of 2 points. The risk in the position lies to the upside, just as in a regular bear spread. If XYZ should advance by a great deal, both options would be at parity and the spread would have widened to 5 points. Since the initial credit was 1½ points, the loss would be 5 minus 1½, or 3½ points in that case. As in all diagonal spreads, the spread will do slightly better to the downside because the long call will hold some value, but it will do slightly worse to the upside if the underlying stock advances substantially.

The reason that a strategist might attempt a diagonal bear spread would *not* be for the slight downside advantage that the diagonalizing effect produces. Rather it would be because he has a chance of *owning the July 35 call*—the longer-term call—*for a substantially reduced cost.* In the example, the cost of the July 35 call was 1½ points and the premium received from the sale of the April 30 call was 3 points. If the spreader can make 1½ points from the sale of the April 30 call, he will have completely covered the cost of his July option. He can then sit back and hope for a rally by the underlying stock. If such a rally occurred, he could make unlimited profits on the long side. If it did not, he loses nothing.

> *Example:* If XYZ is at or below 31½ at April expiration, the April 30 call can be purchased for 1½ points or less. Since the call was originally sold for 3, this would represent a profit of at least 1½ points on the April 30 call. This profit on the near-term option covers the entire cost of the July 35. Consequently, the strategist owns the July 35 for free. If XYZ never rallies above 35, he would make nothing from the overall trade. However, if XYZ were to rally above 35 after April expiration—but before July expiration, of course—he could make potentially large profits. Thus *when one establishes a diagonal spread for a credit, there is always the potential that he could own a call for free.* That is, the profits from the sale of the near-term call could equal or exceed the original cost of the long call. This is, of course, a desirable position to be in, for if the underlying stock should rally substantially after profits are realized on the short side, large profits could accrue.

## DIAGONAL BACKSPREADS

In an analogous strategy, one might buy more than one longer-term call against the short-term call that is sold. Using the foregoing prices, one might sell the April 30 for 3 points and buy 2 July 35's at 1½ points each. This would be an *even money spread.* The credits equal the debits when the position is established. If the April 30 call expires worthless, which would happen if the stock was below 30 in April, the spreader would own 2 July 35 calls for free. Even if the April 30 does not expire totally worthless, but if some profit can be made on the sale of it, the July 35's will be owned at a reduced cost. In Chapter 13, where reverse spreads were discussed, the strategy where one sells a call with a lower strike and then buys more calls at a higher strike was termed a reverse ratio spread, or backspread. The strategy just described is merely the *diagonalizing of a backspread. This is a strategy that is favored by some professionals,* because the short call reduces the risk of owning the longer-term calls if the underlying stock declines. Moreover, if the underlying stock advances, the preponderance of long calls with a longer maturity will certainly outdistance the losses on the written call. The worst situation that could result would be for the underlying stock to rise very slightly by near-term expiration. If this happened, it might be possible to lose money on both sides of the spread. This would have to be considered a rather low probability event, though, and would still represent a limited loss, so it does not substantially offset the positive aspects of the strategy.

Any type of spread may be diagonalized. There are some who prefer to diagonalize even butterfly spreads, figuring that the extra time to maturity in the purchased calls will be of benefit. Overall, the benefits of diagonalizing can be generalized by recalling the way in which the decay of the time value premium of a call takes place. Recall that it was determined that a call loses most of its time value premium in the last stages of its life. When it is a very long-term option, the rate of decay is small. Knowing this fact, it makes sense that one would want to sell options with a short life remaining, so that the maximum benefit of the decay could be obtained. Correspondingly, the purchase of a longer-term call would mean that the buyer is not subjecting himself to a substantial loss in time value premium, at least over the first three months of ownership. A diagonal spread encompasses both of these features—selling a shorter-term call to try to obtain the maximum rate of time decay, while buying a longer-term call to try to lessen the effect of time decay on the long side.

## CALL OPTION SUMMARY

This concludes the description of strategies that utilize only call options. The call option has been seen to be a vehicle which the astute strategist can use to set up a wide variety of positions. He can be bullish or bearish, aggressive or conservative. In addition, he can attempt to be neutral, trying to capitalize on the probability that a stock will not move very far in a short time period.

The investor who is not familiar with options should generally begin with a simple strategy, such as covered call writing or outright call purchases. The simplest types of spreads are the bull spread, the bear spread, and the calendar spread. The more sophisticated investor might consider using ratios in his call strategies—ratio writing against stock or ratio spreading using only calls.

Once the strategist feels that he understands the risk and reward relationships between longer-term and short-term calls, between in-the-money and out-of-the-money calls, and between long calls and short calls, he could then consider utilizing the most advanced types of strategies. This might include reverse ratio spreads, diagonal spreads, and more advanced types of ratios, such as the ratio calendar spread.

A great deal of information, some of it rather technical in detail, has been presented in preceding chapters. The best pattern for an investor to follow would be to attempt only strategies that he fully comprehends. This does not mean that he merely understands the profitability aspects (especially the risk) of the strategy. One must also be able to readily understand the potential effects of early assignments, large dividend payments, striking price adjustments, and the like, if he is going to operate advanced strategies. Without a full understanding of how these things might affect one's position, one cannot operate an advanced strategy correctly.

# Put Option *III*
# Strategies

## *PUT OPTION STRATEGIES*

A *put option* gives the holder the right to *sell* the underlying security at the striking price at any time until the expiration date of the option. Listed put options are even newer than listed call options, having been introduced on June 3, 1977. The introduction of listed puts has provided a much wider range of strategies for both the conservative and aggressive investor. The call option is least effective in strategies where downward price movement by the underlying stock is concerned. The put option is a useful tool in that case.

Not all stocks with listed call options have listed put options as well. In the situations where only listed calls exist, the strategist is limited to the strategies described in earlier chapters. However, where listed puts exist, the use of puts or the combination of puts and calls can provide more versatility to the strategist.

Where listed put options exist, it is no longer necessary to implement strategies involving long calls and short stock. Listed put options can be used more efficiently in such situations. There are many similarities between call strategies and put strategies. For example, put spread strategies and call spread strategies employ similar tactics, although there are technical differences of course. In certain strategies, the tactics for puts may appear largely to be a repetition of those used for calls, but they will be nevertheless spelled out in detail. The strategies that involve the use of both puts and calls together—straddles and combinations—have techniques of their own, but even in this case the reader will recognize certain similarities to strategies previously discussed. Thus the introduction of put options not only widens the realm of potential strategies, but also makes more efficient some of the strategies previously described.

# Put Option Basics 15

Much of the same terminology that is applied to call options also pertains to put options. *Underlying security, striking price, and expiration date are all terms that have the same meaning for puts as they do for calls.* The expiration dates of listed put options agree with the expiration dates of the calls on the same underlying stock. In addition, puts and calls have the same striking prices. This means that if there are options at a certain strike, say on a particular underlying stock that has both listed puts and calls, *both* calls at 50 and puts at 50 will be trading, regardless of the price of the underlying stock. Note that it is no longer sufficient to describe an option as an "XYZ July 50." It must also be stated whether the option is a put or a call, for an XYZ July 50 call and an XYZ July 50 put are two different securities.

In many respects, the put option and its associated strategies will be very nearly the opposite of corresponding call-oriented strategies. However, *it is not correct to say that the put is exactly the opposite of a call.* In this introductory section on puts, the characteristics of puts will be described in an attempt to show where they are similar to calls and where they are not.

## PUT STRATEGIES

In the simplest terms, *the outright buyer of a put is hoping for a stock price decline* in order for his put to become more valuable. If the stock were to decline well *below* the striking price of the put option, the put holder could make a profit. The holder of the put could buy stock in the open market and then exercise his put to sell that stock for a profit at the striking price, which is higher.

> *Example:* If XYZ stock is at 40, an XYZ July 50 put would be worth at least 10 points, for the put grants the holder the right to sell XYZ at 50—10 points above its current price. On the other hand, if the stock price were *above* the striking price of the put option at expiration, the put would be worthless. No one would logically want to exercise a put option to sell stock at the striking price when he could merely go to the open market and sell the stock for a higher price. Thus, *as the price of the underlying stock declines, the put becomes more valuable.* This is, of course, the opposite of a call option's price action.

The meaning of in-the-money and out-of-the-money are altered when one is speaking of put options. *A put is considered to be in-the-money when the underlying stock is below the striking price of the put option; it is out-of-the-money when the stock is above the striking price.* This, again, is the opposite of the call option. If XYZ is at 45, the XYZ July 50 put is in-the-money and the XYZ July 50 call is out-of-the-money. However, if XYZ were at 55, the July 50 put would be out-of-the-money while the July 50 call would then be in-the-money. The broad definition of an in-the-money option as "an option that has intrinsic value" would cover the situation for both puts and calls. Note that a put option has intrinsic value when the underlying stock is below the striking price of the put. That is, the put has some "real" value when the stock is below the striking price.

The intrinsic value of an in-the-money put is merely the difference between the striking price and the stock price. Since the put is an option (to sell), it will generally sell for more than its intrinsic value when there is time remaining until the expiration date. This excess value over its intrinsic value is referred to as the *time value premium,* just as is the case with calls.

> *Example:* XYZ is at 47 and the XYZ July 50 put is selling for 5, the intrinsic value is 3 points (50 − 47), so the time value premium must be 2 points. The time value premium of an in-the-money put option can always be quickly computed by the following formula:

*Time value premium* (in-the-money put) = put option price + stock price − striking price

This is not the same formula that was applied to in-the-money call options, although it is always true that the time value premium of an option is the excess value over intrinsic value.

*Time value premium (in-the-money call)* = call option price + striking price − stock price

If the put is out-of-the-money, the entire premium of the put is composed of time value premium, for the intrinsic value of an out-of-the-money option is always zero. *The time value premium of a put is largest when the stock is at the striking price of the put.* As the option becomes deeply in-the-money or deeply out-of-the-money, the time value premium will shrink substantially. These statements on the magnitude of the time value premium are true for both puts and calls. Table 15-1 will help to illustrate the relationship of stock price and option price for both puts and calls. The reader may want to refer to Table 1-1, which described the time value premium relationship for calls. Table 15-1 describes the prices of an XYZ July 50 call option and an XYZ July 50 put option.

**TABLE 15-1.** *Call and put options compared.*

| XYZ Stock Price | XYZ July 50 Call Price | Call Intrinsic Value | Call Time Value Premium | XYZ July 50 Put Price | Put Intrinsic Value | Put Time Value Premium |
|---|---|---|---|---|---|---|
| 40 | ½ | 0 | ½ | 9½ | 10 | −½a |
| 43 | 1 | 0 | 1 | 7 | 7 | 0 |
| 45 | 2 | 0 | 2 | 6 | 5 | 1 |
| 47 | 3 | 0 | 3 | 5 | 3 | 2 |
| 50 | 5 | 0 | 5 | 4 | 0 | 4 |
| 53 | 7 | 3 | 4 | 3 | 0 | 3 |
| 55 | 8 | 5 | 3 | 2 | 0 | 2 |
| 57 | 9 | 7 | 2 | 1 | 0 | 1 |
| 60 | 10½ | 10 | ½ | ½ | 0 | ½ |
| 70 | 19½ | 20 | −½a | ¼ | 0 | ¼ |

aA deeply in-the-money option may actually trade at a discount from intrinsic value in advance of expiration.

Table 15-1 demonstrates several basic facts. As the stock drops, the actual price of a call option decreases while the value of the put option increases. Conversely, as the stock rises, the call option increases in value and the put option decreases in value. Both the put and the call have their maximum time value premium when the stock is exactly at the striking price. However, *the call will generally sell for more than the put when the stock is at the strike.* Notice in Table 15-1 that, with XYZ at 50, the call is worth 5 points while the put is worth only 4 points. This is true, in general, except in the case of a stock that pays a large dividend. More will be said about this effect later. Table 15-1 also describes an effect of put options that normally holds true— *an in-the-money put (stock is below strike) loses time value premium more quickly than an in-the-money call does.* Notice that with XYZ at 43 in Table 15-1, the put is 7 points in the money and has lost all its time value premium. But when the call is 7 points in the money—XYZ at 57—the call still has 2 points of time value premium. Again, this is a phenomenon that could be affected by the dividend payout of the underlying stock, but is true in general.

## *FACTORS INFLUENCING THE PRICE OF THE PUT OPTION*

The same factors that determined the price of the call option also determine the price of the put option: price of the underlying stock; striking price of the option; time remaining until expiration; volatility of the underlying stock; dividend rate of the underlying stock; and the current risk-free interest rate (Treasury bill rate, for example). Also, market dynamics—supply, demand, and investor psychology—play a part as well.

Without going into as much detail as was shown in Chapter 1, the pricing curve of the put option can be developed. Certain facts remain true for the put option as they did for the call option. The rate of decay of the put option is not linear—that is, the time value premium will decay more rapidly in the weeks immediately preceding expiration. The more volatile the underlying stock, the higher will be the price of its options—both puts and calls. Also, the put option is usually worth at least its intrinsic value at any time, and should be worth exactly its intrinsic value on the day that it expires. Figure 15-1 shows where one might expect the XYZ July 50 put to sell—for any stock price—if there are 6 months remaining until expiration. Compare this with the similar pricing curve for the call option (Figure 1-2). Note that the *intrinsic value line* for the put option faces in the opposite direction from the intrinsic value line for call options—that is, it gains value as the stock falls below the striking price. This put option pricing curve also demonstrates the effect mentioned earlier that a put option loses time value premium more quickly when it is in-the-money and also shows that an out-of-the-money put holds a great deal of time value premium.

**FIGURE 15-1.** *Put option price curve.*

**FIGURE 15-2.** *Call option price curve.*

## THE EFFECT OF DIVIDENDS ON PUT OPTION PREMIUMS

The dividend of the underlying stock is a negative factor on the price of its call options. The opposite is true for puts. *The larger the dividend, the more valuable the puts will be.* This is true because, as

233

the stock goes ex-dividend, it will be reduced in price by the amount of the dividend. That is, the stock will decrease in price and therefore the put will become more valuable. Consequently, the buyer of the put will be willing to pay a higher price for the put and the seller of the put will also demand a high price. As with listed calls, listed puts are not adjusted for the payment of cash dividends on the underlying stock. However, the price of the option itself will reflect the dividend payments on the stock.

*Example:* XYZ is selling for $25 per share and will pay $1 in dividends over the next 6 months. Then a six-month put option should automatically be worth at least $1, regardless of any other factor concerning the underlying stock. During the next 6 months, the stock will be reduced in price by the amount of its dividends—$1—and if everything else remained the same, the stock would then be at 24. With the stock at 24, the put would be 1 point in-the-money and would thus be worth at least its intrinsic value of 1 point. Thus, in advance, this large dividend payout of the underlying stock will help to increase the price of the put options on this stock.

*On the day before a stock goes ex-dividend, the time value premium of an in-the-money put should be at least as large as the impending cash dividend payment.* That is, if XYZ is 40 and is about to pay a $.50 dividend, an XYZ January 50 put should sell for at least 10½. This is true because the stock will be reduced in price by the amount of its dividend on the day of the ex-dividend.

## EXERCISE AND ASSIGNMENT

*When the holder of a put option exercises his option, he sells stock at the striking price.* He may exercise this right at any time during the life of the put option. When this happens, *the writer of a put option with the same terms is assigned an obligation to* buy *stock at the striking price.* It is important to notice the difference between puts and calls in this case. The call holder exercises to *buy* stock and the call writer is obligated to *sell* stock. The reverse is true for the put holder and writer.

The method of assignment via the OCC and the brokerage firm are the same for puts and calls—any fair method of random or first-in/first-out assignment is allowed. Stock commissions are charged on both the purchase and sale of the stock via the assignment and exercise.

When the holder of a put option exercises his right to sell stock, he may be selling stock that he currently holds in his portfolio. Second, he may simultaneously go into the open market and buy stock for sale via the put exercise. Finally, he may want to sell the stock in his short stock account—that is, he may short the underlying stock by exercising his put option. He would have to be able to borrow stock and supply the margin collateral for a short sale of stock if he chose this third course of action.

The writer of the put option also has several choices in how he wants to handle the stock purchase that he is required to make. *The put writer who is assigned must receive stock* (the call writer who is assigned delivers stock). The put writer may currently be short the underlying stock, in which case he will merely use the delivery of stock from the assignment to cover his short sale. He may also decide to immediately sell stock in the open market to offset the purchase that he is forced to make via the put assignment. Finally, he may decide to retain the stock that is delivered to him—he merely keeps the stock in his portfolio. He would, of course, have to pay for (or margin) the stock if he decides to keep it.

The mechanics of which way the put holder wants to deliver the stock and the way in which the put writer wants to receive the stock are relatively simple. Each one merely notifies his brokerage firm of the way in which he wants to operate and, provided that he can meet the federal margin requirements, the exercise or assignment will be made in the desired manner.

### Anticipating Assignment

The writer of a put option can anticipate assignment in the same way that the writer of a call can. *When the time value premium of an in-the-money put option disappears, there is a risk of assignment, regardless of the time remaining until expiration.* In Chapter 1, a form of arbitrage was described in which market makers or firm traders, who pay little or no commissions, can take advantage of an in-the-money call selling at a discount to parity. Similarly, there is a method for these traders to take advantage of an in-the-money put selling at a discount to parity.

*Example:* XYZ is at 40 and an XYZ July 50 put is selling for 9¾—a ¼ discount from parity. That is, the option is selling for ¼ point below its intrinsic value. The arbitrageur could take advantage of this situation through the following actions:

1. Buy the July 50 put at 9¾.
2. Buy XYZ common stock at 40.
3. Exercise the put to sell XYZ at 50.

The arbitrageur makes 10 points on the stock portion of the transaction, buying the common at 40 and selling it at 50 via exercise of his put. He paid 9¾ for the put option and he loses this entire amount upon exercise. However, his overall profit is thus ¼ point, the amount of the original discount from parity. Since his commission costs are minimal, he can actually make a net profit on this transaction.

As was the case with deeply in-the-money calls, this type of arbitrage with deeply in-the-money puts provides a secondary market where one might not otherwise exist. It allows the public holder of an in-the-money put to sell his option at a price near its intrinsic value. Without these arbitrageurs, there might not be a reasonable secondary market in which public put holders could liquidate.

*Dividend payment dates may also have an effect on the frequency of assignment.* For call options, the writer might expect to receive an assignment on the day the stock goes ex-dividend. The holder of the call is able to collect the dividend in this manner. Things are slightly different for the writer of puts. He might expect to receive an assignment on the day *after* the ex-dividend date of the underlying stock. Since the writer of the put is obligated to buy stock, it is unlikely that anyone would put the stock to him until after the dividend has been paid. In any case, the writer of the put can use a relatively simple gauge to *anticipate assignment near the ex-dividend date. If the time value premium of an in-the-money put is less than the amount of the dividend to be paid, the writer may often anticipate that he will be assigned immediately after the ex-dividend of the stock.* An example may show why this is true.

*Example:* XYZ is at 45 and it will pay a $.50 dividend. Furthermore, the XYZ July 50 put is selling at 5¼. Note that the time value premium of the July 50 put is ¼ point—less than the amount of the dividend, which is ½ point. An arbitrageur could take the following actions:

1. Buy XYZ at 45.
2. Buy the July 50 put at 5¼.
3. Collect the ½ point dividend (he must hold the stock until the ex-date to collect the dividend).

4. Exercise his put to sell XYZ at 50 (writer would receive assignment on the day after the ex-date).

The arbitrageur makes 5 points on the stock trades—buying XYZ at 45 and selling it at 50 via exercise of the put. He also collects the ½ point dividend, making his total intake equal to 5½ points. He loses the 5¼ points that he paid for the put but still has a net profit of ¼ point. Thus *as the ex-dividend date of a stock approaches, the time value premium of all in-the-money puts on that stock will tend to equal or exceed the amount of the dividend payment.*

This is quite different from the call option. It was shown in Chapter 1 that the call writer only needs to observe whether or not the call was trading at or below parity, regardless of the amount of the dividend, as the ex-dividend date approaches. The put writer must determine if the time value premium of the put exceeds the amount of the dividend to be paid. If it does, there is a much smaller chance of assignment because of the dividend. In any case, the put writer can anticipate the assignment if he carefully monitors his position.

### Position Limits

When listed puts are involved, the rule for position limits is expanded. Recall that, for a stock that has only listed calls trading, the position limit is 2,000 calls. That is, one could never be long more than 2,000 calls in XYZ options, regardless of the striking prices and expiration dates of the various calls. When a security has both listed puts and listed calls, the definition of position limit is expanded. In this case, *one cannot have a position of more than* 2,000 *options on the same side of the market in the same underlying security.* That is, one cannot have more than 2,000 option contracts on the bullish side of the market—long calls and/or short puts—nor can he have more than 2,000 contracts on the bearish side of the market—short calls and/or long puts. He may, however, have 2,000 contracts on each side of the market—he could simultaneously be long 2,000 calls and long 2,000 puts.

In reality, the "same side of the market" definition is applicable in all cases—whether a stock has listed puts or not. For example, one could be long 2,000 calls and short 2,000 calls (that is, 2,000 spreads), without violating the position limits. The following examples may help to illustrate these points.

Long 2,000 calls, long 2,000 puts —no violation; 2,000 contracts bullish (long calls)
and 2,000 contracts bearish (long puts)
Long 1000 calls, short 1000 puts — no violation; total of 2,000 contracts bullish
Long 1100 calls, short 1000 puts — violation; total of 2,100 contracts bullish

Money managers should be aware that these position limits apply to all "related" accounts, so that someone managing several accounts must total all the accounts' positions when considering the position limit rule.

## CONVERSION

Many of the relationships between call prices and put prices relate to a process known as a *conversion.* This term dates back to the over-the-counter option days when a dealer who owned a put (or could buy one) was able to satisfy the needs of a potential call buyer by "converting" the put to a call. This terminology is somewhat confusing and the actual position that the dealer would take is little more than an arbitrage position. In the listed market, arbitrageurs and firm traders can set up the same position that the converter did.

The actual details of the conversion process, which must include the carrying cost of owning stock and the inclusion of all dividends to be paid by the stock during the time the position is held, will be described later. However, it is important for the put option trader to understand what the arbitrageur is attempting to do in order for him to fully understand the relationship between put and call prices in the listed option market.

A conversion position has no risk. The arbitrageur will do three things:

1. Buy 100 shares of the underlying stock.
2. Buy 1 put option at a certain striking price.
3. Sell 1 call option at the same striking price.

The arbitrageur has no risk in this position. If the underlying stock drops, he can always exercise his long put to sell the stock at a higher price. If the underlying stock rises, his long stock offsets the loss on his short call. Of course, the prices that the arbitrageur pays for the individual securities determine whether or not a conversion will be profitable. At times, a public customer may look at prices in the newspaper and see that he could establish a position similar to the foregoing one for a profit, even after commissions. However, unless prices are out of line, the public customer would not normally be able to make a better return than he could get by putting his money into a bank or a Treasury bill, because of the commission costs that he would pay.

Without needing to understand, at this time, exactly what prices would make an attractive conversion, it is possible to see that it would not always be possible for the arbitrageur to do a conversion. The mere action of many arbitrageurs doing the same conversion would force the prices out of line. The stock price would rise because arbitrageurs are buying the stock, as would the put price, and the call price would drop because of the preponderance of sellers.

When this happens, another arbitrage, known as a *reversal (or reverse conversion),* is possible. In this case, the arbitrageur does the opposite—he shorts the underlying stock, sells 1 put, and buys 1 call. Again, this is a position with no risk. If the stock rises, he can always exercise his call to buy stock at a lower price and cover his short sale. If the stock falls, his short stock will offset any losses on his short put.

The point of introducing this information, which is relatively complicated, at this place in the text is to demonstrate that *there is a relationship between put and call prices.* They are not independent of one another. If the put becomes "cheap" with respect to the call, arbitrageurs will move in to do conversions and force the prices back in line. On the other hand, if the put becomes expensive with relationship to the call, arbitrageurs will do reversals until the prices move back into line.

Because of the way in which the carrying cost of the stock and the dividend rate of the stock are involved in doing these conversions or reversals, two facts come to light regarding the relationship of put prices and call prices. First, *a put option will generally sell for less than a call option when the underlying stock is exactly at the striking price,* unless the stock pays a large dividend. In the older over-the-counter option market, it was often stated that the reason for this relationship was that the demand for calls was larger than the demand for puts. This may have been partially true, but certainly it is no longer true in the listed option markets, where a large supply of both listed puts and calls is available through the OCC. Arbitrageurs again serve a useful function in increasing supply and demand where it might not otherwise exist. The second fact concerning the relationship of puts and calls is that *a put option will lose its time value premium much more quickly in-the-money than a call option will* (and, conversely, a put option will generally hold out-of-the-money time value premium better than a call option will). Again, the conversion and reversal processes play a large role in this price action phenomenon of puts and calls.

In Chapter 27, exact details of conversions and reversals will be spelled out, with specific reasons why these procedures affect the relationship of put and call prices as stated above. However, at this time, it is merely sufficient for the reader to understand that there is an arbitrage process that is quite widely practiced that will, in fact, make true the foregoing relationships between puts and calls.

# Put Option 16 Buying

The purchase of a put option provides leverage in the case of a downward move by the underlying stock. In this manner, *it is an alternative to the short sale of stock,* much as the purchase of a call option is a leveraged alternative to the purchase of stock.

## *PUT BUYING VS. SHORT SALE*

In the simplest case, when an investor expects a stock to decline in price, he must either short the underlying stock or buy a put option on the stock. Suppose that XYZ is at 50 and that an XYZ July 50 put option is trading at 5. If the underlying stock declines substantially, *the buyer of the put could make profits considerably in excess of his initial investment.* However, if the underlying stock rises in price, *the put buyer has limited risk*—he can only lose the amount of money that he originally paid for the put option. In this example, the most that the put buyer could lose would be 5 points, which is equal to his entire initial investment. Table 16-1 and Figure 16-1 depict the results, at expiration, of this simple purchase of the put option.

The put buyer has limited profit potential since a stock can never drop in price below zero dollars per share. However, his potential

**TABLE 16-1.** *Results of put purchase at expiration.*

| XYZ Price at Expiration | Put Price at Expiration | Put Option Profit |
|---|---|---|
| 20 | 30 | +$2,500 |
| 30 | 20 | + 1,500 |
| 40 | 10 | + 500 |
| 45 | 5 | 0 |
| 48 | 2 | − 300 |
| 50 | 0 | − 500 |
| 60 | 0 | − 500 |
| 70 | 0 | − 500 |

**FIGURE 16-1.** *Put option purchase.*

profits can be huge, percentagewise. His loss—which normally would occur if the stock rises in price—is limited to the amount of his initial investment. *The simplest use of a put purchase is for speculative purposes when expecting a price decline in the underlying stock.*

These results for the profit or loss of the put option purchases can be compared to a similar short sale of XYZ at 50 in order to observe the benefits of leverage and limited risk that the put option buyer achieves. In order to sell short 100 XYZ at 50, assume that the trader would have to use $2,500 in margin. Several points can be verified from Table 16-2 and Figure 16-1. If the stock drops in price sufficiently

**TABLE 16-2.** *Results of selling short.*

| XYZ Price at Expiration | Short Sale | Put Option Purchase |
|---|---|---|
| 20 | +$3,000 (+120%) | +$2,500 (+500%) |
| 30 | + 2,000 (+ 80%) | + 1,500 (+300%) |
| 40 | + 1,000 (+ 40%) | + 500 (+100%) |
| 45 | + 500 (+ 20%) | 0 ( 0%) |
| 48 | + 200 (+ 8%) | − 300 (− 60%) |
| 50 | 0 ( 0%) | − 500 (−100%) |
| 60 | − 1,000 (− 40%) | − 500 (−100%) |
| 75 | − 2,500 (−100%) | − 500 (−100%) |
| 100 | − 5,000 (−200%) | − 500 (−100%) |

far, the percentage profits are much greater on the put option purchase than they are on the short sale of the underlying stock. This is the leveraging effect that an option purchase can achieve. If the underlying stock remains relatively unchanged, the short seller would do better because he does not risk losing his entire investment in a limited amount of time if the underlying stock changes only slightly in price. However, if the underlying stock should rise dramatically, the short seller can actually lose more than his initial investment. The short sale of stock has theoretically unlimited risk. Such is not true of the put option purchase, where the risk is limited to the amount of the initial investment. One other point should be made when comparing the purchase of a put and the short sale of stock. The short seller of stock is obligated to pay the dividends on the stock, but the put option holder has no such obligation. This is an additional advantage to the holder of the put.

## SELECTING WHICH PUT TO BUY

Many of the same types of analyses that the call buyer goes through in deciding which call to buy can be used by the prospective put buyer as well. First, when approaching put buying as a speculative strategy, one should not place more than 15% of his risk capital in the strategy. Some investors participate in put buying to add some amount of downside protection to their basically bullishly oriented common stock portfolios. More will be said in Chapter 17 about buying puts on stocks that one actually owns.

*The out-of-the-money put offers both higher reward potentials and higher risk potentials than does the in-the-money put.* If the underlying stock drops substantially, the percentage returns from having purchased a cheaper, out-of-the-money put will be greater. However, should the underlying stock decline only moderately in price, the *in-the-money put* will often prove to be the better choice. In fact, since a put option tends to lose its time value premium quickly as it becomes an in-the-money option, there is an even greater advantage to the purchase of the in-the-money put.

*Example:* XYZ is at 49 and the following prices exist:

XYZ, 49;

XYZ July 45 put, 1; and

XYZ July 50 put, 3.

If the underlying stock were to drop to 40 by expiration, the July 45 put would be worth 5 points, a 400% profit. The July 50 put would be worth 10 points, a 233% profit over its initial purchase price of 3. Thus in a substantial downward move, the out-of-the-money put purchase provides higher reward potential. However, if the underlying stock drops only moderately, to 45 say, the purchaser of the July 45 put would lose his entire investment, since the put would be worthless at expiration. The purchaser of the in-the-money July 50 put would have a 2-point profit with XYZ at 45 at expiration.

The preceding analysis is based on holding the put until expiration. For the option buyer, this is generally an erroneous form of analysis, for the buyer generally tends to liquidate his option purchase in advance of expiration. When considering what happens to the put option in advance of expiration, it is helpful to remember that an in-the-money put tends to lose its time premium rather quickly. In the example above, the July 45 put is completely composed of time value premium. If the underlying stock begins to drop below 45, the price of the put will not increase as rapidly as would the price of a call that is going into-the-money.

*Example:* If XYZ fell by 4 points to 44, definitely a move in the put buyer's favor, he may find that the put has only increased in value to 2 or 2½ points. This is somewhat disappointing because, with call options, one would expect to do significantly better on a 4-point stock movement in his favor. Thus, when purchasing put options for speculation, *it is generally best to concentrate on in-the-money puts unless a very substantial decline in the price of the underlying stock is anticipated.*

Once the put option is in-the-money, the time value premium will decrease even in the longer-term series. Since this time premium is small in all series, the put buyer can often purchase a longer-term option for very little extra money, thus gaining more time to work with. Call option buyers are generally forced to avoid the longer-term series because the extra cost is not worth the risk involved, especially in a trading situation. However, the put buyer does not necessarily have this disadvantage. If he can purchase the longer-term put for nearly the same price as the near-term put, he should do so in case the underlying stock takes longer to drop than he had originally anticipated it would.

It is not uncommon to see such prices as the following:

XYZ common, 46;

XYZ April 50 put, 4;

XYZ July 50 put, 4½; and

XYZ October 50 put, 5.

None of these three puts have much time value premium in their prices. Thus the put buyer might be willing to spend the extra 1 point and buy the longest-term put. If the underlying stock should drop in price immediately, he will profit, but not as much as if he had bought one of the less expensive puts. However, should the underlying stock rise in price, he will own the longest-term put and will therefore suffer less of a loss, percentagewise. If the underlying stock rises in price, some amount of time value premium will come back into the various puts, and the longest-term put will have the largest amount of time premium. For example, if the stock rises back to 50, the following prices might exist:

XYZ common, 50;

XYZ April 50 put, 1;

XYZ July 50 put, 2½; and

XYZ October 50 put, 3½.

The purchase of the longer-term October 50 put would have suffered the least loss, percentagewise, in this event. Consequently, when one is purchasing an in-the-money put, he may often want to consider buying the longest-term put if the time value premium is small when compared to the time premium in the nearer-term puts.

In Chapter 3, the delta of an option was described as the amount by which one might expect the option will increase or decrease in price if the underlying stock moves by a fixed amount (generally considered to be one point, for simplicity). Thus if XYZ is at 50 and a call option is priced at 3 with a delta of ½, one would expect the call to sell for 3½ with XYZ at 51 and to sell at 2½ with XYZ at 49. In reality, the delta changes even on a fractional move in the underlying stock, but one generally assumes that it will hold true for a 1-point move. Obviously, put options have deltas as well. The delta of a put is a negative number, reflecting the fact that the put price and the stock price are inversely related. *As an approximation, one could say that the delta of the call option minus the delta of the put option with the same terms is equal to 1.* That is,

$$\text{delta of put} = \text{delta of call} - 1.$$

This is an approximation and is actually only accurate when either the put or call is deeply in-the-money or when there is very little time left until expiration. It has already been pointed out that the time value premium behavior of puts and calls is different, so it is inaccurate to assume that this formula holds true exactly.

The delta of a put ranges between 0 and minus 1. If a July 50 put has a delta of −½, and the underlying stock *rises* by 1 point, the put will lose ½ point. The delta of a deeply out-of-the-money put is close to zero. It would decrease slowly at first as the stock declined in value, then would begin to decrease much more rapidly as the stock fell through the striking price, and would reach a value of minus 1 (the minimum) as the stock fell only moderately below the striking price. This is reflective of the fact that an out-of-the-money put tends to hold time premium quite well and an in-the-money put comes to parity rather quickly.

The public option speculator who is working with a list of potential call option purchases published by a brokerage house or a data service might try to approximate a put's delta from the corresponding call's delta, since most data services do not publish deltas for puts. In this case, one could use the general rule of thumb that the difference of the deltas of the put and call equals 1, but he could adjust the put's delta slightly by adding something to the delta of an out-of-the-money put and subtracting something from the delta of an in-the-money put. This would present a slightly truer picture for the put buyer.

# RANKING PROSPECTIVE PUT PURCHASES

In Chapter 3, a method of ranking prospective call purchases was developed that encompassed certain factors, such as the volatility of the underlying stock and the expected holding period of the purchased option. The same sort of analysis should be also applied to put option purchases.

The steps are summarized below. The reader may refer to the section entitled "Advanced Selection Criteria" in Chapter 3 for a more detailed description of why this method of ranking is superior.

1. Assume that each underlying stock can decrease in price in accordance with its volatility over a fixed holding period (30, 60, or 90 days).
2. Estimate the put option prices after the decrease.
3. Rank all potential put purchases by the highest reward opportunity for aggressive purchases.
4. Estimate how much would be lost if the underlying stock instead rose in accordance with its volatility, and rank all potential put purchases by best risk/reward ratio for a more conservative list of put purchases.

As was stated earlier, it is necessary to have a computer to make an accurate analysis of all listed options. The average customer is forced to obtain such data from a brokerage firm or data service. He should be sure that the list he is using conforms to the above-mentioned criteria. If the data service is ranking option purchases by how well the puts would do if each underlying stock fell by a fixed percentage (such as 5% or 10%), the list should be rejected because it is not incorporating the volatility of the underlying stock into its analysis. Also, if the list is based on holding the put purchase until expiration, the list should be rejected as well, because this is not a realistic assumption. There are enough reliable and sophisticated data services that one should not have to work with inferior analyses in today's option market.

For those readers who are more mathematically advanced and have the computer capability to construct their own analysis, the details of implementing an analysis similar to the one described above will be presented later, in Chapter 28. An application of put purchases, combined with fixed-income securities, is described in Chapter 25.

## FOLLOW-UP ACTION

The put buyer can take advantage of strategies that are very similar to those the call buyer uses for follow-up action—either to lock in profits or to attempt to improve a losing situation. Before discussing these specific strategies, it should be stated again that it is rarely to the option buyer's benefit to exercise the option in order to liquidate. This precludes, of course, those situations where the call buyer actually wants to own the stock or the put buyer actually wants to sell the stock. If, however, the option holder is merely looking to liquidate his position, the cost of stock commissions makes exercising a prohibitive move. This is true even if he has to accept a price that is a slight discount from parity when he sells his option.

### Locking in Profits

The reader may recall that there were four strategies—perhaps "tactics" is a better word—for the call buyer with an unrealized profit. These same four tactics can be used with only slight variations by the put option buyer. Additionally, there is a fifth strategy that can be employed as well when a stock has both listed puts and calls.

After an underlying stock has moved *down* and the put buyer has a relatively substantial unrealized gain, he might consider one of the following actions:

1. Sell the put and liquidate the position for a profit.
2. Do nothing and continue to hold the put.
3. Sell the in-the-money long put and use part of the proceeds to purchase out-of-the-money puts.
4. Create a spread by selling an out-of-the-money put against the one he currently holds.

These are the same four tactics that were discussed earlier with respect to call buying. In addition, the holder of a listed put who has an unrealized profit might consider buying a listed *call* to protect his position.

*Example:* A speculator originally purchased an XYZ October 50 put for 2 points when the stock was 52. If the stock has now fallen to 45, the put might be worth 6 points, representing an unrealized gain of 4 points and placing the put buyer in a position to implement one of these five

**TABLE 16-3.** *Background table for profit alternatives.*

| Original Trade | Current Prices | |
|---|---|---|
| XYZ common: 52 | XYZ common: | 45 |
| Bought XYZ October 50 put at 2 | XYZ October 50 put: | 6 |
| | XYZ October 45 put: | 2 |

tactics. After some time has passed, with the stock at 45, an at-the-money October 45 put might be selling for 2 points. Table 16-3 summarizes the situation. If the trader merely liquidates his position by selling out the October 50 put, he would realize a profit of 4 points. Since he is terminating the position, he can neither make more nor less than 4 points. This is the most conservative of the tactics, allowing no additional room for appreciation, but also eliminating any chance of losing back the accumulated profits.

If the trader does nothing, merely continuing to hold the October 50 put, he is taking an aggressive action. If the stock should reverse and rise back above 50 by expiration, he would lose everything. However, if the stock continues to fall, he could build up substantially larger profits. This is the only tactic that could eventually result in a loss at expiration.

These two simple strategies—liquidating or doing nothing—are the easiest alternatives. The remaining strategies allow one to attempt to achieve a balance between retaining built-up profits and generating even more profits. The third tactic that the speculator could use would be to sell the put that he is currently holding and use some of the proceeds to purchase the October 45 put. *The general idea in this tactic is to pull one's initial investment out of the market* and then to increase the number of option contracts held by buying the out-of-the-money option.

*Example:* The trader would receive 6 points from the sale of the October 50 put. He should take 2 points of this amount and put it back into his pocket, thus covering his initial investment. Then he could buy 2 October 45 puts at 2 points each, with the remaining portion of the proceeds from the sale. He has no risk at expiration with this strategy, since he has recovered his initial investment. Moreover, if the underlying stock should continue to fall rapidly, he could profit handsomely because he has increased the number of put contracts that he holds.

The fourth choice that the put holder has is to create a spread by selling the October 45 put against the October 50 that he currently holds. This would create a bear spread, technically. This type of spread will be described in more detail later. For the time being, it is sufficient to understand what happens to the trader's risks and rewards by creating this spread. The sale of the October 45 put brings in 2 points, which covers the initial 2 point purchase cost of the October 50 put. Thus *his "cost" for this spread is nothing*—he has no risk, except for commissions. If the underlying stock should rise above 50 by expiration, all the puts would expire worthless (a put expires worthless when the underlying stock is above the striking price at expiration). This would represent the worst case—he would recover nothing from the spread. If the stock should be below 45 at expiration, he would realize the maximum potential of the spread, which is 5 points. That is, no matter how far XYZ is below 45 at expiration, the October 50 put will be worth 5 points more than the October 45 put, and the spread could thus be liquidated for 5 points. His maximum profit potential in the spread situation is 5 points. This tactic would be the best one if the underlying stock stabilized near 45 until expiration.

To analyze the fifth strategy that the put holder could use, it is necessary to introduce a call option into the picture.

*Example:* With XYZ at 45, there is an October 45 *call* selling for 3 points. The put holder could *buy* this call in order to limit his risk and to still retain the potential for large future profits. If the trader buys the call, he will have the following position:

> Long 1 October 50 put
> Long 1 October 45 call     —     combined cost: 5 points

The total combined cost of this put and call combination is 5 points—2 points were originally paid for the put, and now 3 points have been paid for the call. No matter where the underlying stock is at expiration, this combination will be worth at least 5 points. For example, if XYZ is at 46 at expiration, the put will be worth 4 and the call worth 1; or if XYZ is at 48, the put will be worth 2 and the call worth 3. If the stock is above 50 or below 45 at expiration, the combination will be worth *more* than 5 points. Thus the trader has no risk in this combination, since he has paid 5 points for it and will be able to sell it for at least 5 points at expiration. In fact, if the underlying stock continues to drop, the put will become more valuable and he could build up substantial profits. Moreover, if the underlying stock should reverse direction and climb substantially, he could still profit because the call will then become valuable. This tactic is the best one to use if the underlying stock does not stabilize near 45, but instead makes a relatively dramatic move—either up or down—by expiration. The strategy of simultaneously owning both a put and a call will also be discussed in much greater detail in a later chapter.

It is being introduced here merely for the purposes of the put buyer wanting to obtain protection of his unrealized profits.

Each of these five strategies may work out to be the best one under a different set of circumstances. The ultimate result of each tactic is dependent on the direction that XYZ moves in the future. As was the case with call options, *the spread tactic never turns out to be the worst tactic,* although it is the best one only if the underlying stock stabilizes. Tables 16-4 and 16-5 summarize what results the speculator could expect from invoking each of these five tactics. The tactics are:

1. Liquidate—sell the long put for a profit and do not reinvest.
2. Do nothing—continue to hold the long put.
3. "Roll down"—sell the long put, pocket the initial investment, and invest the remaining proceeds in out-of-the-money puts at a lower strike.
4. "Spread"—create a spread by selling the out-of-the-money put against the put already held.
5. "Combine"—create a combination by buying a call at a lower strike while continuing to hold the put.

**TABLE 16-4.** *Comparison of each of the five tactics.*

| By expiration, if XYZ . . . | the best strategy was . . . | and the worst strategy was . . . |
|---|---|---|
| Continues to fall dramatically | "Roll down" | Liquidate |
| Falls moderately further | Do nothing | Combine |
| Remains relatively unchanged | Spread | Combine or roll down |
| Rises moderately | Liquidate | Roll down or do nothing |
| Rises substantially | Combine | Do nothing |

Note that each tactic is the best one under one of the scenarios, but that the spread tactic is never the worst of the five. The actual results of each tactic, using the figures from the example above, are depicted in Table 16-5, where B denotes best tactic and W denotes worst one.

All the strategies are profitable if the underlying stock continues to fall dramatically, although the "roll down," "do nothing," and combinations work out best, because they continue to accrue profits if the stock continues to fall. If the underlying stock rises instead, only the combination outdistances the simplest tactic of all—liquidation.

**TABLE 16-5.** *Results of adopting each of the five tactics.*

| XYZ Price at Expiration | "Roll-Down" Profit | Do-Nothing Profit | Spread Profit | Liquidate Profit | Combine Profit |
|---|---|---|---|---|---|
| 30 | +$3,000 (B) | +$1,800 | +$500 | +$400 (W) | +$1,500 |
| 35 | + 2,000 (B) | + 1,300 | + 500 | + 400 (W) | + 1,000 |
| 41 | + 800 (B) | + 700 | + 500 | + 400 (W) | + 400 |
| 42 | + 600 (B) | + 600 (B) | + 500 | + 400 | + 300 (W) |
| 43 | + 400 | + 500 (B) | + 500 (B) | + 400 | + 200 (W) |
| 45 | 0 (W) | + 300 | + 500 (B) | + 400 | 0 (W) |
| 46 | 0 (W) | + 200 | + 400 (B) | + 400 (B) | 0 (W) |
| 48 | 0 (W) | 0 (W) | + 200 | + 400 (B) | 0 (W) |
| 50 | 0 | − 200 (W) | 0 | + 400 (B) | 0 |
| 54 | 0 | − 200 (W) | 0 | + 400 (B) | + 400 (B) |
| 60 | 0 | − 200 (W) | 0 | + 400 | + 1,000 (B) |

If the underlying stock stabilizes, the "do-nothing" and "spread" tactics work out best. It would generally appear that the combination tactic or the "roll-down" tactic would be the most attractive, since neither one has any risk and both could generate large profits *if* the stock moved substantially. The advantage for the spread was substantial in *call* options, but in the case of puts, the premium received for the out-of-the-money put is not as large, and therefore the spread strategy loses some of its attractiveness. Finally, any of these tactics could be applied partially—for example, selling out half of a profitable long position in order to take some profits, and continuing to hold the remainder.

## LOSS-LIMITING ACTIONS

The foregoing discussion concentrated on how the put holder could retain or increase his profit. However, it is often the case in option buying that the holder of the option is faced with an unrealized loss. The put holder may also have several choices of action to take in this case. His first, and simplest, course of action would merely be to sell the put and take his loss. Although this is advisable in certain cases, especially where the underlying stock seems to have assumed a distinctly bullish stance, it is not always the wisest thing to do. The put holder who has a loss may also consider either "rolling up" to create a bearish spread or may consider a calendar spread. Either of these actions could help him recover part or all of his loss.

### The "Rolling-up" Strategy

The *"rolling-up"* strategy will be described first. The reader may recall that a similar action, termed "rolling down," was available for call options held at a loss and was described in Chapter 3. The put buyer who owns a put at a loss may be able to create a spread that allows him to be able to break even at a more favorable price at expiration. Such action will inevitably limit his profit potential, but is generally useful in recovering something from a put that might otherwise expire totally worthless.

> *Example:* An investor initially purchased an XYZ October 45 put for 3 points when the underlying stock was at 45. However, the stock rises to 48 at a later date and the put that was originally bought for 3 points is now selling for 1½ points. It is not unusual, by the way, for a put to retain this much of its value even though the stock has moved up and some amount of time has passed, since out-of-the-money puts tend to hold time value premium rather well. With XYZ at 48, an October 50 put might be selling for 3 points. The put holder could create a position designed to permit recovery of some of his losses by *selling two of the puts that he is long—October 45's—and simultaneously buying one October 50 put.* The net cost for this transaction would be only commissions, since he receives $300 from selling two puts at 1½ each, which completely covers the $300 cost of buying the October 50 put. The transactions are summarized in Table 16-6.

**TABLE 16-6.** *Summary of rolling up transactions.*

| | | |
|---|---|---|
| Original trade: | Buy 1 October 45 put for 3 with XYZ at 45 | $300 debit |
| Later: | With XYZ at 48, sell 2 October 45's for 1½ each and buy 1 October 50 put for 3 | $300 credit $300 debit |
| Net position: | Long 1 October 50 put Short 1 October 45 put | $300 debit |

By selling two of the October 45 puts, the investor is now short an October 45 put. Since he also purchased an October 50 put, he has a spread (technically, a bear spread). He has spent no money, except commissions, to set up this spread, since the sale of the October 45's covered the purchase of the October 50 put. *This strategy is most attractive when the debit involved to create the spread is small.* In this example, the debit is zero.

The effect of creating this spread is that *the investor has not increased his risk at all, but has raised the break-even point for his position.* That is, if XYZ merely falls a small distance, he will be able to get out even. Without the effect of creating the spread, the put holder would need XYZ to fall back to 42 at expiration in order for him to break even, since he originally paid 3 points for the October 45 put. His original risk was $300. If XYZ continues to rise in price and the puts in the spread expire worthless, the net loss will still be only $300 plus additional commissions. Admittedly, the commissions for the spread will increase the loss slightly, but they are small in comparison to the debit of the position ($300). On the other hand, if the stock should only fall back slightly to 47 by expiration, the spread will break even. At expiration, with XYZ at 47, the in-the-money October 50 put will be worth 3 points and the out-of-the-money October 45 put will expire worthless. Thus the investor will recover his $300 cost, except for commissions, with XYZ at 47 at expiration. His break-even point is raised from 42 to 47, a substantial improvement of his chances for recovery.

*The implementation of this spread strategy reduces the profit potential of the position,* however. The maximum potential of the spread is 2 points. If XYZ is anywhere below 45 at expiration, the spread will be worth 5 points, since the October 50 put will sell for 5 points more than the October 45 put. The investor has limited his potential profit to 2 points—the 5-point maximum width of the spread, less the 3 points that he paid to get into the position. He can no longer gain substantially on a large drop in price by the underlying stock. This is normally of little concern to the put holder faced with an unrealized loss and the potential for a total loss. He generally would be appreciative of getting out even or of making a small profit. The creation of the spread accomplishes this objective for him.

It should also be pointed out that he does not incur the maximum loss of his entire debit plus commissions unless XYZ closes above 50 at expiration. If XYZ is anywhere below 50, the October 50 will have some value and the investor will be able to recover something from the position. This is distinctly different from the original put holding of the October 45, where the maximum loss would be incurred unless the stock were below 45 at expiration. Thus the introduction of *the spread also reduces the chances of having to realize the maximum loss.*

In summary, the put holder faced with an unrealized loss may be able to create a spread by selling twice the number of puts that he is currently long and simultaneously buying the put at the next higher strike. This action should only be used if the spread can be transacted at a small debit or, preferably, at even money (zero debit). The spread position offers a much better chance of breaking even and also reduces the possibility of having to realize the maximum loss in the position.

However, the introduction of these loss-limiting measures reduces the maximum potential of the position if the underlying stock should subsequently decline in price by a significant amount. Using this spread strategy for puts would require a margin account, just as calls do.

### The Calendar Spread Strategy

There is another strategy that is sometimes available to the put holder who has an unrealized loss. If the put that he is holding has an intermediate-term or long-term expiration date, he might be able to create a *calendar spread* by selling the near-term put against the put that he currently holds.

> *Example:* An investor bought an XYZ October 45 put for 3 points when the stock was at 45. The stock rises to 48, moving in the wrong direction for the put buyer, and his put falls in value to 1½. He might, at that time, consider selling the near-term, July 45 put for 1 point. The ideal situation would be for the July 45 put to expire worthless, reducing the cost of his long put by 1 point. Then if the underlying stock declined below 45, he could profit after July expiration.

The major drawback to this strategy is that little or no profit will be made—in fact a loss is quite possible—if the underlying stock falls back to 45 or below before the near-term July option expires. Puts display different qualities in their time value premiums than calls do, as has been noted before. With the stock at 45, the differential between the July 45 put and the October 45 put might not widen much at all. This would mean that the spread has not gained anything, and the spreader has a loss equal to his commissions plus the initial unrealized loss. In the example above, if XYZ dropped quickly back to 45, the July 45 might be worth 1½ and the October 45 worth 2½. At this point, the spreader would have a loss on both sides of his spread—he sold the July 45 put for 1 and it is now 1½; he bought the October 45 for 3 and it is now 2½, plus he has spent two commissions to date and would have to spend two more to liquidate the position.

At this point, the strategist may decide to do nothing and take his chances that the stock will subsequently rally so that the July 45 put will expire worthless. However, if the stock continues to decline below 45, the spread will most certainly become more of a loss as both puts come closer to parity.

This type of spread strategy is not as attractive as the "rolling-up" strategy. In the "rolling-up" strategy, one is not subjected to a loss if the stock declines after the spread is established, although he does limit his profits. The fact that the calendar spread strategy can lead to a loss even if the stock declines makes it a less desirable alternative.

### CONVERTED (SYNTHETIC) PUTS

There is another type of put option that some brokerage firms offer to their customers. This is not actually a listed put, per se, but the *brokerage firm* will *create* a put option on any stock with listed *call* options. This created put is known as a *converted put,* or alternatively as a *synthetic put.* All that the broker needs to create such a put is a market in the underlying stock and a market in the listed calls on that stock. Since both these markets readily exist, there is, in effect, a liquid secondary market for these converted puts.

Since, at this writing, the number of stocks with listed puts is smaller than the number of stocks with listed calls, the speculator who is bearish on one of the stocks without listed puts cannot normally participate in a leveraged bearish strategy. Of course, puts may be bought in the over-the-counter market on any stock, but invariably the only way to realize a profit on an OTC option is to exercise it. There is no secondary market for OTC options. Thus the OTC put buyer cannot take advantage of a short-term move in his favor—he must wait until the stock moves far enough to cover all his costs before he can exercise.

When a stock has listed *calls,* it may be possible for a speculator to buy converted puts. These are not listed puts, trading on national exchanges, but they have nearly all the properties of listed puts—limited risk, potentially large profits, and a secondary market. The converted put is actually created by the customer's brokerage firm through a trading technique known as "conversion." This was described in the introductory material on listed put options. *These converted puts are always priced according to the following formula:*

*Converted put price* $=$ striking price of listed call $+$ price of listed call
$-$ stock price

The speculator can always determine the price of his converted put merely by knowing the price of the underlying stock and the price of the listed call with the same terms. The formula is valid when initially purchasing the put or when determining its value at any time in the secondary market.

*Example:* A speculator is bearish on XYZ, a stock with listed calls but with no listed puts trading. If XYZ is at 52 and the January 50 call is selling for 4, the price of the January 50 converted put would be 2 points.

XYZ: 52     XYZ January 50 listed call:   4

January 50 converted put price $= 50 + 4 - 52 = 2$ points

When the brokerage firm sets up this converted put for the customer, it is necessary for the firm to sell stock short and buy the listed call. The reader will recall that the strategy in which one sells stock short and buys a listed call was termed a "protected short sale" or synthetic put. The risk in this strategy, which was detailed in Chapter 4, was described by the same formula as the one displayed above. That is, the buyer of the converted put is paying an amount of money for the put equal to the risk in the broker's position. The broker has no risk in his side of the position and thus will willingly set up any put that the customer might desire. The broker also has no profit potential on the put itself. It should be stressed that not all brokerage firms provide this service. There is sometimes a slight difficulty in establishing the converted put. Since the broker must sell stock short to establish the converted put for the customer, an "uptick" is required for the short sale. If the underlying stock is being sold down quite heavily and no uptick is available, the stock cannot be sold short, and the converted put cannot be created at that time.

The converted put has other basic properties of the listed put.

*Example:* If the underlying stock, XYZ, were to fall to 46, the January 50 call might be selling for 1 point. Then the price of the converted put could again be computed via the formula:

XYZ:  46                XYZ January 50 call:   1

XYZ January 50 converted put $= 50 + 1 - 46 = 5$ points

The owner of the converted put is therefore able to gain leverage in the case of a downside move by the underlying stock, just as he might with a listed put. Recall, again, that the reason the speculator is dealing in this converted put is that there are no listed puts on this particular stock. If the speculator decided to take his profit from this position, he could sell the converted put back to his broker for 5 points, less commissions. Technically, the broker would cover the short sale and sell the call. The customer should not even care that the broker actually has a position in the stock and the call. To the customer, it appears that he is dealing in a security that is very much like a listed put. The major difference is that a small computation has to be made to determine the price of the converted put.

If things do not work out as well and the underlying stock rises instead of falls, the converted put will generally retain some value before expiration. Suppose that XYZ rises to 56 and that the January 50 call is worth 7 points. Then the converted put will be priced as before:

XYZ:   56                              XYZ January 50 call:   7

XYZ January 50 converted put $= 50 + 7 - 56 = 1$ point

The converted put is out-of-the-money and is worth only 1 point, but it could be sold back to the broker at this time in order to salvage something from the position. In fact, *the converted put is actually a function of the time value premium in the* call *option*. Note that the formula for the put is also the formula for computing the time value premium of an in-the-money call option. Thus the converted put will retain some value as long as the call retains some time value premium.

The observations made with regard to the price and time value premium behavior of listed puts in the earlier parts of this chapter do *not* apply to converted puts, because the converted put's price and time value premium action are merely a reflection of what is happening to the call option.

There are certain other technicalities generally associated with converted puts. Normally, the broker will allow only opening purchase, and closing sale, transactions in converted puts. That is, the customer's initial (opening) trade in an opening put cannot be a sale. This precludes the writing of converted puts and also eliminates the use of converted put spreads.

In addition to the price of the converted put as computed by use of the formula above, *the customer is asked to pay, in advance, the dividends of the underlying stock during the life of the stock*. If the converted put is sold before the ex-dividend date, he will receive that amount back from the broker. This is necessary to cover the broker's risk, since the broker is actually short the underlying stock and thus will be paying those dividends.

*Example:* XYZ pays $.25 per quarter in dividends and the speculator wants to buy a six-month converted put option. In addition to the cost of the converted put, as determined by the formula, he will have to pay another $.50, or ½ point, per put. If he should sell the put before any of the ex-dividend dates, he will receive an extra ½ point from his broker when he sells the put. If he sells the put after the stock goes ex-dividend (for $.25) once, but before the stock goes ex-dividend a second time, he will receive an extra ¼ point ($.25) back from his broker when he sells the put. *In essence, the customer is operating exactly the same strategy as if he had set up a "protected short sale"*—shorting the stock and buying the call—but he is able to do so for a much smaller dollar cost. He also may buy these puts in a cash account. It is not necessary to have a margin account to buy converted puts.

The converted put is only useful to the speculator seeking leverage in a bearish scenario on a stock that does not have listed put options. Therefore, it is not that commonly used, but it may prove useful in special situations. In a broader sense, *the converted put is inferior to the listed put.* This is attributable to the fact that commission costs are normally higher for converted puts and also to the fact that the dividends are a direct payment for the converted put buyer while they are only a factor in determining the price of the listed put. As most investors know, even though a stock is reduced in price by the amount of its dividend payments, they seem to get "lost" over the course of time. That is, a stock that is in a trend will normally keep up the pace of its trend regardless of whether it happens to pay a dividend at that time or not. Thus the listed put buyer generally pays less of a premium for the dividend than does the converted put buyer, who must pay the full rate of the dividend. The point is that *if one is bearish on the market in general, and is looking for stocks on which to purchase puts, he should concentrate his selections in the stocks that have listed puts.* Converted puts should only be purchased when one is particularly bearish on a certain stock that does not have listed puts. If the entire market is going to decine, the listed put stocks will offer enough opportunities to take advantage of the decline without having to accept the disadvantage of the converted puts (higher commissions and full dividend payout).

## EQUIVALENT POSITIONS

Before discussing other put-oriented strategies, the definition of an equivalent position will be presented. Two strategies, or positions, are equivalent when they have the same profit potential. They may have different collateral or investment requirements, but they have similar profit potentials. Many of the call-oriented strategies that were discussed in the first portion of the book have an equivalent put strategy. One such case has already been described: the "protected short sale"—shorting the common stock and buying a call—is equivalent to the purchase of a put. That is, both have limited risk above the striking price of the option and relatively large profit potential to the downside. *An easy way to tell if two strategies are equivalent is to see if their profit graphs have the same shape.* The put purchase and the "protected short sale" have profit graphs with exactly the same shape. As more put strategies are discussed, it will always be mentioned if the put strategy is equivalent to a previously described call strategy. This may help to clarify the put strategies, which understandably may seem more complex to the reader who is not familiar with put options.

# CHAPTER 17

# *Put Buying in Conjunction with Common Stock Ownership*

Another useful feature of put options, in addition to their speculative leverage in a downward move by the underlying stock, is that *the put purchase can be used to limit downside loss in a stock that is owned.* When one simultaneously owns both the common stock and a put on that same stock, he has a position with limited downside risk during the life of the put.

*Example:* An investor owns XYZ stock, which is at 52, and purchases an XYZ October 50 put for 2. The put gives him the right to *sell* XYZ at 50, so the most that the stockholder can lose on his stock is 2 points. Since he pays 2 points for the put protection, his maximum potential loss until October expiration is 4 points, no matter how far XYZ might decline up until that time. If, on the other hand, the price of the stock should move up by October, the investor would realize *any* gain in the stock, less the 2 points that he paid for the put protection. *The put functions much like an insurance policy with a finite life.* Table 17-1 and Figure 17-1 depict the results at October expiration for this position—buying the October 50 put for 2 points to protect a holding in XYZ common stock, which is selling at 52. The dashed line on the graph represents the profit potential of the common stock ownership by itself. Notice that if the stock were below 48 in October, the common stock owner would have been better off buying the put. However, with XYZ above 48 at expiration, the put purchase was a burden that cost a

261

**TABLE 17-1.** *Results at expiration on a protected stock holding.*

| XYZ Price at Expiration | Stock Profit | Put Profit | Total Profit |
|---|---|---|---|
| 30 | −$2,200 | +$1,800 | −$  400 |
| 40 | −  1,200 | +   800 | −   400 |
| 50 | −    200 | −   200 | −   400 |
| 54 | +    200 | −   200 |       0 |
| 60 | +    800 | −   200 | +   600 |
| 70 | +  1,800 | −   200 | + 1,600 |
| 80 | +  2,800 | −   200 | + 2,600 |

**FIGURE 17-1.** *Long common stock and long put.*

small portion of potential profits. This strategy, however, is not necessarily geared to maximizing one's profit potential on the common stock, but rather provides the stock owner with *protection,* eliminating the possibility of any devastating loss on the stock holding during the life of the put. In all the put buying strategies discussed in this chapter and Chapter 18, the put must be paid for in full. That is the only increase in investment.

Although any common stock holder may use this strategy, two general classes of stock owners find it particularly attractive. First, the long-term holder of the stock who is *not* considering selling the stock may utilize the put protection to limit losses over a short-term horizon. Second, the buyer of common stock who wants some *"insurance"* in case he is wrong may also find the put protection attractive.

The long-term holder who strongly feels that his stock will drop should probably sell that stock. However, his cost basis may make the capital gains tax on the sale prohibitive. He also may not be all that sure that the stock will decline—after all, he has owned it a long time—and wants to continue to hold the stock in case it *does* go up. In either case, the purchase of a put will limit the stockholder's downside risk while still allowing room for upside appreciation. There are a large number of individual and institutional investors who have holdings that they might find difficult to sell for one reason or another. The purchase of a low-cost put can often reduce the negative effects of a bear market on their holdings.

The second general class of put buyers for protection includes the investor who is *establishing* a position in the stock. He might want to buy a put at the same time that he buys the stock, thereby creating a position with a profitability as depicted in the previous profit graph. He immediately starts out with a position that has limited downside risk with large potential profits if the stock moves up. In this way, he can feel free to hold the stock during the life of the put without worrying when to sell it if it should experience a temporary setback. Some fairly aggressive stock traders use this technique because it eliminates the necessity of having to place a stop loss order on the stock. It is often frustrating to see a stock fall and touch off one's stop loss limit order, only to subsequently rise in price. The stock owner who has a put for protection need not overreact to a downward move. He can afford to sit back and wait during the life of the put, since he has built-in protection.

## WHICH PUT TO BUY

The selection of which put the stock owner purchases will determine how much of his profit potential he is giving up and how much risk he is limiting. An out-of-the-money put will cost very little. Therefore, it will be less of a hindrance on profit potential if the underlying stock rises in price. Unfortunately, the put's protective feature does not start until the stock falls to the striking price of the put. Therefore, *the purchase of the out-of-the-money put will not provide as much downside protection as an at- or in-the-money put would.* The purchase of a deeply out-of-the-money put as protection is more like "disaster insurance"—it will prevent a stock owner from experiencing a disaster in terms of downside loss during the life of the put, but will not provide much protection in the case of a limited stock decline.

> *Example:* XYZ is at 40 and the October 35 put is selling for ½. The purchase of this put as protection for the common stock would not reduce upside potential much at all—only by ½ point. However, the stock owner could lose 5½ points if XYZ fell to 35 or below. That is his maximum possible loss, for if XYZ were below 35 at October expiration, he could exercise his put to sell the stock at 35—losing 5 points on the stock—and he would have paid ½ of a point for the put, bringing his total loss to 5½ points.

At the opposite end of the spectrum, the stock owner might buy an in-the-money put as protection. This would quite severely limit his profit potential, since the underlying stock would have to rise above the strike and more for him to make a profit. However, the in-the-money put provides vast quantities of downside protection, limiting his loss to a very small amount.

> *Example:* XYZ is again at 40 and there is an October 45 put selling for 5½. The stock owner who purchases the October 45 put would have a maximum risk of ½ point, for he could always exercise the put to sell stock at 45—giving him a 5-point *gain* on the stock—but he paid 5½ points for the put, thereby giving him an overall maximum loss of ½ point. He would have difficulty making any profit during the life of the put, however. XYZ would have to rise by more than 5½ points (the cost of the put) for him to make any total profit on the position by October expiration.

*The in-the-money put purchase is overly conservative and is usually not a good strategy.* On the other hand, it is not wise to purchase a put that is too deeply out-of-the-money as protection. *Generally, one should purchase a slightly out-of-the-money put as protection.* This attempts to achieve a balance between the positive feature of protection for the common stock and the negative feature of limiting profits.

The reader may find it interesting to know that he has actually gone through this analysis, back in Chapter 3. Glance again at the profit graph for this strategy of using the put purchase to protect a common stock holding (Figure 17-1). It has exactly the same shape as the profit graph of a simple call purchase. Therefore, *the call purchase and the long put/long stock strategies are equivalent.* Again, by equivalent it is meant that they have similar profit potentials. Obviously, the ownership of a call differs substantially from the ownership of common stock and a put. The stock owner continues to maintain his position for an indefinite period of time while the call holder does not. Also, the stock holder is forced to pay substantially more for his position than is the call holder, and he also receives dividends whereas the call holder does not. Therefore, "equivalent" does not mean *exactly* the same when comparing call-oriented and put-oriented strategies, but rather denotes that they have similar profit potentials.

In Chapter 3, it was determined that the slightly in-the-money call often offers the best ratio between risk and reward. When the call is slightly in-the-money, the stock is above the striking price. Similarly, the slightly *out*-of-the-money put often offers the best ratio between risk and reward for the common stockholder who is buying the put for protection. Again, the stock is slightly above the striking price. Actually, since the two positions are equivalent, the same conclusions *should* be arrived at—that is why it was stated that the reader has been through this analysis previously.

## TAX CONSIDERATIONS

Although tax considerations will be covered in detail in Chapter 29, there is an important tax law concerning the purchase of puts against a common stock holding that should be mentioned at this time. If the stock owner is already a long-term holder of the stock at the time that he buys the put, the put purchase has no effect on his tax status. Similarly, if the stock buyer buys the stock at the time that he buys the put and identifies the position as a hedge, there is no effect on the tax status of his stock. However, *if one is currently a short-term holder of the common stock at the time that he buys a put, he eliminates any accrued holding period on his common stock. Moreover, the holding period for that stock does not begin again until the put is sold.*

> *Example:* the long-term holding period is 1 year. That is, a stock owner must own the stock for 1 year before it can be considered a long-term capital gain. An investor who bought the stock and held it for 11 months and then purchased a put would wipe out his entire holding period of 11 months. Suppose he then held the put and the stock simultaneously for 6 months, liquidating the put at the end of 6 months. His holding

period would start all over again for that common stock. Even though he has owned the stock for 17 months—11 months prior to the put purchase and 6 months more while he simultaneously owned the put—his holding period for tax purposes is considered to be zero!

This law could have important tax ramifications and one should consult a tax advisor if he is in doubt as to the effect that a put purchase might have on the taxability of his common stock holdings. These tax consequences will be discussed more fully in Chapter 29.

## PUT BUYING AS PROTECTION FOR THE COVERED CALL WRITER

Since put purchases afford protection to the owner of common stock, some investors naturally feel that the same protective feature could be used to limit their downside risk in the covered call writing strategy. Recall that the covered call writing strategy involves the purchase of stock and the sale of a call option against that stock. The covered write has limited upside profit potentials and offers protection, in the amount of the call premium to the downside. The covered writer will make money if the stock falls a little, remains unchanged, or rises by expiration. The covered writer can actually lose money only if the stock falls by more than the call premium received. He has potentially large downside losses.

*The purchase of an out-of-the-money put option can eliminate the risk of large potential losses for the covered write,* although the money spent for the put purchase will reduce the overall return from his covered write. He must therefore include the put cost in his initial calculations to determine if it is worthwhile to buy the put.

*Example:* XYZ is at 39 and there is an XYZ October 40 call selling for 3 points and an XYZ October 35 put selling for ½ point. A covered write could be established by buying the common at 39 and selling the October 40 call for 3. This covered write would have a maximum profit potential of 4 points if XYZ were anywhere above 40 at expiration. The write would lose money if XYZ were anywhere below 36, the break-even point, at October expiration. By also purchasing the October 35 put at the time the covered write is initiated, the covered writer will limit his profit potential slightly, but will also greatly reduce his risk potential. If the put purchase is added to the covered write, the maximum profit potential is reduced to 3½ points at October expiration. The break-even point moves up to 36½, and the writer will experience some

**TABLE 17-2.** *Comparison of regular and protected covered writes.*

| XYZ Price at Expiration | Stock Profit | October 40 Call Profit | October 35 Put Profit | Total Profit |
|---|---|---|---|---|
| 25 | −$1,400 | +$300 | +$950 | −$150 |
| 30 | − 900 | + 300 | + 450 | − 150 |
| 35 | − 400 | + 300 | − 50 | − 150 |
| 36½ | − 250 | + 300 | − 50 | 0 |
| 38 | − 100 | + 300 | − 50 | + 150 |
| 40 | + 100 | + 300 | − 50 | + 350 |
| 45 | + 600 | − 200 | − 50 | + 350 |
| 50 | + 1,100 | − 700 | − 50 | + 350 |

loss if XYZ is below 36½ at expiration. However, the most that the writer could lose would be 1½ points if XYZ were below 35 at expiration. The purchase of the put option produces this loss-limiting effect. Table 17-2 and Figure 17-2 depict the profitability of both the regular covered write and the covered write that is protected by the put purchase.

Commissions should be carefully included in the covered writer's return calculations as well as the cost of the put. It was demonstrated in Chapter 2 that the covered writer must include all commission and margin interest expenses as well as all dividends received in order to

**FIGURE 17-2.** *Covered call write protected by a put purchase.*

produce an accurate "total return" picture of the covered write. Figure
17-2 shows that the break-even point is raised slightly and the overall
profit potential is reduced by the purchase of the put. However, *the
maximum risk is quite small and the writer need never be forced to
roll down in a disadvantageous situation.*

Recall that the covered writer who does not have the protective
put in place is forced to roll down in order to gain increased downside
protection. Rolling down merely means that he buys back the call that
is currently written and writes another call, with a lower striking price,
in its place. This rolling-down action can be helpful if the stock
stabilizes after falling, but if the stock reverses and climbs upward in
price again, the covered writer who rolled down would have limited
his gains. In fact, he may have even *"locked in"* a loss. The writer who
has the protective put need not be bothered with such things. He never
has to roll down, for he has a limited maximum loss. Therefore, he
should never get into a "locked-in" loss situation. This can be a great
advantage, especially from an emotional viewpoint, because the writer
is never forced to make a decision as to the future price of the stock, in
the middle of the stock's decline. With the put in place, he can feel free
to take no action at all since his overall loss is limited. If the stock
should rally upward later, he will still be in a position to make his
maximum profit.

The longer-term effects of buying puts in combination with
covered writes are not easily definable, but it would appear that the
writer reduces his overall rate of return slightly by buying the puts.
This is because he gives something away if the stock falls slightly,
remains unchanged, or rises in price. He only "gains" something if the
stock falls heavily. Since the odds of a stock falling heavily are small in
comparison to the other events—falling slightly, remaining unchanged,
or rising—the writer will be gaining something in only a small percentage of cases. However, the put buying strategy may still prove
useful in that it removes the emotional uncertainty of large losses. The
covered writer who buys puts may often find it easier to operate in a
more rational manner when he has the protective put in place.

This strategy is equivalent to one that has been described before—the bull spread. Notice that the profit graph in Figure 17-2 has
the same shape as the bull spread profit graph (Figure 7-1). This
means that the two strategies are equivalent. In fact, in Chapter 7 it
was pointed out that the bull spread could sometimes be considered a
"substitute" for covered writing. Actually, the bull spread is more akin
to this strategy—the covered write protected by a put purchase. There

are, of course, differences between the strategies. They are equivalent in profit and loss potential, but the covered writer could never lose all his investment in a short period of time, although the spreader could. In order to actually use bull spreads as substitutes for covered writes, one would invest only a small portion of his available funds in the spread and would place the remainder of his funds in fixed-income securities. Such a strategy was discussed in more depth in Chapter 7.

# Buying Puts in *18*
# Conjunction with
# Call Purchases

There are several ways in which the purchases of both puts and calls can be used to the speculator's advantage. One simple method is actually a follow-up strategy for the call buyer. If the stock has advanced and the call buyer has a profit, he might consider *buying a put as a means of locking in his call profits while still allowing for more potential upside appreciation.* In Chapter 3, four basic alternatives were listed for the call buyer who had a profit—he could liquidate the call and take his profit, he could do nothing, he could "roll up" by selling the call for a profit and using part of the proceeds to purchase more out-of-the-money calls, or he could create a bull spread by selling the out-of-the-money call against the profitable call that he holds. If the underlying stock has listed puts, he has another alternative—he could buy a put. This put purchase would serve to lock in some of the profits on the call and would still allow room for further appreciation if the stock should continue to rise in price.

*Example:* An investor initially purchased an XYZ October 50 call for 3 points when the stock was at 48. Sometime later, after the stock had risen to 58, the call would be worth about 9 points. If there was an October 60 put, it might be selling for 4 points, and the call holder could buy this put to lock in some of his profits. His position, after purchasing the put, would be:

Long 1 October 50 call at 3 points
Long 1 October 60 put at 4 points — net cost: 7 points

He would own a *"combination"*—any position consisting of both a put and call with differing terms—that is always worth at least 10 points. The combination will be worth exactly 10 points at expiration if XYZ is anywhere between 50 and 60. For example, if XYZ is at 52 at expiration, the call will be worth 2 points and the put will be worth 8 points. Alternatively, if the stock is at 58 at expiration, the put will be worth 2 points and the call worth 8 points. Should XYZ be above 60 at expiration, the combination's value will be equal to the call's value since the put will expire worthless with XYZ *above 60.* The call would have to be worth *more* than 10 points in that case, since it has a striking price of 50. Similarly, if XYZ were *below 50* at expiration, the combination would be worth more than 10 points, since the put would be more than 10 points in-the-money and the call would be worthless.

The speculator has thus created a position in which he cannot lose money—that is because he only paid 7 points for the combination (3 points for the call and 4 points for the put). No matter what happens, the combination will be worth at least 10 points at expiration, and a 3-point profit is thus "locked in." If XYZ should continue to climb in price, the speculator could make more than 3 points of profit whenever XYZ is above 60 at expiration. Moreover, if XYZ should suddenly collapse in price, the speculator could make more than 3 points of profit if the stock was below 50 by expiration. The reader must realize that such a position can never be created as an initial position. This desirable situation only arose because the call had built up a substantial profit before the put was purchased. The similar strategy for the put buyer—who might buy a call to protect his unrealized put profits—was described in Chapter 16.

## STRADDLE BUYING

*A straddle purchase consists of buying both a put and a call with the same terms—same underlying stock, striking price, and expiration date.* The straddle purchase allows the buyer to make large potential profits if the stock moves far enough in either direction. The buyer has a predetermined maximum loss, equal to the amount of his initial investment.

*Example:* The following prices exist:

XYZ common, 50;

XYZ July 50 call, 3; and

XYZ July 50 put, 2.

If one purchased both the July 50 call and the July 50 put, he would be buying a straddle. This would cost 5 points, plus commissions. The investment required to purchase a straddle is the net debit. If the underlying stock is exactly at 50 at expiration, the buyer would lose all his investment since both the put and the call would expire worthless. If the stock were above 55 at expiration, the call portion of the straddle would be worth more than 5 points and the straddle buyer would make money, even though his put expired worthless. To the downside, a similar situation exists. If XYZ were below 45 at expiration, the put would be worth more than 5 points and he would have a profit despite the fact that the call expired worthless. Table 18-1 and Figure 18-1 depict the results of his example straddle purchase at expiration. The straddle buyer

**TABLE 18-1.** *Results at expiration of straddle purchase.*

| XYZ Price at Expiration | Call Profit | Put Profit | Total Straddle Profit |
|---|---|---|---|
| 30 | −$   300 | +$1,800 | +$1,500 |
| 40 | −   300 | +   800 | +   500 |
| 45 | −   300 | +   300 | 0 |
| 50 | −   300 | −   200 | −   500 |
| 55 | +   200 | −   200 | 0 |
| 60 | +   700 | −   200 | +   500 |
| 70 | + 1,700 | −   200 | + 1,500 |

**FIGURE 18-1.** *Straddle purchase.*

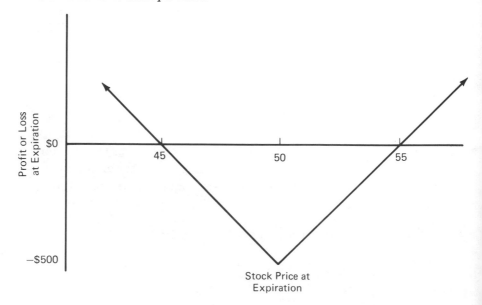

can immediately determine his break-even points at expiration—45 and 55 in this example. He will lose money if the underlying stock is between those break-even points at expiration. He has *potentially large profits* if XYZ should move a great distance away from 50 by expiration.

One would normally purchase a straddle on a relatively volatile stock which has the potential to move far enough to make the straddle profitable in the allotted time. This strategy is particularly attractive when option premiums are low, since low premiums will mean a cheaper straddle cost. Although *losses may occur in a relatively large percentage of cases that are held to expiration,* there is actually only a minute probability of losing one's entire investment. Even if XYZ should be at 50 at expiration, there would still be the opportunity to sell the straddle for a small amount on the final day of trading.

### Equivalences

*Straddle buying is equivalent to the reverse hedge*—a strategy described in Chapter 4, in which one sells the underlying stock short and purchases two calls on the underlying stock. Both strategies have similar profit characteristics—a limited loss which would occur at the striking price of the options involved and potentially large profits if the underlying stock should rise or fall far enough in price. *The straddle purchase is superior to the reverse hedge,* however, and where listed puts exist on a stock, the reverse hedge strategy becomes obsolete. The reason that the straddle purchase is superior is that dividends are not paid by the holder and that commission costs are much smaller in the straddle situation. As with many of these strategies where the put replaces a stock holding, one cannot invest a large sum of money in the straddle strategy since he could lose a significant portion of it in a short time period.

> *Example:* The straddle purchase might require only $500 as investment but could involve a loss of up to $500. The reverse hedge strategy might require an investment of $3,000, but would involve the same $500 maximum loss. Thus, if one wants to operate with straddles instead of reverse hedges, he should invest the $500 in the straddle and place the remaining $2,500 in much more conservative investments. A similar strategy of dollar investment can be followed with any types of equivalent strategies.

### Reverse Hedge with Puts

A third strategy is equivalent to both the straddle purchase and the reverse hedge. It consists of buying the underlying stock and buying two put options. If the stock rises substantially in price, large profits will accrue, for the stock profit will more than offset the fixed loss on the purchase of two put options. If the stock declines in price by a large amount, profits will also be generated. In a decline, the profits generated by 2 long puts will more than offset the loss on 100 shares of long stock. This form of the straddle purchase has limited risk as well. The worst case would occur if the stock were exactly at the striking price of the puts at their expiration date—the puts would both expire worthless. The risk is limited, percentagewise and dollarwise, since the cost of two put options would normally be a relatively small percentage of the total cost of buying the stock. Furthermore, the investor may receive some dividends if the underlying stock is a dividend-paying stock. Buying stock and buying two puts is superior to the reverse hedge strategy, but is still inferior to the straddle purchase—as long as the straddle buyer makes a more conservative investment with the balance of his funds.

## SELECTING A STRADDLE BUY

In theory, one could find the best straddle purchases by applying the analyses for best call purchases and best put purchases simultaneously. Then, if both the puts and calls on a particular stock showed attractive opportunity, the straddle could be bought. It is rare to find both the puts and calls simultaneously attractive. Rather, the straddle should be viewed as an entire position. A similar sort of analysis to that proposed for either put or call purchases could be used for straddles as well. First, one would assume the stock would move up or down in accordance with its volatility within a fixed time period, such as 60 or 90 days. Then, the prices of both the put and the call could be predicted for this stock movement. The straddles that offer the best reward opportunity under this analysis would be the most attractive ones to buy.

To demonstrate this sort of analysis, the previous example can be utilized again.

*Example:* XYZ is at 50 and the July 50 call is selling for 3 while the July 50 put is selling for 2 points. If the strategist is able to determine that XYZ has a 25% chance of being above 54 in 90 days and also a 25% chance of being below 46 in 90 days, he can then predict the option prices. A rigorous method for determining what percentage chance a stock has of making a predetermined price movement is presented in Chapter 28. For now, a general procedure of analysis is more important than its actual implementation. If XYZ were at 54 in 90 days, it might be reasonable to assume that the call would be worth 5½ and the put would be worth 1 point. The straddle would therefore be worth 6½ points. Similarly, if the stock were at 46 in 90 days, the put might be worth 4½ points, and the call worth 1 point, making the entire straddle worth 5½ points. It is fairly common for the straddle to be higher-priced when it is a fixed distance in-the-money on the call side (such as 4 points) than when it is in-the-money on the put side by that same distance. In this example, the strategist has now determined that there is a 25% chance that the straddle will be worth 6½ points in 90 days on an upside movement, and there is a 25% chance that the straddle will be worth 5½ points on a downside movement. The average price of these two expectations is 6 points. Since the straddle is currently selling for 5 points, this would represent a 20% profit. If all potential straddles are ranked in the same manner—allowing for a 25% chance of upside and downside movement by each underlying stock—the straddle buyer will have a common basis for comparing various straddle opportunities.

## FOLLOW-UP ACTION

It has been mentioned frequently that there is a good chance that a stock will remain relatively unchanged over a short time period. This does not mean that the stock will *never* move much one way or the other, but that its *net* movement over the time period will generally be small.

*Example:* If XYZ is currently at 50, one might say that its chances of being over 55 at the end in 90 days are fairly small, perhaps 30%. This may even be supported by mathematical analysis based on the volatility of the underlying stock. This does not imply, however, that the stock only has a 30% chance of *ever* reaching 55 during the 90-day period. Rather, it implies that it only has a 30% chance of being over 55 at the *end* of the 90-day period. These are two distinctly different events, with different probabilities of occurrence. Even though the probability of being over 55 at the *end* of 90 days might be only 30%, the probability of *ever* being 55 during the 90-day period could be amazingly high, perhaps as high as 80%. It is important for the straddle buyer to understand the differences between these events occurring, for he might often be able to take *follow-up action* to improve his position.

Many times, after a straddle is bought, the underlying stock will begin to move strongly, making it appear that the straddle is immediately going to become profitable. However, just as things are going well, the stock reverses and begins to change direction—perhaps so quickly that it would now appear that the straddle will become profitable on the other side. These volatile stock movements often result in little net change, however, and at expiration the straddle buyer may have a loss. One might think that he would take profits on the call side when they became available in a quick upward movement, and then hope for a downward reversal so that he could take profits on the put side as well. *Taking small profits, however, is a poor strategy.* Straddle buying has limited losses and potentially unlimited profits. One might have to suffer through a substantial number of small losses before hitting a big winner, but the magnitude of the gain on that one large stock movement can offset many small losses. By taking small profits, the straddle buyer is immediately cutting off his chances for a substantial gain, and that is why it is a poor strategy to limit the profits.

This is one of those statements that sounds easier in theory than it is in practice. It is emotionally distressing to watch the straddle gain 2 or 3 points in a short time period, only to lose that and more when the stock fails to follow through. By using a different example, it will be possible to demonstrate the types of follow-up action that the straddle buyer might take.

> *Example:* One had initially bought an XYZ January 40 straddle for 6 points when the stock was 40. After a fairly short time, the stock jumps up to 45 and the following prices exist:
>
> XYZ common, 45;
>
> XYZ January 40 call, 7;
>
> XYZ January 40 put, 1; and
>
> XYZ January 45 put, 3.
>
> The straddle itself is now worth 8 points. The January 45 put price is included because it will be part of one of the follow-up strategies. What could the straddle buyer do at this time? First, he might do nothing, preferring to let the straddle run its course—at least for three months or so. Assuming that he is not content to sit tight, however, he might sell the call, taking his profit, and hope for the stock to then drop in price. This would be an inferior course of action since he is cutting off potential large profits to the upside.

In the older, over-the-counter option market, one might have tried a technique known as *"trading against the straddle."* Since there was no secondary market for over-the-counter options, straddle buyers often traded the stock itself against the straddle that they owned. This type of follow-up action dictated that, if the stock rose enough to make the straddle profitable to the upside, one would sell short the underlying stock. This involved no extra risk, since if the stock continued up, the straddle holder could always exercise his call to cover the short sale for a profit. Conversely, if the underlying stock fell at the outset, making the straddle profitable to the downside, one would *buy* the underlying stock. Again this involved no extra risk if the stock continued down, since the put could always be exercised to sell the stock at a profit. The idea was to be able to capitalize on large stock price reversals with the addition of the stock position to the straddle. This strategy worked best for the brokers, who made numerous commissions as the trader tried to gauge the whipsaws in the market. In the listed options market, the same strategic effect can be realized (without as large of a commission expense) by merely selling out the long call on an upward move, and using part of the proceeds to buy a second put similar to the one already held. On a downside move, one could sell out the long put for a profit and buy a second call similar to the one he already owns. In the example above, the call would be sold for 7 points and a second January 40 put purchased for 1 point. This would allow the straddle buyer to recover his initial 6-point cost and would allow for large downside profit potential. This strategy is *not* recommended, however, since the straddle buyer is limiting his profit in the direction that the stock is moving. Once the stock has moved from 40 to 45, as in this example, it would be more reasonable to expect that it could continue up rather than experience a drop of more than 5 points.

*A more desirable sort of follow-up action would be one where the straddle buyer could retain much of the profit already built up without limiting further potential profits if the stock continues to run.* In the example above, the straddle buyer could use the January 45 put—the one at the higher price—for this purpose.

> *Example:* Suppose that when the stock got to 45, he sold the put that he owned, the January 40, for 1 point, and simultaneously bought the January 45 put for 3 points. This transaction would *cost* 2 points, and would leave him in the following position:
>
> > Long 1 January 40 call
> > Long 1 January 45 put — combined cost: 8 points

He now owns a combination at a cost of 8 points. However, no matter where the underlying stock is at expiration, this combination will be worth at least 5 points, since the put has a striking price 5 points higher than the call's striking price. In fact, if the stock is above 45 at expiration or is below 40 at expiration, the combination will be worth more than 5 points. This follow-up action has not limited the potential profits. If the stock continues to rise in price, the call will become more and more valuable. On the other hand, if the stock reverses and falls dramatically, the put will become quite valuable. In either case, the opportunity for large potential profits remains. Moreover, he has improved his risk exposure. The most that the new position can lose at expiration is 3 points, since the combination cost 8 points originally, and can be sold for 5 points at worst.

To summarize, *if the underlying stock moves up to the next strike, the straddle buyer should consider rolling his put up*—selling the one that he is long and buying the one at the next higher striking price. Conversely, *if the stock starts out with a downward move, he should consider rolling the call down*—selling the one that he is long and buying the one at the next lower strike. In either case, he reduces his risk exposure without limiting his profit potential—exactly the type of follow-up result that the straddle buyer should be aiming for.

## BUYING A COMBINATION

*A combination is any position that consists of both a put and a call on the same underlying stock, where the options have differing terms.* They may have different striking prices and/or expiration dates. The most common combination position is one in which the put and call have the same expiration date but have different striking prices.

*Example:* One might buy a combination consisting of an XYZ January 45 put and an XYZ January 50 call. Buying such a combination is quite similar to buying a straddle, although there are some differences, as the following discussion will demonstrate. Suppose the following prices exist:

XYZ common, 47;

XYZ January 45 put, 2; and

XYZ January 50 call, 2.

In this example, both options are out-of-the-money when purchased. This, again, is the most normal application of the combination purchase. If XYZ is still between 45 and 50 at January expiration, both options will expire worthless and the combination buyer will lose his entire investment. This investment—$400 in the example—is generally smaller than that required to buy a straddle on XYZ. If XYZ moves in either direction, rising above 50 or falling below 45, the combination will have some value at expiration. In this example, if XYZ is above 54 at expiration, the call will be worth more than 4 points (the put will expire worthless) and the buyer will make a profit. In a similar manner, if XYZ is below 41 at expiration, the put will have a value greater than 4 points and the combination buyer would make a profit in that case as well. *The potential profits are quite large, if the underlying stock should move a great deal before the options expire.* Table 18-2 and Figure 18-2 depict the potential profits or losses from this position at January expiration. The maximum loss is possible over a much wider range than that of a straddle. The straddle only achieves its maximum loss if the stock is exactly at the striking price of the options at expiration. However, the combination has its maximum loss anywhere between the two strikes at expiration. The actual amount of the loss is smaller for the combination, and that is a compensating factor. The potential profits are large for both strategies.

**TABLE 18-2.** *Results at expiration of a combination purchase.*

| XYZ Price at Expiration | Put Profit | Call Profit | Total Profit |
|---|---|---|---|
| 25 | +$1,800 | −$ 200 | +$1,600 |
| 35 | + 800 | − 200 | + 600 |
| 41 | + 200 | − 200 | 0 |
| 43 | 0 | − 200 | − 200 |
| 45 | − 200 | − 200 | − 400 |
| 47 | − 200 | − 200 | − 400 |
| 50 | − 200 | − 200 | − 400 |
| 54 | − 200 | + 200 | 0 |
| 60 | − 200 | + 800 | + 600 |
| 70 | − 200 | + 1,800 | + 1,600 |

**FIGURE 18.2.** *Combination purchase.*

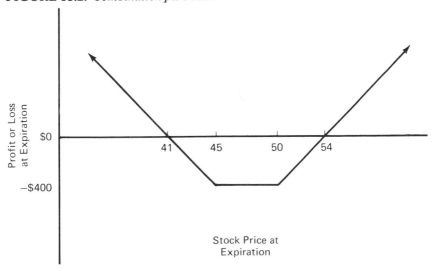

Stock Price at
Expiration

The example above is one in which both options are out-of-the-money. It is also possible to construct a very similar position by utilizing in-the-money options.

> *Example:* With XYZ at 47 as before, the in-the-money options might have the following prices: XYZ January 45 call, 4, and XYZ January 50 put, 4. If one purchased this *in-the-money combination,* he would pay a total cost of 8 points. However, the value of this combination will always be at least 5 points, since the striking price of the put is 5 points higher than that of the call. The reader has seen this sort of position before—when protective follow-up strategies for straddle buying and for call or put buying were described. Because the combination will always be worth at least 5 points, the most that the in-the-money combination buyer can lose is 3 points in this example. His potential profits are still unlimited should the underlying stock move a large distance. Thus, even though it requires a larger initial investment, *the in-the-money combination may often be a superior strategy to the out-of-the-money combination, from a buyer's viewpoint.* The in-the-money combination purchase certainly involves less percentage risk—the buyer can never lose all his investment, since he can always get back 5 points, even in the worst case (when XYZ is between 45 and 50 at expiration). His percentage profits are lower with the in-the-money combination purchase since he paid more for the combination to begin with. These observations should come as no surprise, since when the outright purchase of a call was discussed, it was shown that the purchase of an in-the-money call was more conservative than the purchase of an out-of-the money call, in general. The same was true for the outright purchase of puts—perhaps even more so, because of the smaller time value of an in-the-money put. Therefore, the combination of the two—an in-the-money call and an in-the-money put—should be more conservative than the out-of-the-money combination.

If the underlying stock moves quickly in either direction, the combination buyer may sometimes be able to take action to protect some of his profits. He would do so in a manner similar to that described for the straddle buyer. For example, if the stock moved up quickly, he could sell the put that he originally bought and buy the put at the next higher striking price in its place. This would then place him in a straddle, if he had started from an out-of-the-money combination position. The strategist should not blindly take this sort of follow-up action, however. It may be overly expensive to "roll up" the put in such a manner, depending on the amount of time that has passed and the actual option prices involved. Therefore, it is best to analyze each situation on a case-by-case basis to see whether it is logical to take any follow-up action at all.

As a final point, the out-of-the-money combinations may appear deceptively cheap—both options selling for fractions of a point as expiration nears. However, the probability of realizing the maximum loss equal to one's initial investment is fairly large with combinations. This is distinctly different from straddle purchases, where the probability of losing the entire investment is small. The aggressive speculator should *not* place a large portion of his funds in out-of-the-money combination purchases. The percentage risk is smaller with the in-the-money combination—being equal to the amount of time value premium paid for the options initially—but commission costs will be somewhat larger, and in either case the underlying stock still needs to move by a relatively large amount in order for the buyer to profit.

# The Sale of a Put $19$

The buyer of a put stands to profit if the underlying stock drops in price. As might then be expected, the seller of a put will make money if the underlying stock increases in price. The uncovered sale of a put is a more common strategy than the covered sale of a put, and will therefore be described first. It is a bullishly oriented strategy.

## THE UNCOVERED PUT SALE

Since the buyer of a put has a right to sell stock at the striking price, the writer of a put is obligating himself to buy that stock at the striking price. For assuming this obligation he receives the put option premium. If the underlying stock advances and the put expires worthless, the put writer will not be assigned and *he could make a maximum profit equal to the premium received.* He has large downside risk, since the stock could fall substantially, thereby increasing the value of the written put and causing large losses to occur. An example will aid in explaining these general statements about risk and reward.

*Example:* XYZ is at 50 and a 6-month put is selling for 4 points. The naked put writer has a fixed potential profit to the upside—$400 in this example—and a large potential loss to the downside (Table 19-1 and

**TABLE 19-1.** *Results from the sale of an uncovered put.*

| XYZ Price at Expiration | Put Price at Expiration (Parity) | Put Sale Profit |
|---|---|---|
| 30 | 20 | −$1,600 |
| 40 | 10 | −  600 |
| 46 | 4 | 0 |
| 50 | 0 | +   400 |
| 60 | 0 | +   400 |
| 70 | 0 | +   400 |

**FIGURE 19-1.** *Uncovered sale of a put.*

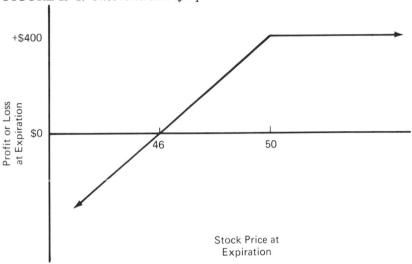

Figure 19-1). This downside loss is only limited by the fact that a stock cannot go below zero.

The collateral requirement for writing naked puts is the same as that for writing naked calls. The requirement is equal to 30% of the current stock price plus or minus the difference between the striking price and the stock price.

*Example:* If XYZ is at 45, the collateral requirement for writing a put with a striking price of 50 would be $1,350 (30% of 45) plus $500 for the in-the-money amount. If the stock were above the striking price, the striking price differential would be subtracted from the requirement. The minimum requirement is $250, even if the computation above yields a smaller result.

*The uncovered put writing strategy is similar in many ways to the covered call writing strategy.* Note that the profit graphs have the same shape—this means that the two strategies are equivalent. It may be helpful to the reader to describe the aspects of naked put writing by comparing it to similar aspects of covered call writing.

In either strategy, one needs to be somewhat bullish, or at least neutral, on the underlying stock. If the underlying stock moves upward, the uncovered put writer will make a profit, possibly profiting by the entire amount of the premium received. If the underlying stock should be unchanged at expiration—a neutral situation—the put writer will profit by the amount of the time value premium received when he initially wrote the put. This could represent the maximum profit if the put was out-of-the-money initially, since that would mean that the entire put premium was composed of time value premium. For an in-the-money put, however, the time value premium would represent something less than the entire value of the option. These are similar qualities to those inherent in covered call writing. If the stock moves up, the covered call writer can make his maximum profit. However, if the stock is unchanged at expiration, he will only make his maximum profit if the stock is above the call's striking price. So, *in either strategy, if the position is established with the stock above the striking price, there is a greater probability of achieving the maximum profit.* This represents the less aggressive application—writing an out-of-the-money put initially, which is equivalent to the covered write of an in-the-money call.

The more aggressive application of naked put writing is to write an in-the-money put initially. The writer will receive a larger amount of premium dollars for the in-the-money put and if the underlying stock advances far enough, he will thus make a large profit. By increasing his profit potential in this manner, he assumes more risk. If the underlying stock should fall, the in-the-money put writer will lose money more quickly than one who initially wrote an out-of-the-money put. Again, these facts were demonstrated much earlier with covered call writing. An in-the-money covered call write affords more downside protection but less profit potential than does an out-of-the-money covered call write.

It is fairly easy to summarize all of this by noting that in either the naked put writing strategy or the covered call writing strategy, *a less aggressive position is established when the stock is higher than the striking price of the written option. If the stock is below the striking price initially, a more aggressive position is created.*

There are, of course, some basic differences between covered call writing and naked put writing. First, the naked put write will generally require a smaller investment, since one is only collateralizing 30% of the stock price plus any in-the-money amount as opposed to 50% for the covered call write on margin. Also, the naked put writer is not actually investing cash—collateral is used, so he may finance his naked put writing through the value of his present portfolio, whether it be stocks, bonds, or government securities. However, any losses would create a debit and might therefore cause him to disturb a portion of this portfolio. The covered call writer receives the dividends on the underlying stock, but the naked put writer does not. In certain cases, this may be a substantial amount, but it should also be pointed out that the puts on a high-yielding stock will have more value and the naked put writer will thus be taking in a higher premium initially. Basically, there is a different psychology involved in writing naked puts than that required for covered call writing. The covered call write is a comfortable strategy for most investors, since it involves common stock ownership. Writing naked options, however, is a more foreign concept to the average investor, even if the strategies are equivalent. Therefore, it is relatively unlikely that the same investor would be a participant in both strategies.

## FOLLOW-UP ACTION

The naked put writer would take protective follow-up action if the underlying stock drops in price. His simplest form of follow-up action is to merely close the position at a small loss if the stock drops. Since in-the-money puts tend to rapidly lose time value premium, he may find that his loss is often quite small if the stock goes against him. In the example above, XYZ was at 50 with the put at 4. If the stock falls to 45, the writer may be able to quite easily repurchase the put for 5½ or 6 points, thereby incurring a fairly small loss.

In the covered call writing strategy, it was recommended that the strategist roll down wherever possible. One reason for doing so, rather than closing the covered call position, was that stock commissions are quite large and one cannot generally afford to be moving in and out of stocks all the time. It is more advantageous to try to preserve the stock position and roll the calls down. This commission disadvantage does not exist with naked put writing. When one closes the naked put position, he merely buys in the put. Therefore, *rolling down is not as advantageous for the naked put writer.* For example, in the paragraph above, the put writer buys in the put for 5½ or 6 points. He could roll down by selling a put with striking price 45 at that time. However, there may be better put writing situations in other stocks and there should be no reason for him to continue to preserve a position in XYZ stock.

In fact, this same reasoning can be applied to any sort of rolling action for the naked put writer. It is extremely advantageous for the covered call writer to roll forward—that is, to buy back the call when it has little or no time value premium remaining in it and sell a longer-term call at the same striking price. By doing so, he takes in additional premium without having to disturb his stock position at all. However, the naked put writer has little advantage in rolling forward. He can also take in additional premium, but when he closes the initial uncovered put, he should then evaluate other available put writing positions before deciding to again write another put on the same underlying stock. His commission costs are the same if he remains in XYZ stock or if he goes on to a put writing position in a different stock.

## EVALUATING A NAKED PUT WRITE

The computation of potential returns from a naked put write is not as straightforward as were the computations for covered call writing. The reason for this is that the collateral requirement changes as the stock moves up or down, since any naked option position is marked to the market. *The most conservative approach is to allow enough collateral in the position if the underlying stock should fall,* thus increasing the requirement. In this way, the naked put writer would not be forced to prematurely close a position because he cannot maintain the margin required.

*Example:* XYZ is at 50 and the October 50 put is selling for 4 points. The initial collateral requirement is 30% of 50, or $1,500. There is no additional requirement, since the stock is exactly at the striking price of the put. Furthermore, let us assume that the writer is going to close the position should the underlying stock fall to 45. To maintain his put write, he should therefore allow enough margin to collateralize the position if the stock were at 45. The requirement at that stock price would be $1,850 (30% of 45 plus the 5 points for the in-the-money amount). Thus the put writer who is establishing this position should allow $1,850 of collateral value for each put written. In Chapter 6, it was pointed out that the naked call writer could quickly figure the additional collateral needed by noting that the requirement for a call increases by $130 for each point that the stock moves up in price. A similar short cut is availble for the naked put writer. The collateral for a naked put increases by $70 for each point that the stock falls in price. In this example, the writer wants to allow for the stock to fall 5 points. So, at $70 per point, he should allow $350 in addition to the $1,500 initial requirement. This would give a result of $1,850, confirming the calculation made above. Of course, this collateral requirement can be reduced by the amount of the proceeds received from the put sale— $400 less commissions in this example. If we assume that the writer sells 5 puts, his gross premium inflow would be $2,000 and his commission expense would be about $75, for a net premium of $1,925.

Once this information has been determined, it is a simple matter to determine the maximum potential return and also the downside break-even point. To achieve the maximum potential return, the put would expire worthless with the underlying stock above the striking price. Therefore, the maximum potential profit is equal to the net premium received. The return is merely that profit divided by the collateral used. In the example above, the maximum potential profit is $1,925. The collateral required is $1,850 per put (allowing for the stock to drop to 45) or $9,250 for 5 puts, reduced by the $1,925 premium received, for a total requirement of $7,325. The potential return is then $1,925 divided by $7,325, or 26.3%. Table 19-2 summarizes these calculations.

There are differences of opinion on how to compute the potential returns from naked put writing. The method presented above is a more conservative one in that it takes into consideration a larger collateral requirement than the initial requirement. Of course, since one is not really investing cash, but is merely using the collateral value of his present portfolio, it may even be correct to claim that one has no investment at all in such a position. This may be true, but it would be impossible to compare various put writing opportunities without having a return computation available.

One other feature of return computations that is important is the return if unchanged. If the put is initially out-of-the-money, the return if unchanged is the same as the maximum potential return. However, if the put is initially in-the-money, the computation must take into consideration what the writer would have to pay to buy back the put when it expires.

*Example:* XYZ is 48 and the XYZ January 50 put is selling for 5 points. The profit that could be made if the stock were unchanged at expiration would be only 3 points, less commissions, since the put would have to be repurchased for 2 points with XYZ at 48 at expiration. Commissions for the buy-back should be included as well, to make the computation as accurate as possible.

**TABLE 19-2.** *Calculation of the potential return of uncovered put writing.*

XYZ:    50
XYZ January 50 put:    4

*Potential profit:*

| | |
|---|---:|
| Sell 5 puts | $2,000 |
| Less commissions | − 75 |
| Potential maximum profit (premium received) | $1,925 |

*Break-even point:*

| | |
|---|---:|
| Striking price | $ 50.00 |
| Less premium per pet ($1,925/5) | − 3.85 |
| Break-even stock price | 46.15 |

*Collateral required* (allowing for stock to drop to 45):

| | |
|---|---:|
| 30% of 45 | $1,350 |
| Plus in-the-money amount | 500 |
| | $1,850 |
| | × 5 |
| Requirement for 5 puts | $9,250 |
| Less premium received | − 1,925 |
| Net collateral | $7,325 |

*Potential return:*

| | |
|---|---:|
| Premium divided by net collateral | $1,925/$7,325 = 26.3% |

As was the case with covered call writing, one can create several rankings of naked put writes. One list might be the *highest potential returns*. Another list would be the put writes that provided the *most downside protection*—that is, the ones that have the least chance of losing money. Both lists need some screening applied to them, however. When considering the maximum potential returns, one should take care to ensure at least some room for downside movement.

*Example:* If XYZ were at 50, the XYZ January 100 put would be selling at 50 also and would most assuredly have a tremendously large maximum potential return. However, there is no room for downside movement at all, and one would surely not write such a put. One simple way of allowing for such cases would be to reject any put that did not offer at least 5% downside protection. Alternatively, *one could also reject situations in which the return if unchanged is below 5%.*

The other list—involving maximum downside protection—also must have some screens applied to it.

*Example:* With XYZ at 70, the XYZ January 50 put would be selling for ½ at most. Thus it is extremely unlikely that one would lose money in this situation—the stock would have to fall 20 points to do so. However, there is practically nothing to be made from this position, and one would most likely not ever write such a deeply out-of-the-money put.

*A minimum acceptable level of return must accompany the items on this list of put writes.* For example, one might decide that the return would have to be at least 12% on an annualized basis in order for the put write to be on the list of positions offering the most downside protection. Such a requirement would preclude an extreme situation as that shown above. Once these screens have been applied, the lists can then be ranked in a normal manner. The put writes offering the highest returns would be at the top of the more aggressive list, and those offering the highest percentage of downside protection would be at the top of the more conservative list. In the strictest sense, a more advanced technique to incorporate the volatility of the underlying stock should rightfully be employed. As mentioned previously, that technique will be presented in Chapter 28.

## BUYING STOCK BELOW ITS MARKET PRICE

In addition to viewing naked put writing as a strategy unto itself, as was the case in the previous discussion, *some investors who actually want to acquire stock will often write naked puts as well.*

*Example:* XYZ is a $60 stock and an investor feels it would be a good buy at 55. He places an open buy order with a limit of 55. Three months later, XYZ has drifted down to 57 but no lower. It then turns and rises heavily, but the buy limit was never reached, and the investor misses out on the advance.

This hypothetical investor could have perhaps used a naked put to his advantage. Suppose that when XYZ was originally at 60, this investor wrote a naked three-month put for 5 points instead of placing an open buy limit order. Then, if XYZ is anywhere below 60 at expiration, he will have stock put to him at 60. That is, he will have to buy stock at 60. However, since he received 5 points for the put sale, his *net* cost for the stock is 55. Thus, even if XYZ is 57 at expiration and has never been any lower, the investor can still buy XYZ for a net cost of 55.

Of course, if XYZ rose right away and was above 60 at expiration, the put will not be assigned and the investor will not own XYZ. However, he will still have made $500 from selling the put, which is now worthless. The put writer thus assumes a more active role in his investments by acting rather than waiting. He at least receives some compensation for his efforts, even though he did not get to buy the stock.

If, instead of rising, XYZ fell considerably—say to 40—by expiration, the investor will be forced to purchase stock at a net cost of 55, thereby giving himself an immediate paper loss. He was, however, going to buy stock at 55 in any case, so the put writer and the investor using a buy limit have the same result in this case. Critics may point out that any buy order for common stock may be canceled if one's opinion changes about purchasing the stock. The put writer, of course, may do the same thing by closing out his obligation through a closing purchase of the put.

This technique is useful to many types of investors who are oriented toward eventually owning the stock. Large portfolio managers as well as individual investors may find the sale of puts useful for this purpose. *It is a method of attempting to accumulate a stock position at prices lower than today's market price.* If the stock rises and the stock is not bought, the investor will at least have received the put premium as compensation for efforts.

## *THE COVERED PUT SALE*

By definition, a put sale is covered only if the investor also owns a corresponding put with striking price equal to or greater than the strike of the written put. This is a spread. However, *for margin purposes, one is covered if he sells a put and is also short the underlying stock.* This creates a position with limited profit potential that is obtained if the underlying stock is anywhere *below* the striking price of the put at expiration. There is unlimited upside risk, since if the underlying stock rises, the short sale of stock will accrue losses, while the profit from the put sale is limited. This is really a position equivalent to a naked call write, except that the covered put writer must pay out the dividend on the underlying stock, if one exists. The naked sale of a call also has an advantage over this strategy in that commission costs are considerably smaller. In addition, the time value premium of a call is generally higher than that of a put, so that the naked call writer is taking in more time premium. The covered put sale is a little-used strategy that appears to be inferior to naked call writing. As a result, the strategy will not be described more fully.

## RATIO PUT WRITING

A ratio put write would involve the short sale of the underlying stock plus the sale of 2 puts for each 100 shares sold short. This strategy has a profit graph exactly like that of a ratio call writing—achieving its maximum profit at the striking price of the written options, and having large potential losses if the underlying stock should move too far in either direction. The ratio call write is a highly superior strategy, however, for the reasons just outlined. The ratio call writer receives dividends while the ratio put writer would have to pay them out. In addition, the ratio call writer will generally be taking in larger amounts of time value premium because calls have more time premium than puts do. Therefore, the ratio put writing strategy is not a viable one.

# *The Sale* 20
# *of a Straddle*

Selling a straddle involves selling both a put and call with the same terms. As with any type of option sale, the straddle sale may be either covered or uncovered. Both uses are fairly common. The covered sale of a straddle is very similar to the covered call writing strategy and would generally appeal to the same type of investor. The uncovered straddle write is more similar to ratio call writing, and is attractive to the more aggressive strategist who is interested in selling large amounts of time premium in hopes of collecting larger profits if the underlying stock remains fairly stable.

## *THE COVERED STRADDLE WRITE*

In this strategy, *one owns the underlying stock and simultaneously writes a straddle on that stock.* This may be particularly appealing to investors who are already involved in covered call writing. In reality, this position is not totally covered—only the sale of the call is covered by the ownership of the stock. The sale of the put is uncovered. However, the name "covered" straddle is generally used for this type of position in order to distinguish it from the uncovered straddle write.

*Example:* XYZ is at 51 and an XYZ January 50 call is selling for 5 points while an XYZ January 50 put is selling for 4 points. A covered straddle write would be established by buying 100 shares of the underlying stock and simultaneously selling one put and one call. The similarity between this position and a covered call writer's position should be obvious. The covered straddle write is actually a covered write—long 100 shares of XYZ plus short one call—coupled with a naked put write. Since the naked put write has already been shown to be equivalent to a covered call write, *this position is quite similar to a 200-share covered call write.* In fact, all the profit and loss characteristics of a covered call write are the same for the covered straddle write. There is limited upside profit potential and potentially large downside risk.

The maximum profit is attained if XYZ is anywhere above the striking price of 50 at expiration. The amount of maximum profit in this example would be $800—the premium received from selling the straddle, less the 1 point loss on the stock if it is called away at 50. In fact, the maximum profit potential of a covered straddle write is quickly computed by the following formula:

$$\text{Maximum profit} = \text{straddle premium} + \text{striking price} - \text{initial stock price}$$

The break-even point in this example is 46. Note that the covered writing portion of this example—buying stock at 51 and selling a call for 5 points—has a break-even point of 46. Additionally, the naked put portion of the position has a break-even point of 46 as well, since the January 50 put was sold for 4 points. Therefore, the combined position—the covered straddle write—must have a break-even point of 46. Again, this observation is easily defined by an equation:

$$\text{Break-even price} = \frac{\text{stock price} + \text{strike price} - \text{straddle premium}}{2}$$

Table 20-1 and Figure 20-1 compare the covered straddle write to a 100-share covered call write of the XYZ January 50 at expiration.

*The attraction for the covered call writer to become a covered straddle writer is that he may be able to increase his return without altering the parameters of his covered call writing position substantially.* Using the prices in Table 20-1, if one had decided to establish a covered write by buying XYZ at 51 and selling the January 50 call at 5 points, he would have a position with its maximum potential return anywhere above 50 and with a break-even point of 46. By adding the naked put to his covered call position, he does not change the price

**TABLE 20-1.** *Results at expiration of covered straddle write.*

| Stock Price | (A) 100-Share Covered Write | (B) Put Write | Covered Straddle Write (A + B) |
|---|---|---|---|
| 35 | −$1,100 | −$1,100 | −$2,200 |
| 40 | − 600 | − 600 | − 1,200 |
| 46 | 0 | 0 | 0 |
| 50 | + 400 | + 400 | + 800 |
| 60 | + 400 | + 400 | + 800 |

**FIGURE 20-1.** *Covered straddle write.*

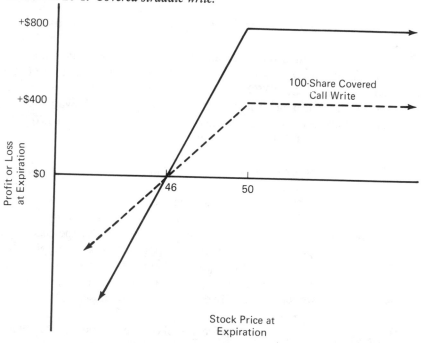

parameters of his position—he still makes his maximum profit anywhere above 50 and he still has a break-even point of 46. Therefore, he does not have to change his outlook on the underlying stock in order to become a covered straddle writer.

The investment is increased by the addition of the naked put, as are the potential dollars of profit if the stock is above 50 and the potential dollars of loss if the stock is below 46 at expiration. The covered straddle writer loses money twice as fast on the downside, since his position is similar to a 200-share covered write. Because the commissions are smaller for the naked put write than for the covered call write, the covered call writer who adds a naked put to his position will generally be increasing his return somewhat.

Follow-up action can be implemented in much the same way that it would be for a covered call write. Whenever one would normally roll his call in a covered situation, he now rolls the entire straddle—rolling down for protection, rolling up for an increase of profit potential, and rolling forward when the time value premium of the straddle dissipates. Rolling up or down would probably involve debits, unless one rolled to a longer maturity.

Some writers might prefer to make a slight adjustment to the covered straddle writing strategy. Instead of selling the put and call at the same price, they prefer to sell an out-of-the-money put against the covered call write. That is, if one is buying XYZ at 50 and selling the call, he might then also sell a put at 45. This would increase his upside profit potential and would allow for the possibility of both options expiring worthless if XYZ were anywhere between 45 and 50 at expiration. Such action would, of course, increase the potential dollars of risk if XYZ fell below 45 by expiration, but the writer could always roll the call down to obtain additional downside protection.

One final point should be made with regard to this strategy. The covered call writer who is writing on margin and is fully utilizing his borrowing power for call writing will have to add additional collateral in order to write covered straddles. This is because the put write is uncovered. However, the covered call writer who is operating on a cash basis can switch to the covered straddle writing strategy without putting up additional funds. He merely needs to move his stock to a margin account and use the collateral value of the stock he already owns in order to sell the puts necessary to implement the covered straddle writes.

## THE UNCOVERED STRADDLE WRITE

In an uncovered straddle write, *one sells the straddle without owning the underlying stock.* In broad terms, this is a neutral strategy with limited profit potential and large risk potential. However, the probability of making a profit is generally quite large and there are methods that can be implemented to reduce the risks of the strategy.

Since one is selling both a put and a call in this strategy, he is initially taking in large amounts of time value premium. If the underlying stock is relatively unchanged at expiration, the straddle writer will be able to buy the straddle back for its intrinsic value, which would normally leave him with a profit.

*Example:* The following prices exist:

    XYZ common, 45;

    XYZ January 45 call, 4; and

    XYZ January 45 put, 3.

A straddle could be sold for 7 points. If the stock were above 38 and below 52 at expiration, the straddle writer would profit since the in-the-money option could be bought back for less than 7 points in that case, while the out-of-the-money option expires worthless (Table 20-2).

**TABLE 20-2.** *The naked straddle write.*

| XYZ Price at Expiration | Call Profit | Put Profit | Total Profit |
|---|---|---|---|
| 30 | +$  400 | −$1,200 | −$800 |
| 35 | +   400 | −   700 | −  300 |
| 38 | +   400 | −   400 | 0 |
| 40 | +   400 | −   200 | +  200 |
| 45 | +   400 | +   300 | +  700 |
| 50 | −   100 | +   300 | +  200 |
| 52 | −   300 | +   300 | 0 |
| 55 | −   600 | +   300 | −  300 |
| 60 | − 1,100 | +   300 | −  800 |

    Notice that Figure 20-2 has a shape like a roof. *The maximum potential profit point is at the striking price at expiration, and large potential losses exist in either direction if the underlying stock should move too far.* The reader may recall that the ratio call writing

**FIGURE 20-2.** *Naked straddle sale.*

strategy—buying 100 shares of the underlying stock and selling two calls—has the same profit graph. These two strategies, the naked straddle write and the ratio call write, are equivalent. The two strategies do have some differences, of course, as do all equivalent strategies, but they are similar in that both are highly probabilistic strategies that can be somewhat complex. In addition, both have large potential risks under adverse market conditions or if follow-up strategies are not applied.

The investment required for a naked straddle is the greater of the requirement on the call or the put. In general, this would mean that the margin requirement is equal to the requirement for the in-the-money option in a simple naked write. This requirement is 30% of the stock price plus the in-the-money amount. *The straddle writer should allow enough collateral so that he can take whatever follow-up actions he deems necessary without having to incur a margin call.* If he is intending to close out the straddle if the stock should reach the upside break-even point—52 in the example above—then he should allow enough collateral to finance the position with the stock at 52. If, however, he is planning on taking other action that might involve staying with the position if the stock goes to 55 or 56, he should allow enough collateral to be able to finance that action. If the stock never gets that high, he will have excess collateral while the position is in place.

## SELECTING A STRADDLE WRITE

Ideally, one would like to receive a premium for the straddle write that produces a profit range that is wide in relation to the volatility of the underlying stock. In the example above, the profit range is 38 to 52. This may or may not be extraordinarily wide, depending on the volatility of XYZ. This is a somewhat subjective measurement, although one could construct a simple straddle writer's index that ranked straddles based on the following simple formula:

$$\text{Index} = \frac{\text{straddle time value premium}}{\text{stock price} \times \text{volatility}}$$

Refinements would have to be made to such a ranking, such as eliminating cases in which either the put or the call sells for less than ½ point (or even 1 point, if a more restrictive requirement is desired) or where the in-the-money time premium is small. Furthermore, the index would have to be annualized to be able to compare straddles for different expiration months. More advanced selection criteria, in the form of an expected return analysis, will be presented in Chapter 28.

More screens can be added to produce a more conservative list of straddle writes. For example, one might want to ignore any straddles that are not worth at least a fixed percentage, say 10%, of the underlying stock price. Also, straddles that are too short-term, such as ones with less than 30 days of life remaining, might be thrown out as well. The remaining list of straddle writing candidates should be ones that will provide reasonable returns under favorable conditions, and also should be readily adaptable to some of the follow-up strategies to be discussed later. Finally, one would generally like to have some amount of technical support at or above the lower break-even price and some technical resistance at or below the upper break-even point. Thus, once the computer has generated a list of straddles ranked by an index such as the one listed above, the straddle writer can further pare down the list by looking at the technical pictures of the underlying stocks.

## FOLLOW-UP ACTION

*The risks involved in straddle writing can be quite large.* When market conditions are favorable, one can make considerable profits, even with restrictive selection requirements, and even by allowing considerable extra collateral for adverse stock movements. However, in an extremely volatile market, especially a bullish one, losses can occur rapidly and follow-up action must be taken. Since the time value premium of a put tends to shrink when it goes into-the-money, there is actually slightly less risk to the downside than there is to the upside. In an extremely bullish market, the time value premiums of call options will not shrink much at all and might even expand. This may force the straddle writer to pay excessive amounts of time value premium to buy back the written straddle, especially if the movement occurs well in advance of expiration.

*The simplest form of follow-up action is to buy the straddle back when and if the underlying stock reaches a break-even point.* The idea behind doing so is to limit the losses to a small amount, because the straddle should be selling for only slightly more than its original value when the stock has reached a break-even point. In practice, there are several flaws in this theory. If the underlying stock arrives at a break-even point well in advance of expiration, the amount of time value premium remaining in the straddle may be extremely large and the writer will be losing a fairly large amount by repurchasing the straddle.

Thus a break-even point at expiration is probably a loss point prior to expiration.

> *Example:* After the straddle is established with the stock at 45, there is a sudden rally in the stock and it climbs quickly to 52. The call might be selling for 9 points, even though it is 7 points in the money. This is not unusual in a bullish situation. Moreover, the put might be worth 1½ points. This is also not unusual, as out-of-the-money puts with a large amount of time remaining tend to hold time value premium very well. Thus the straddle writer would have to pay 10½ points to buy back this straddle, even though it is at the break-even point, 7 points in the money on the call side.

This example is included merely to demonstrate that *it is a misconception to believe that one can always buy the straddle back at the break-even point and hold his losses to mere fractions of a point by doing so.* This type of buy-back strategy works best when there is little time remaining in the straddle. In that case, the options will indeed be close to parity and the straddle will be able to be bought back for close to its initial value when the stock reaches the break-even point.

Another follow-up strategy that can be employed, similar to the previous one, but with certain improvements, is to *buy back only the in-the-money option when it reaches a price equal to that of the initial straddle price.*

> *Example:* Again using the same XYZ situation, suppose that when XYZ began to climb heavily, the call was worth 7 points when the stock reached 50. The in-the-money option—the call—is now worth an amount equal to the initial straddle value. It could then be bought back, leaving the out-of-the-money put naked. As long as the stock then remained above 45, the put would expire worthless. In practice, the put could be bought back for a small fraction after enough time had passed or if the underlying stock continued to climb in price.

This type of follow-up action does not depend on taking action at a fixed stock price, but rather is triggered by the option price itself. It is therefore a *dynamic* sort of follow-up action—one in which the same action could be applied at various stock prices, depending on the amount of time remaining until expiration. One of the problems with closing the straddle at the break-even points is that the break-even point is only a valid break-even point at expiration. A long time before expiration, this stock price will not represent much of a break-even point, as was pointed out in the last example. Thus buying back only the in-the-money option at a fixed price may often be a superior strategy. The drawback is that one does not release much collateral by buying back the in-the-money option, and he is therefore stuck in a position with little potential profit for what could amount to a considerable amount of time. The collateral release amounts to the in-the-money amount—the writer still needs to collateralize 30% of the stock price.

One could adjust this follow-up method to attempt to retain some profit. For example, he might decide to buy the in-the-money option when it has reached a value that is 1 point less than the total straddle value initially taken in. This would then allow him the chance to make a 1-point profit overall, if the other option expired worthless. In any case, there is always the risk that the stock would suddenly reverse direction and cause a loss on the remaining option as well. This method of follow-up action is akin to the ratio writing follow-up strategy of using buy and sell stops on the underlying stock.

Before describing other types of follow-up action that are designed to combat the problems described above, it might be worthwhile to address the method used in ratio writing—rolling up or rolling down. *In straddle writing, there is often little to be gained from rolling up or rolling down.* This is a much more viable strategy in ratio writing—one does not want to constantly be moving in and out of stock positions, because of the commissions involved. However, with straddle writing, once one position is closed, there is no need to pursue a similar straddle in that same stock. It may be more desirable to look elsewhere for a new straddle position.

There are two other very simple forms of follow-up action that one might consider using also, although neither one is for most strategists. *First, one might consider doing nothing at all,* even if the underlying stock moves by a great deal, figuring that the advantage lies in the probability that the stock will be back near the striking price by the time the options expire. This should only be used by the most diversified and well-heeled investors, for in extreme market periods, almost all stocks may move in unison, generating tremendous losses to anyone who does not take some sort of action. *A more aggressive type of follow-up action would be to attempt to "leg out" of the straddle,* by buying in the profitable side and then hoping for a stock price reversal in order to buy back the remaining side. In the example above, when XYZ ran up to 52, an aggressive trader would buy in the put at 1½, taking his profit, and then hope for the stock to fall back in order to buy the call in cheaper. This is a very aggressive type of follow-up action because the stock could easily continue to rise in price, thereby generating larger losses. This is a trader's sort of action, not that of a disciplined strategist, and it should be avoided.

*In essence, follow-up action should be designed to do two things: first, to limit the risk in the position, and, second, to still allow room for a potential profit to be made.* None of the above types of follow-up action accomplish both of these purposes. There is, however, a follow-up strategy that does allow the straddle writer to limit his losses while still allowing for a potential profit.

*Example:* After the straddle was originally sold for 7 points when the stock was at 45, the stock experiences a rally and the following prices exist:

XYZ common, 50;

XYZ January 45 call, 7;

XYZ January 45 put, 1; and

XYZ January 50 call, 3.

The January 50 call price is included because it will be part of the follow-up strategy. Notice that this straddle has a considerable amount of time value premium remaining in it, and thus would be rather expensive to buy back at the current time. Suppose, however, that the straddle writer does not touch the January 45 straddle that he is short, but instead buys the January 50 call for protection to the upside. Since this call costs 3 points, he will now have a position with a total credit of 4 points (the straddle was originally sold for 7 points credit and he is now spending 3 points for the call at 50). This action of buying a call at a higher strike than the striking price of the straddle has limited the potential loss to the upside, no matter how far the stock might run up. If XYZ is anywhere above 50 at expiration, the put will expire worthless and the writer will have to pay 5 points to close the call spread—short January 45, long January 50. This means that his maximum potential loss is 1 point plus commissions if XYZ is anywhere above 50 at expiration.

In addition to be able to limit the upside loss, this type of follow-up action still allows room for potential profits. If XYZ is anywhere between 41 and 49 at expiration—that is, less than 4 points away from the striking price of 45—the writer will be able to buy the straddle back for less than 4 points, thereby making a profit.

Thus the straddle writer has both limited his potential losses to the upside and has also allowed room for profit potential should the underlying stock fall back in price toward the original striking price of 45. Only a severe price reversal, with the stock falling back below 40, would cause a large loss to be taken. In fact, by the time that the stock could reverse its current strong upward momentum and fall all the way back to 40, a significant amount of time should have passed, thereby allowing the writer to purchase the straddle back with only a relatively small amount of time premium left in it.

This follow-up strategy has an effect on the margin requirement of the position. When the calls are bought as protection to the upside, the writer has—for margin purposes—a bearish spread in the calls and an uncovered put. The margin for this position would normally be less than that required for the straddle which is 5 points in the money.

*A secondary move is available in this strategy.*

*Example:* The stock continues to climb over the short term and the out-of-the-money put drops to a price of less than ½ of a point. The straddle writer might now consider buying back the put, thereby leaving himself with a bear spread in the calls. His net credit left in the position, after buying back the put at ½ point, would be 3½ points credit. Thus if XYZ should reverse direction and be within 3½ points of the striking price—that is, anywhere below 48½—at expiration, the position will produce a profit. In fact, if XYZ should be below 45 at expiration, the entire bear spread will expire worthless and the strategist will have made a 3½-point profit. Finally, this repurchase of the put releases the margin requirement for the naked put, and will generally free up excess funds so that a new straddle position can be established in another stock while the low-requirement bear spread remains in place.

In summary, this type of follow-up action is broader in purpose than any of the simpler buy-back strategies described earlier. It will limit the writer's loss, but not prevent him from making a profit. Moreover, he may be able to release enough margin to be able to establish a new position in another stock by buying in the uncovered puts at a fractional price. This would prevent him from tying up his money completely while waiting for the original straddle to reach its expiration date. The same type of strategy also works in a downward market. If the stock falls after the straddle was written, one can buy the put at the next lower strike to limit the downside risk, while still allowing for profit potential if the stock rises back to the striking price.

## STARTING OUT WITH THE PROTECTION IN PLACE (PEACE OF MIND)

In certain cases, the straddle writer may be able to initially establish a position that has no risk in one direction—he can buy an out-of-the-money put or call at the same time that the straddle is written. This accomplishes the same purposes as the follow-up action described in the last few paragraphs, but the protective option will cost less since it is out-of-the-money when it is purchased. There are, of course, both positive and negative aspects involved in adding an out-of-the-money long option to the straddle write at the outset.

> *Example:* Given the following prices:
>
> XYZ, 45;
>
> XYZ January 45 straddle, 7; and
>
> XYZ January 50 call, 1½,
>
> the upside risk will be limited. If one writes the January 45 straddle for 7 points and buys the January 50 call for 1½ points, his overall credit will be 5½ points. He has no upside risk in this position, for if XYZ should rise and be over 50 at expiration, he will be able to close the position by buying back the call spread for 5 points. The put will expire worthless. The out-of-the-money call has eliminated any risk above 50 on the position. Another advantage of buying the protection initially is that one is protected if the stock should experience a gap opening or a trading halt. If he already owns the protection, such stock price movement in the direction of the protection is of little consequence. However, if he was planning to buy the protection as a follow-up action, the sudden surge in the stock price may ruin his strategy.

The overall profit potential of this position is smaller than that of the normal straddle write, since the premium paid for the long call will be lost if the stock is below 50 at expiration. However, the automatic risk-limiting feature of the long call may prove to be worth more than the decrease in profit potential. The strategist has peace of mind in a rally and does not have to worry about unlimited losses accruing to the upside.

Downside protection for a straddle writer can be achieved in a similar manner by buying an out-of-the-money put at the outset.

> *Example:* With XYZ at 45, one might write the January 45 straddle for 7 and buy a January 40 put for 1 point if he is concerned about the stock dropping in price. Generally, however, the straddle writer should be more concerned with upside risk. As was mentioned earlier, the in-the-money call will carry more time value premium than an in-the-money put. Thus, when the stock rises quickly, the straddle writer will encounter more of a problem than when the stock falls quickly.

It should now be fairly easy to see that the straddle writer could limit risk in either direction by initially buying both an out-of-the-money call and an out-of-the-money put at the same time that the straddle is written. The major benefit in doing this is that risk is limited in either direction. Moreover, the margin requirements are significantly reduced, since the whole position consists of a call spread and a put spread. There are no longer any naked options. The detriment of buying protection on both sides initially is that commission costs increase and the overall profit potential of the straddle write is reduced, perhaps significantly, by the cost of two long options. Therefore, one must evaluate whether the cost of the protection is too large in comparison to what is received for the straddle write. This completely protected strategy can be very attractive when available, and it will be described again when butterfly spreads are discussed in Chapter 23.

In summary, any strategy in which the straddle writer also decides to buy protection presents both advantages and disadvantages. Obviously, the risk-limiting feature of the purchased options is an advantage. However, the seller of options does not like to purchase time value premium at any time. He would generally prefer to buy intrinsic value. The reader will note that, in each of the protective buying strategies discussed above, the purchased option has a large amount of time value premium left in it. Therefore, the writer must often try to strike a delicate balance between trying to limit his risk on one hand and trying to hold down the expenses of buying long options on the other hand. In the final analysis, however, the risk must be limited regardless of the cost.

## COMBINATION WRITING

Recall that a combination is any position involving both puts and calls, where there is some difference in the terms of the options. Commonly, the puts and calls will have the same expiration date, but will have differing striking prices. *A combination write is usually established by selling both an out-of-the-money put and an out-of-the-money call with the stock approximately centered between the two striking prices.* In this way, the naked option writer can remain neutral on the outlook for the underlying stock, even when the stock is not near a striking price.

This is a strategy that is quite similar to straddle writing, except that *the combination writer makes his maximum profit over a much wider range than the straddle writer does.* In this or any other naked writing strategy, the most money that the strategist can make is the amount of the premium received. The straddle writer has only a minute chance of making a profit of the entire straddle premium, since the stock would have to be exactly at the striking price at expiration in order for both the written put and call to expire worthless. The combination writer will make his maximum profit potential if the stock is anywhere between the two strikes at expiration, for both options will expire worthless in that case. This strategy is equivalent to the variable ratio write, described in Chapter 6, in which two calls at two different striking prices were written against 100 shares of the underlying stock.

   *Example:* Given the following prices:
   XYZ common, 65;
   XYZ January 70 call, 4; and
   XYZ January 60 put, 3,

a combination write would be established by selling the January 70 call and the January 60 put. If XYZ is anywhere between 60 and 70 at January expiration, both options will expire worthless and the combination writer will make a profit of 7 points, the amount of the original credit taken in. If XYZ is above 70 at expiration, the strategist will have to pay something to buy back the call. For example, if XYZ is at 77 at expiration, the January 70 call will have to be bought back for 7 points, thereby creating a break-even situation. To the downside, if XYZ were at 53 at expiration, the January 60 put would have to be bought back for 7 points, thereby defining that as the downside break-even point. Table 20-3 and Figure 20-3 outline the potential results of this combination write. The profit range in this example is quite wide, extending from 53 on the downside to 77 on the upside. With the stock presently at 65, this is a relatively neutral position.

   At first glance, this may seem to be a more conservative strategy than straddle writing because the profit range is wider and the stock

**TABLE 20-3.** *Results of a combination write.*

| Stock Price at Expiration | Call Profit | Put Profit | Total Profit |
|---|---|---|---|
| 40 | +$ 400 | −$1,700 | −$1,300 |
| 50 | + 400 | − 700 | − 300 |
| 53 | + 400 | − 400 | 0 |
| 57 | + 400 | 0 | + 400 |
| 60 | + 400 | + 300 | + 700 |
| 65 | + 400 | + 300 | + 700 |
| 70 | + 400 | + 300 | + 700 |
| 73 | + 100 | + 300 | + 400 |
| 77 | − 300 | + 300 | 0 |
| 80 | − 600 | + 300 | − 300 |
| 90 | − 1,600 | + 300 | − 1,300 |

**FIGURE 20-3.** *Sale of a combination.*

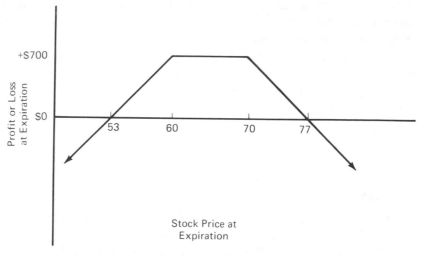

needs to move a great deal to reach the break-even points. In the absence of follow-up action, this is a true observation. However, if the stock begins to rise quickly or to drop dramatically, the combination writer often has little recourse but to buy back the in-the-money option in order to limit his losses. This can, as has been shown previously, entail a purchase price involving excess amounts of time value premium, thereby generating a significant loss.

The only other alternative that is available to the combination writer (outside of attempting to trade out of the position) is to convert the position into a straddle if the stock reaches either break-even point.

> *Example:* If XYZ rose to 70 or 71 in the previous example, the January 70 put would be sold. Depending on the amount of collateral available, the January 60 put may or may not be bought back when the January 70 put is sold. This action of converting the combination write into a straddle write will work out well if the stock stabilizes. It will also lessen the pain if the stock continues to rise. However, if the stock reverses direction, the January 70 put write will prove to be unprofitable. Technical analysis of the underlying stock may prove to be of some help in deciding whether or not to convert the combination write into a straddle. If there appears to be a relatively large chance that the stock could fall back in price, it is probably not worthwhile to roll the put up.

This example of a combination write is one in which the writer received a large amount of premium for selling the put and the call. Many times, however, an aggressive combination writer is tempted to sell two out-of-the-money options that have only a short life remaining.

These options would generally be sold at fractional prices. This can be an extremely aggressive strategy at times, for if the underlying stock should move quickly in either direction through a striking price, there is little the combination writer can do. He must buy in the options to limit his loss. Nevertheless, this type of combination writing—selling short-term, fractionally priced, out-of-the-money options—appeals to many writers. This is a similar philosophy to the naked call writer, described in Chapter 5, who writes calls that are nearly restricted, figuring there will be a large probability that the option will expire worthless. It also has the same risk—a large price change or gap opening can cause such devastating losses that many profitable trades are wiped away. To sell fractionally-priced combinations is a poor strategy and should be avoided.

Before leaving the topic of combination writing, it may be useful to define how the margin requirements apply to a combination write. Recall that the margin requirement for writing a straddle is 30% of the stock price plus the amount by which either the put or the call is in-the-money. In a combination write, however, both options may be out-of-the-money, as in the example above. When this is the case, the straddle writer is allowed to deduct the smaller out-of-the-money amount from his requirement. Thus, if XYZ were at 68 and the January 60 put and the January 70 call had been written, the collateral requirement would be $2,040 (30% of 68) less $200—the lesser out-of-the-money amount. The call is 2 points out-of-the-money and the put is 8 points out-of-the-money. Actually, the true collateral requirement for any write involving both puts and calls—straddle write or combination write—is *the greater of the requirement on the put or the call, plus the amount by which the other option is in-the-money.* The last phrase—the amount by which the other option is in-the-money— would apply to a situation in which a combination had been constructed by selling two in-the-money options. This is a less popular strategy, since the writer generally receives less time value premium by writing two in-the-money options. An example of an in-the-money combination would be to sell the January 60 call and the January 70 put with the stock at 65.

## FURTHER COMMENTS ON
## UNCOVERED STRADDLE AND COMBINATION WRITING

When ratio writing was discussed, it was noted that it was a strategy with a high probability of making a limited profit. Since the straddle write is equivalent to the ratio write and the combination write is equivalent to the variable ratio write, the same statement applies to these strategies as well. The practitioner of straddle and combination writing must realize, however, that protective follow-up action is mandatory in limiting losses in a very volatile market. There are other techniques that the straddle writer can sometimes use to help reduce his risk.

It has often been mentioned that puts lose their time value premium more quickly when they become in-the-money options than calls do. *One can often construct a neutral position by writing an extra put or two.* That is, if one sells 5 or 6 puts and 4 calls with the same terms, he may often have created a more neutral position than a straddle write. If the stock moves up and the call picks up time premium in a bullish market, the extra puts will help to offset the negative effect of the calls. On the other hand, if the stock drops, the 5 or 6 puts will not hold as much time premium as the 4 calls are losing—again a neutral, standoff position. If the stock begins to drop too much, the writer can always balance out the position by selling another call or two. The advantage of writing an extra put or two is that it counterbalances the straddle writer's most severe enemy—a quick, extremely bullish rise by the underlying stock.

### Using the Deltas

This analysis, that adding an extra short put is a neutral position, can be substantiated more rigorously. Recall that a ratio writer or ratio spreader can use the deltas of the options involved in his position to determine a neutral ratio. The straddle writer can do the same thing, of course. It was stated that the difference in a call's delta and a put's delta is approximately one. Using the same prices as in the previous straddle writing example, and assuming the call's delta to be .60, a neutral ratio can be determined.

| *Prices* | | *Deltas* |
|---|---|---|
| XYZ common: | 45 | |
| XYZ January 45 call: | 4 | .60 |
| XYZ January 45 put: | 3 | $-.40 \, (.60 - 1)$ |

The put has a negative delta, to indicate that the put and the underlying stock are inversely related. A neutral ratio is determined by dividing the call's delta by the put's delta and ignoring the minus sign. The resultant ratio—1.5:1 (.60/.40) in this case—is the ratio of puts to sell for each call that is sold. Thus, one should sell 3 puts and sell 2 calls to establish a neutral position. The reader may wonder if the assumption that an in-the-money call has a delta of .60 is a fair one. It generally is, although very long term calls will have slightly smaller at-the-money deltas, and very short term calls will have a higher delta. Consequently, a 3:2 ratio is often a neutral one. When neutral ratios were discussed with respect to ratio writing, it was mentioned that selling 5 calls and buying 300 shares of stock is often a neutral ratio. The reader should note that a straddle constructed by selling 3 puts and 2 calls is equivalent to the ratio write in which one sells 5 calls and buys 300 shares of stock.

If a straddle writer is going to use the deltas to determine his neutral ratio, he should compute each one at the time of his initial investment, of course, rather than relying on a generality such as that 3 puts and 2 calls is often neutral. The deltas can be used as a follow-up action, by adjusting the ratio to remain neutral after a move by the underlying stock.

### *Avoid Excess Trading*

In any of the straddle and combination writing strategies described above, too much follow-up action can be detrimental because of the commission costs involved. Thus, although it is important to take protective action, the straddle writer should plan in advance to make the minimum number of strategic moves to protect himself. This is why buying protection is often useful, because not only does it limit the risk in the direction that the stock is moving, but it also involves only one additional option commission. In fact, if it is feasible, buying protection at the outset is often a better strategy than protecting as a secondary action.

An extension of this concept of trying to avoid too much follow-up action is that *the strategist should not attempt to anticipate movement in an underlying stock.* For example, if the straddle writer has planned to take defensive action should the stock reach 50, he should not anticipate by taking action with the stock at 48 or 49. It is possible that the stock could retreat back down and the writer would have taken a defensive action that not only cost him commissions, but reduced his profit potential. Of course, there is a little trader in everyone, and the temptation to anticipate (or wait too long, also) is always there. Unless there are very strong technical reasons for doing so, the strategist should resist the temptation to trade, and should operate his strategy according to his original plan. The ratio writer may actually have an advantage in this respect, because he can use buy and sell stops on the underlying stock to remove the emotion from his follow-up strategy. This technique was described in Chapter 6. Unfortunately, no such emotionless technique exists for the straddle or combination writer.

### Using the Credits

In previous chapters, it was mentioned that the sale of uncovered options does not require any cash investment on the part of the strategist. He may use the collateral value of his present portfolio to finance the sale of naked options. Moreover, once he sells the uncovered options, he can take the premium dollars that he has brought in from the sales to buy fixed-income securities, such as Treasury bills. The same statements naturally apply to the straddle writing and combination writing strategies. However, the strategist should not be overly obsessed with continuing to maintain a credit balance in his positions, nor should he strive to hold onto the Treasury bills at all costs. If one's follow-up actions dictate that he must take a debit to avoid losses or that he should sell out his Treasury bills to keep a credit, he should by all means do so.

# Synthetic Stock 21
# Positions Created
# by Puts and Calls

It is possible for a strategist to establish a position that is essentially the same as a stock position, but he can do this using only options. The option position generally requires a smaller margin investment and may have other residual benefits over simply buying stock or simply selling stock short. In brief, the strategies are summarized by:

1. Buy call and sell put instead of buying stock.
2. Buy put and sell call instead of selling stock short.

## SYNTHETIC LONG STOCK

*When one buys a call and sells a put, he sets up a position that is equivalent to owning the stock.* His position is sometimes called "synthetic" long stock.

*Example:* To verify that this option position acts much like a long stock position would, suppose that the following prices exist:

XYZ common, 50;

XYZ January 50 call, 5; and

XYZ January 50 put, 4.

**TABLE 21-1.** *Synthetic long stock position.*

| XYZ Price at Expiration | January 50 Call Result | January 50 Put Result | Total Option Result | Long Stock Result |
|---|---|---|---|---|
| 40 | −$500 | −$600 | −$1,100 | −$1,000 |
| 45 | − 500 | − 100 | − 600 | − 500 |
| 50 | − 500 | + 400 | − 100 | 0 |
| 55 | 0 | + 400 | + 400 | + 500 |
| 60 | + 500 | + 400 | + 900 | + 1,000 |

If one were bullish on XYZ and wanted to buy stock at 50, he might consider the alternative strategy of buying the January 50 call and selling (uncovered) the January 50 put. By using the option strategy, the investor has nearly the same profit and loss potential as the stock buyer, as shown in Table 21-1. The two right-hand columns of the table compare the results of the option strategy with the results that would be attained by merely owning the stock at 50.

The table shows that the result of the option strategy is exactly $100 less than the stock results for any price at expiration. Thus the "synthetic" long stock and the actual long stock have nearly the same profit and loss potentials. The reason that there is a difference in the results of the two equivalent positions lies in the fact that the option strategist had to pay 1 point of time premium in order to set up his position. This time premium represents the $100 by which the "synthetic" position underperforms the actual stock position at expiration. Note that, with XYZ at 50, both the put and the call are completely composed of time value premium initially. The synthetic position consists of paying out 5 points of time premium for the call and receiving in 4 points of time premium for the put. The net time premium is thus a 1-point payout.

The reason that one would consider using the synthetic long stock position rather than the stock position itself is that the synthetic position may require a much smaller investment than buying the stock would require. The purchase of the stock requires $5,000 in a cash account or $2,500 in a margin account (if the margin rate is 50%). However, the synthetic position requires only a $100 debit plus a collateral requirement—30% of the stock price, plus or minus the difference between the striking price and the stock price. In this example, the collateral requirement would be 30% of $5,000, or $1,500, plus the $100 debit incurred by paying 5 for the call and only receiving 4 for the put. This is a total of $1,600 initially. There is no initial difference between the stock price and the striking price. Of course, this collateral requirement would increase if the stock fell in price, and would decrease if the stock rose in price, since there is a naked put. Also notice that buying stock creates a $5,000 debit in the account, whereas the option strategy's debit is $100—the rest is a collateral requirement, not a cash requirement.

The effect of this reduction in margin required is that some leverage is obtained in the position. If XYZ rose to 60, the stock position profit would be $1,000 for a return of 40% on margin ($1,000/$2,500). With the option strategy, the percentage return would be higher. The profit would be $900 and the return thus over 50% ($900/$1,600). Of course, leverage works to the downside as well, so that the percent risk is also greater in the option strategy.

The synthetic stock strategy is generally not applied merely as an alternative to buying stock. Besides possibly having a smaller profit potential, *the option strategist does not collect dividends, whereas the stock owner does.* Either of these facts could make the synthetic strategy inferior to the outright purchase of stock. It is important, however, for the strategist to understand that a long call plus a short put is equivalent to long stock. It thus may be possible for the strategist to substitute the synthetic option position in certain option strategies that normally call for the purchase of stock.

## SYNTHETIC SHORT SALE

*A position that is equivalent to the short sale of the underlying stock can be established by selling a call and simultaneously buying a put.* This alternative option strategy, in general, offers significant benefits when compared with selling the stock short. Using the prices above—XYZ at 50, January 50 call at 5, and January 50 put at 4—Table 21-2 depicts the potential profits and losses at January expiration.

Both the option position and the short stock position have similar results—large potential profits if the stock declines and unlimited losses if the underlying stock rises in price. However, the option

**TABLE 21-2.** *Synthetic short sale position.*

| XYZ Price at Expiration | January 50 Call Result | January 50 Put Result | Total Option Result | Short Stock Result |
|---|---|---|---|---|
| 40 | + 500 | +$600 | +$1,100 | +$1,000 |
| 45 | + 500 | + 100 | + 600 | + 500 |
| 50 | + 500 | − 400 | + 100 | 0 |
| 55 | 0 | − 400 | − 400 | − 500 |
| 60 | − 500 | − 400 | − 900 | − 1,000 |

strategy does better than the stock position because the option strategist is getting the benefit of the time value premium. Again, this is because the call has more time value premium than the put, which works to the option strategist's advantage in this case, where he is selling the call and buying the put.

Leverage is a factor in this strategy also. The short seller would need $2,500 to collateralize this position, assuming that the margin rate is 50%. The option strategist only needs, initially, 30% of the stock price less the credit received, for a $1,400 requirement. Moreover, one of the major disadvantages that was mentioned with the synthetic long stock position is not a disadvantage in the synthetic short sale strategy. The option trader does not have to pay out dividends on the options, but the short seller of stock would have to.

Because of the advantages of the option position in not having to pay out the dividend and also having a slightly larger profit potential from the excess time value premium, it may often be feasible for the trader who is looking to sell stock short to instead sell a call and buy a put. It is also important for the strategist to understand the equivalence between the short stock position and the option position. He might be able to substitute the option position in certain cases where the short sale of stock is called for normally.

## SPLITTING THE STRIKES

The strategist may be able to use a slight variation of the synthetic strategy to set up an aggressive, but attractive position. Rather than using the same striking price for the put and call, he can use a lower striking price for the put and a higher striking price for the call. This action of splitting apart the striking prices gives him some room for error, while still retaining the potential for large profits.

### Bullishly Oriented

If an out-of-the-money put is sold naked, and an out-of-the-money call is simultaneously purchased, an aggressive bullish position is established—often for a credit. If the underlying stock rises far enough, profits can be generated on both the long call and the short put. If the stock remains relatively unchanged, the call purchase will be a loss, but the put sale will be a profit. The risk occurs if the underlying stock drops in price, producing losses on both the short put and the long call.

*Example:* The following prices exist: XYZ is at 53, a January 50 put is selling for 2, and a January 60 call is selling for 1. An investor who is bullish on XYZ sells the January 50 put naked and simultaneously buys the January 60 call. This position brings in a credit of 1 point, less commissions. There is a collateral requirement necessary for the naked put. If XYZ is anywhere between 50 and 60 at January expiration, both options would expire worthless, and the investor would make a small profit equal to the amount of the initial credit received. If XYZ rallies above 60 by expiration, however, his potential profits are unlimited since he owns the call at 60. His losses could be very large if XYZ should decline well below 50 before expiration, since he has written the naked put at 50. Table 21-3 and Figure 21-1 depict the results at expiration of this strategy.

**FIGURE 21-1.** *Bullishly Split Strikes.*

**TABLE 21-3.** *Bullishly split strikes.*

| XYZ Price at Expiration | January 50 Put Profit | January 60 Call Profit | Total Profit |
|---|---|---|---|
| 40 | −$800 | −$100 | −$ 900 |
| 45 | − 300 | − 100 | − 400 |
| 50 | + 200 | − 100 | + 100 |
| 55 | + 200 | − 100 | + 100 |
| 60 | + 200 | − 100 | + 100 |
| 65 | + 200 | + 400 | + 600 |
| 70 | + 200 | + 900 | + 1,100 |

Essentially, the investor who uses this strategy is bullish on the underlying stock and is attempting to buy an out-of-the-money call for free. If he is moderately wrong and the underlying stock only rallies slightly or even declines slightly, he can still make a small profit. If he is correct, of course, large profits could be generated in a rally. He may lose heavily if he is very wrong and the stock falls by a large amount instead of rising.

### Bearishly Oriented

There is a companion strategy for the investor who is bearish on a stock. He could attempt to buy an out-of-the-money put, giving himself the opportunity for substantial profits in a stock price decline, and could "finance" the purchase of the put by writing an out-of-the-money call naked. The sale of the call would provide profits if the stock stayed below the striking price of the call, but could cost him heavily if the underlying stock rallies too far.

*Example:* With XYZ at 65, the bearish investor buys a February 60 put for 2 points, and simultaneously sells a February 70 call for 3 points. These trades bring in a credit of 1 point, less commissions. He must collateralize the sale of the call. If XYZ should decline substantially by February expiration, large profits are possible because the February 60 put is owned. Even if XYZ does not perform as expected, but still ends up anywhere between 60 and 70 at expiration, the profit will be equal to the initial credit because both options will expire worthless. However, if the stock rallies above 70, unlimited losses are possible because there is a naked call at 70. Table 21-4 and Figure 21-2 show the results of this strategy at expiration.

This is clearly an aggressively bearish strategy. The investor would like to own an out-of-the-money put for downside potential. In

**TABLE 21-4.** *Bearishly split strikes.*

| XYZ Price at Expiration | February 60 Put Profit | February 70 Call Profit | Total Profit |
|---|---|---|---|
| 50 | +$800 | +$300 | +$1,100 |
| 55 | + 300 | + 300 | + 600 |
| 60 | − 200 | + 300 | + 100 |
| 65 | − 200 | + 300 | + 100 |
| 70 | − 200 | + 300 | + 100 |
| 75 | − 200 | − 200 | − 400 |
| 80 | − 200 | − 700 | − 900 |

FIGURE 21-2. *Bearishly Split Strikes.*

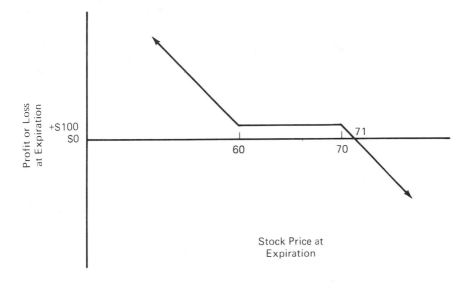

Profit or Loss
at Expiration

+$100
$0

60

70

71

Stock Price at
Expiration

addition, he sells an out-of-the-money call, normally for a price greater
than that of the purchased put. The call sale essentially lets him own
the put for free. In fact, he can still make profits even if the underlying
stock rises slightly or only falls slightly. His risk is realized if the stock
rises above the striking price of the written call.

### Summary

In either of these aggressive strategies, *the investor must have a
definite opinion about the future price movement of the underlying
stock.* He buys an out-of-the-money option to provide profit potential
for that stock movement. However, an investor can lose the entire
purchase proceeds of an out-of-the-money option if the stock does not
perform as expected. An aggressive investor, who has sufficient collateral, might attempt to counteract this effect by also writing an out-
of-the-money option to cover the cost of the option that he bought.
Then, he will not only make money if the stock performs as expected,
but will also make money if the stock remains relatively unchanged.
He will lose quite heavily, however, if the underlying stock goes in the
opposite direction from his original anticipation. That is why he must
have a definite opinion on the stock and also be fairly certain of his
timing.

CHAPTER **22**

# *Basic Put Spreads*

## *PUT SPREADS*

Put spreading strategies do not differ substantially in theory from their accompanying call spread strategies. Both bullish and bearish positions can be constructed with put spreads, as was also the case with call spreads. However, because puts are more oriented toward downward stock movement than calls are, some bearish put spread strategies are superior to their equivalent bearish call spread strategies.

The three simplest forms of option spreads are the bull spread, the bear spread, and the calendar spread. The same types of spreads that were constructed with calls can be established with puts, but there are some differences.

## *BEAR SPREAD*

In a call bear spread, a call with a lower striking price was sold while a call at a higher striking price was bought. The same thing is true for puts—*a put bear spread is established by selling a put at a lower strike while buying a put at a higher strike.* The put bear spread is a debit spread. This is true because a put with a *higher* striking price will sell for more than a put with a lower striking price. Thus on a stock with both puts and calls trading, one could set up a bear spread for a credit (using calls) or alternatively set one up for a debit (using puts):

| Put Bear Spread | Call Bear Spread |
|---|---|
| Buy XYZ January 60 put | Buy XYZ January 60 call |
| Sell XYZ January 50 put | Sell XYZ January 50 call |
| (debit spread) | (credit spread) |

The put bear spread has the same sort of profit potential as the call bear spread. There is a limited maximum potential profit and this profit would be realized if XYZ were below the lower striking price at expiration. The put spread would widen, in this case, to equal the difference between the striking prices. The maximum risk is also limited and would be realized if XYZ were anywhere above the higher striking price at expiration.

*Example:* The following prices exist:

   XYZ common, 55;

   XYZ January 50 put, 2; and

   XYZ January 60 put, 7.

Buying the January 60 put and selling the January 50 would establish a bear spread for a 5-point debit. Table 22-1 will help verify that this is indeed a bearish position. The reader will note that Figure 22-1 has the same shape as the call bear spread's graph (Figure 8-1). The investment required for this spread is the net debit, and it must be paid in full. Notice that *the maximum profit potential is realized anywhere below 50 at expiration, and the maximum risk potential is realized anywhere above 60 at expiration.* The maximum risk is always equal to the initial debit

**TABLE 22-1.** *Put bear spread.*

| XYZ Price at Expiration | January 50 Put Profit | January 60 Put Profit | Total Profit |
|---|---|---|---|
| 40 | −$800 | +$1,300 | +$500 |
| 45 | − 300 | + 800 | + 500 |
| 50 | + 200 | + 300 | + 500 |
| 55 | + 200 | − 200 | 0 |
| 60 | + 200 | − 700 | − 500 |
| 70 | + 200 | − 700 | − 500 |
| 80 | + 200 | − 700 | − 500 |

FIGURE 22-1. *Put bear spread.*

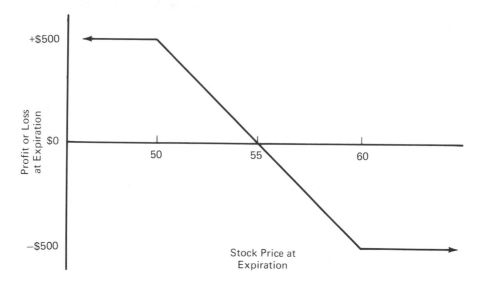

required to establish the spread. The break-even point is 55 in this example. The following formulae allow one to quickly compute the meaningful statistics regarding a put bear spread.

Maximum risk = initial debit

Maximum profit = difference between strikes − initial debit

Break-even price = higher striking price − initial debit

Put bear spreads have an advantage over call bear spreads. With puts, one is selling an out-of-the-money option when setting up the spread. Thus *one is not risking early exercise of his written option before the spread becomes profitable.* For the written put to be in-the-money, and thus in danger of being exercised, the spread would have to be profitable, because the stock would have to be below the lower striking price. Such is not the case with call bear spreads. In the call spread, one sells an in-the-money call as part of the bear spread, and thus could be at risk of early exercise before the spread has a chance to become profitable.

Besides this difference in the probability of early exercise, the put bear spread holds another advantage over the call bear spread. *In the put spread, if the underlying stock drops quickly, the spread will normally widen quickly as well.* This is because—as has been mentioned previously—put options tend to lose time value premium rather quickly when they go into-the-money. In the example above, if XYZ rapidly dropped to 48, the January 60 put would be near 12, retaining very little time premium. However, the January 50 put which is short would also not retain much time value premium, perhaps selling at 4 points or so. Thus the spread would have widened to 8 points. Call bear spreads often do not produce a similar result on a short-term downward movement. Since the call spread involves being short a call with a lower striking price, this call may actually pick up time value premium as the stock falls close to the lower strike. Thus, even though the call spread might have a similar profit *at expiration,* it often will not perform as well on a quick downward movement.

For these two reasons—less chance of early exercise and better profits on a short-term movement—the put bear spread is superior to the call bear spread. Some investors still prefer to use the call spread, since it is established for a credit and thus does not require a cash investment. This is a rather weak reason to avoid the superior put spread and should not be an overriding consideration. Note that the margin requirement for a call bear spread will result in a reduction of one's buying power by an amount approximately equal to the debit required for a similar put bear spread (the margin required for a call bear spread is the difference in the striking prices less the credit received from the spread). Thus the only accounts that gain any substantial advantage from a credit spread are those that are near the minimum equity requirement to begin with. For most brokerage firms, the minimum equity requirement for spreads is $2,000.

## BULL SPREAD

*A bull spread can be established with put options by buying a put at a lower striking price and simultaneously selling a put with a higher striking price.* This, again, is the same way that a bull spread was constructed with calls—selling the higher strike and buying the lower strike.

*Example:* The same prices can be used:

XYZ common, 55;

XYZ January 50 put, 2; and

XYZ January 60 put, 7.

The bull spread is constructed by buying the January 50 put and selling the January 60 put. This would be a credit spread. The credit is five points in this example. If the underlying stock advances by January expiration, and is anywhere above 60 at that time, the maximum profit potential of the spread will be realized. In that case, with XYZ anywhere above 60, both puts would expire worthless and the spreader would make a profit of the entire credit—5 points in this example. Thus *the maximum profit potential is limited, and the maximum profit occurs if the underlying stock rises in price.* These are the same qualities that were displayed by a call bull spread (Chapter 7). The name "bull spread" is derived from the fact that this is a bullish position—that the strategist wants the underlying stock to rise in price.

The risk is limited in this spread. If the underlying stock should decline by expiration, the maximum loss will be realized with XYZ anywhere below 50 at that time. The risk is five points in this example. To see this, note that if XYZ were anywhere below 50 at expiration, the differential between the two puts would widen to 10 points, since that is the difference in their striking prices. Thus the spreader would have to pay 10 points to buy the spread back, or to close out the position. Since he initially took in a 5-point credit, this means his loss is equal to 5 points—the 10-point cost of closing out less the 5 points he initially received.

The investment required for a bullish put spread is actually a collateral requirement since the spread is a credit spread. The amount of collateral required is equal to the difference in the striking prices less the net credit received for the spread. In this example, the collateral requirement would be $500—the $1,000, or 10-point differential in the striking prices less the $500 credit received from the spread. Note that *the maximum possible loss is always equal to the collateral requirement in a bullish put spread.*

There is a break-even point in a bullish spread. In this example, the break-even point before commissions would be 55 at expiration. With XYZ at 55 in January, the January 50 put would expire worthless and the January 60 put would have to be bought back for 5 points. It would be 5 points in-the-money with XYZ at 55. Thus the spreader would break even since he originally received 5 points credit for the spread and would then pay out 5 points to close the spread. The following formulae allow one to quickly compute the details of a bullish put spread.

Maximum potential risk = initial collateral requirement
          = difference in striking prices − net credit received

Maximum potential profit = net credit

Break-even price = higher striking price − net credit

*In general, bullish call spreads are superior to bullish put spreads.* This is mostly due to the fact that in a bullish call spread one is selling an out-of-the-money option, while in a bullish put spread he is selling an in-the-money option. This means that the put spread, which contains a short in-the-money option, is much more subject to early exercise than is the call spread. The early exercise could come before the spread is profitable, thus causing the position to be terminated early at a loss. Such is not the case with a bullish call spread, since the written option would not be in-the-money until the stock was in the maximum profit area—above the higher strike.

## CALENDAR SPREADS

In a calendar spread, a near-term option is sold and a longer-term option is bought, both with the same striking price. This definition applies to either a put or a call calendar spread. In Chapter 9, it was shown that there were two types of philosophies available for call calendar spreads, either a neutral strategy or a bullish one. Similarly, there are two philosophies available for put calendar spreads: neutral or bearish.

In a neutral calendar spread, one sets up the spread with the idea of closing the spread when the near-term call or put expires. In this type of spread, the maximum profit would be realized if the stock is exactly at the striking price at expiration. The spreader is merely attempting to capitalize on the fact that the time value premium disappears more rapidly from a near-term option than it does from a longer-term one.

> *Example:* XYZ is at 50 and a January 50 put is selling for 2 points while an April 50 put is selling for 3 points. A neutral calendar spread can be established for a 1-point debit by selling the January 50 put and buying the April 50 put. The investment required for this position is the amount of the net debit, and it must be paid for in full. If XYZ is exactly at 50 at January expiration, the January 50 put will expire worthless and the April 50 put will be worth about 2 points. The neutral spreader would then sell the April 50 put for 2 points and take his profit. The profit in this case would be one point before commissions—he originally paid a 1-point debit to set up the spread and then liquidates the position by selling the April 50 put for 2 points. Since commission costs can substantially cut into available profits, spreads should be established in a large enough quantity to minimize the percentage cost of commissions. This would mean that at least ten spreads should be set up initially.

In any type of calendar spread, *the risk is limited to the amount of the net debit.* This maximum loss would be realized if the underlying stock moved substantially far away from the striking price by the time the near-term option expires. If this happened, both options would trade at nearly the same price and the differential would shrink to practically nothing, the worst case for the calendar spreader. For example, if the underlying stock drops very substantially, say to 20, both the near-term and the longer-term put would trade at nearly 30 points. On the other hand, if the underlying stock rose substantially, say to 80, both puts would trade at a very low price—say 1/16 or 1/8—and again the spread would shrink to nearly zero.

*Neutral call calendar spreads are generally superior to neutral put calendar spreads.* Since the amount of time value premium is usually greater in a call option (unless the underlying stock pays a large dividend), the spreader who is interested in selling time value would be better off utilizing call options.

The second philosophy of calendar spreading is a more aggressive one. *With put options, a bearish strategy can be constructed using a calendar spread.* In this case one would establish the spread with out-of-the-money puts.

> *Example:* With XYZ at 55, one would sell the January 50 put for 1 point and buy the April 50 put for 1½ points. He would then like the underlying stock to remain above the striking price until the near-term January put expires. If this happens, he would make the 1-point profit from the sale of that put, reducing his net cost for the April 50 put to ½ point. Then, he would become bearish, hoping for the underlying stock to decline in price substantially before April expiration in order that he might be able to generate large profits on the April 50 put that he holds.

Just as the bullish calendar spread with calls can be a relatively attractive strategy, so can the bearish calendar spread with puts. Granted, two criteria have to be fulfilled in order for the position to work to the optimum—the near-term put must expire worthless and then the underlying stock must drop in order to generate profits on the long side. Although these conditions may not occur frequently, one profitable situation can more than make up for several losing ones. This is true because the initial debit for a bearish calendar spread is small—½ point in the example above. Thus the losses will be small and the potential profits could be very large if things work out right.

The aggressive spreader must be careful *not* to "leg out" of his spread, since he could generate a large loss by doing so. The object of the strategy is to accept a rather large number of small losses, with the idea that the infrequent large profits will more than offset the sum of the losses. If one generates a large loss somewhere along the way, this may ruin the overall strategy. Also, if the underlying stock should fall to the striking price before the near-term put expires, the spread will normally have widened enough to produce a small profit, and that profit should be taken by closing the spread at that time.

CHAPTER **23**

# Spreads
# Combining
# Calls and Puts

Certain types of spreads can be constructed that utilize both puts and calls. One of these strategies has been discussed before—the butterfly spread. However, other strategies exist that uniquely offer potentially large profits to the spreader. These other strategies are all variations of calendar spreads and/or straddles that involve both put and call options.

## THE BUTTERFLY SPREAD

This is a strategy that has been described previously, although its usage in Chapter 10 was restricted to constructing the spread with calls only. Recall that the butterfly spread is a neutral position that has limited risk as well as limited profits. The position involves three striking prices by utilizing a bull spread between the lower two strikes and also a bear spread between the higher two strikes. The maximum profit is realized at the middle strike at expiration, and the maximum loss is realized if the stock is above the higher strike or below the lower strike at expiration.

Since either a bull spread or a bear spread can be constructed with puts or calls, it should be obvious that a butterfly spread (consisting of both a bull spread and a bear spread) can be constructed in a number of ways. In fact, there are four ways in which the spread can be established. If option prices are fairly balanced—that is, the arbitrageurs are keeping prices in line—any of the four ways will have the same potential profits and losses at expiration of the options. However, because of the ways in which puts and calls behave prior to their expiration, there are certain advantages or disadvantages connected with some of the methods of establishing the butterfly spread.

*Example:* the following prices exist:

| XYZ common: | | 60 | |
|---|---|---|---|
| Strike: | 50 | 60 | 70 |
| Call: | 12 | 6 | 2 |
| Put: | 1 | 5 | 11 |

The method using only the calls indicates that one would buy the call at 50, sell two calls at 60, and buy the call at 70. Thus there would be a bull spread in the calls between the 50 and 60 strikes, and a bear spread in the calls between the 60 and 70 strikes. In a similar manner, one could establish a butterfly spread by combining either type of bull spread between the 50 and 60 strikes with any type of bear spread between the 60 and 70 strikes. Some of these spreads would be credit spreads, while others would be debit spreads. In fact, one's personal choice between two rather equivalent makeups of the butterfly spread might be decided by whether there were a credit or debit involved.

**TABLE 23-1.** *Butterfly spread.*

| *Bull Spread*<br>*(Buy Option at 50,* ... *plus* ... *Sell at 60)* | *Bear Spread*<br>*(Buy Option at 70,*<br>*Sell at 60)* | *Total Money* |
|---|---|---|
| Calls (6 debit) | Calls (4 credit) | 2 debit |
| Calls (6 debit) | Puts (6 debit) | 12 debit |
| Puts (4 credit) | Calls (4 credit) | 8 credit |
| Puts (4 credit) | Puts (6 debit) | 2 debit |

Table 23-1 summarizes the four ways in which the butterfly spread might be constructed. In order to verify the debits and credits listed, the reader should recall that a bull spread consists of buying a lower strike and selling a higher strike, whether puts or calls are used. Similarly, bear spreads with either puts or calls consist of buying a higher strike and selling a lower strike.

In each of the spreads above, the maximum potential profit at expiration is 8 points if the underlying stock is exactly at 60 at that time. The maximum possible loss in any of the four spreads is 2 points, if the stock is above 70 at expiration or is below 50 at expiration. For example, either the top line in the table, where the spread is set up only with calls, or the bottom line, where the spread is set up only with puts, has a risk equal to the debit involved—2 points. The large debit spread (second line of table) will be able to be liquidated for a minimum of 10 points at expiration, no matter where the stock is, so the risk is also 2 points (it cost 12 points to begin with). Finally, the credit combination (third line) has a maximum buy-back of 10 points, so it also has risk of 2 points. In addition, since the striking prices are 10 points apart, the maximum potential profit is 8 points (maximum profit = striking price differential minus maximum risk) in all the cases.

The factor that causes all these combinations to be equal in risk and reward is the arbitrageur. If put and call prices get too far out of line, the arbitrageur can take riskless action to force them back. This particular form of arbitrage, known as the box spread, is described in Chapter 27.

Even though all four ways of constructing the butterfly spread are equal at expiration, some are superior to others for certain price movements prior to expiration. Recall that it was previously stated that bull spreads are best constructed with calls, and bear spreads are best constructed with puts. Since the butterfly spread is merely the combination of a bull spread and a bear spread, the best way to set up the butterfly spread is to use calls for the bull spread and puts for the bear spread. This combination is the one listed on the second line of Table 23-1. This strategy involves the largest debit of the four combinations, and as a result, many investors shun this approach. However, all the other combinations involve selling an in-the-money put or call at the outset, a situation that could lead to early exercise. The reader may also recall that the credit combination, listed on the third line of Table 23-1, was previously described as a protected straddle position. That is, one sells a straddle and simultaneously buys both an out-of-the-money put and an out-of-the-money call with the same expiration month as protection for the straddle. Thus a butterfly spread is actually the equivalent of a completely protected straddle write.

Butterfly spreads are not an overly attractive strategy, although they may be useful from time to time. The commissions required are extremely high and there is no chance of making a large profit on the position. The limited risk feature is good to have in a position, but it alone cannot compensate for the less attractive features of the strategy. Essentially, the strategist is looking for the stock to remain in a neutral pattern until the options expire. If the potential profit is at least three times the maximum risk (and preferably four times) and the underlying stock appears to be in a trading range, the strategy is feasible. Otherwise, it is not.

## THREE USEFUL, BUT COMPLEX, STRATEGIES

The three strategies to be presented in this section are all designed to limit risk while allowing for large potential profits if correct market conditions develop. Each is a combination strategy—that is, it involves both puts and calls—and each is a calendar strategy, in which near-term options are sold and longer-term options are bought. A fourth strategy that is similar in nature to those about to be discussed will be presented in Chapter 24. Although all of these are somewhat complex, and are for the most advanced strategist, they do provide attractive risk/reward opportunities. In addition, they are strategies that are able to be employed by the public customer—they are not designed strictly for professionals. All three strategies will be described conceptually before specific selection criteria are presented in a later section.

### A Two-Pronged Attack (The Calendar Combination)

A bullish calendar spread was shown to be a rather attractive strategy. A bullish call calendar spread is established with out-of-the-money calls for a relatively small debit. If the near-term call expires worthless and the stock then rises substantially before the longer-term call expires, the potential profits could be large. In any case, the risk is limited to the small debit required to establish the spread. In a similar manner, the bearish calendar spread which uses put options can be an attractive strategy as well. In this strategy, one would set up the spread with out-of-the-money puts. He would then want the near-term put to expire worthless, followed by a substantial drop in the stock price in order to profit on the longer-term put.

Since both strategies are attractive by themselves, the combination of the two should be attractive as well. That is, *with a stock midway between two striking prices, one might set up a bullish out-of-the-money call calendar spread and simultaneously establish a bearish out-of-the-money put calendar spread.* If the stock remains relatively stable, both near-term options would expire worthless. Then a substantial stock price movement *in either direction* could produce large profits. With this strategy, the spreader does not care which direction the stock moves after the near-options expire worthless—he only hopes that the stock becomes volatile and moves a large distance in either direction.

*Example:* Suppose that the following prices exist 3 months before the January options expire:

| XYZ common: | | 65 | |
|---|---|---|---|
| January 70 call: | 3 | January 60 put: | 2 |
| April 70 call: | 5 | April 60 put: | 3 |

The bullish portion of this combination of calendar spreads would be set up by selling the shorter-term January 70 call for 3 points and simultaneously buying the longer-term April 70 call for 5 points. This portion of the spread requires a two-point debit. The bearish portion of the spread would be constructed using the puts. The near-term January 60 put would be sold for 2 points while the longer-term April 60 put would be bought for 3. Thus the put portion of the spread is a 1-point debit. Overall, then, the combination of the calendar spreads requires a 3-point debit, plus commissions. This debit is the required investment—no additional collateral is required. Since there are four options involved, the commision cost will be large. Again, establishing the spreads in quantity can reduce the percentage cost of commissions.

Note that all the options involved in this position are initially out-of-the-money. The stock is below the striking price of the calls and is above the striking price of the puts. One has sold a near-term put and call combination and purchased a longer-term combination. For nomenclature purposes, this strategy is called a "calendar combination."

There are a variety of possible outcomes from this position. First, it should be understood that *the risk is limited to the amount of the initial debit*—three points in this example. If the underlying stock should rise dramatically or fall dramatically before the near-term options expire, both the call spread and the put spread will shrink to nearly nothing. This would be the least desirable result. In actual practice, the spread would probably have a small positive differential left even after a premature move by the underlying stock so that the probability of a loss of the entire debit would be small.

If the near-term options both expire worthless, a profit will generally exist at that time.

*Example:* If XYZ were still at 65 at January expiration in the prior example, the position should be profitable at that time. The January call and put would expire worthless with XYZ at 65, and the April options might be worth a total of 5 points. The spread could thus be closed for a profit with XYZ at 65 in January, since the April options could be sold for 5 points, and the initial "cost" of the spread was only 3 points. Although commissions would substantially reduce this 2-point gross profit, there would still be a good percentage profit on the overall position. If the strategist decides to take his profit at this time, he would be operating in a conservative manner.

However, the strategist may want to be more aggressive and hold onto the April combination in hope that the stock might experience a substantial movement before those options expire. Should this occur, *the potential profits could be quite large.*

*Example:* If the stock were to undergo a very bullish move and rise to 100 before April expiration, the April 70 call could be sold for 30 points (the April 60 put would expire worthless in that case). Alternatively, if the stock plunged to 30 by April expiration, the put at 60 could be sold for 30 points while the call expired worthless. In either case, the strategist would have made a substantial profit on his initial 3-point investment.

It may be somewhat difficult for the strategist to decide what he wants to do after the near-term options expire worthless. He may be torn between taking the limited profit that is at hand or holding onto the combination that he owns in hopes of larger profits. A reasonable approach for the strategist to take is to do nothing immediately after the near-term options expire worthless. He can hold the longer-term options for some time before they will decay enough to produce a loss in the position. Referring again to the previous example, when the January options expire worthless, the strategist then owns the April combination, which is worth 5 points at that time. He can continue to hold the April options for perhaps 6 or 8 weeks before they decay to a value of three points, even if the stock remains close to 65. At this point, the position could be closed for a net loss of the commission costs involved in the various transactions.

As a general rule, one should be willing to hold the combination, even if this means that he lets a small profit decay into a loss. The reason for this is that *one should give himself the maximum opportunity to realize large profits.* He will probably sustain a number of small losses by doing this, but by giving himself the opportunity for large profits, he has a reasonable chance of having the profits out-distance the losses.

*There is a time to take small profits in this strategy.* This would be when either the puts or the calls were slightly in-the-money as the near-term options expire.

> *Example:* If XYZ moved to 71 just as the January options were expiring, the call portion of the spread should be closed. The January 70 call could be bought back for 1 point and the April 70 call would probably be worth about 5 points. Thus the call portion of the spread could be "sold" for 4 points, enough to cover the entire cost of the position. The April 60 put would not have much value with the stock at 71, but it should be held just in case the stock should experience a large price decline. Similar results would occur on the put side of the spread if the underlying stock were slightly in-the-money—say at 58 or 59—at January expiration. At no time does the strategist want to risk being assigned on an option that he is short, so he must always close the portion of the position that is in-the-money at near-term expiration. This is only necessary, of course, if the stock has risen above the striking price of the calls or has fallen below the striking price of the puts.

In summary, this is a reasonable strategy if one operates it over a period of time long enough to encompass several market cycles. The strategist must be careful not to place a large portion of his trading capital in the strategy, however, since even though the losses are limited, they still represent his entire net investment. A variation of this strategy, whereby one sells more options than he buys, is described in Chapter 24.

### The Calendar Straddle

Another strategy that combines calendar spreads on both put and call options can be constructed by selling a near-term straddle and simultaneously purchasing a longer-term straddle. Since the time value premium of the near-term straddle will decrease more rapidly than that of the longer-term straddle, one could make profits on a limited investment. This strategy is somewhat inferior to the one described in the previous section, but is interesting enough to examine.

> *Example:* Again, suppose that three months before January expiration, the following prices exist:

| XYZ common: | 40 |
| --- | --- |
| January 40 straddle: 5 | April 40 straddle: 7 |

A calendar spread of the straddles could be established by selling the January 40 straddle and simultaneously buying the April 40 straddle. This would involve a cost of 2 points, the debit of the transaction, plus commissions.

The risk is limited to the amount of this debit *up until the time the near-term straddle expires.* That is, even if XYZ moves up in price by a substantial amount or declines in price by a substantial amount, the worst that can happen is that the difference between the straddle prices shrinks to zero. This could cause one to lose an amount equal to his original debit, plus commissions. *This limit on the risk only applies until the near-term options expire.* If the strategist decides to buy back the near-term straddle and continue to hold the longer-term one, his risk then increases by the cost of buying back the near-term straddle.

*Example:* XYZ is at 43 when the January options expire. The January 40 straddle can now be bought back for 3 points. The April 40 straddle might be selling for 6 points at that time. If the strategist wants to hold on to the April straddle, in hopes that the stock might experience a large price swing, he is free to do so after buying back the January 40 straddle. However, he has now invested a total of 5 points in the position—the original 2-point debit plus the 3 points that he paid to buy back the January 40 straddle. Hence his risk has increased to 5 points. If XYZ were to be at exactly 40 at April expiration, he would lose the entire 5 points. While the probabilities of losing the entire 5 points must be considered small, there is a substantial chance that he might lose more than 2 points—his original debit. Thus he has increased his risk by buying back the near-term straddle and continuing to hold the longer-term one.

*This is actually a neutral strategy.* Recall that when calendar spreads were discussed previously, it was pointed out that one establishes a neutral calendar spread with the stock near the striking price. This is true for either a call calendar spread or a put calendar spread. This strategy—a calendar spread with straddles—is merely the combination of a neutral call calendar spread and a neutral put calendar spread. Moreover, recall that the neutral calendar spreader generally establishes the position with the intention of closing it out once the near-term option expires. He is mainly interested in selling time in an attempt to capitalize on the fact that a near-term option loses time value premium more rapidly than a longer-term option does. The straddle calendar spread should be treated in the same manner. It is generally best to close it out at near-term expiration. If the stock is near the striking price at that time, a profit will generally result. To verify this, refer again to the prices in the preceding paragraph, where XYZ is at 43 at January expiration. The January 40 straddle can be bought back for 3 points and the April 40 straddle can be sold for 6. Thus the differential between the two straddles has widened to 3 points. Since the original differential was 2 points, this represents a profit to the strategist.

*The maximum profit would be realized if XYZ were exactly at the striking price at near-term expiration.* In this case, the January 40 straddle could be bought back for a very small fraction and the April 40 straddle might be worth about 5 points. The differential would have widened from the original 2 points to nearly 5 points in this case.

*This strategy is inferior to the one described in the previous section* (the "calendar combination"). It has unlimited profits only if the strategist is willing to increase his debit, and thus his risk, when the near-term straddle expires. Consequently, this strategy should only be used in cases where the near-term straddle appears to be extremely overpriced. Furthermore, the position should be closed at near-term expiration unless the stock is so close to the striking price at that time that the near-term straddle can be bought back for a fractional price. This fractional buy-back would then give the strategist the opportunity to make large potential profits with only a small increase in his risk. This situation of being able to buy back the near-term straddle at a fractional price will occur very infrequently—much more infrequently than the case where both the out-of-the-money put and call expire worthless in the previous strategy. Thus the "calendar combination" strategy will afford the spreader more opportunities for large profits, and also never forces him to increase his risk.

### Owning a "Free" Combination (The "Diagonal Butterfly Spread")

The strategies described in the previous sections are established for debits. This means that even if the near-term options expire worthless, the strategist still has risk. The long options which he then holds could proceed to expire worthless as well, thereby leaving him with an overall loss equal to his original debit. There is another strategy involving both put and call options that gives the strategist the opportunity to own a "free" combination. That is, the profits from the near-term options could equal or exceed the entire cost of his long-term options.

*This strategy consists of selling a near-term straddle and simultaneously purchasing both a longer-term, out-of-the-money call and a longer-term, out-of-the-money put. This differs from the protected straddle write previously described in that the long options have a more distant maturity than do the short options.*

*Example:*

| XYZ common: | 40 |
|---|---|
| April 35 put: | 1½ |
| January 40 straddle: | 7 |
| April 45 call: | 2½ |

If one were to sell the short-term January 40 straddle for 7 points and simultaneously purchase the out-of-the-money put and call combination—April 35 put and April 45 call—*he would establish a credit spread.* The credit for the position is 3 points less commissions, since 7 points are brought in from the straddle sale and 4 points are paid for the out-of-the-money combination. Note that the position technically consists of a bearish spread in the calls—buy the higher strike and sell the lower strike—coupled with a bullish spread in the puts—buy the lower strike and sell the higher strike. The investment required is in the form of collateral since both spreads are credit spreads, and is equal to the differential in the striking prices, less the net credit received. In this example, then, the investment would be 10 points for the striking price differential (5 points for the calls and 5 points for the puts) less the 3-point credit received, for a total collateral requirement of $700, plus commissions.

The potential results from this position may vary widely. However, *the risk is limited before near-term expiration.* If the underlying stock should advance substantially before January expiration, the puts would be nearly worthless and the calls would both be trading near parity. With the calls at parity, the strategist would have to pay, at most, 5 points to close the call spread since the striking prices of the calls are 5 points apart. In a similar manner, if the underlying stock had declined substantially before the near-term January options expired, the calls would be nearly worthless and the puts would be at parity. Again, it would cost a maximum of 5 points to close the put spread since the difference in the striking prices of the puts is also 5 points. The worst result would be a 2-point loss in this example—3 points of credit were initially received and the most that the strategist would have to pay to close the position is 5 points. This is the theoretical risk. In actual practice, it is very unlikely that the calls would trade as much as 5 points apart, even if the underlying stock advanced by a large amount, because the longer-term call should retain some small time value premium even if it is deeply in-the-money. A similar analysis might apply to the puts. The risk can always be quickly computed as being equal to the difference in two contiguous striking prices (two strikes next to each other), less the net credit received.

*The strategist's objective with this position is to be able to buy back the near-term straddle for a price less than the original credit received.* If he can do this, he will own the longer-term combination for *free.*

> *Example:* Near January expiration, the strategist is able to repurchase the January 40 straddle for 2 points. Since he initially received a 3-point credit and is then able to buy back the written straddle for 2 points, he is left with an overall credit in the position of 1 point, less commissions. Once he has done this, the strategist retains the long options, the April 35 put and April 45 call. *If the underlying stock should then advance substantially or decline substantially, he could make very large profits.* However, even if the long combination expires worthless, the strategist still makes a profit since he was able to buy the straddle back for less than the amount of the original credit.

In this example, the strategist's objective is to buy back the January 40 straddle for less than 3 points, since that is the amount of the initial credit. At expiration, this would mean that the stock would have to be between 37 and 43 for the buy-back to be made for 3 points or less. Although it is possible, certainly, that the stock will be in this fairly narrow range at near-term expiration, it is not probable. However, the strategist who is willing to add to his risk slightly can often achieve the same result by "legging out" of the January 40 straddle. It has repeatedly been stated that one should not attempt to leg out of a spread, but this is an exception to that rule, since one owns a long combination and therefore is protected, so he is not subjecting himself to large risks by attempting to "leg out" of the straddle that he has written.

> *Example:* XYZ rallies before January expiration and the January 40 put drops to a price of ½ during the rally. Even though there is time remaining until expiration, the strategist might decide to buy back the put

at ½. This could potentially increase his overall risk by ½ point if the stock continues to rise. However, if the stock then reversed itself and fell, he could attempt to buy the call back at 2½ points or less. In this manner, he would still achieve his objective of buying the short-term straddle back for 3 points or less. In fact, he might be able to close both sides of the straddle well before near-term expiration if the underlying stock first moves quickly in one direction and then reverses direction by a large amount.

The maximum risk and the optimum potential objectives have been described, but there are also interim results that might occur in this strategy.

> *Example:* XYZ is at 44 at January expiration. The January 40 straddle must be bought back for 4 points. This means that the long combination will not be owned free, but will have a cost of 1 point plus commissions. The strategist, at this time, must decide if he wants to hold on to the April options or if he wants to sell them, possibly producing a small overall profit on the entire position. There is no iron-clad rule in this type of situation. If the decision is made to hold on to the longer-term options, the strategist realizes that he has assumed additional risk by doing so. Nevertheless, he may decide that it is worth owning the long combination at a relatively low cost. The cost in this example would be 1 point, plus commissions, since he paid 4 points to buy back the straddle after only taking in a 3-point credit initially. The more expensive the buy-back of the near-term straddle is, the more the strategist should be readily willing to sell his long options at the same time. For example, if XYZ were at 48 at January expiration and the January 40 straddle had to be bought back for 8 points, there should be no question that he should simultaneously sell his April options as well. The most difficult decisions come when the stock is just outside the optimum buy-back area at near-term expiration. In this example, the strategist would have a fairly difficult decision if XYZ were in the 44 to 45 area or in the 35 to 36 area at January expiration.

The reader may recall that, back in Chapter 14, it was mentioned that one is sometimes able to own a call free by entering into a diagonal credit spread. A diagonal bear spread was given as an example. The same thing happens to be true of a diagonal bullish put spread, since that is a credit spread as well. The strategy being discussed in this section is merely a combination of a diagonal bearish call spread and a diagonal bullish put spread *and is known as a "diagonal butterfly spread."* The same concept that was described in Chapter 14—being able to make more on the short-term call than one originally paid for the long-term call—applies here as well. *One enters into a credit position with the hopes of being able to buy back the near-term written options for a profit greater than the cost of the long options.* If he is able to do this, he will own options for free and could make large profits if the underlying stock moves substantially in either direction. Even if the stock does not move after the buy-back, he still has no risk. *The risk occurs prior to the expiration of the near-term options, but this risk is limited.* As a result, this is an attractive strategy that, when operated over a period of market cycles, should produce some large profits. Ideally, these profits would offset any small losses that had to be taken. Since there are large commission costs involved in this strategy, the strategist is reminded that establishing the spreads in quantity can help to reduce the percentage effect of the commissions.

## SELECTING THE SPREADS

Now that the concepts of these three strategies have been laid out, let us define selection criteria for them. The "calendar combination" is the easiest one of these strategies to spot. One would like to have the stock nearly halfway between two striking prices. The most attractive positions can normally be found where the striking prices are at least 10 points apart and the underlying stock is relatively volatile. The optimum time to establish the "calendar combination" is two or three months before the near-term options expire. Additionally, one would like the sum of the prices of the near-term options to be equal to at least one-half of the cost of the longer-term options. In the example given in the previous section on the "calendar combination," the near-term combination was sold for 5 points, while the longer-term combination was bought for 8 points. Thus the near-term combination was worth more than one-half of the cost of the longer-term combination. These five criteria can be summarized as follows:

1. Relatively volatile stock.
2. Stock price nearly midway between two strikes.
3. Striking prices at least 10 points apart.
4. 2 or 3 months remaining until near-term expiration.
5. Price of near-term combination greater than one-half the price of the longer-term combination.

Even though 5 criteria have been stated, it is relatively easy to find a position that satisfies all five conditions. The strategist may also be able to rely upon technical input. If the stock seems to be in a near-term trading range, the position may be more attractive, for that would indicate that the chances of the near-term combination expiring worthless are enhanced.

The "calendar straddle" is a strategy that looks deceptively attractive. As the reader should know by now, options do not decay in a linear fashion. Instead, options will tend to hold time value premium until they get quite close to expiration, when the time value premium disappears at a fast rate. Consequently, the sale of a near-term straddle and the simultaneous purchase of a longer-term straddle will often appear to be attractive because the debit seems small. Again, certain criteria can be set forth that will aid in selecting a reasonably attractive position. The stock should be at or very near the striking price when the position is established. Since this is basically a neutral strategy—one that offers the largest potential profits at near-term expiration—one should want to sell the most time premium possible. This is why the stock must be near the striking price initially. The underlying stock does not have to be a volatile one, although volatile stocks will most easily satisfy the next two criteria. The near-term credit should be at least two-thirds of the longer-term debit. In the example used to explain this strategy, the near-term straddle was sold for 5, while the longer-term straddle was bought for 7 points. Thus the near-term straddle was worth more than two-thirds of the longer-term straddle's price. Finally, the position should be established with two to four months remaining until near-term expiration. If positions with a longer time remaining are used, there is a significant probability that the underlying stock will have moved some distance away from the striking price by the time the near-term options expire. Summarizing, the three criteria for a "calendar straddle" are:

1. Stock near striking price initially.
2. 2 to 4 months remaining until near-term expiration.
3. Near-term straddle price at least two-thirds of longer-term straddle price.

The "diagonal butterfly" is the most difficult of these three types of positions to locate. Again, one would like the stock to be near the middle striking price when the position is established. Also, one would like the underlying stock to be somewhat volatile, since there is the possibility that long-term options will be owned for free. If this comes to pass, the strategist wants the stock to be capable of a large move in order to have a chance of generating large profits. The most restrictive criterion—one that will eliminate all but a few possibilities on a daily basis—is that the near-term straddle price should be at least one and one-half times that of the longer-term, out-of-the-money combination. By adhering to this criterion, one gives himself a reasonable chance of being able to buy the near-term straddle back for a price low enough to result in owning the longer-term options for free. In the example used to describe this strategy, the near-term straddle was sold for 7 while the out-of-the-money, longer-term combination cost 4 points. This satisfies the criterion. Finally, one should limit his possible risk before near-term expiration. Recall that the risk is equal to the difference in any two contiguous striking prices less the net credit received. In the example, the risk would be 5 minus 3, or 2 points. The risk should always be less than the credit taken in. This precludes selling a near-term straddle at 80 for 4 points and buying the put at 60 and the call at 100 for a combined cost of 1 point. Although the credit is substantially more than one and one-half times the cost of the long combination, the risk would be ridiculously high. The risk, in fact, is 20 points (the difference in two contiguous striking prices) less the 3 points credit, or 17 points—much too high.

The criteria can be summarized as follows:

1. Stock near middle striking price initially.
2. Three to four months to near-term expiration.
3. Price of written straddle at least one and one-half times that of the cost of the longer-term, out-of-the-money combination.
4. Risk before near-term expiration less than the net credit received.

One way in which the strategist may notice this type of position is when he sees a relatively short-term straddle selling at what seems to be an outrageously high price. Professionals, who often have a good feel for a stock's short-term potential, will sometimes bid up straddles when the stock is about to make a volatile move. This will cause the near-term straddles to be very overpriced. When a straddle seller notices that a particular straddle looks too attractive as a sale, he should consider establishing a diagonal butterfly spread instead. He still sells the overpriced straddle, but also buys a longer-term, out-of-the-money combination as a hedge against large loss. Both factions can be right. Perhaps the stock will experience a very short-term volatile movement, proving that the professionals were correct. However, this will not worry the strategist holding a diagonal butterfly, for he has limited risk. Once the short-term move is over, the stock may drift back toward the original strike, allowing the near-term straddle to be bought back at a low price—the eventual objective of the strategist utilizing the diagonal butterfly spread.

These are admittedly three quite complex strategies and thus are not to be attempted by a novice investor. If one wants to gain experience in how he would operate such a strategy, it would be far better to operate a "paper strategy" for a while. That is, one would not actually make investments, but would instead follow prices in the newspaper and make day-to-day decisions without actual risk. This will allow the inexperienced strategist to gain a feel for how these complex strategies perform over a particular time period. The astute investor can, of course, obtain price history information and track a number of market cycles in this same way.

## SUMMARY

These three various types of strategies that involve calendar combination of puts and calls may all be attractive. One should be especially alert for these types of positions when near-term calls are overpriced. Typically, this would be during, or just after, a bullish period in the stock market. For nomenclature purposes, these three strategies are called the "calendar combination," the "calendar straddle," and the "diagonal butterfly."

All three strategies offer the possibility of large potential profits if the underlying stock remains relatively stable until the near-term options expire. In addition, all three strategies have limited risk, even if the underlying stock should move explosively in either direction prior to near-term expiration. If an intermediate result occurs—for example, the stock moves a moderate distance in either direction before near-term expiration—it is still possible to realize a limited profit in any of the strategies, because of the fact that the time premiums will decay much more rapidly in the near-term options than they will in the longer-term options.

The three strategies have many things in common, but each one has its own advantages and disadvantages. The "diagonal butterfly" is the only one of the three strategies where the strategist has a possibility of owning free options. Admittedly, the probability of actually being able to own the options completely for free is small. However, there is a relatively large probability that one can substantially reduce the cost of the long options. The "calendar combination"—the first of the three strategies discussed—offers the largest probability of capturing the entire near-term premium. This is because both near-term options are out-of-the-money to begin with. The "calendar straddle" offers the largest potential profits at near-term expiration. That is, if the stock is relatively unchanged from the time the position was established until the time that the near-term options expire, the "calendar straddle" will show the best profit of the three strategies at that time.

Looking at the negative side, the "calendar straddle" is the least attractive of the three strategies, primarily because one is forced to increase his risk after near-term expiration, if he wants to continue to hold the longer-term options. It is often difficult to find a "diagonal butterfly" which offers enough credit to make the position attractive. Finally, the "calendar combination" has the largest probability of losing the entire debit eventually, because one may find that the longer-term options expire worthless also (they are out-of-the-money to begin with, just as the near-term options were).

The strategist will not normally be able to find a large number of these positions available at attractive price levels at any particular time in the market. However, since they are attractive strategies with little or no margin collateral requirements, the strategist should constantly be looking for these types of positions. A certain amount of cash or collateral should be reserved for the specific purpose of utilizing it for these types of positions—perhaps 15 to 20% of one's dollars.

# Ratio Spreads Using Puts $24$

The put option spreader may want to sell more puts than he owns. This creates a ratio spread. Basically, there are two types of put ratio spreads that may prove to be attractive: the standard ratio put spread and the ratio calendar spread using puts. Both strategies are designed for the more aggressive investor, but, when operated properly, can both present attractive reward opportunities.

## THE RATIO PUT SPREAD

This strategy is designed for a neutral to slightly bearish outlook on the underlying stock. In a ratio put spread, one buys a number of puts at a higher strike and sells more puts at a lower strike. This position involves naked puts, since one is short more puts than he is long. *There is limited upside risk in the position,* but the downside risk can be very large. The maximum profit can be obtained if the stock is exactly at the striking price of the written puts at expiration.

*Example:* Given the following:

XYZ common, 50;

XYZ January 45 put, 2; and

XYZ January 50 put, 4.

A ratio put spread might be established by buying one January 50 put and simultaneously selling two January 45 puts. Since one would be paying $400 for the purchased put and would be collecting $400 from the sale of the two out-of-the-money puts, the spread could be done for even money. There is no upside risk in this position. If XYZ should rally and be above 50 at January expiration, all the puts would expire worthless and the result would be a loss of commissions. However, there is downside risk. If XYZ should fall by a great deal, one would have to pay much more to buy back the two short puts than he would receive from selling out the one long put. The maximum profit would be realized if XYZ were at 45 at expiration, since the short puts would expire worthless, but the long January 50 put would be worth 5 points and could be sold at that price. Table 24-1 and Figure 24-1 summarize the position. Note that there is a range within which the position is profitable—40 to 50 in this example. If XYZ is above 40 and below 50 at

**TABLE 24-1.** *Ratio put spread.*

| XYZ Price at Expiration | Long January 50 Put Profit | Short 2 January 45 Put Profit | Total Profit |
|---|---|---|---|
| 20 | +$2,600 | −$4,600 | −$2,000 |
| 30 | + 1,600 | − 2,600 | − 1,000 |
| 40 | + 600 | − 600 | 0 |
| 42 | + 400 | − 200 | + 200 |
| 45 | + 100 | + 400 | + 500 |
| 48 | − 200 | + 400 | + 200 |
| 50 | − 400 | + 400 | 0 |
| 60 | − 400 | + 400 | 0 |

**FIGURE 24-1.** *Ratio put spread.*

January expiration, there will be some profit, before commissions, from the spread. Below 40 at expiration, losses will be generated, and, although these losses are limited by the fact that a stock cannot decline in price below zero, these losses could become very large. There is no upside risk, however, as was pointed out earlier. The following formulae summarize the situation for any ratio:

Maximum upside risk = net debit of spread (no upside risk if done for a credit)

Maximum profit potential = striking price differential × number of long puts − net debit (or plus net credit)

Downside break-even price = lower strike price − maximum profit potential ÷ number of naked puts

The investment required for the put ratio spread consists of the collateral requirement necessary for a naked put, plus or minus the credit or debit of the entire position. Since the collateral requirement for a naked option is 30% of the stock price, plus or minus the amount by which the stock is in- or out-of-the-money, the actual dollar requirement in this example would be $1,000 (30% of $5,000 minus the $500 by which the January 45 put is out-of-the-money). As with all types of naked writing positions, the strategist should allow enough collateral for an adverse stock move to occur. This will allow enough room for stock movement without forcing early liquidation of the position due to a margin call. If, in this example, the strategist felt that he might stay with the position until the stock declined to 39, he should allow $1,770 in collateral (30% of $3,900 plus the $600 in-the-money amount).

The ratio put spread is generally most attractive when the underlying stock is initially between the two striking prices. That is, if XYZ were somewhere between 45 and 50, one might find the ratio put spread used in the example attractive. If the stock is initially below the lower striking price, a ratio put spread is not as attractive, since the stock is already too close to the downside risk point. Alternatively, if the stock is too far above the striking price of the written calls, one would have to normally pay a large debit to establish the position. Although one could eliminate the debit by writing four or five short options to each put bought, large ratios have extraordinarily large downside risk and are therefore very aggressive.

Follow-up action is rather simple in the ratio put spread. There is very little that one need do, except for closing the position if the stock breaks below the downside break-even point. Since put options tend to lose time value premium rather quickly after they become in-the-money options, there is not normally an opportunity to roll down. Rather, one should be able to close the position with the puts close to parity if the stock breaks below the downside break-even point. The spreader may want to buy in additional long puts, as was described for call spreads in Chapter 11, but this is not as advantageous in the put spread because of the time value premium shrinkage.

This strategy may prove psychologically pleasing to the less experienced investor because he will not lose money on an upward move by the underlying stock. Many of the ratio strategies that involve call options have upside risk, and there is a large number of investors who do not like to lose money when stocks move up. Thus, although these investors might be attracted to ratio strategies because of the possibility of collecting the profits on the sale of multiple out-of-the-money options, they may often prefer ratio put spreads to ratio call spreads because of the small upside risk in the put strategy.

## USING DELTAS

The "delta spread" concept can also be used for establishing and adjusting neutral ratio put spreads. The delta spread was first described in Chapter 11. A neutral put spread can be constructed by using the deltas of the two put options involved in the spread. The neutral ratio is determined by dividing the delta of the put at the higher strike by the delta of the put at the lower strike. Referring to the previous example, suppose that the delta of the January 45 put is −.30 and the delta of the January 50 put is −.50. Then a neutral ratio would be 1.67 (−.50 divided by −.30). That is, 1.67 puts would be sold for each put bought. One might thus sell 16 January 45 puts and buy 10 January 50 puts.

This type of spread would not change much in price for small fluctuations in the underlying stock price. However, as time passes, the preponderance of time value premium sold via the January 45 puts would begin to turn a profit. As the underlying stock moves up or down by more than a small distance, the neutral ratio between the two puts will change. The spreader can adjust his position back into a neutral one by selling more January 45's or buying more January 50's in order to produce a neutral position once more.

## THE RATIO PUT CALENDAR SPREAD

The ratio put calendar spread consists of buying a longer-term put and selling a larger quantity of shorter-term puts, all with the same striking price. The position is generally established with out-of-the-money puts—that is, the stock is above the striking price—so that there is a greater probability that the near-term puts will expire worthless. Also, the position should be established for a credit, where the money brought in from the sale of the near-term puts more than covers the cost of the longer-term put. If this is done and the near-term puts expire worthless, the strategist will then own the longer-term put free, and large profits could result if the stock subsequently experiences a sizable downward movement.

> *Example:* If XYZ were at 55, and the January 50 put was at 1½ with the April 50 at 2, one could establish a ratio put calendar spread by buying the April 50 and selling two January 50 puts. This would be a credit position, for the sale of the two January 50 puts would bring in $300 while the cost of the April 50 put is only $200. If the stock remains above 50 until January expiration, the January 50 puts will expire worthless and the April 50 put will be owned for free. In fact, even if the April 50 put should then expire worthless, the strategist will make a small profit on the overall position in the amount of his original credit—$100—less commissions. However, after the Januarys have expired worthless, if XYZ should drop dramatically to 25 or 20, a very large profit would accrue on the April 50 put that is still owned.
>
> The risk in the position could be very large if the stock should drop well below 50 before the January puts expire. For example, if XYZ fell to 30 prior to January expiration, one would have to pay $4,000 to buy back the January 50 puts and would only receive $2,000 from selling out his long April 50 put. This would represent a rather large loss. Of course, this type of tragedy can be avoided by taking appropriate follow-up action. *Normally, one would close the position if the stock fell more than 8 to 10% below the striking price before the near-term puts expire.*
>
> As with any type of ratio position, there are naked options involved. This increases the collateral requirement for the position and also means that the strategist should allow enough collateral in order for the follow-up action point to be reached. In this example, the initial requirement would be $1,150 (30% of $5,500 less the $500 by which the naked January 50 put is out-of-the-money). However, if the strategist decides that he will hold the position until XYZ falls to 46, he should allow $1,780 in collateral (30% of $4,600 plus the $400 in-the-money amount). Of course, the $100 credit, less commissions, generated by the initial position can be applied against these collateral requirements.

This strategy is a sensible one for the investor who is willing to accept the risk of writing a naked put. Since the position should be established with the stock above the striking price of the put options, there is a reasonable chance that the near-term puts will expire worthless. This means that some profit will be generated, and that the profit could be large if the stock should then experience a large downward move before the longer-term puts expire. One should take care, however, to limit his losses before near-term expiration, since the eventual large profits will be able to overcome a series of small losses, but could not overcome a preponderance of large losses.

## A LOGICAL EXTENSION
## (THE RATIO CALENDAR COMBINATION)

The previous section demonstrated that ratio put calendar spreads can be attractive. The ratio call calendar spread was described earlier as a reasonably attractive strategy for the bullish investor. A logical combination of these two types of ratio calendar spreads (put and call) would be the *ratio combination*—buying a longer-term out-of-the-money combination and selling several near-term out-of-the-money combinations.

*Example:* The following prices exist:

| | |
|---|---|
| XYZ common: | 55 |
| XYZ January 50 put:  1½ | XYZ April 50 put:  2 |
| XYZ January 60 call:  3½ | XYZ April 60 call:  5 |

One could sell the near-term January combination (January 50 put and January 60 call) for 5 points. It would cost 7 points to buy the longer-term April combination (April 50 put and April 60 call). By selling more January combinations than April combinations bought, a ratio calendar combination could be established. For example, suppose that a strategist sold two of the near-term January combinations, bringing in 10 points, and simultaneously bought one April combination for 7 points. This would be a credit position—a credit of 3 points in this example. If the near-term, out-of-the-money combination expires worthless, a guaranteed profit of 3 points will exist, even if the longer-term options proceed to expire totally worthless. *If the near-term combination expires worthless, the longer-term combination is owned for free, and a large profit could result on a substantial stock price movement in either direction.*

Although this is a superbly attractive strategy if the near-term options do, in fact, expire worthless, it must also be monitored closely so that large losses do not occur. These large losses would be possible if the stock broke out in either direction too quickly—before the near-term options expire. In the absence of a technical opinion on the underlying stock, one can generally compute a stock price where it might be reasonable to take follow-up action. This is a similar analysis to the one described for ratio call calendar spreads in Chapter 12. Suppose the stock in this example began to rally. There would be a point at which the strategist would have to pay 3 points of debit to close the call side of the combination. That would be his break-even point.

> *Example:* With XYZ at 65 at January expiration (5 points above the higher strike of the original combination), the near-term January 60 call would be worth 5 points and the longer-term April 60 call might be worth 7 points. If one closed the call side of the combination, he would have to pay 10 points to buy back two January 60 calls and would receive 7 points from selling out his April 60. This closing transction would be a 3-point debit. This represents a break-even situation up to this point in time, except for commissions, since a 3-point credit was initially taken in. The strategist would continue to hold the April 50 put (the January 50 put would expire worthless) just in case the improbable occurs and the underlying stock plunges below 50 before April expiration. A similar analysis could be performed for the put side of the spread in case of an early downside breakout by the underlying stock. It might be determined that the downside break-even point at January expiration is 46, for example. Thus the strategist has two parameters to work with in attempting to limit losses in case the stock moves by a great deal before near-term expiration: 65 on the upside and 46 on the downside. In practice, if the stock should reach these levels *before*, rather than *at*, January expiration, the strategist would incur a small loss by closing the in-the-money side of the combination. This action should still be taken, however, as *the objective of risk management of this strategy is to take small losses, if necessary.* Eventually, large profits may be generated that could more than compensate for any small losses that were incurred.

The foregoing follow-up action was designed to handle a volatile move by the underlying stock prior to near-term expiration. Another, perhaps more common, time that follow-up action is necessary is when the underlying stock is relatively unchanged at near-term expiration. If XYZ in the example above were near 55 at January expiration, a relatively large profit would exist at that time: the near-term combination would expire worthless for a gain of 10 points on that sale, and the longer-term combination would probably still be worth about 5 points, so that the unrealized loss on the April combination would only be 2 points. This represents a total (realized and unrealized) gain of 8 points. In fact, *as long as the near-term combination can be bought back for less than the original 3-point credit of the position, the position will show a total unrealized gain at near-term expiration.* Should the gain be taken or should the longer-term combination be held in hopes of a volatile move by the underlying stock? Although the strategist will normally handle each position on a case-by-case basis, the general philosophy should be to hold on to the April combination. A profit is already guaranteed at this time—the worst that can happen is a 3-point profit (the original credit). Consequently, the strategist should allow himself the opportunity to make large profits. The strategist may want to attempt to trade out of his long combination, since he will not risk making the position a losing one by doing so. Technical analysis may be able to provide him with buy or sell zones on the stock, and he would then consider selling out his long options in accordance with these technical levels.

In summary, *this strategy is very attractive and should be utilized by strategists who have the expertise to trade in positions with naked options.* As long as risk management principles of taking small losses are adhered to, there will be a large probability of overall profit from this strategy.

## PUT OPTION SUMMARY

This concludes the section on put option strategies. The put option is useful in a variety of situations. First, it represents a more attractive way to take advantage of a bearish attitude with options. Second, the use of the put options opens up a new set of strategies—straddles and combinations—that can present reasonably high levels of profit potential. Many of the strategies that were described in Part II for call options have been discussed again in this part. Some of these strategies were described more fully in terms of philosophy, selection procedures, and follow-up action when they were first discussed. The second description—the one involving put options—was often shortened to a more mechanical description of how puts fit into the strategy. This format is intentional. The reader who is planning to employ a certain strategy that can be established with either puts or calls (a bear spread, for example) should familiarize himself with both applications by a simultaneous review of the call chapter and its analogous put chapter.

The combination strategies generally introduced new concepts to the reader. The combination allows the construction of positions that are attractive with either puts or calls (out-of-the-money calendar spreads, for example) to be combined into one position. The four combination strategies that involved selling short-term options and simultaneously buying longer-term options are complex, but are most attractive in that they have the desirable features of limited risk and large potential profits.

PART **IV**

# Additional Considerations

# Buying Options 25
# and
# Treasury Bills

Numerous strategies have been described, ranging from the simple to the complex. Each one has advantages, but there are disadvantages as well. In fact, some of them may be too complex for the average investor to seriously consider implementing. The reader may feel that there should be an easier answer. Isn't there a strategy that might not require such a large investment or so much time spent in monitoring the position, but would still have a chance of returning a reasonable profit? In fact, there is a strategy that has not yet been described, a strategy considered by some experts in the field of mathematical analysis to be the best of them all. Simply stated, *the strategy consists of putting 90% of one's money in risk-free investments (such as short-term Treasury bills) and buying options with the remaining 10% of one's funds.*

It has been previously pointed out that some of the more attractive strategies are those that involve small levels of risk with the potential for large profits. Usually, these types of strategies inherently have a rather large frequency of small losses, and a small probability of realizing large gains. Their advantage lies in the fact that one or two large profits can conceivably more than make up for numerous small losses. This Treasury-bill/option strategy is another strategy of this type.

## HOW THE TREASURY BILL/OPTION
## STRATEGY OPERATES

Although there are certain details involved in operating this strategy, it is basically a simple one to approach. First, the most that one can lose is 10%, less the interest earned on the fixed-income portion of his portfolio (the remaining 90% of his assets), during the life of the purchased options. It is a simple matter to space out one's commitments to option purchases so that his overall risk in a one-year period can be kept down to nearly 10%.

> *Example:* An investor might decide to put 4% of his money into three-month option purchases. Thus, in any one year, he would be risking 16%. At the same time he would be earning perhaps 6% from the overall interest generated on the fixed-income securities which make up the remaining 90% of his assets. This would keep his overall risk down to approximately 10% per year.

There are better ways to monitor this risk, and they will be described shortly. The potential profits from this strategy are limited only by time. Since one is owning options—say call options—he could profit handsomely from a large upward move in the stock market. As with any strategy in which one has limited risk and the potential of large profits, a small number of large profits could offset a large number of small losses. In actual practice, of course, his profits will never be overwhelming, since only approximately 10% of the money is committed to option purchases.

In total, *this strategy has greatly reduced risk with the potential of making above-average profits.* Since the 10% of the money that is invested in options gives great leverage, it might be possible for that portion to double or triple in a short time under favorable market conditions. This strategy is something like owning a convertible bond. A convertible bond, since it is convertible into the common stock, moves up and down in price with the price of the underlying stock. However, if the stock should fall a great deal, the bond will not follow it all the way down because eventually its yield will provide a "floor" for the price. In fact, there is a strategy that is not used too often, called the "synthetic convertible bond." One buys a debenture and a call option on the same stock. If the stock rises in price, the call does too and so the combination of the debenture and the call acts much like a convertible bond would to the upside. If, on the other hand, the stock falls, the call will expire worthless, but the investor will retain most of his investment because he will still have the debenture plus any interest that the bond has paid. The strategy of placing 90% of one's money into risk-free, interest-bearing certificates and buying options with the remainder is superior to the convertible bond or the "synthetic convertible bond" since there is no risk of price fluctuation in the largest portion of the investment.

The Treasury bill/option strategy is fairly easy to operate, although one does have to do some work every time that new options are purchased. Also, periodic adjustments need to be made to keep the level of risk approximately the same at all times. As for which options to buy, the reader may recall that specific criteria were outlined in Chapters 3 and 16 on how to select the best option purchases. These criteria can be briefly summarized as follows:

1. Assume that each underlying stock can advance or decline in accordance with its volatility over a fixed time period (30, 60, or 90 days).
2. Estimate the call prices after the advance, or put prices after the decline.
3. Rank all potential purchases by the highest reward opportunity.

*The user of this strategy need only be interested in those option purchases which provide the highest reward opportunity* under this ranking method. In the previous chapters on option buying, it was mentioned that one might want to look at the risk/reward ratios of his potential option purchases in order to have a more conservative list. However, that is not necessary in the Treasury bill/option strategy, since the risk has already been accounted for by the inclusion of the Treasury bills in the strategy. A ranking of option purchases via the foregoing criteria will generally give a list of at- or slightly out-of-the-money options. These are not necessarily "underpriced" options, although if an option is truly underpriced, it will have a better chance of ranking higher on the selection list than one that is "overpriced."

A list of potential option purchases that is constructed with criteria similar to those outlined above is available from many data services and brokerage firms. The strategist who is willing to select his option purchases in this manner will find that he does not have to spend a great deal of time in his selection process. The reader should note that *this type of option purchase ranking completely ignores the outlook for the underlying stock.* If one would rather make his purchases based on an outlook for the underlying stock—preferably a technical outlook—he will be forced to spend more time in his selection process. Although this may be appealing to some investors, it will probably yield worse results in the long run than the previously described unbiased approach to option purchases unless the strategist is extremely adept at stock selection.

### Keeping the Risk Level Equal

The second function that the strategist has to perform in this Treasury bill/option strategy is to *keep his risk level approximately equal at all times.*

*Example:* An investor starts the strategy with $90,000 in Treasury bills (T-bills) and $10,000 in option purchases. After some time has passed, the option purchases may have worked out well and perhaps he now has $90,000 in T-bills plus $30,000 worth of options, plus interest from the T-bills. Obviously, he no longer has 90% of his money in fixed-income securities and 10% in option purchases. The ratio is now 75% in T-bills and 25% in option purchases. This is too risky a ratio, and the strategist must consequently sell some of his options and buy T-bills with the proceeds. Since his total assets are $120,000 currently, he must sell out $18,000 of options to bring his option investment down from the current $30,000 figure to $12,000—10% of his total assets. If one fails to adhere to this readjustment of his funds after profits are made, he will eventually lose those profits. Since options can lose a great percentage of their worth in a short time period, the investor is always running the risk that the option portion of his investment may be nearly wiped out. If he has kept all his profits in the option portion of his strategy, he is constantly risking nearly all of his accumulated profits, and that is not wise.

One must also adjust his ratio of T-bills to options after losses occur.

*Example:* In the first year, the strategist loses all of the $10,000 he originally placed in options. This would leave him with total assets of $90,000 plus interest (possibly $6,000 of interest might be earned). He could readjust to a 90:10 ratio by selling out some of the T-bills and using the proceeds to buy options. If one follows this strategy, he will be risking 10% of his funds each year. Thus a series of loss years could depreciate the initial assets, although the net losses in one year would be smaller than 10% because of the interest earned on the T-bills. It is recommended that the strategist pursue this method of readjusting his ratios in both up and down markets in order to constantly provide himself with essentially similar risk/reward opportunities at all times.

The individual can blend the option selection process and the adjustment of the T-bill/option ratio to fit his individual portfolio. The larger portfolio can be diversified into options with differing holding periods, and the ratio adjustments can be made quite frequently, perhaps once a month. The smaller investor should concentrate on somewhat longer holding periods for his options, and would adjust the ratio less often. Some examples might help to illustrate the way in which both the large and small strategist might operate. It should be noted that this T-bill/option strategy is quite adaptable to fairly small sums of money, as long as the 10% that is going to be put into option purchases allows one to be able to participate in a reasonable manner. A tactic for the extremely small investor will also be described below.

### *Annualized Risk*

Before getting into portfolio size, the concept of *annualized risk* will be described. One might want to purchase options with the intent of holding some of them for 30 days, some for 90 days, and some for 180 days. Recall that at any one time he does not want his option purchases to represent more than 10% annual risk. In actual practice, if one purchases an option that has 90 days of life, but he is planning on holding the option only 30 days, he will most likely not lose 100% of his investment in the 30-day period. However, for purposes of computing annualized risk easily, the assumption that will be made is that the risk during any *holding period* is 100%, regardless of the length of time remaining in the life of the option. Thus a 30-day option purchase represents an annualized risk of 1,200% (100% risk every 30 days and there are twelve 30-day periods in one year). Ninety-day purchases have 400% annualized risk, and 180-day purchases have 200% annualized risk. There are multitudes of ways to combine purchases in these three holding periods so that the overall risk is 10% annualized.

*Example:* An investor could put 2½% of his total money into 90-day purchases four times a year. That is, 2½% of his total assets are being subjected to a 400% annualized risk; 400 times 2½% equals 10% annualized risk on the total assets. Of course, the remainder of the assets would be placed in risk-free, income-bearing securities. Another of the many combinations might be to place 1% of the total assets in 90-day purchases and also place 3% of the total assets in 180-day purchases. Thus 1% of one's total money would be subjected to a 400% annual risk and 3% would be subjected to a 200% annual risk. (.01 times 400 plus .03 times 200 equals 10% annualized risk on the entire assets). If one prefers a formula, annualized risk can be computed as:

$$\text{Annualized risk on entire porfolio} = \frac{\text{percent of total}}{\text{assets invested}} \times \frac{360}{\text{holding period}}$$

If one is able to diversify into several holding periods, the annualized risk is merely the sum of the risks for each holding period.

With this information in mind, the strategist can then utilize option purchases of 1 month, 3 months, and 6 months—preferably each generated by a separate computer analysis similar to the one described earlier. He will know how much of his total assets he can place into purchases of each holding period because he will know his annualized risk.

*Example:* A very large investor, or pool of investors, has $1 million committed to this T-bill/option strategy. Further, suppose ½ of 1% of the money is to be committed to 30-day option purchases with the idea of reinvesting every 30 days. Similarly, ½ of 1% is to be placed in 90-day purchases and 1% in 180-day purchases. The annualized risk is 10%:

$$\text{Total annualized risk} = \frac{1}{2}\% \times \frac{360}{30} + \frac{1}{2}\% \times \frac{360}{90} + 1\% \times \frac{360}{180}$$

$$= .06 \quad + \quad .02 \quad + \quad .02 \ = 10\%$$

With assets of $1 million, this means that $5,000 would be committed to 30-day purchases, $5,000 to 90-day purchases, and $10,000 to 180-day purchases. This money would be reinvested in similar quantities at the end of each holding period.

### Risk Adjustment

*The subject of adjusting the ratio to constantly reflect 10% risk must be addressed at the end of each holding period.* Although it is correct for the investor to keep his percentage commitments constant, he must not be deluded into automatically reinvesting the same amount of dollars each time.

*Example:* At the end of 30 days, the value of the entire portfolio, including potential option profits and losses, and interest earned, was down to $990,000. Then only ½ of 1% of *that* amount should be invested in the next 30-day purchase ($4,950).

By operating in this manner—first computing the annualized risk and balancing it through predetermined percentage commitments to holding periods of various lengths, and second, readjusting the actual dollar commitment at the end of each holding period—the overall risk/reward ratios will be kept close to the levels described in the earlier, simple description of this strategy. This may require a relatively large amount of work on the part of the strategist, but large portfolios usually do.

The smaller investor does not have the luxury of such complete diversification, but he also does not have to adjust his total position as often.

*Example:* An investor decided to commit $50,000 to this strategy. Since there is a 1,200% annualized risk in 30-day purchases, it does not make much sense to even consider purchases that are so short-term for assets that are of this size. Rather, he might decide to commit 1% of his assets to a 90-day purchase and 3% to a 180-day purchase. In dollar amounts, this would be $500 in a 90-day option and $1,500 in 180-day options. Admittedly, this does not leave much room for diversification, but to risk more in the short-term purchases would expose the investor to too much risk. In actual practice, this investor would probably just invest 5% of his assets in 180-day purchases, also a 10% annualized risk. This would mean that he would only have to operate with one option buyer's analysis (the 180-day one) and could place $2,500 into selections from that list.

His adjustments of the assets committed to option purchases could not be done as frequently as the large investor, because of the commissions involved. He certainly would have to adjust every 180 days, but might prefer to do so more frequently—perhaps every 90 days—to be able to space his 180-day commitments over different option expiration cycles. It should also be pointed out that T-bills can only be bought and sold in amounts of at least $10,000 and in increments of $5,000 thereafter. That is, one could buy or sell $10,000 or $15,000 or $20,000 or $25,000, and so on, but could not buy or sell $5,000 or $8,000 or $23,000 T-bills. This is of little concern to the investor with $1 million, since it is only a fraction of a percentage of his assets to be able to round up to the next $5,000 increment for a T-bill sale or purchase. However, the medium-sized investor with a $50,000 portfolio might run into problems. While short-term T-bills do represent the best risk-free investment, the medium-sized investor might want to utilize—at least partially—one of the no-load, money market funds for part of his income-bearing assets. Such funds have only slightly more risk than T-bills and offer the ability to deposit and withdraw in any amount.

The truly small investor might be feeling somewhat left out.

Could it be possible to operate this strategy with a very small amount of money, such as $5,000? Yes it could, but there are several disadvantages.

> *Example:* It would be extremely difficult to keep the risk level down to 10% annually with only $5,000. For example, 5% of the money invested every 180 days is only $250 in each investment period. Since the option selection process that is described will tend to select at- or slightly out-of-the-money calls, many of these will cost more than 2½ points for one option. The small investor might decide to raise his risk level slightly, although the risk level should never exceed 20% annually, no matter how small the actual dollar investment. To exceed this risk level would be to completely defeat the whole purpose of the fixed-income/option purchase strategy. Obviously, this small investor cannot buy T-bills, for his total investable assets are below the minimum $10,000 purchase level. He might consider utilizing one of the money market funds, but this could drain him of money that is close at hand at a local bank. The easiest approach for this small investor might be to leave the fixed-income portion of his investable assets in his savings account, only withdrawing the small portion required for option purchases as it becomes necessary. Clearly, an investor of this small magnitude is operating at a double disadvantage—his small dollar commitment to option purchases may preclude him from buying some of the more attractive items, and his fixed-income portion will be earning a smaller percentage interest rate in a savings account than that of the larger investor who is in T-bills or some other form of relatively risk-free, income-bearing security. Consequently, the *small investor should carefully consider his financial capability and willingness to adhere strictly to the criteria of this strategy before actually committing his dollars.*

It may appear to the reader that the actual dollars being placed at risk in each option purchase are quite small in these examples. In fact, they are rather small, but they have been shown to represent 10% annualized risk. An assumption was made in these examples that the risk in each option purchase was 100% for the holding period. This is a fairly restrictive assumption and, if it were lessened, would allow for larger dollar commitment in each holding period. It is difficult and dangerous, however, to assume that the risk in holding a call option is less than 100% in a holding period as long as 30 days. The strategist may feel that he is disciplined enough to sell out when losses occur and thereby hold the risk to less than 100%. Alternatively, mathematical analysis will generally show that the expected loss in a fixed time period is less than 100%. Adhering to either of these criteria can lead one to become too aggressive and therefore be too heavily committed to option purchases. It is far safer to stick to the simpler, more restrictive assumption that one is risking all his money—even over a fairly short holding period—when he buys an option.

### Avoiding Excessive Risk

One final word of caution must be inserted. *The investor should not attempt to get "fancy" with the income-bearing portion of his assets.* T-bills may appear to be too "tame" to some investors, and they consider using GNMA's (Government National Mortgage Association certificates), corporate bonds, convertible bonds, or municipal bonds for the fixed-income portion. Although the latter securities may yield a slightly higher return than do T-bills, they may also prove to be less liquid and quite clearly involve more risk than a short-term T-bill does. Moreover, some investors might even consider placing the balance of their funds in other places, such as high-yield stock or covered call writing. While high-yield stock purchases and covered call writing are conservative investments, as most investments go, they would have to be considered very speculative in comparison to the purchase of a 90-day T-bill. In this strategy, the profit potential is represented by the option purchases. The yield on short-term T-bills will quite adequately offset the risks, and one should take great care not to attempt to generate much higher yields on the fixed-income portion of his investment, for he may find that he has assumed risk with the portion of his money that was not intended to have any risk at all.

A fair amount of rigorous, mathematical work has been done on the evaluation of this strategy. *The theoretical papers are quite favorable.* These scholars have generally only considered the purchase of call options as the risk portion of the strategy. Obviously, the strategist is quite free to purchase put options without harming the overall intent of the strategy. When only call options are purchased, both static and down markets harm the performance. If some puts are included in the option purchases, only static markets could produce the worst results.

There are trade-offs involved as well. If, after purchasing the options, the market has a substantial rally, that portion of the option purchase money that is devoted to put option purchases will be lost. Thus the combination of both put and call purchases would do better in a down market than a strategy of buying only calls, but would do worse in an up market. In a broad sense, it makes sense to include some put purchases—if one has the funds to diversify—since the frequency of market rallies is smaller than the combined frequency of market rallies and declines. The investor who owns both puts and calls will be able to profit from substantial moves in either direction, because the profitable options will be able to overcome the limited losses on the unprofitable ones.

## SUMMARY

In summary, the T-bill/option strategy is attractive from several viewpoints. *Its true advantage lies in the fact that it has predefined risk and does not have a limit on potential profits.* Some theorists claim it is the best strategy available, if the options are "underpriced" when they are purchased. The strategy is also relatively simple to operate—it is not necessary to have a margin account or to compute collateral requirements for uncovered options. The strategy can be operated completely from a cash account. There are no spreads involved, nor is it necessary to worry about details such as early assignment (there are no short options in this strategy).

The investor who is going to employ this strategy must, however, not be deluded into thinking that it is so simple that it does not take any work at all. The concepts and application of annualized risk management are very important to the strategy. So are the mechanics of option buying—particularly a disciplined, rational approach to the selection of which calls and/or puts to buy. Consequently, this strategy is suitable only for the investor who has both the time and discipline to operate it correctly.

# CHAPTER 26

# *The Best Strategy?*

There is no one best strategy. Although this statement may appear to be unfair and disappointing to some, it is nevertheless the truth. Its validity lies in the fact that there are many types of investors, and no one strategy can be best for all of them. Knowledge and suitability are the keys to determining which strategy may be the best one for an individual. The previous 25 chapters have been devoted to imparting much of the knowledge required to understand an individual strategy. This chapter will attempt to point out how the investor might incorporate his own risk/reward attitude and financial condition to select the most feasible strategies for his own use. The final section of this chapter describes which strategies have the better probabilities of success.

## GENERAL CONCEPTS—MARKET ATTITUDE AND EQUIVALENT POSITIONS

A wide variety of strategies have been described. Certain ones are geared to capitalizing on one's (hopefully correct) outlook for a particular stock, or for the market in general. These tend to be the more aggressive strategies, such as outright put or call buying, and low-debit (high-potential) bull and bear spreads. Other strategies are much more conservative, having as their emphasis the possibility of making a reasonable, but limited, return coupled with a decreased risk exposure.

These would include covered call writing and in-the-money (large debit) bull or bear spreads. Even in these strategies, however, one has a general attitude about the market. He is bullish or bearish, but not overly so. If he is proven slightly wrong, he can still make money. However, if he is gravely wrong, relatively large percentage losses might occur. The third broad category of strategies is the one that is not oriented toward picking stock market direction, but is rather a neutral approach that allows one to earn time value premiums. If the net change in the market is small over a period of time—and there are historical indications that it is—these strategies should perform well. These strategies would include ratio writing, ratio spreading (especially "delta spreads"), straddle and combination writing, neutral calendar spreading, and butterfly spreads.

Certain other strategies overlap into more than one of the three broad categories. For example, the bullish or bearish calendar spread is initially a neutral position. It only assumes a bullish or bearish bias after the near-term option expires. In fact, any of the diagonal or calendar strategies whose ultimate aim is to generate profits on the sale of shorter-term options are similar in nature. If these near-term profits are generated, they can offset, partially or completely, the cost of long options. Thus one might potentially own options at a reduced cost and could profit from a definitive move in his favor at the right time. It was shown in Chapters 14, 23, and 24 that diagonalizing a spread can often be very attractive.

This brief grouping into three broad categories does not cover all the strategies that have been discussed. For example, some strategies are generally so poor that they are to be avoided by most investors— reverse calendar spreads, high-risk naked option writing (selling options for fractional prices), and covered or ratio *put* writing. In essence, the investor will normally do best with a position that has limited risk and the potential of large profits. Even if the profit potential is a low-probability event, one or two successful cases may be able to overcome a series of limited losses. Complex strategies that fit this description are the diagonal put and call combinations described in Chapters 23 and 24. The simplest strategy fitting this description is the T-bill/option purchase program.

Finally, many strategies may be implemented in more than one way. The method of implementation may not alter the profit potential, but the percentage risk levels can be substantially different. Equivalent strategies fit into this category.

*Example:* Buying stock and then protecting the stock purchase with a put purchase is an equivalent strategy in profit potential to buying a call. That is, both have limited dollar risk and large potential dollar profit if the stock rallies. However, they are substantially different in their structure. The purchase of stock and a put requires substantially more initial investment dollars than does the purchase, but the limited dollar risk of the strategy would normally be a relatively small percentage of the initial investment. The call purchase, on the other hand, involves a much smaller capital outlay, and while it also has limited dollar risk, the loss may easily represent the entire initial investment. The stockholder will receive cash dividends while the call holder will not. Moreover, the stock will not expire as the call will. This provides the stock/put holder with an additional alternative of choosing to extend his position for a longer period of time by buying another put or possibly by just continuing to hold the stock after the original put expires.

Many equivalent positions have similar characteristics. The straddle purchase and the reverse hedge (short stock and buy calls) have similar profit and loss potential when measured in dollars. Their percentage risks are substantially different, however. In fact, as was shown in Chapter 20, there is another strategy that is equivalent to both of these—buying stock and buying several puts. That is, buying a straddle is equivalent to buying 100 shares of stock and simultaneously buying two puts. The "buy stock and puts" strategy has a larger initial dollar investment, but the percentage risk is smaller and the stockholder will receive any dividends paid by the common stock.

In summary, the investor must know two things well—the strategy that he is contemplating using and his own attitude toward risk and reward. His own attitude represents suitability, a topic that will be discussed more fully in the following section. Every strategy has risk. It would not be proper for an investor to pursue the best strategy in the universe (such a strategy does not exist, of course) if the risks of that strategy violated the investor's own level of financial objectives or accepted investment methodology. On the other hand, it is also not sufficient for the investor to merely feel that a strategy is suitable for his investment objectives. Suppose an investor felt that the T-bill/ option strategy was suitable for him because of the profit and risk levels. Even if he understands the philosophies of option purchasing, it would be improper for him to utilize the strategy unless he also understands the mechanics of buying Treasury bills and, more important, the concept of annualized risk.

## WHAT IS BEST FOR ME
## MIGHT NOT BE BEST FOR YOU

*It would be impossible to classify any one strategy as the best one.* The conservative investor would certainly not want to be an outright buyer of options. For him, covered call writing might be the best strategy. Not only would it accomplish his financial aims—moderate profit potential with reduced risk—but it would be much more appealing to him psychologically. The conservative investor normally understands and accepts the risks of stock ownership. It is only a small step from that understanding to the covered call writing strategy. The aggressive investor would not consider covered call writing to be the best strategy, most likely, because he would consider the profit potential too small. He is willing to take larger risks for the opportunities of making larger profits. Outright option purchases might suit him best, and he would accept, by his aggressive nature, that he could lose nearly all his money in a relatively short time period. (Of course, one would hope that he only uses 15 to 20% of his assets for speculative option buying.)

Many investors fit somewhere in between the conservative description and the aggressive description. They might want to have the opportunity to make large profits, but certainly are not willing to risk a large percentage of their available funds in a short period of time. Spreads might therefore appeal to this type of investor—especially the low-debit bullish or bearish calendar spreads. He might also consider occasional ventures into other types of strategies—bullish or bearish spreads, straddle buys or writes, and so on—but would generally not be into a wide range of these types of positions. The T-bill/option strategy might work well for this investor also.

The wealthy aggressive investor may be attracted by strategies that offer the opportunity of making money from credit positions, such as straddle or combination writing. Although ratio writing is not a credit strategy, it might also appeal to this type of investor because of the large amounts of time value premium that are gathered in. These are generally strategies for the wealthier investor because he needs the "staying power" to be able to ride out adverse cycles. If he can do this, he should be able to operate the strategy for a sufficient period of time in order to profit from the constant selling of time value premiums.

In essence, the answer to the question of "which strategy is best" again revolves around that familiar word *suitability. The financial needs and investment objectives of the individual investor are more important than the merits of the strategy itself.* It sounds nice to be able to say that one would like to participate in strategies with limited risk and potentially large profits. Unfortunately, if the actual mechanics of the strategy involve risk that is not suitable for the investor, he should not use the strategy—no matter how attractive it sounds.

*Example:* The T-bill/option strategy seems attractive: limited risk because only 10% of one's assets are subjected to risk annually; the remaining 90% of one's assets earn interest; and if the option profits materialize, they could be large. What if the worst scenario unfolds? Suppose that poor option selections are continuously made and there are three or four years of losses, coupled with a declining rate of interest earned from the Treasury bills (not to mention the commission charges for trading the securities). The portfolio might have lost 15 or 20% of its assets over those years. *A good test of suitability is for the investor to ask himself, in advance: "How will I react if this worst case occurs?"* If there will be sleepless nights, pointing of fingers, threats, and so forth, the strategy is unsuitable. If, on the other hand, the investor feels that he would be disappointed (because no one likes to lose money), but that he can withstand the risk, the strategy may indeed be suitable.

## *MATHEMATICAL RANKING*

The discussion above demonstrates that it is not possible to ultimately define the best strategy when one considers the background—both financial and psychological—of the individual investor. However, the reader may be interested in knowing which strategies have the best mathematical chances of success, regardless of the investor's personal feelings. Not unexpectedly, *those strategies which take in large amounts of time value premium have high mathematical expectations.* These would include ratio writing, ratio spreading, straddle writing, and naked call writing (but only if the "rolling for credits" follow-up strategy is adhered to). The ratio strategies would have to be operated according to a delta neutral ratio in order to be mathematically optimum. Unfortunately, these strategies are not for everyone. All involve naked options, and also require that the investor have a substantial amount of money (or collateral) available to make the strategies work properly. Moreover, naked option writing in any form is not suitable for some investors, regardless of their protests to the contrary.

*Another group of strategies that rank high on an expected profit basis are those that have limited risk with the potential of occasionally attaining large profits.* The T-bill/option strategy is a prime example of this type of strategy. The strategies in which one attempts to reduce the cost of longer-term options through the sale of near-term options would fit in this broad category also, although one should limit his dollar commitment to 15 to 20% of his portfolio. Calendar spreads such as the combinations described in Chapter 23 (calendar combination, calendar straddle, and diagonal butterfly spread) or bullish call calendar spreads or bearish put calendar spreads are all examples of such strategies. These strategies may have a rather frequent probability of losing a small amount of money, coupled with a low probability of earning large profits. Still, a few large profits may be able to more than overcome the frequent, but small, losses.

*Ranking behind these strategies would be the ones that offer limited profits with a reasonable probability of attaining that profit.* Covered call writing, large debit bull or bear spreads (purchased option well in-the-money and possibly written option as well), neutral calendar spreads, and butterfly spreads would fit into this category. Unfortunately, all these strategies involve relatively large commission costs. Even though these are not normally strategies which require a large investment, the investor who wants to reduce the percentage effect of commissions must take larger positions and will therefore be advancing a sizable amount of money.

*Speculative buying and spreading strategies rank the lowest on a mathematical basis.* The T-bill/option strategy is not a speculative buying strategy. In-the-money purchases, including the in-the-money combination, generally outrank out-of-the-money purchases. This is because one has the possibility of making a large percentage profit but has decreased the chance of losing all his investment, since he starts out in-the-money. In general, however, the constant purchase of time value premiums—which must waste away by the time the options expire—will be a burdensome negative effect. The chances of large profits and large losses are relatively equal, on a mathematical basis, and thus become subsidiary to the time premium effect in the long run. This mathematical outlook of course precludes those investors who are able to predict stock movements with an above-average degree of accuracy. Although the true mathematical approach holds that it is not possible to accurately predict the market, there are undoubtedly some who can and many who try.

## SUMMARY

Mathematical expectations for a strategy do not make it suitable even if the expected returns are good, for the improbable may occur. Profit potentials also do not determine suitability—risk levels do. In the final analysis, one must determine suitability of a strategy by determining if he will be able to withstand the inherent risks if the worst scenario should occur. For this reason, no one strategy can be designated as the best one, because there are numerous attitudes as to the degree of risk that is acceptable.

CHAPTER

# *Arbitrage* 27

Arbitrage in the securities market often connotates that one is buying something in one marketplace and selling it in another market-place, for a small profit with little or no risk. For example, one might buy XYZ at 55 in New York and sell it at 55¼ in Chicago. Arbitrage—especially option arbitrage—involves a far wider range of tactics than this simple example. Many of the option arbitrage tactics involve buying one side of an equivalent position and simultaneously selling the other side. Since there is a large number of equivalent strategies—many of which have been pointed out in earlier chapters—a full-time option arbitrageur is able to construct a rather large number of positions, most of which have little or no risk. The public customer cannot generally operate arbitrage-like strategies because of the commission costs involved. Arbitrageurs are firm traders or floor traders who are trading through a seat on the appropriate securities exchange, and therefore have only minimal transaction costs.

*The public customer can benefit from understanding arbitrage techniques, even if he does not personally employ them.* The arbitrageurs perform a useful function in the option marketplace—often being the ones who make markets where a market might not otherwise exist (deeply in-the-money options, for example). This chapter is written in a tone directed at the strategist who is actually going to be participating in arbitrage. This should not be confusing to the public customer, for he will better understand the arbitrage strategies if he temporarily places himself in the arbitrageur's shoes.

It may infrequently be possible to perform pure arbitrage on dually listed options. That is, one might be able to buy an option on the CBOE and sell it on the American Exchange in New York for a profit. Such discrepancies occur so infrequently and in such small size that an option arbitrageur could never hope to be fully employed in this type of simple arbitrage. Rather, the more complex forms of arbitrage described below are the ones on which he would normally concentrate.

## BASIC PUT AND CALL ARBITRAGE ("DISCOUNTING")

The basic call and the basic put arbitrages are two of the simpler forms of option arbitrage. In these situations, *the arbitrageur attempts to buy the option at a discount while simultaneously taking an opposite position in the underlying stock.* He can then exercise his option immediately and make a profit equal to the amount of the discount.

The basic call arbitrage will be described first. This was also outlined in Chapter 1, under the section on anticipating exercise.

*Example:* XYZ is trading at 58 and the XYZ July 50 call is trading at 7¾. The call is actually at a discount from parity of ¼ point. Discount options are generally either quite deeply in-the-money or have only a short time remaining until expiration, or both. The call arbitrage would be constructed by:

1. Buying the call at 7¾.
2. Selling the stock at 58.
3. Exercising the call to buy the stock at 50.

The arbitrageur would make 8 points of profit from the stock—having sold it at 58 and bought it back at 50 via the option exercise. He loses the 7¾ points that he paid for the call option, but this still leaves him with an overall profit of ¼ point. Since he is a member of the exchange, or is trading the seat of an exchange member, the arbitrageur pays only a small charge to transact the trades.

In reality, the stock is not sold *short,* per se, even though it is sold before it is bought. Rather, the position is designated, at the time of its inception, as an "irrevocable exercise"—the arbitrageur is promising to exercise the call. As a result, no uptick is required to sell the stock.

*The main goal in the call arbitrage is to be able to buy the call at a discount from the price at which the stock is sold.* The differential is the profit potential of the arbitrage. *The basic put arbitrage is quite similar* to the call arbitrage. Again, the arbitrageur is looking to buy the put option at a discount from parity. The put arbitrage is completed with a stock *purchase* and option exercise.

> *Example:* XYZ is at 58 and the XYZ July 70 put is at 11¾. With the put at a ¼ discount from parity, the arbitrageur might take the following action:
>
> 1. Buy put at 11¾.
> 2. Buy stock at 58.
> 3. Exercise the put to sell stock at 70.
>
> The stock transaction is a 12-point profit, since the stock was bought at 58 and is sold at 70 via the put exercise. The cost of the put—11¾ points—is lost, but the arbitrageur still makes a ¼-point profit. Again, *this profit is equal to the amount of the discount in the option when the position was established.* Generally, the arbitrageur would exercise his put option immediately because he would not want to tie up his capital to carry the long stock. An exception to this would be if the stock were about to go ex-dividend. Dividend arbitrage is discussed in the next section.

The basic call and put arbitrages may exist at any time, although they will be more frequent when there is an abundance of deeply in-the-money options or when there is a very short time remaining until expiration. After market rallies, the call arbitrage may be easier to establish, and after market declines, the put arbitrage will be easier to find. As an expiration date draws near, an option that is even slightly in-the-money on the last day or two of trading could be a candidate for discount arbitrage. The reason that this is true is that public buying interest in the option will normally wane. The only public buyers would be those who are short and want to cover. Many covered writers will elect to let the stock be called away, so that will reduce even further the buying potential of the public. This leaves it to the arbitrageurs to supply the buying interest.

The arbitrageur obviously wants to establish these positions in as large a size as possible, since there is no risk in the position if it is established at a discount. Usually, there will be a larger market for the stock than there will be for the options, so that the arbitrageur spends more of his time on the option position. However, there may be occasions when the option markets are larger than the corresponding stock quotes. When this happens, the arbitrageur has an alternative available to him—*he might sell an in-the-money option at parity rather than taking a stock position.*

> *Example:* XYZ is at 58 and the XYZ July 50 call is at 7¾. These are the same figures as in the previous example. Furthermore, suppose that the trader is able to buy more options at 7¾ than he is able to sell stock at 58. If there were another in-the-money call that could be sold at parity, it could be used in place of the stock sale. For example, if the XYZ July 40 call could be sold at 18 (parity), the arbitrage could still be established. If he is assigned on the July 40 that he is short, he will then be short stock at a net price of 58—the striking price of 40, plus the 18 points that were brought in from the sale of the July 40 call. Thus *the sale of the in-the-money call at parity is equivalent to shorting the stock for the arbitrage purpose.*

In a similar manner, an in-the-money put can be used in the basic put arbitrage.

> *Example:* With XYZ at 58 and the July 70 put at 11¾, the arbitrage could be established. However, if the trader is having trouble buying enough stock at 58, he might be able to use another in-the-money put. Suppose the XYZ July 80 put could be sold at 22. This would be the same as buying the stock at 58, for if the put were assigned the arbitrageur would be forced to buy stock at 80—the striking price—but his net cost would be 80 minus the 22 points he received from the sale of the put, for a net cost of 58. Again, the arbitrageur is able to use the sale of a deeply in-the-money option as a substitute for the stock trade.

The examples above assumed that the arbitrageur sold a deeper in-the-money option at parity. In actual practice, if an in-the-money is at a discount, an even deeper in-the-money option will generally be at a discount as well. The arbitrageur would normally try to sell, at parity, an option that was *less* deeply in-the-money than the one he is discounting.

In a broader sense, this technique is applicable to any arbitrage that involves a stock trade as part of the arbitrage, except where the dividend on the stock itself is important. *Thus any time that the arbitrageur is having trouble buying or selling stock as part of his arbitrage, he can always check to see if there is an in-the-money option that could be sold to produce a position equivalent to the stock position.*

## *DIVIDEND ARBITRAGE*

There is a dividend arbitrage that is actually quite similar to the basic put arbitrage. The trader can lock in profits by buying both the stock and the put, then waiting to collect the dividend on the underlying stock before exercising his put. *In theory, on the day before a stock goes ex-dividend, all puts should have a time value premium at least as large as the dividend amount.* This is true even for deeply in-the-money puts.

> *Example:* XYZ closes at 45 and is going to go ex-dividend by $1 tomorrow. Then a put with striking price of 50 should sell for at least 6 points—the in-the-money amount plus the amount of the dividend—because the stock will go ex-dividend and will open at 44, six points in-the-money.
>
> If, however, the put's time value premium should be less than the amount of the dividend, the arbitrageur can take a riskless position. Suppose the XYZ July 50 put is selling for 5¾, with the stock at 45 and about to go ex-dividend by $1. The arbitrageur can take the following steps:
>
> 1.  Buy the put at 5¾.
> 2.  Buy the stock at 45.
> 3.  Hold the put and stock until the stock goes ex-dividend (1 point in this case).
> 4.  Exercise the put to sell the stock at 50.
>
> The trader makes 5 points from the stock trade—buying it at 45 and selling it at 50 via the put exercise—and also collects the one point dividend, for a total inflow of 6 points. Since he loses the 5¾ points he paid for the put, his net profit is ¼ point.

Far in advance of the ex-dividend date, a deeply in-the-money put may trade very close to parity. Thus it would seem that the arbitrageur could "load up" on these types of positions and merely sit back and wait for the stock to go ex-dividend. There is a flaw in this line of thinking, however, because *the arbitrageur has a carrying cost for the money that he must tie up in the long stock.* This carrying cost fluctuates with short-term interest rates.

> *Example:* If the current rate of carrying charges were 6% annually, this would be equivalent to 1% every two months. If the arbitrageur were to establish this example position two months prior to expiration, he would

have a carrying cost of .5075 point (his total outlay is 50¾ points, 45 for the stock and 5¾ for the options, and he would pay 1% to carry that stock and option for the two months until the ex-dividend date). This is more than ½ point in costs—clearly more than the ¼ point potential profit. Consequently, the arbitrageur must be aware of his carrying costs if he attempts to establish a dividend arbitrage well in advance of the ex-dividend date. Of course, if the ex-dividend date is only a short time away, the carrying cost has little effect, and the arbitrageur can gauge the profitability of his position mostly by the amount of the dividend and the time value premium in the put option.

The arbitrageur should note that this strategy of buying the put and buying the stock to pick up the dividend might have a residual, rather profitable, side effect. If the underlying stock shall rally up to, or above, the striking price of the put, there could be rather large profits in this position. Although it is not likely that such a rally could occur, it would be an added benefit if it did. Even a rather small rally might cause the put to pick up some time premium, allowing the arbitrageur to trade out of his position for a profit larger than he could have made by the arbitrage discount.

This form of arbitrage lends itself occasionally to a limited form of risk arbitrage. Risk arbitrage is a strategy that is designed to lock in a profit, if a certain event occurs. If that event does not occur, there could be a loss (usually quite limited), and hence the position has risk. *This risk element differentiates a risk arbitrage from a standard, no-risk arbitrage.* Risk arbitrage will be described more fully in a later section, but the following example concerning a special dividend is one form of risk arbitrage.

*Example:* XYZ has been known to declare extra, or special, dividends with a fair amount of regularity. There are several stocks that do so—Eastman Kodak and General Motors, for example. In this case, assume that a hypothetical stock, XYZ, has generally declared a special dividend in the fourth quarter of each year, but that its normal quarterly rate is $1.00 per share. Suppose the special dividend in the fourth quarter has ranged from an extra $1.00 to $3.00 over the past five years. If the arbitrageur were willing to speculate on the size of the upcoming dividend, he might be able to make a nice profit. Even if he overestimates the size of the special dividend, he has a limited loss. Suppose XYZ is trading at 55 about two weeks before the company is going to announce their dividend for the fourth quarter. There is no guarantee that there will, in fact, be a special dividend, but assume that XYZ is having a relatively good year, profitwise, and that some special dividend seems forthcoming. Furthermore, suppose the January 60 put is trading at 7½. This put has 2½ points of time value premium. If the arbitrageur buys XYZ at 55 and also buys the January 60 put at 7½, he is setting up a risk arbitrage. He will profit—regardless of how far the stock falls or how much time value premium the put loses—if the special dividend is larger than $1.50. A special dividend of $1.50 plus the regular dividend of $1.00 would add up to $2.50, or 2½ points, thus covering his risk in the position. Note that $1.50 is in the low end of the $1.00 to $3.00 recent historical range for the special dividends, so the arbitrageur might be tempted to speculate a little by establishing this dividend risk arbitrage. Even if the company were to unexpectedly decide to declare no special dividend at all, it would most likely still pay out the $1.00 regular dividend. Thus the most that the arbitrageur would lose would be 1½ points (his 2½-point initial time value premium cost, less the 1 point dividend). In actual practice, the stock would probably not change in price by a great deal—it is a high-yield stock— over the next two weeks, and therefore the January 60 put would probably have some time value premium left in it after the stock goes ex-dividend. Thus the practical risk is even less than 1½ points.

While these types of dividend risk arbitrage are not frequently available, the arbitrageur who is willing to do some homework and also take some risk may find that he is able to put on a position with a small risk and a profitability quite a bit larger than the normal discount dividend arbitrage.

*There is really not a direct form of dividend arbitrage involving call options.* If a relatively high-yield stock is about to go ex-dividend, holders of the calls will attempt to sell. They do so because the stock will drop in price, thereby generally forcing the call to drop in price as well, because of the ex-dividend. However, the holder of a call does not receive cash dividends and therefore is not willing to hold the call if the stock is going to drop by a relatively large amount (perhaps ¾ point or more). The effect of these call holders attempting to sell their calls may often produce a discount option—and therefore a basic call arbitrage may be possible. The arbitrageur should be careful, however, if he is attempting to arbitrage a stock that is going ex-dividend on the following day. Since he must sell the stock to set up the arbitrage, he cannot afford to wind up the day being short any stock, for he will then have to pay out the dividend the following day (the ex-dividend date). Furthermore, his records must be accurate so that he exercises all his long options on the day before the ex-dividend rate. If the arbitrageur is careless and is still short some stock on the ex-date, he may find that the dividend he has to pay out wipes out a large portion of the discount profits that he has established.

## CONVERSIONS AND REVERSALS

In the introductory material on puts, it was shown that put and call prices are related through a process known as conversion. This is an arbitrage process whereby a trader may sometimes be able to lock in a profit at absolutely no risk. *A conversion consists of buying the underlying stock, and also buying a put option and selling a call option where both options have the same terms. This position will have a locked-in profit if the total cost of the position is less than the striking price of the options.*

*Example:* The following prices exist:

XYZ common, 55;

XYZ January 50 call, 6½; and

XYZ January 50 put, 1.

The total cost of this position is 49½—55 for the stock, plus 1 for the put, less 6½ for the call. Since 49½ is less than the striking price of 50, there is a locked-in profit on this position. To see that such a profit exists, suppose the stock is somewhere above 50 at expiration. It makes no difference how far above 50 the stock might be, for the result will be the same. With the stock above 50, the call will be assigned and the stock will be sold at a price of 50. The put will expire worthless. Thus the profit is ½ point, since the initial cost of the position was 49½ and it can eventually be liquidated for a price of 50 at expiration. A similar result occurs if XYZ is below 50 at expiration. In this case, the trader would exercise his put to sell his stock at 50, and the call would expire worthless. Again, the position is liquidated for a price of 50 and, since it only cost 49½ to establish, the same ½-point profit can be made. No matter where the stock is at expiration, this position has a locked-in profit of ½ point.

This example is rather simplistic because it does not include two very important factors—the possible dividend paid by the stock and the cost of carrying the position until expiration. The inclusion of these factors complicates things somewhat, and its discussion will be deferred momentarily while the companion strategy, the reversal, is explained.

A reversal (or reverse conversion, as it is sometimes called) is exactly the opposite of a conversion. *In a reversal, the trader sells stock short, sells a put and buys a call.* Again, the put and call have the same terms. *A reversal will be profitable if the initial credit (sale price) is greater than the striking price of the options.*

*Example:* A different set of prices will be used to describe a reversal:

XYZ common, 55;

XYZ January 60 call, 2; and

XYZ January 60 put, 7½.

The total credit of the reversal is 60½—55 from the stock sale, plus 7½ from the put sale, less the 2-point cost of the call. Since 60½ is greater than the striking price of the options, 60, there is a locked-in profit equal to the differential of ½ point. To verify this, first assume that XYZ is anywhere below 60 at January expiration. The put will be assigned— stock is bought at 60—and the call will expire worthless. Thus the reversal position is liquidated for a cost of 60. A ½-point profit results since the original sale value (credit) of the position was 60½. On the other hand, if XYZ were above 60 at expiration, the trader would exercise his call, thus buying stock at 60, and the put would expire worthless. Again, he would liquidate the position at a cost of 60 and would make a ½-point profit.

Dividends and carrying costs are important in reversals, too, and these factors will now be addressed. The *conversion* involves buying stock and the trader will thus receive any dividends paid by the stock during the life of the arbitrage. However, the converter also has to pay out a rather large sum of money to set up his arbitrage, and must therefore deduct the cost of carrying the position from his potential profits. In the example above, the conversion position cost 49½ points to establish. If the trader's cost of money were ½ of 1% per month, he would thus lose .005 times 49½, or .2475 point per month for each month that he holds the position. This is nearly ¼ of a point per month. Recall that the potential profit in the example is ½ point, so that if he held the position for more than two months, his carrying costs would wipe out his profit. *It is extremely important that the arbitrageur compute his carrying costs accurately prior to establishing any conversion arbitrage.*

If one prefers formulae, the profit potentials of a conversion or a reversal can be stated as:

$$\text{Conversion profit} = \text{striking price} + \text{call price} - \text{stock price} - \text{put price} + \text{dividends to be received} - \text{carrying cost of position}$$

$$\text{Reversal profit} = \text{Stock} + \text{put} - \text{strike} - \text{call} + \text{carrying cost} - \text{dividends}$$

Note that during any one trading day, the only items in the formulae that can change are the prices of the securities involved. The other items—*dividends and carrying cost—are fixed for the day.* Thus one could merely have a small computer program prepared that listed the fixed charges on a particular stock and all the strikes on that stock.

*Example:* It is assumed that XYZ stock is going to pay a ½-point dividend during the life of the position, and that the position will have to be held for three months at a carrying cost of ½ of 1% per month. If the arbitrageur were interested in a conversion with a striking price of 50, his fixed cost would be:

Conversion fixed cost = carrying charge per month $\times$ months held $\times$ striking price − dividend to be received

$$= .005 \times 3 \times 50 - ½$$

$$= .75 - ½ = .25, \text{ or } ¼ \text{ of a point}$$

The arbitrageur would know that if the profit potential, computed in the simplistic manner using only the prices of the securities involved, was greater than ¼ of a point, he could establish the conversion for an eventual profit, including all costs. Of course, the carrying costs would be different if the striking price were 40 or 60, so a small computer printout of all the possible striking prices on each stock with both puts and calls would be useful in order for the trader to be able to quickly refer to a table of his fixed costs each day. To keep things workable for the trader, such a program should round the cost up to the nearest eighth of a point, so that the trader does not have to bother with decimal calculations during the trading day. In actual practice, the carrying costs should be computed using days to expiration, not months.

## MORE ON CARRYING COSTS

The computation of carrying costs can be made more involved than the simple method used above. Simplistically, the carrying cost is computed by multiplying the debit of the position by the interest rate charged and by the time that the position will be held. That is, it could be formulated as:

$$\text{Carrying cost} = \text{strike} \times r \times t$$

where $r$ is the interest rate per month and $t$ is the number of months that the position will be held. Relating this formula for the carrying cost to the conversion profit formula given above, one would get:

Conversion profit = − stock − put + div + strike − carrying cost

$$= \text{call} - \text{stock} - \text{put} + \text{div} + \text{strike} (1 - rt)$$

In an actuarial sense, the carrying cost could be expressed in a slightly more complex manner. The simple formula (strike $\times r \times t$) ignores two things: the compounding effect of interest rates and the "present value" concept—the present value of a future amount. The absolutely correct formula to include both present value and the compounding effect would necessitate replacing the factor strike $(1 - rt)$ in the profit formula by the factor

$$\frac{\text{strike}}{(1 + r)^t}$$

Is this effect large? No, not when $r$ and $t$ are small, as they would be for most option calculations. The interest rate per month would be normally less than 1% and the time would be less than 9 months. Thus it is generally acceptable, and is the common practice among many arbitrageurs, to use the simple formula for carrying costs. In fact, this is often a matter of convenience for the arbitrageur if he is computing the carrying costs on a hand calculator that does not do exponentiation. However, in periods of high interest rates when longer-term options are being analyzed, the arbitrageur who is using the simple formula should double-check his calculations with the correct formula to assure that his error is not too large.

For purposes of simplicity, the remaining examples will use the simple formula for carrying-cost computations. The reader should remember, however, that it is only a convenient approximation that works best when the interest rate and the holding period are small. Also, since the arbitrageur must round his calculations to the nearest eighth, most differentials between the approximation formula and the exact formula will be wiped away. This discussion of the compounding effect of interest rates also raises another interesting point: any investor using margin should, in theory, calculate his potential interest charge using the compounding formula. However, as a matter of practicality, extremely few investors do. An example of this compounding effect on a covered call write is presented in Chapter 2.

## BACK TO CONVERSIONS AND REVERSALS

Profit calculation similar to the conversion profit formula is necessary for the reversal arbitrage. Since the reversal necessitates shorting stock, the trader must pay out any dividends on the stock during the time in which the position is held. However, he is now bringing in a credit when the position is established, and this money can be put to work to earn interest. In a reversal, then, the dividend is a cost and the interest earned is a profit.

> *Example:* Use the same XYZ details described above—the stock is going to pay a ½-point dividend, the position will be held for three months, and the money will earn interest at a rate of ½ of 1% per month. If the trader were contemplating an arbitrage with a striking price of 30, the fixed cost would be:
>
> $$\text{Reversal fixed cost} = \text{dividend to be paid} - \text{interest rate per month} \times$$
> $$\text{months held} \times \text{striking price}$$
>
> $$= \tfrac{1}{2} - .005 \times 3 \times 30$$
>
> $$= \tfrac{1}{2} - .045 = .005 \text{ point}$$

The fixed cost in this reversal is extremely small. In fact, the reader should be able to see that it is often possible—even probable—that there will be a fixed profit, not a fixed cost, in a reversal arbitrage. To verify this, rework the example with a striking price of 50 or 60. As in a conversion, the fixed cost (or profit) in a reversal is a number that can be used for the entire trading day. It will not change.

*Reversals are generally easier positions for the arbitrageur to locate than are conversions.* This is because the fixed cost of the conversion is a rather burdensome effect. Only if the stock pays a rather large dividend that outweighs the carrying cost could the fixed portion of the conversion formula ever be a profit as opposed to a cost. In practice, the interest rate paid to carry stock is probably higher than the interest earned from being short stock, but any reasonable computer program should be able to handle two different interest rates.

The novice trader may find the term "conversion" somewhat illogical. In the over-the-counter option markets, the dealers create a position similar to the one shown here as a result of actually converting a put to a call.

> *Example:* When someone owns a conventional put on XYZ with striking price of 60 and the stock falls to 50, there is often little chance of being able to sell the put profitably in the secondary market. The over-the-counter option dealer might offer to convert the put into a call. To do this, he would buy the put from the holder, then buy the stock itself, and then offer a call—at the original striking price of 60—to the holder of the put. Thus the dealer would be long the stock, long the put, and short the call—a conversion. The customer would then own a call on

XYZ with a striking price of 60, due to expire on the same date that the put was destined to. The put that the customer owned has been converted into a call. To effect this conversion, the dealer pays out to the customer the difference between the current stock price, 50, and the striking price, 60. Thus the customer receives $1,000 for this conversion. Also, the dealer would charge the customer for costs to carry the stock, so that the dealer had no risk. If the stock rallied back above 60, the customer could make more money, because he owns the call. The dealer has no risk, as he has an arbitrage position to begin with. In a similar manner, the dealer can effect a reverse conversion—converting a call to a put—but will charge the dividends to the customer for doing so.

*The practice of conversion and reversal arbitrage in the listed option markets helps to keep put and call prices in line.* If arbitrageurs are active in a particular option, the prices of the put and call will relate to the stock price in line with the formulae given earlier. Note that this is also a valid reason why puts tend to sell at a lower price than calls do. The cost of money is the determining factor in the difference between put and call prices. In essence, the "cost" (although it may sometimes be a credit) is subtracted from the theoretical put price. Refer again to the formula given above for the profit potential of a conversion. Assume that things are in perfect alignment. Then the formula would read:

Put price = striking price + call price − stock price − fixed cost

Furthermore, if the stock is at the striking price, the formula reduces to:

Put price = call price − fixed cost

So, whenever the fixed cost, which is equal to the carrying charge less the dividends, is greater than zero (and it usually is), the put will sell for less than the call if a stock is at the striking price. Only in the case of a large-dividend-paying stock, where the fixed cost becomes negative (that is, it is not a cost, but a profit), does the reverse hold true. This is supportive evidence for statements made earlier that calls sell for more than puts, all other things being equal. The reader can see quite clearly that it has nothing to do with supply and demand for the puts and calls—a fallacy that is sometimes proferred. This same sort of analysis can also be used to prove the broader statement that calls have a greater time value premium than puts do, except in the case of a large-dividend-paying stock.

One final word of advice should be offered to the public customer. He may sometimes be able to find conversions or reversals, by using the simplistic formula, that appear to have profit potentials that exceed commission costs. Such positions do exist from time to time, but the rate of return to the public customer will almost assuredly be less than the short-term cost of money. If it were not, arbitrageurs would be onto the position very quickly. The public option trader may not actually be thinking in terms of comparing the profit potential of a position with what he could get by placing the money into a bank, but he must do so to convince himself that he cannot feasibly attempt conversion or reversal arbitrages.

## THE "INTEREST PLAY"

In the preceding discussion of reversal arbitrage, it is apparent that a substantial portion of the arbitrageur's profits may be due to the interest earned on the credit of the position. Another type of position is used by many arbitrageurs to take advantage of this interest earned. The arbitrageur sells the underlying stock short and simultaneously buys an in-the-money call that is trading slightly over parity. The actual amount over parity that the arbitrageur can afford to pay for the call is determined by the amount of interest that he will earn from his short sale. He does not use a put in this type of position. In fact, this "interest play" strategy is merely a reversal arbitrage without the short put. This slight variation has a residual benefit for the arbitrageur—if the underlying stock should drop dramatically in price, he could make large profits because he is short the underlying stock. In any case, *he will make his interest credit less the amount of time value premium paid for the call.*

> *Example 1:* XYZ is at sold short at 60, and a January 50 call is bought for 10¼ points. Assume that the prevailing interest rate is 1% per month and that the position is established one month prior to expiration. The total credit brought in from the trades is $4975, so the arbitrageur will earn $49.75 in interest over the course of 1 month. If the stock is above 50 at expiration, he will exercise his call to buy stock at 50 and close the position. His loss on the security trades will be $25— the amount of time value premium paid for the call option (he makes 10 points by selling stock at 60 and buying at 50, but loses 10¼ points on the exercised call). His overall profit is thus $24.75.

> *Example 2:* A real-life example may point out the effect of interest rates

even more dramatically. In early 1979, IBM options with about six weeks of life remaining were over 60 points in-the-money. Normally, such a deeply in-the-money option would be trading at parity or even a discount when the time remaining to expiration is so short. However, these calls were trading 3½ points over parity because of the prevailing high interest rates at the time. IBM was at 300, the April 240 calls were trading at 63½, and the prevailing interest rate was approximately 1% per month. The credit from selling the stock and buying the call was $23,700, so the arbitrageur earned $365.50 in interest for 1½ months, and lost $350—the 3½ points of time value premium that he paid for the call. This still left enough room for a profit.

In Chapter 1, it was stated that interest rates affect option prices. The above examples of the "interest play" strategy quite clearly show why. As interest rates rise, the arbitrageur can afford to pay more for the long call in this strategy, thus causing the call price to increase in times of high interest rates. If call prices are higher, so will put prices be, as the relationships necessary for conversion and reversal arbitrage are preserved. Similarly, if interest rates decline, the arbitrageur will make lower bids, and call and put prices will be lower. While arbitrageurs cannot possibly keep every call and put on every underlying stock "in line"; they are active enough to give truth to the theory that option prices are directly related to interest rates.

## THE BOX SPREAD

*An arbitrage consists of simultaneously buying and selling the same security or equivalent securities at different prices.* For example, the reversal consists of selling a put and simultaneously shorting stock and buying a call. The reader should recall that the short stock/long call position was called a synthetic put. That is, shorting the stock and buying a call is equivalent to buying a put. The reversal arbitrage therefore consists of selling a (listed) put and simultaneously buying a (synthetic) put. In a similar manner, the conversion is merely the purchase of a (listed) put and the simultaneous sale of a (synthetic) put. Many equivalent strategies can be combined for arbitrage purposes. One of the more common ones is the box spread.

Recall that it was shown that a bull spread or a bear spread could be constructed with either puts or calls. Thus if one were to simultaneously buy a (call) bull spread and buy a (put) bear spread, he could have an arbitrage. In essence, he is merely buying and selling equivalent spreads. If the price differentials work out correctly, a risk-free arbitrage may be possible.

*Example:* The following prices exist:

XYZ common, 55

XYZ January 50 call, 7

XYZ January 50 put, 1

XYZ January 60 call, 2

XYZ January 60 put, 5½

The arbitrageur could establish the box spread in this example by executing the following transactions:

|  |  |  |
|---|---|---|
| Buy a call bull spread: | | |
| Buy XYZ January 50 call | 7 debit | |
| Sell XYZ January 60 call | 2 credit | |
| Net call cost | | 5 debit |
| | | |
| Buy a put bear spread: | | |
| Buy XYZ January 60 put | 5½ debit | |
| Sell XYZ January 50 put | 1 credit | |
| Net put cost | | 4½ debit |
| Total cost of position | | 9½ debit |

No matter where XYZ is at January expiration, this position will be worth 10 points. *The arbitrageur has locked in a risk-free profit* of ½ points, since he "bought" the box spread for 9½ points and will be able to "sell" it for 10 points at expiration. To verify this, the position will be evaluated at expiration, first with XYZ above 60, then with XYZ between 50 and 60, and finally with XYZ below 50. If XYZ is above 60 at expiration, the puts will expire worthless and the call bull spread will be at its maximum potential of 10 points—the difference between the striking prices. Thus the position can be liquidated for 10 points if XYZ is above 60 at expiration. Now assume that XYZ is between 50 and 60 at expiration. In that case, the out-of-the-money, written options would expire worthless—the January 60 call and the January 50 put. This would leave a long, in-the-money combination consisting of a January 50 call and a January 60 put. These two options must have a total value of 10 points at expiration with XYZ between 50 and 60 (for example, the arbitrageur could exercise his call to buy stock at 50 and exercise his put to sell stock at 60). Finally, assume that XYZ is below 50 at expiration. The calls would expire worthless if that were true, but the remaining put spread—actually a bear spread in the puts—would be at its maximum potential of 10 points. Again, the box spread could be liquidated for 10 points.

In essence, a bull spread (using calls) was purchased while a bear spread (using puts) was bought. The box spread was described in these terms only to illustrate the fact that the arbitrageur is buying and selling equivalent positions. The arbitrageur who is utilizing the box spread should *not* think in terms of bull or bear spread, however. Rather, he should be concerned with "buying" the entire box spread at a cost of less than the differential between the two striking prices. By "buying" the box spread, it is meant that both the call spread portion and the put spread portion are debit spreads. *Whenever the arbitrageur observes that a call spread and a put spread using the same strikes—and where both are debit spreads—can be bought for less than the difference in the strikes, he should execute the arbitrage.*

Obviously, there is a companion strategy to the one just described. It might sometimes be possible for the arbitrageur to "sell" both spreads. That is, he would establish a credit call spread and a credit put spread, using the same strikes. *If this credit were greater than the difference in the striking prices, a risk-free profit would be locked in.*

*Example:* Assume that a different set of prices exists:

XYZ common, 75

XYZ April 70 call, 8½

XYZ April 70 put, 1

XYZ April 80 call, 3

XYZ April 80 put, 6

By executing the following transactions, the box spread could be "sold":

| | | |
|---|---|---|
| Sell a call (bear) spread: | | |
| Buy April 80 call | 3   debit | |
| Sell April 70 call | 8½ credit | |
| Net credit on calls | | 5½ credit |
| Sell a put (bull) spread: | | |
| Buy April 70 put | 1 debit | |
| Sell April 80 put | 6 credit | |
| Net credit on puts | | 5   credit |
| Total credit of position | | 10½ credit |

In this case, no matter where XYZ is at expiration, the position can be bought back for 10 points. This means that the arbitrageur has locked in a risk-free profit of ½ point. To briefly verify this statement, first assume that XYZ is above 80 at April expiration. The puts will expire worthless, and the call spread will have widened to 10 points—the cost to buy it back. Alternatively, if XYZ were between 70 and 80 at April expiration, the long, out-of-the-money options would expire worthless and the in-the-money combination would cost 10 points to buy back (for example, the arbitrageur could let himself be put at 80, buying stock there, and called at 70, selling the stock there—a net "cost" to liquidate of 10 points). Finally, if XYZ were below 70 at expiration, the calls would expire worthless and the put spread would have widened to 10 points. It could then be closed out at a cost of 10 points. In each case, the arbitrageur is able to liquidate the box spread by buying it back at 10.

These box spreads are not easy to find. If one does appear, the act of doing the arbitrage will soon make the arbitrage impossible. In fact, this is true of any type of arbitrage—it cannot be executed indefinitely because the mere act of arbitraging will force the prices back into line. Occasionally, the arbitrageur will be able to find the option quotes to his liking, especially in volatile markets, and can establish a risk-free arbitrage with the box spread. It can be evaluated at a glance. Only two questions need to be answered:

1. If one were to establish a debit call spread and a debit put spread, using the same strikes, would the total cost be *less than* the difference in the striking prices? If the answer is yes, an arbitrage exists.
2. Alternatively, if one were to sell both spreads—establishing a credit call spread and a credit put spread—would the total credit received be *greater than* the difference in the striking prices? If the answer is yes, an arbitrage exists.

## VARIATIONS ON EQUIVALENCE ARBITRAGE

Other variations of arbitrage on equivalent positions are possible, although they are relatively complicated and probably not worth the arbitrageur's time to analyze. For example, one could buy a butterfly spread with calls and simultaneously sell a butterfly spread using puts. A listed straddle could be sold and a synthetic straddle could be bought—short stock and long 2 calls. Inversely, a listed straddle could be bought against a ratio write—long stock and short 2 calls. The only time that the arbitrageur should even consider anything like this is when there are more sizable markets in certain of the puts and calls than there are in others. If this were the case, he might be able to take an ordinary box spread, conversion, or reversal, and add to it, keeping the arbitrage intact by ensuring that he is, in fact, buying and selling equivalent positions.

## THE EFFECTS OF ARBITRAGE

The arbitrage process serves a useful purpose in the listed options market because it may provide a secondary market where one might not otherwise exist. Normally, public interest in an in-the-money option dwindles as the option becomes deeply in-the-money or if the time remaining until expiration is very short. There would be few public buyers of these options. In fact, public selling pressure might increase because the public would rather liquidate in-the-money options held long than exercise them. The few public buyers of such options might be writers who are closing out. However, if the writer is covered—especially where call options are concerned—he might decide to be assigned rather than close out his option. This means that the public seller is creating a rather large supply that is not offset by a public demand. The market created by the arbitrageur—especially in the basic put or call arbitrage—essentially creates the demand. Without these arbitrageurs, there could conceivably be no buyers at all, for those options which are short-lived and in-the-money, after public writers have finished closing out their positions.

Equivalence arbitrage—conversion, reversals, and box spreads—helps to keep the relative prices of puts and calls in line with each other and with the underlying stock price. This creates a more efficient and rational market for the public to operate in. The arbitrageur would help eliminate, for example, the case where a public customer buys a call, sees the stock go up, but cannot find anyone to sell his call to at higher prices. If the call were too cheap, arbitrageurs would do reversals, which involve call purchases, and would therefore provide a market to sell into.

Questions have been raised as to whether option trading affects stock prices, especially at or just before an expiration. If the amount of arbitrage in a certain issue becomes very large, it could appear to temporarily affect the price of the stock itself. For example, take the call arbitrage. This involves the sale of stock in the market. The corresponding stock purchase, via the call exercise, is not executed on the exchange. Thus, as far as the stock market is concerned, there may appear to be an inordinate amount of selling in the stock. If a large number of basic call arbitrages are taking place, they might thus hold the price of the stock down until the calls expire.

The put arbitrage has an opposite effect. This arbitrage involves buying stock in the market. The offsetting stock sale, via the put exercise, takes place off the exchange. If a large amount of put arbitrage is being done, there may appear to be an inordinate amount of buying in the stock. Such action might temporarily hold the stock price up.

In a vast majority of cases, however, the arbitrage has no visible effect on the underlying stock price, because the amount of arbitrage being done is very small in comparison to the total number of trades in a given stock. Even if the open interest in a particular option is large, allowing for plenty of option volume by the arbitrageurs, the actual act of doing the arbitrage will force the prices of the stock and option back into line, thus destroying the arbitrage.

Rather elaborate studies, including doctoral theses, have been written which try to prove or disprove the theory that option trading affects stock prices. Nothing has been conclusively proven, and may never be, because of the complexity of the task. Logic would seem to dictate that arbitrage could temporarily affect a stock's movement if it has discount, in-the-money options shortly before expiration. However, one would have to reasonably conclude that the size of these arbitrages could almost never be large enough to overcome a directional trend in the underlying stock itself. Thus, in the absence of a definite direction in the stock, arbitrage might help to perpetuate the inertia, but if there were truly a preponderance of investors wanting to buy or sell the stock, these investors would totally dominate any arbitrage that might be in progress.

## RISK ARBITRAGE USING OPTIONS

Risk arbitrage is a strategy that is well described by its name. It is basically an arbitrage—the same or equivalent securities are bought and sold. However, *there is generally risk because the arbitrage usually depends on a future event occurring in order for the arbitrage to be successful.* One form of a risk arbitrage was described earlier concerning the speculation on the size of a special dividend that an underlying stock might pay. That arbitrage consisted of buying the stock and buying the put, where the put's time value premium is less than the amount of the projected special dividend. The risk lies in the arbitrageur's speculation on the size of the anticipated special dividend.

Risk arbitrage is an age-old type of arbitrage in the stock market. *Generally, it concerns speculation on whether a proposed merger or acquisition will actually go through as proposed.*

*Example:* XYZ, which is selling for $50 per share, offers to buy out LMN and is offering to swap one share of its (XYZ's) stock for every two shares of LMN. This would mean that LMN should be worth $25 per share if the acquisition goes through as proposed. On the day the takeover is proposed, LMN stock would probably rise to about $22 per share. It would not trade all the way up to 25 until the takeover was approved by the shareholders of LMN stock. The arbitrageur who feels that this takeover will be approved can take action. He would sell short XYZ and, for every share that he is short, he would buy 2 shares of LMN stock. If the merger goes through, he will profit. The reason that he shorts XYZ as well as buying LMN is to protect himself in case the market price of XYZ drops before the acquisition is approved. In essence, he has sold XYZ and also bought the equivalent of XYZ (two shares of LMN will be equal to one share of XYZ if the takeover goes through). This, then, is clearly an arbitrage. However, it is a risk arbitrage because if the stockholders of LMN reject the offer, he will surely lose money. His profit potential is equal to the remaining differential between the current market price of LMN (22) and the takeover price (25). If the proposed acquisition goes through, the differential disappears, and the arbitrageur has his profit.

*If either or both of the stocks involved in the proposed takeover has options, the arbitrageur may be able to work options into his strategy.*

*Example:* If XYZ has options, *the arbitrageur might decide to sell a slightly in-the-money naked call on XYZ rather than short the stock itself.* This sale of the naked call has two advantages. First, the arbitrageur takes in some time premium from the call sale, and therefore might make a little extra money on the short side if the deal takes a lengthy amount of time to go through. Second, the arbitrageur does not need to borrow stock to sell short—he merely sells calls if there is a market for them. The *disadvantage* of the naked call write versus the short sale is that if XYZ falls by a substantial amount before the deal goes through—an unlikely, but still possible, occurrence—then the call will stop providing protection at its striking price, whereas a short sale would never stop providing protection.

In a similar manner, *the arbitrageur might sell an in-the-money put on LMN*—if listed puts are trading on the stock—rather than buy the stock itself. The put sale has a slight advantage over the purchase of LMN stock if the stock price remains relatively stable, because the arbitrageur would be collecting the time premium on the put. However, *the disadvantages here are rather large.* If LMN were to rally heavily and exceed the striking price of the in-the-money put, the arbitrageur would not be participating fully to the upside. At first glance, it might seem that such a situation could be avoided merely by writing a put whose striking price is quite a bit above the market. This still might not provide enough leeway, however, because the takeover price of LMN will rise if XYZ rises substantially in price. Moreover, there is always the possibility that a bidding war will develop between XYZ and some other company over the LMN stock. If this were to happen, then LMN could run up in price very dramatically before a final takeover offer was accepted.

*Option purchases might also be used by the risk arbitrageur.* A call purchase could be used as a substitute for buying stock and a put purchase could be used as a substitute for selling stock. In either case, the arbitrageur would like to be able to buy an in-the-money option with as little time value premium as possible. Purchasing options rather than taking a stock position can reduce the investment requirements of the position also. More positions could thus be established with the same amount of trading capital.

The real risk in this type of risk arbitrage is that the proposed takeover will not go through and, therefore, that LMN stock might drop in price rather dramatically. *The purchase of an out-of-the-money put option (if one exists) on LMN could help to reduce the arbitrageur's risk in case the takeover is not approved.* Althouth the sale of a call on LMN might also be a protective measure, it is generally not as advisable, because it offers only limited downside protection.

Since the potential profits in risk arbitrage situations of this type may be quite large—perhaps 3 or 4 points per 100 shares—the public can participate in this strategy. Commission charges will make the risk arbitrage less profitable for a public customer than it would be for an arbitrageur. The profit potential is often large enough, however, to make this type of risk arbitrage viable even for the public customer.

In summary, the risk arbitrageur may be able to use options in his strategy, either as a replacement for the actual stock position or as protection for the stock position. Although the public cannot normally participate in arbitrage strategies because of the small profit potential, risk arbitrages may often be exceptions. The profit potential can be large enough to overcome the commission burden for the public customer.

## FACILITATION (BLOCK POSITIONING)

Facilitation is the process whereby a trader seeks to aid in making markets for the purchase or sale of large blocks of stock. This is not really an arbitrage, and its description is thus deferred to Chapter 28.

# *Mathematical* 28
# *Applications*

In previous chapters, many references have been made to the possibility of applying mathematical techniques to option strategies. Those techniques will be developed in this chapter. Although the average investor—public, institutional, or floor trader—normally has a limited grasp of advanced mathematics, the information in this chapter should still prove useful. It will allow the investor to see what sorts of strategy decisions could be aided by the use of mathematics. It will allow the investor to evaluate techniques of an information service. Additionally, if the investor is contemplating hiring someone knowledgeable in mathematics to do work for him, the information to be presented may be useful as a focal point for the work. The investor who does have a knowledge of mathematics and perhaps also has access to a computer will be able to directly use the techniques in this chapter.

## THE BLACK-SCHOLES MODEL

Since an option's price is a function of stock price, striking price, volatility, and time to expiration, *it is logical that a formula could be drawn up to calculate option prices* from these variables. Many models have been conceived since listed options began trading in 1973. Many of these have been attempts to improve on one of the first models introduced, the *Black-Scholes model.* This model was introduced in early 1973, very near to the time that listed options began trading. It was made public at that time and, as a result, gained a rather large number of adherents. The formula is rather easy to use in that the equations are short and the number of variables is small.

The actual formula is

$$\text{Theoretical option price} = pN(d_1) - se^{-rt}N(d_2)$$

$$\text{where } d_1 = \frac{\ln\left(\dfrac{p}{s}\right) + \left(r + \dfrac{v^2}{2}\right)t}{v\sqrt{t}}$$

$$d_2 = d_1 - v\sqrt{t}$$

The variables are:

$p$ = stock price
$s$ = striking price
$t$ = time remaining until expiration, expressed as a percent of a year
$r$ = current risk-free interest rate
$v$ = volatility measured by annual standard deviation
$\ln$ = natural logarithm
$N(x)$ = cumulative normal density function

*An important by-product of the model is the exact calculation of the delta*—that is, the amount by which the option price can be expected to change for a small change in the stock price. The delta was described in Chapter 2, and is more formally known as the *hedge ratio.*

$$\text{Delta} = N(d_1)$$

The formula is so simple to use that it can fit quite easily on most programmable calculators. In fact, some of these calculators can be observed on the exchange floors as the more theoretical floor traders attempt to monitor the present value of option premiums. Of course, a computer can handle the calculations easily and with great speed. A large number of Black-Scholes computations can be performed in a very short period of time.

The cumulative normal distribution function can be found—in tabular form—in most statistical books. However, for computation purposes, it would be wasteful to repeatedly keep looking up values in a table. Since the normal curve is a smooth curve (it is the "bell-shaped" curve used to describe population distributions most commonly), the cumulative distribution can be approximated by a formula:

$$x = 1 - z(1.330274y^5 - 1.821256y^4 + 1.781478y^3 - .356538y^2 + .3193815y)$$

$$\text{where } y = \frac{1}{1 + .2316419|\sigma|} \quad and \quad z = .3989423e^{-\sigma^2/2}$$

$$\text{Then } N(\sigma) = x \quad \text{if } \sigma > 0 \quad \text{or} \quad N(\sigma) = 1 - x \quad \text{if } \sigma < 0$$

This approximation is quite accurate for option pricing purposes, since one is not really interested in thousandths of a point where option prices are concerned.

The reader interested in a more in-depth description of the model, possibly including the actual derivation, should refer to the article "Fact and Fantasy in the Use of Options."[1] One of the less obvious relationships in the model is that option prices will increase as the risk-free interest rate increases. It may also be observed that the model correctly preserves relationships such as increased volatility, higher stock prices, or more time to expiration, which all imply higher option prices.

### Characteristics of the Model

Several aspects of this model are worth further discussion. First, the reader will notice that *the model does not include dividends paid by the common stock*. As has been demonstrated, dividends act as a negative effect on call prices. Thus direct application of the model will tend to give inflated call prices, especially on stocks that pay relatively large dividends. There are ways of handling this. Fisher Black, one of the coauthors of the model, suggests the following method. Adjust the stock price to be used in the formula by subtracting, from the current stock price, the present worth of the dividends likely to be paid before maturity. Then calculate the option price. Second, assume that the option expires just prior to the last ex-dividend date preceding actual option expiration. Again adjust the stock price and calculate the option price. Use the higher of the two option prices calculated as the theoretical price. Another, less exact method would be to apply a weighting

[1]Fisher Black,**Financial Analysts Journal**, July–August 1975, pp. 36–70.

factor to call prices. The weighting factor would be based on the dividend payment, with a heavier weight being applied to call options on high-yielding stock. It should be pointed out that, in many of the applications that are going to be prescribed, it is not necessary to know the exact theoretical price of the call. Therefore, the dividend "correction" might not have to be applied for certain strategy decisions.

*The model is based on a lognormal distribution of stock prices.* Even though the normal distribution is part of the model, the inclusion of the exponential functions makes the distribution lognormal. For those less familiar with statistics, a normal distribution has a bell-shaped curve. This is the most familiar mathematical distribution. The problem with using a normal distribution is that it allows for negative stock prices, an impossible occurrence. Therefore, the lognormal distribution is generally used for stock prices, because it implies that the stock price can only have a range between zero and infinity. Furthermore, the upward (bullish) bias of the lognormal distribution appears to be logically correct, since a stock can only drop 100% but can rise in price by more than 100%. Many option pricing models that antedate the Black-Scholes model have attempted to use empirical distributions. An empirical distribution has a different shape than either the normal or the lognormal distribution. Reasonable empirical distributions for stock prices do not differ tremendously from the lognormal distribution, although they often assume that a stock has a greater probability of remaining stable than does the lognormal distribution. Critics of the Black-Scholes model claim that the model, largely because it uses the lognormal distribution, tends to overprice in-the-money calls and underprice out-of-the-money calls. This criticism is true, in some cases, but does not materially subtract from many applications of the model in strategy decisions. True, if one is going to buy or sell calls solely on the basis of their computed value, this would create a large problem. However, if strategy decisions are to be made on other factors that outweigh the overpriced/underpriced criteria, small differentials will not matter.

The computation of volatility is always a difficult problem for mathematical application. In the Black-Scholes model, volatility is defined as the annual standard deviation of the stock price. This is the regular statistical definition of standard deviation:

$$v^2 = \frac{\sum\limits_{i=1}^{n} (P_i - P)^2}{n - 1}$$

where $P$ = average stock price of all $P_i$'s
$P_i$ = daily stock price
$n$ = number of days observed
$v$ = volatility

*The volatilities of stocks tend to change over time.* Certain predictable factors, such as a large stock split increasing the float of the stock, can reduce the volatility. The entry of a company into a more speculative area of business may increase the volatility. Other, less well defined factors can alter the volatility as well. Since the volatility is a very crucial element of the pricing model, it is important that the modeler be using a reasonable estimate of the current volatility. *It has become apparent that an annual standard deviation is not accurate because it encompasses too long of a period of time.* Recent efforts by many modelers have suggested that one should perhaps weight the recent stock price action more heavily than older price action in arriving at a current volatility. This is a possible approach, but the computation of such factors may introduce as much error as using the annual standard deviation does. The problem of accurately computing the volatility is critical, because the model is so sensitive to it.

There is, in fact, a way in which *the strategist can let the market compute the volatility for him.* This is called using the *implied volatility*—that is, the volatility that the market itself is implying. This concept makes the assumption that, for options with striking prices close to the current stock price and for options with relatively large trading volume, the market is fairly priced. This is something like an efficient market hypothesis. If there is enough trading interest in an option that is close to the money, that option will generally be fairly priced. Once this assumption has been made, a corollary arises: *if the actual price of an option is the fair price, it can be fixed in the Black-Scholes equation while letting volatility be the unknown variable.* The volatility can be determined by iteration. In fact, this process of iterating to compute the volatility can be done for each option on a particular underlying stock. This might result in several different volatilities for the stock. If one weights these various results by volume of trading and by distance in- or out-of-the-money, a single volatility can be derived for the underlying stock. This volatility is based on the closing price of all the options on the underlying stock for that given day.

*Example:* XYZ is 33 and the closing prices are given in Table 28-1. Each option has a different implied volatility as computed by determin-

**TABLE 28-1.** *Implied volatilities, closing price, and volume.*

| Option | Option Price | Volume | Implied Volatility |
|--------|-------------|--------|-------------------|
| January 30 | 4½ | 50 | .34 |
| January 35 | 1½ | 90 | .28 |
| April 35 | 2½ | 55 | .30 |
| April 40 | 1½ | 5 | .38 |
| | | 200 | |

ing what volatility in the Black-Scholes model would result in the closing price for each option: That is, if .34 were used as the volatility, the model would give 4½ as the price of the January 30 call. In order to rationally combine these volatilities, weighting factors must be applied before a volatility for XYZ stock itself can be arrived at.

The weighting factors for volume are easy to compute. The factor for each option is merely that option's daily volume divided by the total option volume on all XYZ options (Table 28-2). The weighting functions for distance from the striking price should probably not be linear. For example, if one option is 2 points out-of-the-money and

**TABLE 28-2.** *Volume weighting factors.*

| Option | Volume | Volume Weighting Factor |
|--------|--------|------------------------|
| January 30 | 50 | .25 (50/200) |
| January 35 | 90 | .45 (90/200) |
| April 35 | 55 | .275 (55/200) |
| April 40 | 5 | .025 ( 5/200) |

another is 4 points out-of-the-money, the former option should not necessarily get twice as much weight as the latter. Once an option is too far in- or out-of-the-money, it should not be given much if any weight at all, regardless of its trading volume. Any parabolic function of the following form should suffice:

$$\text{Weighting factor} \begin{cases} = \dfrac{(x-a)^2}{a^2} & \text{if } x \text{ is less than } a \\ = 0 & \text{if } x \text{ is greater than } a \end{cases}$$

where $x$ is the percentage distance between stock price and strike price and $a$ is the maximum percentage distance at which the modeler wants to give any weight at all to the option's implied volatility.

*Example:* An investor decides that he wants to discard options from the weighting criterion which have striking prices more than 25% from the current stock price. The variable, *a*, would then be equal to .25. The weighting factors, with XYZ at 33, could thus be computed as shown in Table 28-3. To combine the weighting factors for both volume and

**TABLE 28-3.** *Distance weighting factors.*

| Option | Distance from Stock Price | Distance Weighting Factor |
|---|---|---|
| January 30 | .091 (3/33) | .41 |
| January 35 | .061 (2/33) | .57 |
| April 35 | .061 (2/33) | .57 |
| April 40 | .212 (7/33) | .02 |

distance from strike, the two factors are multiplied by the implied volatility for that option. These products are summed up for all the options in question. This sum is then divided by the products of the weighting factors, summed over all the options in question. As a formula, this would read:

$$\frac{\text{Implied}}{\text{volatility}} = \frac{\Sigma \ (\text{volume factor} \times \text{distance factor} \times \text{implied volatility})}{\Sigma \ (\text{volume factor} \times \text{distance factor})}$$

In our example, this would give an implied volatility for XYZ stock of 29.8% (Table 28-4). Note that the implied volatility, .298, is not

**TABLE 28-4.** *Option's implied volatility.*

| Option | Volume Factor | Distance Factor | Option's Implied Volatility |
|---|---|---|---|
| January 30 | .25 | .41 | .34 |
| January 35 | .45 | .57 | .28 |
| April 35 | .275 | .57 | .30 |
| April 40 | .025 | .02 | .38 |

$$\frac{\text{Implied}}{\text{volatility}} = \frac{.25 \times .41 \times .34 + .45 \times .57 \times .28 + .275 \times .57 \times .30 + .025 \times .02 \times .38}{.25 \times .41 + .45 \times .57 + .275 \times .57 + .025 \times .02}$$

$$= .298$$

equal to any of the individual option's implied volatilities. Rather, it is a composite figure that gives the most weight to the heavily traded, near-the-money options, and very little weight to the lightly traded (5 contracts), deeply out-of-the-money April 40 call. This implied volatility is still a form of standard deviation, and can thus be used whenever a standard deviation volatility is called for.

*This method of computing volatility is quite accurate and proves to be sensitive to changes in the volatility of a stock.* For example, as markets become bullish or bearish (generating large rallies or declines), most stocks will react in a volatile manner as well. Option premiums expand rather quickly, and this method of implied volatility is able to pick up the change quickly. One final bit of *fine tuning needs to be done* before the final volatility of the stock is arrived at. On a day-to-day basis, the implied volatility for a stock—especially one whose options are not too active—may fluctuate more than the strategist would like. A smoothing effect can be obtained by taking a moving average of the last 20 or 30 days' implied volatilities. An alternative, which does not require the saving of many previous days' worth of data, would be to use a momentum calculation on the implied volatility. For example, today's final volatility might be computed by adding 5% of today's implied volatility to 95% of yesterday's final volatility. This method requires saving only one previous piece of data—yesterday's final volatility—and still preserves a "smoothing" effect.

*Once this implied volatility has been computed, it can then be used in the Black-Scholes model (or any other model) as the volatility variable.* Thus one could compute the theoretical value of each option according to the Black-Scholes formula utilizing the implied volatility for the stock. Since the implied volatility for the stock will most likely be somewhat different than the implied volatility of this particular option, there will be a discrepancy between the option's actual closing price and the theoretical price as computed by the model. This differential represents the amount by which the option is theoretically overpriced or underpriced, *compared to other options on that same stock.*

## EXPECTED RETURN

There are certain investors who will enter positions only when the historical percentages are on their side. When one enters into a transaction, he normally has a feeling as to the possibility of making a profit. For example, when he buys stock he may feel that there is a "good chance" that there will be a rally or that earnings will increase. The investor may consciously or unconsciously evaluate the probabilities, but, invariably, an investment is made based on a positive expectation of profit. Since options have fixed terms, they lend themselves to a more rigorous computation of expected profit than the aforementioned intuitive appraisal. This more rigorous approach consists of computing the expected return. *The expected return is nothing more than the return that the position should yield over a large number of cases.*

A simple example may help to explain the concept. The crucial variable in computing expected return is to outline what the chances are of the stock being at a certain price at some future time.

*Example:* XYZ is selling at 33, and an investor is interested in determining where XYZ will be in 6 months. Assume that there is a 20% chance of XYZ being below 30 in 6 months, and that there is a 40% chance that XYZ will be above 35 in 6 months. Finally, assume that XYZ has an equal 10% chance of being at 31, 32, 33, or 34 in 6 months. All other prices are ignored for simplification. Table 28-5 summarizes these assumptions.

**TABLE 28-5.** *Calculation of expected returns.*

| Price of XYZ in 6 months | Chance of XYZ Being at That Price |
|---|---|
| Below 30 | 20% |
| 31 | 10% |
| 32 | 10% |
| 33 | 10% |
| 34 | 10% |
| Above 35 | 40% |
| | 100% |

Since the percentages total 100%, all the outcomes have theoretically been allowed for. Now suppose a February 30 call is trading at 4 and a February 35 call is trading at 2 points. A bull spread could be established by buying the February 30 and selling the February 35. This position would cost 2 points—that is, it is a 2-point debit. The spreader could make 3 points if XYZ were above 35 at expiration for a return of 150%, or he could lose 100% if XYZ were below 30 at expirtion. The expected return for this spread can be computed by multiplying the outcome at expiration for each price by the probability of being at that price, and then summing the results. For example, if XYZ is below 30 at expiration, the spreader loses $200. It was assumed that there is a 20% chance of XYZ being below 30 at expiration, so the expected loss is 20% times $200, or $40. Table 28-6 shows the computation of the expected results at all the prices. The total expected profit is $100. This means that the expected return (profit divided by investment) is 50% ($100/$200). This would appear to be an attractive spread, because the spreader could "expect" to make 50% of his money, less commissions.

**TABLE 28-6.** *Computation of expected profit.*

| XYZ Price at Expiration | (A) Chance of Being at That Price | (B) Profit at That Price | Expected Profit: (A) × (B) |
|---|---|---|---|
| Below 30 | 20% | −$200 | −$ 40 |
| 31 | 10% | − 100 | − 10 |
| 32 | 10% | − 0 | 0 |
| 33 | 10% | + 100 | + 10 |
| 34 | 10% | + 200 | + 20 |
| Above 35 | 40% | + 300 | + 120 |
| | | Total expected profit | $100 |

What has really been calculated in this example is merely *the return that one would expect to make in the long run if he invested in the same position many times throughout history.* Saying that a particular position has an expected return of 8 or 9% is no different from saying that common stocks return 8 or 9% in the long run. Of course, in bull markets stock would do much better and in bear markets much worse. In a similar manner, this example bull spread with an expected return of 50% may do as well as the maximum profit or as poorly as losing 100% in any *one* case. It is the total return on *many* cases that has the expected return of 50%. *Mathematical theory holds that, if one constantly invests in positions with positive expected returns, he should have a better chance of making money.*

As is readily observable, the selection of what percentages to assign to the possible outcomes in the stock price is a *crucial* choice. In the example above, if one altered his assumption slightly so that XYZ had a 30% chance of being below 30 and a 30% chance of being above 35 at expiration, the expected return would drop considerably, to 25%. Thus *it is important to have a reasonably accurate and consistent method of assigning these percentages.* Furthermore, the example above was too simplistic, in that it did not allow for the stock to close at any fractional prices, such as 32½. A correct expected return computation must take into account all possible outcomes for the stock.

Fortunately, there is a straightforward method of computing the expected percentage chance of a given stock being at a certain price at a certain point in time. This computation involves using the distribution of stock prices. As mentioned earlier, the Black-Scholes model assumes a lognormal distribution for stock prices, although many modelers today are using nonstandard (empirical or heuristic) distributions. No matter what the distribution, *the area under the distribution curve between any two points gives the probability of being between those two points.*

**FIGURE 28-1.** *Typical lognormal distribution.*

Figure 28-1 is a graph of a typical lognormal distribution. The peak always lies at the "mean," or average, of the distribution. For stock price distributions, under the random walk assumption, *the "mean" is generally considered to be the current stock price.* The graph allows one to visualize the probability of being at any given price. Note that there is a fairly great chance that the stock will be relatively unchanged, there is no chance that the stock will be below zero, and there is a bullish bias to the graph—the stock could rise infinitely, although the chances of it doing so are extremely small.

The chance that XYZ will be below the mean at the end of the time period is 50% in a random walk distribution. This also means that 50% of the area under the graph lies to the left of the mean and 50% lies to the right of the mean. Note point A on the graph. Forty percent of the area under the distribution curve lies to the left of point A and 60% lies above point A. This means that there is a 40% chance that the stock will be below price A at the end of the time period and a 60% chance that the stock will be above point A. Consequently, the distribution curve can be used to determine the probabilities necessary for the expected return computation. The reader should take note of the fact that these probabilities apply to the *end of the time period.* They say nothing about the chances that XYZ might dip below price A at some time *during* the time period. To compute that percentage, an involved computation is necessary.

The height and width of the distribution graph are determined by the volatility of the underlying stock, when volatility is expressed as a standard deviation. This is consistent with the method of computing volatility described earlier in this chapter. Implied volatility can, of course, be used. Since the option modeler is generally interested in time periods other than one year, *the annual volatility must be converted into a volatility for the time period in question.* This is easily accomplished by the following formula:

$$v_t = v\sqrt{t}$$

*where* $v$ = annual volatility
$\quad t$ = time, in years
$\quad v_t$ = volatility for time, $t$

As an example, a 3-month volatility would be equal to one-half of the annual volatility. In this case, $t$ would equal .25 (one-fourth of a year), so $v_{.25} = v\sqrt{.25} = .5v$.

The necessary groundwork has been laid for the computation of the probability necessary in the expected return calculation. The following formula gives the probability of a stock, which is currently at price $p$, being below some other price, $q$, at the end of the time period. The lognormal distribution is assumed.

Probability of stock being below price $q$ at end of time period, $t$:

$$P\text{ (below)} = N\left(\frac{\ln\left(\frac{q}{p}\right)}{v_t}\right)$$

where $N$ = cumulative normal distribution
$\quad p$ = current price of the stock
$\quad q$ = price in question
$\quad \ln$ = natural logarithm
$\quad v_t$ = volatility for the time period in question

If one is interested in computing the probability of the stock being *above* the given price, the formula is

$$P(\text{above}) = 1 - P(\text{below})$$

With this formula, the computation of expected return is quickly accomplished with a computer. One merely has to start at some price—the lower strike in a bull spread, for example—and work his way up to a higher price—the high strike for a bull spread. At each eighth of a point in between, the outcome of the spread is multiplied by the probability of being at that price and a running sum is kept.

Simplistically, the following iterative equation would be used.

$$P(\text{of being at price } x) = P(\text{below } x) - P(\text{below } y)$$

where $y$ is close to but less than $x$ in price. As an example:

$$P(\text{of being at } 32\tfrac{3}{8}) = P(\text{below } 32\tfrac{3}{8}) - P(\text{below } 32\tfrac{1}{4})$$

Thus once the low starting point is chosen and the probability of being below that price is determined, one can compute the probability of being at prices that are successively higher merely by iterating with the preceding formula. In reality, *one is using this information to integrate the distribution curve.* Any method of approximating the integral that is used in basic calculus—such as the Trapezoidal Rule or Simpson's Rule—would be applicable here for more accurate results, if they are desired.

A partial example of an expected return calculation follows.

*Example:* XYZ is currently at 33 and has an annual volatility of 25%. The previous bull spread is being established—buy the February 30 and sell the February 35 for a two-point debit—and these are 6-month options. Table 28-7 gives the necessary components for computing the expected return. Column (A), the probability of being below price $q$, is computed according to the previously given formula, where $p = 33$ and $v_t = .177$ ($v_t = .25\sqrt{\tfrac{1}{2}}$). The first stock price that needs to be looked at is 30, since all results for the bull spread are equal below that price—a 100% loss on the spread. The calculations would be performed for each eighth of a point up through a price of 35. The expected return is computed by multiplying the two right-hand columns, (B) and (C), and summing the results. Note that column (B) is determined by subtracting

**TABLE 28-7.** *Calculation of expected returns.*

| Price at Expiration (q) | (A) P(below q) | (B) P(of being at q) | (C) Profit on Spread |
|---|---|---|---|
| 30 | .295 | .295 | −$200 |
| 30⅛ | .301 | .006 | − 187.50 |
| 30¼ | .308 | .007 | − 175 |
| 30⅜ | .316 | .008 | − 162.50 |
| . | . | . | . |
| . | . | . | . |
| . | . | . | . |

successive numbers in column (A). It would not be particularly enlightening to carry this example to completion, since the rest of the computations are similar and there is a large number of them.

In theory, if one had the data and computer power, he could evaluate a wide range of strategies every day and come up with the best positions on an expected return basis. He would probably get a few option buys (puts or calls), some bull spreads, some naked writes and ratio calendar spreads, fewer straddles, ratio writes, and a few covered call writes. This theory would be somewhat difficult to apply in practice because of the massive amounts of calculations involved and also because of the inaccuracy of closing price data. It was mentioned previously that a computer will assume that "bad" closing prices are actually attainable. By a "bad" closing price, it is meant that the option did not trade simultaneously with the stock later in the day, and that the actual market for the option is somewhat different in price than is reflected by the closing price for the option. A daily contract volume "screen" will help alleviate this problem— for example, one may want to discard any option from his calculations if that option did not trade a predetermined, minimum amount of contracts during the previous day. Data that give closing bids and offers for each option are more expensive but also more reliable and would alleviate the problem of "bad" closing prices. In addition to a volume screen, another way of reducing the calculations required is to limit oneself to strategies in which one has interest, or which one is reasonably certain will fit in well with his investment objectives. Regardless of the limitations that one places upon the quantity of computations, some computer power is necessary to compute expected return. A sophisticated programmable calculator may be able to provide a real-time calculation, but could never be used to evaluate the entire option universe and come up with a ranking of the preferable situations each day. On-line computer systems are also available which can provide these types of calculations using up-to-the-minute prices. While real-time prices may occasionally be useful, it is not an absolute necessity to have them.

One other by-product of the expected return calculation is that it could be used as another model for predicting the theoretical value of an option. All one would have to do is compute the probabilities of the stock being at each successive price above the striking price of the option by expiration and sum them up. The result would be the theoretical option value. These data are published by some services and generally give a different theoretical value than would the Black-Scholes model. The reason for the difference most readily lies in the inclusion of the risk-free interest rate in the Black-Scholes model and its omission in the expected return model.

## APPLYING THE CALCULATIONS TO STRATEGY DECISIONS

### Call Writing

One method of ranking covered call writes that was described in Chapter 2 was to rank all the writes that provided at least a minimal acceptable level of return by their probability of not losing money. If one were interested in safety, he might decide to use this approach. Suppose that he decided that he would consider any write that provided an annualized total return (capital gains, dividends, and commissions) of at least 12%. This would eliminate many potential writes but would leave him with a fairly large number of writing candidates each day. He knows the downside break-even point at expiration in each write. Therefore, the probability of the stock being below that break-even point at expiration can be quickly computed. His final list would *rank those writes with the least chance of being below the break-even point at expiration as the best writes.* Again, this ranking is based on an expected probability and is of course no guarantee that the stock will not, in reality, fall below the break-even point. However, over time, *a list of this sort should provide the most conservative covered writes.*

> *Example:* XYZ is selling for 43 and a 6-month July 40 call is selling for 8 points. After including dividends and commission costs for a 500-share position, the downside break-even point at expiration is 36. If the annualized volatility of XYZ is 25%, the probability of making money at expiration can be computed. The 6-month volatility is 17.7% (25% times the square root of ½ year). The probability of being below 36 can be computed by using the formula given earlier in this section:
>
> $$P \text{ (below 36 in 6 months)} = N\left(\frac{\ln\left(\frac{36}{43}\right)}{.177}\right) = N\left(\frac{-.178}{.177}\right) = .159$$
>
> The expected probability of XYZ being below 36 in 6 months is 15.9%. Therefore, this would be an attractive write on a conservative basis, because it has a large probability of making money (nearly 85% chance

of not being below the break-even point at expiration). The return if exercised in this example is approximately 20% annualized, so it should be acceptable from a profit potential viewpoint as well. It is a relatively easy matter to perform a similar calculation, with the aid of a computer, on all covered writing candidates.

The ability to measure downside protection in terms of a common denominator—volatility—can be useful in other types of covered call writing analyses. The writer interested in writing out-of-the-money calls, which generally have higher profit potential, is still interested in having an idea of what his downside protection is. He might, for example, decide that he wants to invest in situations in which the probability of making money is at least 60%. This is not an unusually difficult requirement to fulfill, and will leave many attractive covered writes with a high profit potential to choose from. A downside requirement stated in terms of probability of success removes the necessity of having to impose arbitrary requirements. Typical arbitrary requirements would be including only calls that sell for one point or more, or stating that the downside protection must be a certain percentage of the stock price. These obviously cannot suffice for stocks with different volatilities. Rather, the downside protection criterion should be stated in terms of "probability of downside protection" or, alternatively, in terms of the volatility itself. In this manner, a uniform comparison can be made between volatile and nonvolatile stocks.

### *Call Buying*

The option buyer can also constructively use the measurement of volatility to aid him in his option buying decisions. In Chapter 3, it was shown that *evaluating the profitability of calls based on the volatility of the underlying stock is the correct way to analyze an option purchase.* One specific method of analysis will be described. There are certain variables in this analysis that may be altered to fit the call buyer's individual preferences, but the general logic is applicable to all cases.

As a first step, *one should decide upon a uniform stock movement for ranking call purchases.* One might decide to rank all purchases by how they would perform if the underlying stock moved up in accordance with its volatility. The phrase "in accordance with its volatility" must be quantified. For example, one might decide to assume that every stock could move up one standard deviation, and then rank all call purchases on that basis. *The prospective call buyer must also fix the time period that he wants to use.* Generally, one looks at purchases to be held for 30 days, 60 days, and 90 days.

The exact steps to be followed in the analysis of profitability and risk can be listed as follows:

1. Specify the distance that underlying stock can move, up or down, in terms of its volatility.
2. Select the holding period over which the analysis is to take place.

*Profitability*
3. Calculate the stock price which the stock would move up to, when the foregoing assumptions are implemented.
4. Using a pricing model, such as the Black-Scholes model, estimate what the option price would become after the upward stock movement.
5. Calculate the percent profit, after deducting commissions.
6. Repeat steps 4 and 5 for each option on the stock.

A final ranking of all potential call buys can be obtained by performing steps 3 through 6 on all stocks, and ranking the purchases by their percentage reward.

*Risk*
7. Calculate the stock price that the stock could fall to, when the assumptions in steps 1 and 2 are applied.
8. With a model, price the option after the stock's decline.
9. Calculate the percentage loss after commissions.
10. Compute a reward/risk ratio: Divide the percentage profit from step 5 by the percentage risk from step 9.
11. Repeat steps 8 through 10 for each option on the stock.

A final ranking of less aggressive option purchases can be constructed by performing steps 7 through 11 on all stocks, and ranking the purchases by their reward/risk ratio.

The higher profitability list of option purchases will tend to be at- or slightly out-of-the-money calls. The less aggressive list, ranked by reward/risk potential, will tend to be in-the-money options.

*Example:* Steps 1 and 2: Suppose an investor wants to look at option purchases for a 90-day holding period, under the assumption that each stock could move up by one standard deviation in that time. (There is only about a 16% chance that a stock will move more than one standard deviation in a given time period. Therefore, in actual practice, one might want to use a smaller stock movement in his ranking calculations). Furthermore, assume that the following data are known:

XYZ common, 41;

XYZ volatility, 30% annually;

XYZ January 40 call, 4; and

time to January expiration, 6 months.

Step 3: Calculate upward stock potential. This is accomplished by the following formula:

$$q = pe^{av_t}$$

where

$p$ = current stock price

$q$ = potential stock price

$v_t$ = volatility for the time period, $t$

$a$ = a constant (see below)

The constants, $a$ and $t$, are fixed under the assumptions in steps 1 and 2. The first constant, $a$, is the number of standard deviations of movement to be allowed. In our example, $a = 1$. That is, the analysis is being made under the assumption that the stock could move up by one standard deviation. The second constant, $t$, is .25, since the analysis is for a 90-day holding period, which is 25% of a year. In this example,

$$v_t = v\sqrt{t} = .30\ \sqrt{.25} = .30 \times .50 = .15$$

so

$$q = 41e^{.15} = 41 \times 1.16 = 47.64$$

Thus this stock would move up to approximately 47⅝ if it moved one standard deviation in exactly 90 days.

Step 4: Using the Black-Scholes model, the XYZ January 40 call can be priced. It would be worth approximately 8⅛ if XYZ were at 47⅝ and there were 90 days' less life in the call.

Step 5: Calculate the profit potential. For this example, commissions will be ignored, but they should be included in a real-life situation.

$$\text{Percent profit} = \frac{8\frac{1}{8} - 4}{4} = \frac{4\frac{1}{8}}{4} = 103\%$$

Thus if XYZ stock moves up by one standard deviation over the next 90 days, this call would yield a projected profit of 103%. Recall again that there is only about a 16% chance of the stock actually moving this far. If all options on all stocks are ranked under this same assumption, however, a fair comparison of profitable options will be obtained.

Step 6 is omitted from this example—it would consist of performing a similar profit analysis (steps 4 and 5) on all other XYZ options, with the assumption that XYZ is at 47⅝ after 90 days.

Step 7: Calculate the downside potential of XYZ. The formula for the downside potential of the stock is nearly the same as that used in step 3 for the upside potential:

$$q = pe^{-av_t}$$
$$= 41e^{-.15} = 41 \times .86 = 35.29$$

XYZ could fall to approximately 35¼ in 90 days if it fell by one standard deviation. Note that the actual distances that XYZ could rise and fall are not the same. The upward potential was 6⅝ points, while the downward potential is about 5¾ points. This difference is due to the use of the lognormal distribution.

Step 8: Using the Black-Scholes model, one could estimate that the XYZ January 40 call would be worth about 1⅛ if XYZ were at 35¼ in 90 days.

Step 9: The risk potential in the January 40 call would be

$$\text{Percent risk} = \frac{4 - 1⅛}{4} = \frac{2⅞}{4} = 72\%$$

Step 10: The reward/risk ratio is merely the percentage reward divided by the percentage risk:

$$\text{Reward/risk ratio} = \frac{103\%}{72\%} = 1.43$$

Step 11: This analysis would be repeated for all XYZ options, and then for all other optionable stocks. The less aggressive call purchases would be ranked by their reward/risk ratios, with higher ratios representing more attractive purchases. More aggressive purchases would be ranked by the potential rewards only (step 5).

This completes the call buying example. Before leaving this section, it should be noted that the assumption of ranking the purchases after one full standard deviation movement by the underlying stock is probably excessive. A more moderate assumption would be that the stock might be able to move .7 standard deviation. There is about a 25% expected chance that a stock could move .7 standard deviation at the end of a fixed time period.

### *Pricing a Put Option*

Theoretical models for pricing put options have been derived—that is, ones which are separate from call pricing models. Black and Scholes presented such a model in their original paper. However, as has been demonstrated, there is a relationship between put and call prices in the listed option market due to the conversion and reversal strategies.

*One could use the basic call pricing model for the purpose of predicting put prices if he assumes that arbitrageurs will efficiently influence the market via conversions.* Theoreticians will argue that such a method of pricing puts assumes that the arbitrage process is always present and works efficiently, and that this is not true. The "conversion efficiency" assumption could be a serious fault if one were trying to determine the exact overpriced or underpriced nature of the put option. However, if one is merely comparing various put strategies under constant assumptions, the arbitrage model for pricing puts works quite well.

The listed put's price can be estimated by using the call pricing model and the arbitrage formula. Recall that the arbitrageur must include the cost of carrying the position as well as the dividends to be received.

$$\text{Theoretical put price} = \text{theoretical call price} + \text{strike price} - \text{stock price} - \text{carrying cost} + \text{dividends}$$

The "theoretical call price" is obtained from the Black-Scholes model. The carrying cost is the cost of money (interest rate) times the striking price multiplied by the time to expiration. Recall that this is the approximation formula for carrying cost (see Chapter 27 for comments on present value and compounding). Consequently, if XYZ were at 41 and a 6-month January 40 call option were valued at 4 points by the Black-Scholes model, the theoretical put price could be estimated. Assume that the cost of money interest rate is 10%, annually, and that the stock will pay \$.50 in dividends in 6 months ($t = \frac{1}{2}$ year).

$$\text{Theoretical put price} = 4 + 40 - 41 - (.10 \times 40 \times \tfrac{1}{2}) + .50$$
$$= 3 - 2 + \tfrac{1}{2}$$
$$= 1\tfrac{1}{2}$$

This means that if the call could be sold for 4 points, the arbitrageur would be willing to pay up to 1½ points for the put to establish a conversion. The arbitrageur's price is used as the theoretical listed put price estimate.

### Put Buying

*Put option purchases can be ranked in a manner very similar to that described for call option buying.* Reward opportunities occur when the stock falls in accordance with its volatility. An upward stock movement represents risk for the put buyer. All of the 11 steps in the previous section on call buying would be applicable to put buying. The pricing of the put necessary for steps 4 and 8 would be done in accordance with the arbitrage model just presented.

If an underlying stock does not have listed puts trading, the synthetic put can be considered. Recall that synthetic puts are created for customers by some brokerage houses. The brokerage sells the stock short and buys a call. The customer can purchase the synthetic put for the amount of the risk involved, plus any dividends to be paid by the underlying stock. The synthetic put pricing formula—which would be used in steps 4 and 8 of the option buying analysis—is exactly the same as the arbitrage model for listed puts, except that the carrying costs are omitted:

$$\begin{matrix} \text{Theoretical synthetic} \\ \text{put price} \end{matrix} = \begin{matrix} \text{theoretical} \\ \text{call price} \end{matrix} + \begin{matrix} \text{strike} \\ \text{price} \end{matrix} - \begin{matrix} \text{stock} \\ \text{price} \end{matrix} + \text{dividends}$$

When the ranking analysis is performed, very few synthetic puts will appear as attractive put buys. This is because when the customer buys a synthetic put, he must advance the full cost of the dividend, but receives no offsetting cost reduction for the credit being earned by the short stock position. Consequently, synthetic puts are always more expensive, on a relative basis, than are listed puts. However, if one is particularly bearish on a stock that has no listed puts, a synthetic put may still prove to be a worthwhile investment. The recommended analysis can give him a feeling for the reward and risk potential of the investment.

### Calendar Spreads

*The pricing model can help in determining which neutral calendar spreads are most attractive.* Recall that in a neutral calendar spread, one is selling a near-term call and buying a longer-term call, when the stock is relatively close to the striking price of the calls. The object of the spread is to capture the time decay differential between the two options. The neutral calendar spread is normally closed at the expiration of the near-term option. The pricing model can aid the spreader by estimating what the profit potential of the spread is, as well as aiding in the determination of the break-even points of the position at near-term expiration.

To determine the maximum profit potential of the spread, assume that the near-term call expires worthless and use the pricing model to estimate the value of the longer-term call with the stock exactly at the striking price. Since commission costs are relatively large in spread transactions, it would be best to have the computations include commissions. A second profit potential is sometimes useful as well—*the profit if unchanged.* To determine how much profit would be made if the stock were unchanged at near-term expiration, assume that the spread is closed with the near-term call equal to its intrinsic value (zero if the stock is currently below the strike, or the difference between the stock price and the strike if the stock is initially above the strike). Then use the pricing model to estimate the value of the longer-term call, which will then have three or six months of life remaining, with the stock unchanged. The resulting differential between the near-term call's intrinsic value and the estimated value of the longer-term call is an estimate of the price at which the spread could be liquidated. The profit, of course, is that differential minus the current (initial) differential, less commissions.

In the earlier discussion of calendar spreads, it was pointed out that there is both an upside break-even point and a downside break-even point at near-term expiration. These *break-even points can be estimated with the use of the pricing model.* One method of determination involves estimating the liquidating value of the spread at successive stock prices. When the liquidating value is found to be equal to the initial value, plus commissions, a break-even point has been located.

*Example:* If the spread in question is using options with a striking price of 30, one would begin his break-even point calculations at a price of 30. Estimate the liquidating value of the spread at 30, 29⅞, 29¾, 29⅝, and so forth until the break-even point is found. Once the downside break-even point has been determined in this manner, the iterations to locate the upside break-even point should begin again at the striking price. Thus one would evaluate the liquidating value at 30, 30⅛, 30¼, and so on. This is somewhat of a brute-force method, but with a large computer it is fairly fast. The number of calculations can be reduced by adopting a more complicated iteration process.

One word of caution should be added about the determination of the break-even points. As previously stated, the Black-Scholes model tends to overprice in-the-money calls. Thus, *at times, one may not be able to locate an upside break-even point for low-debit calendar spreads.* To counteract this, one should set some sort of reasonable upside limit on his iterations so that he does not waste excessive amounts of computing in an attempt to find a break-even point that is indeterminate with the pricing model.

A final useful piece of information can be obtained with the aid of the pricing model—*the theoretical value of the spread.* Recompute the estimated value of both the near-term and longer-term calls at the current time and stock price, using the implied volatility for the underlying stock. The resultant differential between the two estimated call prices may differ substantially from the actual differential, perhaps highlighting an attractive calendar spread situation. One would want to establish spreads where the theoretical differential is *greater than* the actual differential (that is, he would want to buy a "cheap" calendar spread).

Once these pieces of information have been computed, the strategist can rank the spread possibilities by whatever criterion he finds most workable. *The logical method of ranking the spreads would be by their return if unchanged.* The spreads with the highest return if unchanged—at near-term expiration—would be those in which the stock price and striking price were close together initially, a basic requirement of the neutral calendar spread. More complicated ranking systems should try to include the theoretical value of the spread and possibly even the maximum potential of the spread. *A similar analysis can, of course, be worked out for put calendar spreads,* using the arbitrage pricing model for puts.

### Ratio Strategies

Ratio strategies involve selling naked options. Therefore, the strategist has potentially large risk—either to the upside or to the downside or both. He should attempt to get a feeling for how probable this risk is. The formulae for determining the probability of a stock being above or below a certain price at some time in the future can give him these probabilities. For example, in a straddle writing situation, the strategist would want to compute such arithmetic quantities as maximum profit potential, return if unchanged, collateral required at upside break-even point or at upside action point (recall that the collateral requirement increases for naked options on an adverse stock movement), and the break-even points themselves. The probability of being above the upper break-even point at expiration and the probability of being below the lower break-even point should be computed as well. Moreover, an expected return analysis could be performed on the position to determine the general level of profitability of the position with respect to all other positions of the same type on other stocks. Such an expected return analysis need not assume that the position is held to expiration. Firm traders, paying little or no commissions, might be interested in seeing the expected results for a holding period as short as 30 days or less. Public customers might use a longer holding period, on the assumption that they would not trade the position as readily because of commission costs. Ratio positions should be ranked either by return if unchanged, or by expected return.

*The analyses described for calendar spreads and ratio positions should not be relied upon as gospel.* In the proposed forms of analysis, one is projecting future option prices and stock prices under the assumption that the volatility of the underlying stock will remain the same. Although this may be true in some cases, there will also be many times when the volatility of the underlying stock will change during the life of the position. If the volatility decreases, the projected break-even points for a calendar spread will be too far away from the striking price. Thus a loss would result at some prices where the spreader expected to make money. If the volatility increases, the expected return of a ratio position will drop, because the probabilities of the stock moving outside the profit range will increase, thereby increasing the probability of loss.

The effect of a changing volatility can be counteracted, in theory, by continuing to monitor the position daily after it has been established. In a straddle write, for example, if the stock begins to move dramatically, the expected return may become very low. If this happens, adjustments could be made to the position to improve it. Such monitoring is difficult to apply in practice for the public customer, because the commission costs involved in constant position adjustments would mount rapidly. There is no exact method that would allow for infrequent, periodic adjustments, but *by using a follow-up analysis the public customer may be able to get a better feeling for the timing of adjusting a position.* For example, suppose that one initially wrote a 5-point straddle when the stock was at 30. Sometime later, the stock is at 34. The expected return of writing a 5-point straddle with a strike of 30 when the stock is at 34 could be computed for the shorter time period remaining until expiration. If the expected return is negative, an adjustment needs to be made. Adopting this form of adjusting would keep the number of trades to a minimum, but would still allow the strategist to see when his position has become improperly balanced. Of course, the current volatility would be used in making these determinations. Another follow-up monitoring technique, using the deltas of the options involved, is presented later in this chapter, and has been described several times previously.

## FACILITATION OR
## INSTITUTIONAL BLOCK POSITIONING

In this and the following section, *the advantages of using the hedge ratio will be outlined.* These strategies are primarily member firm, not public customer, strategies since they are best applied in the absence of commission costs. An institutional block trader may be able to use options to help him in his positioning, particularly when he is trying to help a client in a stock transaction.

Suppose that a block trader wants to make a bid for stock to facilitate a customer's sell order. If he wants some sort of a hedge until he can sell the stock that he buys, and the stock has listed options, he can sell some options to hedge his stock position. To determine the quantity of options to sell, he can use the hedge ratio. The exact formula for the hedge ratio was given earlier in this chapter in the section on the Black-Scholes pricing model. It is one of the components of the formula. Simply stated, the hedge ratio is merely the delta of the option—that is, the amount by which the option will change in price for small changes in the stock price. By selling the correct number of calls against his stock purchase, the block trader will have a neutral position. This position would, in theory, neither gain nor lose for small changes in the stock price. He is therefore buying himself time until he can unwind the position in the open market.

> *Example:* A trader buys 10,000 shares of XYZ and a January 30 call is trading with a hedge ratio of .50. To have a neutral position, the trader should sell options against 20,000 shares of stock (10,000 divided by .50 equals 20,000). Thus, he should sell 200 of the January 30's. If the hedge ratio is correct—largely a function of the volatility estimate of the underlying stock—the trader will have no risk or reward on the position for small stock movements. Of course, if the block trader *wants* to assume some risk, that is a different matter. However, for the purposes of this discussion, the assumption is made that the block trader merely wants to facilitate the trade in the most risk-free manner possible. In this sample position, if the stock moves up by 1 point, the option should move up by ½ point. The trader would make $10,000 on his stock

position and would lose $10,000 on his 200 short options—he has no gain or loss. Once the trader has the neutral position established, he can then begin to concentrate on unwinding the position.

*In actual practice, this hedge ratio may not work exactly because of the fact that it tends to change constantly as the stock price changes.* If the trader finds the stock moving more than fractionally, he may have to add more calls or buy some in, to maintain a neutral hedge ratio. This would expose him to some risk, but the risk is substantially smaller than if he had not hedged at all. Of course, there would also be certain cases in which he would profit by the stock price change as well.

A similar hedge can be established by the block trader who sells stock to accommodate a customer buy order. He could buy calls in accordance with the hedge ratio, to set up a neutral position.

*This process of facilitation is quite widely practiced,* especially by brokerage houses that are trying to attract the large business of the institutional customer. Since the introduction of listed call options and their applications for facilitating orders, many quotes for large blocks of stock have improved considerably. The block trader (who works for the brokerage house) is willing to make a higher bid or a lower offer if he can use options to hedge his position. This facilitation with options results in a better market (higher bid or lower offer) from the point of view of the institutional customer. Without the availability of such listed options, the block trader would probably make a bid or an offer that was substantially away from the prevailing market price in order to work out of his stock-only position with a lessened degree of risk. This would obviously present a poorer market for the institutional customer.

### The Neutral Spread

*The hedge ratios of two or more options may be used to determine a neutral spread.* This strategy is especially useful to market markers on the options exchanges who may want to reduce the risk of options bought or sold in the process of providing a public market. If the hedge ratios of two options are known, *the neutral ratio is determined by dividing the two hedge ratios.*

*Example:* An XYZ January 35 has a hedge ratio of .25 and an XYZ January 30 has a hedge ratio of .50, so a neutral ratio would be 2:1 (.50 divided by .25). That is, one would sell 2 January 35's against one long January 30, or, conversely, would buy 2 January 35's against one short January 30. Thus a market-maker who has just bought 50 January 30's in an effort to provide a market for a public seller of that call could hedge his position by selling 100 January 35's. This should keep his risk small—for small stock price changes—until he can unwind the position. The ratio for the neutral spread is not as sensitive to the volatility estimate of the underlying stock as is the ratio concerning stock and options. This is because the same volatility estimate is applied to both options, and the resultant ratio for the spread would not tend to change greatly.

*The risk trader can also use the neutral spread ratio to his advantage.* This concept was illustrated several times in previous chapters describing ratio writing, ratio spreads, and straddle writes. Ratio spreads are quite popular with member firm traders and floor traders. Recall that a ratio spread consists of buying options at a certain strike, and selling more options further out-of-the-money. The hedge ratios can, of course, be used by the trader, or by a public customer, to initially establish a neutral position. Perhaps more important, the hedge ratio can also be used as a follow-up action to keep the position neutral after the stock changes in price. This strategy is the "delta spread" described in Chapter 11.

*The risk trader is not attempting to establish the spread with the idea of minimizing risk for small stock movements.* Rather, he is looking to make a profit, but would prefer to remain as neutral as possible on the underlying stock. He is implementing a risk strategy that has a neutral outlook on the underlying stock. He is selling much more time value premium than he is buying.

> *Example:* The purchase of 15 January 30 calls and the sale of 30 January 35 calls—a ratio call spread—may be a position taken for profit potential. It would be a neutral position if the deltas were .60 and .30, for example. This spread would do best if the stock were at exactly 35 at expiration. However, if the stock rose quickly before expiration, the spread ratio would decrease from 2:1 to perhaps 3:2. That is, the neutral ratio between the January 30 call and the January 35 call should be 3 short January 35's to 2 long January 30's. If the trader wants to balance his position, he could buy 5 more January 30's, giving him a total of 20 long versus the 30 short January 35's that he originally sold. Conversely, if the stock dropped in price, the neutral spread ratio might increase, indicating that more calls should be sold. For example, if this stock declines, the neutral ratio might be 3:1. In that case, 15 more January 35's could be sold, making the position short 45 calls versus 15 long calls, which would produce the neutral 3:1 ratio.

*It would not be proper to adjust the ratio constantly,* because the frequent whipsaw losses on trading movements would wipe out the profit potential of the position. However, the trader may want to pick out points, in advance, at which he wants to reevaluate his position before something drastic goes wrong. For example, if the foregoing spread were established with the stock at a price of 30, the spreader might want to readjust at 33 or 27, whichever comes first.

By monitoring the spread using the hedge ratio, the trader may also be able to discern whether he has established too bullish or too bearish of a position.

> *Example:* The trader starts with the example described above—long 15 January 30 calls and short 30 January 35 calls—when the hedge ratios were .60 and .30, respectively. Some later time, the stock falls to 27 and the trader needs to reevaluate his position. The hedge ratios may have become .42 for the January 30 and .14 for the January 35, indicating that a 3:1 ratio would be neutral (.42/.14 = 3). He now has a bullish position because his 2:1 ratio is *less than* the neutral 3:1 ratio. It is not mandatory that the trader act on this information. He may actually be bullish on the stock at this point and decide to remain with his position. The usefulness of the hedge ratio is that it allows him to see that his position is bullish and therefore he can make a correct judgment. Without this knowledge, he might still think his position to be neutral, a critical mistake if he indeed wants to be neutral. If the trader's ratio is greater than the neutral ratio (2:1 vs. 3:2, for example), he is bearishly positioned.

As a final point, it should be noted that the ratio can be adjusted by buying or selling either option.

> *Example:* If the stock falls and it is desired that the ratio be increased to 3:1, one might sell more January 35's or might decide to sell out some of his January 30's. A bullish adjustment could be made by buying on either side of the spread in a similar manner. In general, one should adjust by selling time premium or buying intrinsic value. That is, out-of-the-moneys are usually sold and in-the-moneys are usually bought, when adjusting.

## AIDING IN FOLLOW-UP ACTION

The computer can also be an invaluable aid to the strategist in that it can help him monitor his positions. It is generally necessary for the strategist to have some way of inputting his positions into an inventory data base and also to have some way of identifying different securities that are grouped within the same trading position. Once this has been done, *the computer can simultaneously read a pricing tape and the inventory data base to generate information concerning the current status of any position.*

A current mark to market (profit and loss) statement is of obvious use in that the trader can see how he is doing each day. The computer can also easily generate a set of warning flags that may be of interest to the trader and could print out a list summarizing possible positions that need action. In most of the strategies that were described, it was shown that the strategist should avoid early assignment if at all possible. It is a simple matter for the computer to calculate the remaining time value premium of any short options, and to warn the trader if there is only a small amount of time value premium remaining—perhaps ½ point or less. For similar reasons, the trader may want to have a daily list of positions that are nearing maturity—perhaps with less than 1 month of life remaining in the options. A flag indicating an approaching ex-dividend date might also be useful for this purpose. If the trader inputs another piece of information into the data base, the computer can help him in another follow-up action. In most strategies that were described, especially those involving uncovered options, the trader wants to take some sort of follow-up action based on the price movement of the underlying stock. If the stock rallies too far, he may want to cover short calls or buys other calls as protection. If the stock declines too far, similar maneuvers would apply to put options or to rolling down short calls. If the trader inputs the stock prices at which he would like to take action, the computer can monitor each day's closing price of the stock and generate a list of positions that have exceeded their upside or downside action points.

The computer can also do more sophisticated types of position monitoring. Recall that it was pointed out that the deltas of the options involved in a position can be compared to each other to tell whether the position is bullish or bearish. The Black-Scholes model can be used to calculate the deltas of the options in one's positions. Then the net position can be determined by the computer, thereby telling the trader whether his position has become "delta long" (bullish), "delta short" (bearish), or neutral. If he sees that a position is bearish and he does not want to be structured in that way, he can make bullish adjustments. The delta spread and neutral spread strategies very conveniently lend themselves to such types of follow-up action, although any of the more complicated straddle writing, and protected straddle writing positions can be monitored usefully in this way as well.

The computation of determining whether a position is net short or net long generally involves computing the "equivalent stock position" (ESP). If one owns 10 calls which have a delta of .45, his equivalent stock position from those calls is 10 × 100 shares per call × .45 =

450. That is, owning those 10 calls is equivalent to owning 450 shares of the underlying stock, according to the delta. All puts and calls can be reduced to an ESP and can then, of course, be combined with any actual long or short stock in the position to produce an ESP for the entire strategy. The resultant ESP for each of the trader's positions can be printed out by the computer along with the items described above.

## *IMPLEMENTATION*

Many of the analyses described in this chapter can be obtained from a reliable data service or brokerage firm. The strategist who plans to prepare his own analysis—either by himself or by contracting the programming work out—should be aware that computer programs cannot be written in the COBOL language, for the mathematics are far too complicated for a business language. FORTRAN or ALGOL would suffice as programming languages, as would any higher-level language, such as PL/I. Reliable option pricing data that include dividend information on the underlying stock are also necessary. The larger programmable calculators can handle calculations such as the Black-Scholes model, computing the hedge ratio, and determining the probability of a stock being above or below a certain price at some future time. However, more involved calculations, such as computing the implied volatility or determining the expected return of a position, would require the use of a computer.

## *SUMMARY*

Two basic mathematical aids have been presented—the pricing model and the ability to predict the probability of a stock's movement. The hedge ratio and the expected return analysis are extensions of the basic aids. Any strategy can be evaluated with these tools. Such an analysis should be able to give the trader or strategist some idea of the relative attractiveness of establishing the position and may also aid in follow-up adjustments to the position. All the analyses rely heavily on one's estimate of the volatility of the underlying stock. The implied volatility seems to be one of the best ways to obtain an accurate, current volatility estimate, since it is derived from the prices in the market itself. The applications presented here are not all-inclusive. The strategist who is, or becomes, familiar with the advantages of rigorous mathematical analysis will be able to constuct many other aids for his trading, which utilize the basic mathematics that have been described in this chapter.

# *Taxes*

In this chapter, the basic tax treatment of listed options will be outlined and several tax strategies will be presented. The reader should be aware of the fact that tax laws change, and therefore should consult tax counsel before actually implementing any tax-oriented strategy. The interpretation of certain tax strategies by the Internal Revenue Service is subject to reclarification or change, as well.

An option is a capital asset and any gains or losses are capital gains or losses. Differing tax consequences apply, depending on whether the option trade is a complete transaction by itself, or whether it becomes part of a stock transaction via exercise or assignment. Listed option transactions which are closed out in the options market or are allowed to expire worthless are short-term capital transactions. Gains from option purchases could possibly be long-term gains if the holding period of the option exceeds the current long-term capital gains holding period. This is not possible at the current time, since the longest options have lives of nine months, and the minimum holding period for long-term capital gains is more than one year. However, there is always the possibility that listed options with longer maturities will be introduced.

Listed options which are exercised or assigned fall into a different category for tax purposes. The original premium of the option transaction is combined into the stock transaction. There is no tax liability on this stock position until the stock position itself is closed out. There are four different combinations of exercising or assigning puts or calls. Table 29-1 summarizes the method of applying the option premium to the stock cost or sale price.

**TABLE 29-1.** *Applying the option premium to the stock cost or sale price.*

| Action | Tax Treatment |
|---|---|
| Call buyer exercises | Add call premium to stock cost |
| Put buyer exercises | Subtract put premium from stock sale price |
| Call writer assigned | Add call premium to stock sale price |
| Put writer assigned | Subtract put premium from stock cost |

Examples of how to treat these various transactions are given in the following sections. In addition to examples explaining the basic tax treatment, some supplementary strategies are included as well.

## BASIC TAX TREATMENT

### Call Buyer

If a call holder subsequently sells the call or allows it to expire worthless, he has a short-term capital gain or loss. Technically, the holding period of the option determines whether the gain or loss is long-term or short-term, but, as mentioned previously, a long-term gain would not be possible until listed options with a maturity of more than one year are available. For tax purposes, an option that expires worthless is considered to have been sold at zero dollars on the expiration date.

*Example:* An investor purchases an XYZ October 50 call for 5 points on July 1. He sells the call for 9 points on September 1. That is, he realizes a capital gain via a closing transaction. His taxable gain would be computed as follows, assuming that a $25 commission was paid on both the purchase and the sale.

| | |
|---|---|
| Net proceeds of sale ($900 − $25) | $875 |
| Net cost ($500 + $25) | 525 |
| Short-term gain: | $350 |

Alternatively, if the stock had fallen in price by October expiration and the October 50 call had expired worthless, the call buyer would have lost $525—his entire net cost. If he had held the call until it expired worthless, he would have a short-term capital loss of $525 to report among his taxable transactions.

## Put Buyer

The holder of a put has much the same tax consequences as the holder of a call, provided that he is not also long the underlying stock. This initial discussion of tax consequences to the put holder will assume that he does *not* simultaneously own the underlying stock. If the put holder sells his put in the option market or allows it to expire worthless, the gain or loss is treated as short-term capital gain. Historically, the purchase of a put was viewed as perhaps the only way an investor could attain a long-term gain in a declining market. However, unless put options with a maturity of longer than one year are introduced, it would be impossible for put holders in today's market to achieve a long-term gain.

Example: An investor buys an XYZ April 40 put for 2 points with the stock at 43. Later, the stock drops in price and the put is sold for 5 points. The commissions were $25 on each option trade, so the tax consequences would be:

|                              |          |
| ---------------------------- | -------- |
| Net sale proceeds ($500 − $25) | $475   |
| Net cost ($200 + $25)          | − 225  |
| Short-term capital gain        | $250   |

Alternatively, if he had sold the put at a loss, perhaps in a rising market, he would have a short-term capital loss. Furthermore, if he allowed the put to expire totally worthless, his short-term loss would be equal to the entire net cost of $225.

## Call Writer

Written calls that are bought back in the listed option market or are allowed to expire worthless are short-term capital gains. This would be true even if options with a maturity of more than one year are eventually introduced, since a written call cannot produce a long-term gain, regardless of the holding period. This treatment of a written call holds true even if the investor simultaneously owned the underlying stock (that is, he had a covered write). As long as the call is bought back or allowed to expire worthless, the gain or loss on the call is treated separately from the underlying stock for tax purposes.

*Example:* A trader sells naked an XYZ July 30 call for 3 points and buys it back three months later at a price of 1. The commissions were $25 for each trade, so the tax gain would be:

| | |
|---|---|
| Net sale proceeds ($300 − $25) | $275 |
| Net cost ($100 + $25) | − 125 |
| Short-term gain | $150 |

If the investor had not bought the call back, but had been fortunate enough to be able to allow it expire worthless, his gain for tax purposes would have been the entire $275, representing his net sale proceeds. The purchase cost is considered to be zero for an option that expires worthless.

### Put Writer

The tax treatment of written puts is quite similar to that of written calls. If the put is bought back in the open market or is allowed to expire worthless, the transaction is a short-term capital item.

*Example:* An investor writes an XYZ July 40 put for 4 points, and later buys it back for 2 points after a rally by the underlying stock. The commissions were $25 on each option trade, so the tax situation would be:

| | |
|---|---|
| Net put sale price ($400 − $25) | $375 |
| Net put cost ($100 + $25) | − 125 |
| Short-term capital gain | $250 |

If the put were allowed to expire worthless, the investor would have a net gain of $375, and this gain would be short-term.

## EXERCISE AND ASSIGNMENT

### Call Exercise

A call holder who has an in-the-money call might decide to exercise the call rather than sell it in the options market. If he does this, there are no tax consequences on the option trade itself. Rather, the cost of the stock is increased by the net cost of the original call option. Moreover, the holding period begins on the day the stock is purchased (the day after the call was exercised). The option's holding period has no bearing on the stock position that resulted from the exercise.

*Example:* An XYZ October 50 call was bought for 5 points on July 1. The stock had risen by October expiration, and the call holder decided to exercise the call on October 20. The option commission was $25 and the stock commission was $85. The cost basis for the stock would be computed as follows:

Buy 100 XYZ at 50 via exercise
($5,000 plus $85 commission)          $5,085
Original call cost ($500 plus $25)        525
    Total tax basis of stock                $5,610
    Holding period of stock begins on October 21.

When this stock is eventually sold, it will be a gain or a loss, depending on the stock's sale price as compared to the tax basis of $5,610 for the stock. Furthermore, it will be a short-term transaction unless the stock is held until October 21 of the following year.

### Call Assignment

If a written call is not closed out, but is instead assigned, the call's net sale proceeds are added to the sale proceeds of the underlying stock. The call's holding period is lost, and the stock position is considered to have been sold on the date of the assignment, which is the day after the exercise.

*Example:* A naked writer sells an XYZ July 30 call for 3 points, and is later assigned rather than buying back the option when it was in-the-money near expiration. The stock commission is $75. His net sale proceeds for the stock would be computed as follows:

Net call sale proceeds ($300 −$25)          $  275
Net stock proceeds from assignment
  of 100 shares at 30 ($3,000 − $75)         2,925
    Net stock sale proceeds                   $3,200

In the case where the investor writes a naked, or uncovered, call, he sells stock short upon assignment. He may, of course, cover the short sale by purchasing stock in the open market for delivery. Such a short sale of stock is governed by the applicable tax rules pertaining to short sales—that any gains or losses from the short sale of stock are short-term gains or losses.

*Tax Treatment for the Covered Writer.* If, on the other hand, the investor was assigned on a covered call—that is, he was operating the covered writing strategy—and he elects to deliver the stock that he owns against the assignment notice, he has a complete stock transaction. The net cost of the stock was determined by its purchase price at an earlier date and the net sale proceeds are, of course, determined by the assignment in accordance with the preceding example. It is important to note that the sale of a call against the underlying stock does not, in any way, affect the holding period of the underlying stock. Thus, if the covered call writer has held the stock long enough to qualify for long-term capital treatment by the time that the call is assigned, he is allowed to treat the entire stock transaction as a long-term capital gain. This is true even if the call was written just prior to the stock's qualifying for long-term treatment.

*Example:* On January 1, an investor bought 100 shares of XYZ at 32, paying $75 in commissions, and simultaneously wrote a 3-month April 35 call for 2 points. The April 35 expired worthless, and the investor then wrote an October 35 call for 3 points. In October, the investor bought back the October 35 call for 6 points (it was in-the-money) and sold a January 40 call for 4 points. In January, on the expiration day, the stock was called away at 40. The investor would have a long-term capital gain on his stock because he had held it for more than one year. He would also have two short-term capital transactions from the April 35 and October 35 calls. Tables 29-2 and 29-3 show his net tax treatment from operating this covered writing strategy for slightly over one year. The option commission on each trade was $25.

Things have indeed worked out quite well, both profitwise and taxwise, for this covered call writer. Not only has he made a net profit of $850 from his transactions on the stock and options over the period of one year, but he has received very favorable tax treatment. He can take a short-term loss of $175 from the combined April and October option transactions, and is able to take the $1,025 gain as a long-term gain.

This example demonstrates an important tax consequence for the covered call writer: his optimum scenario taxwise is a rising market, for he may be able to achieve a long-term gain on the underlying stock if he holds it for at least one year, while simultaneously subtracting short-term losses from written calls that were closed out at higher prices. Unfortunately, in a declining market the opposite result could

**TABLE 29-2.** *Summary of trades.*

| | |
|---|---|
| January 1 | Bought 100 XYZ at 32 |
| | Sold 1 April 35 call at 2 |
| April | April call expired worthless |
| | Sold 1 October 35 call at 3 |
| October | Bought back October 35 call for 6 points |
| | Sold 1 January 40 call for 4 points |
| January | (of the following year) |
| | 100 XYZ called away at 40 |

**TABLE 29-3.** *Tax treatment of trades.*

Short-term capital items:

| | | |
|---|---|---|
| April 35 call: | Net proceeds ($200 − $25) | $175 |
| | Net cost (expired worthless) | 0 |
| | Short-term capital gain | $175 |
| October 35 call: | Net proceeds ($300 − $25) | $275 |
| | Net cost ($600 + $25) | − 625 |
| | Short-term capital loss | ($350) |

Long-term capital item:

| | | |
|---|---|---|
| 100 shares XYZ: | Purchased January 1 of one year and sold at January expiration of the following year. Therefore, held for more than one year, qualifying for long-term treatment. | |
| | Net sale proceeds of stock (assigned call): | |
| |    January 40 call sale proceeds | |
| |      ($400 − $25) | $ 375 |
| |    Sold 100 XYZ at 40 strike | |
| |      ($4,000 − $75) | + 3,925 |
| | | $4,300 |
| | Net cost of stock (January 1 trade): | |
| |    Bought 100 at 32 ($3,200 + $75) | − 3,275 |
| | Long-term capital gain | $1,025 |

occur: short-term option gains coupled with the possibility of a long-term loss on the underlying stock. There are ways to avoid long-term stock losses, such as buying a put (discussed later in the chapter), or going short against the box before the stock becomes long-term. However, these maneuvers would interrupt the covered writing strategy, which may not be a wise tactic.

In summary, then, the covered call writer who finds himself with an in-the-money call written and expiration date drawing near, may have several alternatives open to him. If the stock is not yet held long-term, he might elect to buy back the written call and to write another call whose expiration date is beyond the date required for a long-term holding period on the stock. This is apparently what the hypothetical investor in the preceding example did with his October 35 call. Since that call was in-the-money, he could have elected to let the call be assigned and to take his profit on the position at that time. However, this would have produced a short-term gain, since the stock had not yet been held for one year, so he elected instead to terminate the October 35 call through a closing purchase transaction and to simultaneously write a call whose expiration date exceeded the one-year period required to make the stock a long-term item. He thus wrote the January 40 call, expiring in the next year. Note that this investor not only decided to hold the stock for a long-term gain, but also decided to try for more potential profits—he rolled the call up to a higher striking price. If the investor makes the decision to attempt to hold the stock for a long-term gain, it is often advisable for him to write an in-the-money call in order to receive as much protection of his current profit as is possible. Thus any investor with a short-term stock gain should weigh the possibility of realizing that gain versus writing a call option and attempting to hold the stock for long-term gains. A third alternative that is also open to the call writer who feels assignment is drawing near is to allow the assignment to occur, but to go into the open market and buy new stock for delivery against the assignment. The following discussion describes a scenario where this action might be sensible.

### *Delivering "New" Stock to Avoid A Large Long-Term Gain*

Some covered call writers may not want to deliver the stock that they are using to cover the written call, if that call is assigned. For example, if a covered writer were writing against stock that had an extremely low cost basis, he might not be willing to take the tax consequences of selling that particular stock holding. Thus the writer of a call that is assigned may sometimes wish to buy stock in the open market to deliver against his assignment, rather than deliver the stock he previously owns. Recall that it is completely in accordance with the Options Clearing Corporation rules for a call writer to buy stock in the open market to deliver against an assignment. For tax purposes, the confirmation that the investor receives from his broker for the sale of the stock via assignment should clearly specify which particular shares of stock are being sold. This is usually accomplished by having the confirmation read "Versus Purchase" and listing the purchase date of the stock being sold. This is done to clearly identify that the "new" stock, and not the older long-term stock, is being delivered against the assignment.

> *Example:* An investor owns 100 shares of XYZ and his cost basis—after multiple stock splits and stock dividends over the years—is $2 per share. With XYZ at 50, this investor decides to sell an XYZ July 50 call for 5 points to bring in some income to his portfolio. Subsequently,

the call is assigned, but the investor does not want to deliver his XYZ, which he owns at a cost basis of $2 per share, because he would have to pay capital gains on a large profit. He may go into the open market and buy another 100 shares of XYZ at its current market price for delivery against the assignment notice. Suppose he does this on July 20—the day he receives the assignment notice on his XYZ July 50 call. The confirmation that he receives from his broker for the sale of 100 XYZ at 50—that is, the confirmation for the call assignment—should be marked "Versus Purchase July 20, 19??." This long-term holder of XYZ stock must, of course, pay for the additional XYZ bought in the open market for delivery against the assignment notice. Thus it is imperative that such an investor have a reserve of funds that he can fall back on if he feels that he must ever implement this sort of strategy to avoid the tax consequences of selling his low-cost-basis stock.

## *Put Exercise*

If the put holder does not choose to liquidate the option in the listed market, but instead exercises the put—thereby selling stock at the striking price—the net cost of the put is subtracted from the net sale proceeds of the underlying stock.

*Example:* Assume an XYZ April 45 put was bought for 2 points. XYZ had declined in price below 45 by April expiration, and the put holder decides to exercise his in-the-money put rather than sell it in the option market. The commission on the stock sale is $85, so the net sale proceeds for the underlying stock would be:

| | |
|---|---:|
| Sale of 100 XYZ at 45 strike ($4,500 − $85) | $4,415 |
| Net cost of put ($200 + 25) | −   225 |
| Net sale proceeds of stock for tax purposes: | $4,190 |

If the stock sale represents a new position—that is, the investor has shorted the underlying stock—it will eventually be a short-term gain or loss, according to present tax rules governing short sales. If the put holder already owns the underlying stock and is using the put exercise as a means of selling that stock, his gain or loss on the stock transaction is computed, for tax purposes, by subtracting his original net stock cost from the sale proceeds as determined above.

## *Put Assignment*

If a written put is assigned, stock is bought at the striking price. The net cost of this purchased stock is reduced by the amount of the original put premium received.

*Example:* If one initially sold an XYZ July 40 put for 4 points, and it was assigned, the net cost of the stock would be determined as follows, assuming a $75 commission charge on the stock purchase:

| | |
|---|---|
| Cost of 100 XYZ assigned at 40 ($4,000 + $75) | $4,075 |
| Net proceeds of put sale ($400 − $25) | − 375 |
| Net cost basis of stock | $3,700 |

The holding period for stock purchased via a put assignment begins on the day of the put assignment. The period during which the investor was short the put has no bearing on the holding period of the stock. Obviously, the put transaction itself does not become a capital item—it becomes part of the stock transaction.

## SPECIAL TAX PROBLEMS

### The Wash Sale Rule

The call buyer should be aware of the *wash sale rule.* In general, the wash sale rule denies a tax deduction for a security sold at a loss if a substantially identical security, or an option to acquire that security, is purchased within 30 days before or 30 days after the original sale. This means that one cannot sell XYZ to take a tax loss and also purchase XYZ within the 61-day period that extends 30 days before and 30 days after the sale. Of course, an investor can legally make such a trade, he just cannot take the tax loss on the sale of the stock. A call option is certainly an option to acquire the security. *It would thus invoke the wash sale rule for an investor to sell XYZ stock to take a loss and also purchase any XYZ call within 30 days before or after the stock sale.*

Various series of call options are not generally considered to be substantially identical securities, however. If one sells an XYZ January 50 call to take a loss, he may then buy any other XYZ call option without jeopardizing his tax loss from the sale of the January 50. It is not clear whether he could repurchase another January 50 call—that is, an identical call—without jeopardizing the taxable loss on the original sale of the January 50.

It would also be acceptable for an investor to sell a call to take a loss and then immediately buy the underlying security. This would not invoke the wash sale rule.

*Avoiding a Wash Sale.* It is generally held that the sale of a put is not the acquisition of an option to buy stock, even though that is the effect of assignment of the written put. This fact may be useful in certain cases. If an investor holds a stock at a loss, he may want to sell that stock in order to take the loss on his taxes for the current year. The wash sale rule prevents him from repurchasing the same stock, or a call option on that stock, within 30 days after the sale. Thus the investor will be "out of" the stock for a month—that is, he will not be able to participate in any rally in the stock in the next 30 days. If this underlying stock has listed put options, the investor may be able to partially offset this negative effect. By selling an in-the-money put at the same time that the stock is sold, the investor will be able to take his stock loss on the current year's taxes and also will be able to participate in price movements on the underlying stock.

If the stock should rally, the put will decrease in price. However, if the stock rallies above the striking price of the put, the investor will not make as much from the put sale as he would have from the ownership of the stock. Still, he does realize some profits if the stock rallies.

Conversely, if the stock falls in price, the investor will lose on the put sale. This certainly represents a risk—although no more of a risk than owning the stock did. An additional disadvantage is that the investor who has sold a put will not receive the dividends, if any are paid by the underlying stock.

Once 30 days have passed, the investor can cover the put and repurchase the underlying stock. The investor who utilizes this tactic should be careful to select a put sale in which early assignment is minimal. Therefore, he should sell a long-term, in-the-money put when utilizing this strategy (he needs the in-the-money put in order to participate heavily in the stock's movements). Note that if stock should be put to the investor before 30 days had passed, he would thus be forced to buy stock, and the wash sale rule would be invoked, preventing him from taking the tax loss on the stock at that time—he would have to postpone taking the loss until he makes a sale that does not invoke the wash sale rule.

Finally, this strategy must be employed in a margin account because the put sale will be uncovered. Obviously, the money from the sale of the stock itself can be used to collateralize the sale of the put. If the stock should drop in value, it is always possible that additional collateral will be required for the uncovered put.

### The Short Sale Rule—Put Holder's Problem

A put purchase made by an investor who also owns the underlying stock may have an effect on the holding period of the stock. If a stock holder buys a put, he would normally do so to eliminate some of the downside risk in case the stock falls in price. However, if a put option is purchased to protect stock that is not yet held long enough to qualify for long-term capital treatment, the entire holding period of the stock is wiped out. Furthermore, the holding period for the stock will not begin again until the put is disposed of. For example, if an investor has held XYZ for 11 months—not quite long enough to qualify as a long-term holding—and then buys a put of XYZ, he will wipe out the entire accrued holding period on the stock. Furthermore, when he finally disposes of the put, the holding period for the stock must begin all over again—the previous 11-month holding period is lost, as is the holding period during which the stock and put were held together. This tax consequence of a put purchase is derived from the general rules governing short sales, which state that the acquisition of an option to sell property at a fixed price (that is, a put) is treated as a short sale. This ruling has serious tax consequences for an investor who has bought a put to protect stock that is still in a short-term tax status.

*"Married" Put and Stock.*    There are two cases in which the put purchase does *not* affect the holding period of the underlying stock. First, if the stock has already been held long enough to qualify for long-term capital treatment, the purchase of a put has no bearing on the holding period of the underlying stock. Second, if the put and the stock that it is intended to protect are bought at the same time, *and* the investor indicates that he intends to exercise that particular put to sell those particular shares of stock, the put and the stock are considered to be "married" and the normal tax rulings for a stock holding would apply. The investor must actually go through with the exercise of the put in order for the "married" status to remain valid. If he instead should allow the put to expire worthless, he could not take the tax loss on the put itself but would be forced to add the put's cost to the net cost of the underlying stock. Finally, if the investor neither exercises the put nor allows it to expire worthless but sells both the put and the stock in their respective markets, it would appear that the short sale rules would come back into effect.

This definition of "married" put and stock, and its resultant ramifications, are quite detailed. What exactly are the consequences? The "married" rule was originally intended to allow an investor to buy stock, protect it, and still have a chance of realizing a long-term gain. Unfortunately, this is not possible in the current listed option market and will not be unless options with a maturity of longer than one year are introduced. The reader must be aware of the fact that, if he initially "marries" stock and a listed nine-month put, for example, there is no way that he can replace that put at its expiration with another put and still retain the "married" status. Once the original "married" put is disposed of—through sale, exercise, or expiration—no other put may be considered to be "married" to the stock. Does this tax ruling mean that buying stock and a put simultaneously is not worthwhile? Absolutely not.

> *Example:* An investor bought XYZ at 50 and simultaneously purchased a nine-month, XYZ April 45 put for 1 point. If the stock declines substantially, the investor will want to exercise the put to limit his loss. There is no tax reason why he would want to keep this stock at a substantial loss because it will soon be in danger of becoming a long-term loss. On the other hand, if the stock rises in price, the investor can allow the put to expire worthless. This does not affect his holding period on the stock. The rule merely states that he cannot take the loss on the put immediately—he must add the put's cost to the stock's cost. Once the put has expired worthless, the investor has a stock with a gain that he has held for nine months. He would only have to protect that gain for 3 more months in order to make it long-term. He cannot do this with a put purchase, however, because that would involve the short sale rules. He could, however, sell an in-the-money call with an expiration slightly longer than 3 months. In this way he would enhance his prospects of "locking in" his stock gain while holding it for the additional time needed to make it long-term.

*Protecting a Long-Term Gain or Avoiding a Long-Term Loss.* The investor may be able, at times, to use the short-sale aspect of put purchases to his advantage. The most obvious use is that he can protect a long-term gain with a put purchase. He might want to do this if he has decided to take the long-term gain, but would prefer to delay realizing it until the following tax year. A purchase of a put with a maturity date in the following year would accomplish that purpose.

Another usage of the put purchase, for tax purposes, might be to avoid a long-term loss on a stock position. If an investor owns a stock that has declined in price and also is about to become a long-term holding, he can buy a put on that stock to eliminate the holding period. This avoids having to take a long-term loss. Once the put is removed— either by its sale or by its expiring worthless—the stock holding period would begin all over again and it would be a short-term position. In addition, if the investor should decide to exercise the put that he purchased, the result would be a short-term loss. The sale basis of the stock upon exercise of the put would be equal to the striking price of the put less the amount of premium paid for the put, less all commission costs. Furthermore, note that this strategy does not lock in the loss on the underlying stock. If the stock rallies, the investor would be able to participate in that rally, although he would probably lose all of the premium that he paid for the put.

## SUMMARY

This concludes the section of the tax chapter dealing with listed option trades and their direct consequences on option strategies. In addition to the basic tax treatment to option traders of liquidation, expiring worthless, or assignment or exercise, several other useful tax situations have been described. The call buyer should be aware of the wash sale rule. The put buyer must be aware of the short sale rules involving both put and stock ownership. The call writer should realize the beneficial effects of selling an in-the-money call to protect the underlying stock, while either waiting for a realization of profit in the following tax year or for even potentially making the stock a long-term gain. The put writer may be able to avoid a wash sale by utilizing an in-the-money put write, yet still retaining profit potential from a rally by the underlying stock.

Either put or call buyers may be able to employ various tactics to defer taking a gain on the long option into the following tax year. Options may also be used to defer any sort of capital gain—from any source—from one year to the next. The next section describes strategies applicable to these purposes.

## TAX PLANNING STRATEGIES

### Deferring a Short-Term Call Gain

The call holder may be interested in either deferring a gain until the following year or possibly converting a short-term gain on the call into a long-term gain on the stock. It is much easier to do the former than the latter. A holder of a profitable call that is due to expire in the following year can take any of three possible actions that might let him retain his profit while deferring the gain until the following tax year. One way in which to do this would be to buy a put option. Obviously, he would want to buy an in-the-money put for this purpose. By so doing, he would be spending as little as possible in the way of time value premium for the put option and he would also be locking in his gain on the call. The gains and losses from the put and call combination would nearly equal each other as the stock moves up or down, unless the stock rallies strongly, thereby exceeding the striking price of the put. This would be a happy event, however, since even larger gains would accrue. The combination could be liquidated in the following tax year, thus achieving a gain.

*Example:* On September 1, an investor bought an XYZ January 40 call for 3 points. The call is due to expire in the following year. XYZ has risen in price by December 1, and the call is selling for 6 points. The call holder might want to take his 3-point gain on the call, but would also like to defer that gain until the following year. He might be able to do this by buying an XYZ January 50 put for 5 points, for example. He would then hold this combination until after the first of the new year. At that time, he could liquidate the entire combination for at least 10 points, since the striking price of the put is 10 points greater than that of the call. In fact, if the stock should have climbed to or above 50 by the first of the year, or should have fallen to or below 40 by the first of the year, he would be able to liquidate the combination for more than 10 points. The increase in time value premium at either strike would also be a benefit. In any case, he would have a gain—his original cost was 8 points (3 for the call and 5 for the put). Thus he has effectively deferred taking the gain on the original call holding until the next tax year. The risk that the call holder incurs in this type of transaction is the increased commission charges of buying and selling the put as well as the possible loss of any time value premium in the put itself. The investor must decide for himself whether these risks—although they may be relatively small—outweigh the potential benefit from deferring his tax gain into the next year.

Another way in which the call holder might be able to defer his tax gain into the next year would be to sell another XYZ call against the one that he currently holds. That is, he would create a spread. To assure that he retains as much of his current gain as possible, he should sell an in-the-money call. In fact, he should sell an in-the-money call with a lower striking price than the call held long, if possible, to ensure that his gain remains intact even if the underlying stock should collapse substantially. Once the spread has been established, it could be held until the following tax year before being liquidated. The obvious risk in this means of deferring gain is that one could receive an assignment notice on the short call. This is not a remote possibility, necessarily, since an in-the-money call should be used as protection for the current gain. Such an assignment would result in large commission costs on the resultant purchase and sale of the underlying stock, and could substantially reduce one's gain. Thus the risk in this strategy is greater than that in the previous one (buying a put), but it may be the only alternative available if puts are not traded on the underlying stock in question.

> *Example:* An investor bought an XYZ February 50 call for 3 points in August. In December, the stock is at 65 and the call is at 15. The holder would like to "lock in" his 12-point call profit, but would prefer deferring the actual gain into the following tax year. He could sell an XYZ February 45 call for approximately 20 points to do this. If no assignment notice is received, he will be able to liquidate the spread at a cost of 5 points with the stock anywhere above 50 at February expiration. Thus in the end he would still have a 12-point gain—having received 20 points for the sale of the February 45 and having paid out 3 points for the February 50 plus 5 points to liquidate the spread to take his gain. If the stock should fall below 50 before February expiration, his gain would be even larger, since he would not have to pay out the entire 5 points to liquidate the spread.

The third way in which a call holder could lock in his gain and still defer the gain into the following tax year would be to sell the stock short while continuing to hold the call. This would obviously lock in the gain, since the short sale and the call purchase will offset each other in profit potential as the underlying stock moves up or down. In fact, if the stock should plunge downward, large profits could accrue. However, there is risk in using this strategy as well. The commission costs of the short sale will reduce the call holder's profit. Furthermore, if the underlying stock should go ex-dividend during the time that the stock is held short, the strategist will be liable for the dividend as well. In addition, more margin will be required for the short stock.

The three tactics discussed above showed how to defer a profitable call gain into the following tax year. The gain would still be short-term when realized. The only way in which a call holder could hope to convert his gain into a long-term gain would be to exercise the call and then hold the stock for more than one year. Recall that the holding period for stock acquired through exercise begins on the day of exercise—the option's holding period is lost. If the investor chooses this alternative, he of course is spending some of his gains for the commissions on the stock purchase as well as subjecting himself to an entire year's worth of market risk. There are ways to protect a stock holding—for example, writing in-the-money calls—but the investor who chooses this alternative should carefully weigh the risks involved against the possible benefits of eventually achieving a long-term gain. The investor should also note that he will have to advance considerably more money to hold the stock.

## *Deferring a Put Holder's Short-Term Gain*

Without going into as much detail, there are similar ways in which a put holder who has a short-term gain in a put due to expire in the following tax year can attempt to defer the realization of that gain into the following tax year. One simple way in which he could protect his gain would be to buy a call option to protect his profitable put. He would want to buy an in-the-money call for this purpose. This resulting combination is similar in nature to the one described for the call buyer in the previous section.

A second way that he could attempt to protect his gain and still defer its realization into the following tax year would be to sell another XYZ put option against the one that he holds long. This would create a vertical spread. This put holder should attempt to sell an in-the-money put if possible. Of course, he would not want to sell a put that was so deeply in-the-money that there is risk of early assignment. The results of such a spread are analogous to the call spread described in detail in the last section.

Finally, the put holder could buy the underlying stock if he had enough available cash or collateral to finance the stock purchase. This would lock in the profit, as the stock and the put would offset each other in terms of gains or losses while the stock moved up or down. In fact, if the stock should experience a large rally—rising above the striking price of the put—even larger profits would become possible.

In each of the tactics described, the position would be removed in the following tax year, thereby realizing the gain that was deferred.

## *Difficulty of Deferring Gains from Writing*

As a final point in this section on deferring gains from option transactions, it might be appropriate to describe the risks associated with the strategy of attempting to defer gains from uncovered option writing into the following tax year. Recall that in the previous sections, it was shown that a call or put holder who has an unrealized profit in an option that is due to expire in the following tax year could attempt to "lock in" the gain and defer it. The dollar risks to a holder attempting such a tax deferral were mainly commission costs and/or small amounts of time value premium paid for options. However, the option writer who has an unrealized profit may have a more difficult time finding a way to both "lock in" the gain and also defer its realization into the following tax year. It would seem, at first glance, that the call writer could merely take actions opposite to those that the call buyer takes: buying the underlying stock, buying another call option, or selling a put. Unfortunately, none of these actions "locks in" the call writer's profit—in fact, he could lose substantial investment dollars in his attempt to defer the gain into the following year.

> *Example:* An investor has written an uncovered XYZ January 50 call for 5 points and the call has dropped in value to 1 point in early December. He might want to take the 4-point gain, but would prefer to defer realization of the gain until the following tax year. Since the call write is at a profit, the stock must have dropped and is probably selling around 45 in early December. Buying the underlying stock would not accomplish his purpose, because if the stock continued to decline through year-end, he could lose a substantial amount on the stock purchase and could only make 1 more point on the call write. Similarly, a call purchase would not work well either. A call with a lower striking price—for example, the XYZ January 45 or the January 40—could lose substantial value if the underlying stock continued to drop in price. An out-of-the-money call—the XYZ January 60—is also unacceptable, because if the underlying stock rallied to the high 50's, the writer would lose money both on his January 50 call write and on his January 60 call purchase at expiration. Writing a put option would not "lock in" the profit either. If the underlying stock continued to decline, the losses on the put write would certainly exceed the remaining profit potential of one point in the January 50 call. Alternatively, if the stock rose, the losses on the January 50 call could offset the limited profit potential provided by a put write. Thus there is no relatively safe way for an uncovered call writer to attempt to "lock in" an unrealized gain for the purpose of deferring it to the following tax year. The put writer seeking to defer his gains faces similar problems.

### Deferring a Gain from One Tax Year to the Next

The following two strategies may be used by anyone who has already realized a capital gain in the current tax year and wants to attempt to move that gain into the following tax year. This capital gain may have arisen from a variety of sources—stocks, bonds, commodities, the sale of a business, and so on. It makes no difference in these strategies.

The first such strategy involves using a calendar spread. Although the spread can be established with either puts or calls, it is more common to use call options and they will thus be the basis for the following example. Suppose an investor has a short-term capital gain that he would prefer to take in the following tax year rather than the current one. *He may be able to defer all or part of this gain by establishing a calendar spread with in-the-money call options.* If the underlying stock were then to move up or down substantially in price by the end of the calendar year, the investor would have a gain on one side of the spread and a loss on the other side. He could conceivably take the loss in the current tax year—thereby offsetting some of his gain from other sources—and then hold the profitable side of the spread until the following year before realizing it.

> *Example:* An investor has a $10,000 gain in the current tax year, and the following prices exist on November 15 of the year:
>
> XYZ common, 47;
>
> April 40 call, 8; and
>
> July 40 call, 9.

Both call options have very little time value premium because they are so deeply in-the-money. If the underlying stock advances in price by the end of the year, both options will increase in price as well—moving very nearly point for point with the underlying stock. On the other hand, if the stock drops in price, both options will fall in price. To the downside, the rate of decrease in the price of the options will slow down as the stock falls nearer to the striking price of 40. In either case, the spreader would have both a loss on one option and a gain on the other one at year-end.

If XYZ rises to 55 on the last trading day of the year, then the April 40 call might be selling for 15½ and the July 40 call for 16. He would thus have a 7½-point loss on each April 40 call that had been sold and would have a 7-point gain on each July 40 call that had been bought. He could take the loss in this year and then take his gain on the first trading day of the next year. The loss taken in the current year would be used to reduce all or part of his capital gain that had been realized from other sources. The gain taken in the next year would then be taxable in that year.

If the underlying stock had declined instead, the short side of the spread (April 40) would be a gain and the long side (July 40) would be a loss. Again, the loss could be taken in the current year and the gain in the following year. Note that the amount of the gain and the loss would probably be smaller in a stock decline than in a stock rise.

There are certain fine points that must be observed if this strategy is to be utilized. Although it is generally the rule that losses are taken in the tax year of the *trade date* of the loss, and gains are taken in the tax year of the *settlement date* of the gain, this does not necessarily apply to option writing transactions. Interpretation of the exact method of taking gains and losses on option writing transaction may change—that is why any investor should consult a tax advisor before making a trade for tax purposes. *Some advisors feel that both gains and losses from option writing transactions should be taken in the year of the settlement date of the trade.* If this opinion is upheld, the timing of the closing trade in this tax strategy is important. In the example, the loss side of the spread was the short side, the April 40, and thus would need to be closed out on the next-to-last trading day of the year in order to settle on the last day of year. This means the loss would qualify for the current tax year. This does not harm the strategy, however, since the long call could still be sold the next day—the last trading day of the year. It is a gain and would thus be taken on settlement date, which is the first trading day of the new year. *There is a risk in the spread when the two sides are closed out on different trading days.*

The number of spreads used is important to the investor, of course, because he would like to defer as much of his gain as is possible. Unfortunately, *there is no exact way of knowing how many spreads to establish to attempt to defer a specific gain.* The best way is to estimate how many points the underlying stock could move by the end of the year, and also to estimate what this stock movement would mean in terms of gains and losses on the options used in the spread. In the example, if one felt that the stock was capable of moving 8 points, he could estimate that he would have about 7 points in losses (on the April 40 call). Since this represents about $700 per spread, 15 spreads would have to be established to defer $10,000 worth of gains. Of course, if the underlying stock moved down instead of up, the loss per spread would be smaller and 15 spreads would probably not be able to defer all of the gain. There is no way of knowing exactly how many spreads to use.

*This calendar spread strategy has risk.* If the underlying stock advances or declines by an extremely large amount, the spread differential will shrink to zero and the strategist will have an actual economic loss. Moreover, since there are numerous commissions involved in the transaction, he will lose money there also. Thus there is a cost involved in establishing this strategy. Usually, the cost of commissions is small in comparison to the benefits of tax deferral, but this is a matter that should be carefully investigated before actually utilizing the strategy.

Note that *there is no requirement for establishing this spread, other than the original debit* of the spread, plus commissions. A margin account is necessary, but there are no collateral requirements involved which could change during the life of the position. Since in-the-money options are used, the debit is normally quite small. In the example, the debit is one point, so the investment for 15 spreads would be $1,500 plus commissions. The spreader is also desirous of avoiding early assignment—that is why, in the example, the inter-mediate-term, April call was used for the short side of the spread and the longest-term, July call was used for the long side.

### Using the In-the-Money Combination

*Another strategy is also useful in attempting to defer capital gains from one year to the next: the purchase of an in-the-money combination.* The investor buys both an in-the-money call and an in-the-money put. If the stock moves up in price by the end of the year, he will have a gain on the call and a loss on the put. He can take the loss in this tax year and the gain in the next year. If the stock instead moves down in price, the gain would be on the put and the loss would be on the call. Again, he takes the loss in this year and the gain in the next year.

This strategy, although considerably more expensive to imple-ment than the calendar spread—because of the cost of the in-the-money options—avoids certain of the problems that were pointed out in the calendar spread strategy. *There are no short options involved,* so one does not have to be concerned with the interpretation of when losses and gains are taken on written options. In this strategy, the long options have constant tax interpretation—losses are taken in the year of the trade date and gains are taken in the year of the settlement date. Thus *one would close the combination simultaneously and in its entirety on the last trading day of the year.* There would be no need to risk holding one of the options overnight, or over the year-end weekend as there may be in the calendar spread strategy. Also, there is no risk of early assignment, because there are no short options in this strategy. Of course, this strategy is only applicable on stocks that have both listed puts and calls.

*The investment required for this strategy is rather large.* Using the same example stock as in the last section, suppose it is felt that the stock could move far enough by the end of the year to produce $700 of deferral. Again, 15 combinations would have to be set up in order to defer $10,000 of gains. A combination would require over $1,000 each to buy if the striking prices of the put and call were 10 points apart. Thus 15 combinations would require over $15,000 to establish, plus commissions. This is considerably more than the calendar spread strategy.

The risk in the in-the-money combination strategy is that the time value premium of the purchased options may be lost. If one utilizes fairly short-term options which do not have much time value premium to begin with, he can keep this risk small. Thus if the spread were being established in the month of November, options with a January expiration date would be used.

## *SUMMARY*

Options can be used for many tax purposes. Short-term gains can be protected with options until they mature into long-term gains. Long-term losses can be avoided with the purchase of a put. Wash sales can be avoided without giving up the entire ownership potential of the stock. Finally, capital gains from many sources can potentially be deferred from one tax year into the next. There are risks as well as rewards in any of these strategies. Commission costs and the dissipation of time value premium in purchased options will both work against the strategist.

*A tax advisor should be consulted before actually implementing any tax strategy,* whether that strategy employs options or not. Tax rules change from time to time. It is even possible that a certain strategy is not covered by a written rule, and only a tax advisor is qualified to give consultation on how such a strategy might be interpreted by the IRS.

Finally, the options strategist should be careful not to confuse tax strategies with his profit-oriented strategies. It is generally a good idea to separate profit strategies and tax strategies. That is, if one finds himself in a position that conveniently lends itself to tax applications—fine. However, one should not attempt to stay in a position too long or to close it out at an illogical time just to take advantage of a tax break. *The tax consequences of options should never be considered to be more important than sound strategy management.*

# *Postscript*

Option strategies cannot be unilaterally classified as aggressive or conservative. There are certainly many aggressive applications—the simplest being the outright purchase of calls or puts. However, options can also have conservative applications, most notably in reducing some of the risks of common stock ownership. In addition, there are less polarized applications, particularly spreading techniques, which allow the investor to take a middle-of-the-road approach.

Consequently, *the investor himself—not options—becomes the dominant force in determining whether an option strategy is too risky.* It is imperative that the investor understands what he is trying to accomplish in his portfolio before actually implementing an option strategy. Not only should he be cognizant of the factors that go into determining the initial selection of the position, but he must also have in mind a plan of follow-up action. If he has thought out, in advance, what action he will take if the underlying stock rises or falls, he will be in a position to make a more rational decision when and if the stock does indeed make a move. The investor must also determine if the risk of the strategy is acceptable according to his financial means and objectives. If the risk is too high, the strategy is not suitable.

Every serious investor owes it to himself to acquire an understanding of listed option strategies. Since various options strategies are available for a multitude of purposes, *almost every money manager or dedicated investor will be able to use options in his strategies at one time or another.* For a stock-oriented investor to ignore the potential advantages of using options would be as serious a mistake as it would be for a large grain company to ignore the hedging properties available in the futures market, or as it would be for an income-oriented investor to concentrate only in utilities and Treasury bills while ignoring less well known, but equally compatible, alternatives, such as GNMA's.

PART V

# *Appendixes*

# *Strategy Summary* A

Except for arbitrage strategies and tax strategies, the strategies we have described deal with risk. It is therefore often convenient to summarize option strategies by their risk and reward characteristics and by their market outlook—bullish, bearish, or neutral. Table A-1 lists all the risk strategies that were discussed and gives a general classification of their risks and rewards. If a strategist has a definite attitude about the market's outlook or about his own willingness to accept risks, he can scan Table A-1 and select the strategies that most closely resemble his thinking. the number in parentheses after the strategy name indicates the chapter in which the strategy was discussed.

Table A-1 gives a *broad* classification of the various risk and reward potentials of the strategies. For example, a bullish call calendar spread does not actually have unlimited profit potential unless its near-term call expires worthless. In fact, *all calendar spread or diagonal spread positions have limited profit potential at best until the near-term options expire.*

Also, the definition of limited risk can vary widely. Some strategies do have a risk that is truly limited to a relatively small percentage of the initial investment—the protected stock purchase, for example. *In other cases, the risk is limited but is also equal to the entire initial investment.* That is, one could lose 100% of his investment in a short

**TABLE A-1.** *General strategy summary.*

| Strategy (Chapter) | Risk | Reward |
|---|---|---|
| *Bullish strategies* | | |
| Call purchase (3) | Limited | Unlimited |
| Synthetic long stock (short put/long call) (21) | Unlimited[a] | Unlimited |
| Bull spread—puts or calls (7 and 22) | Limited | Limited |
| Protected stock purchase (long stock/long put) (17) | Limited | Unlimited |
| Bullish call calendar spread (9) | Limited | Unlimited |
| Covered call writing (2) | Unlimited[a] | Limited |
| Uncovered put write (19) | Unlimited[a] | Limited |
| *Bearish Strategies* | | |
| Put purchase (16) | Limited | Unlimited[a] |
| Protected short sale (synthetic put) (4 and 16) | Limited | Unlimited[a] |
| Synthetic short sale (long put/short call) (21) | Unlimited | Unlimited[a] |
| Bear spread—put or call ( and 22) | Limited | Limited |
| Covered put write (19) | Unlimited | Limited |
| Bearish put calendar spread (22) | Limited | Unlimited[a] |
| Naked call write (5) | Unlimited | Limited |
| *Neutral strategies* | | |
| Straddle purchase (18) | Limited | Unlimited |
| Reverse hedge (simulated straddle buy) (4) | Limited | Unlimited |
| Fixed income + option purchase (25) | Limited | Unlimited |
| Diagonal spread (14, 23, and 24) | Limited | Unlimited |
| Neutral calendar spread—puts or calls (9 and 22) | Limited | Limited |
| Butterfly spread (10 and 23) | Limited | Limited |
| Calendar straddle or combination (23) | Limited | Unlimited |
| Reverse spread (13) | Limited | Unlimited |
| Ratio write—put or call (6 and 19) | Unlimited | Limited |
| Straddle or combination write (20) | Unlimited | Limited |
| Ratio spread—put or call (11 and 24) | Unlimited | Limited |
| Ratio calendar spread—put or call (12 and 24) | Unlimited | Unlimited |

[a]Wherever the risk or reward is limited only by the fact that a stock cannot fall below zero in price, the entry is marked. Obviously, although the potential may technically be limited, it could still be quite large if the underlying stock did fall a large distance.

time period—option purchases, and bull, bear, or calendar spreads are examples.

Thus, although Table A-1 gives a broad perspective on the outlook for various strategies, one must be aware of the differences in reward, risk, and market outlook when actually implementing one of the strategies.

Some strategies can be constructed with either puts or calls to attain the same profit potential. These are called equivalent strategies and are given in Table B-1. They do not necessarily have the same potential *returns*, because the investment required may be quite different. However, equivalent positions have profit graphs with exactly the same shape.

**TABLE B-1.** *Equivalent strategies.*

| *This Strategy . . .* | *is equivalent to . . .* | *This Strategy* |
|---|---|---|
| Call purchase | | Long stock/long put |
| Put purchase | | Short stock/long call (synthetic put) |
| Long stock | | Long call/short put (synthetic stock) |
| Short stock | | Long put/short call (synthetic short sale) |
| Naked call write | | Short stock/short put |
| Naked put write | | Covered call write (long stock/short call) |
| Bullish call spread (long call at lower strike/ short call at higher strike) | | Bullish put spread (long put at lower strike/ short put at higher strike) |
| Bearish call spread (long call at higher strike/ short call at lower strike) | | Bearish put spread (long put at higher strike/ short put at lower strike) |
| Ratio call write (long stock/short calls) . . . and is also equivalent to . . . | | Straddle write (short put/short call)  Ratio put write (short stock/short puts) |

**TABLE B-1.** (*continued*)

| *This Strategy . . .* | *is equivalent to . . .* *This Strategy* |
|---|---|
| Straddle buy (long call/long put) | Reverse hedge (short stock/long calls) *or* buy stock/buy puts |
| Butterfly call spread (long 1 call at each outside strike/ short 2 calls at middle strike) | Butterfly put spread (long 1 put at each outer strike/ short 2 puts at middle strike) |

*All four of these "butterfly" strategies are equivalent*

| | |
|---|---|
| Butterfly combination (bullish call spread at two lower strikes/bearish put spread at 2 higher strikes) | Protected straddle write (short straddle at middle strike/ long call at highest strike/ long put at lowest strike) |

Other equivalences can be determined by combining any two strategies in the left-hand column and setting that combination equivalent to the two corresponding strategies in the right-hand column.

*Arbitrage*—the process in which professional traders simultaneously buy and sell the same or equivalent securities for a riskless profit. *See also* Risk Arbitrage.

*Assign*—to designate an option writer for fulfillment of his obligation to sell stock (call option writer) or buy stock (put option writer). The writer receives an assignment notice from the Options Clearing Corporation. *See also* Early Exercise.

*Assignment Notice*—*see* Assign.

*Automatic Exercise*—a protection procedure whereby the Options Clearing Corporation attempts to protect the holder of an expiring in-the-money option by automatically exercising the option on behalf of the holder.

*Average Down*—to buy more of a security at a lower price, thereby reducing the holder's average cost. (Average Up: to buy more at a higher price.)

*Backspread*—*see* Reverse Strategy.

*Bearish*—an adjective describing an opinion or outlook that expects a decline in price, either by the general market or by an underlying stock, or both. *See also* Bullish.

*Bear Spread*—an option strategy that makes its maximum profit when the underlying stock declines and has its maximum risk if the stock rises in price. The strategy can be implemented with either puts or calls. In either case, an option with a higher striking price is purchased and one with a lower striking price is sold, both options generally having the same expiration date. *See also* Bull Spread.

*Beta*—a measure of how a stock's movement correlates to the movement of the entire stock market. The Beta is not the same as volatility. *See also* Standard Deviation *and* Volatility.

*Board Broker*—the exchange member in charge of keeping the book of public orders on exchanges utilizing the "market-maker" system, as opposed to the "specialist system," of executing orders. *See also* Market-Maker *and* Specialist.

*Box Spread*—a type of option arbitrage in which both a bull spread and a bear spread are established for a riskless profit. One spread is established using put options and the other is established calls. The spreads may both be debit spreads (call bull spread vs. put bear spread), or both credit spreads (call bear spread vs. put bull spread).

*Break-even Point*—the stock price (or prices) at which a particular strategy neither makes nor loses money. It generally pertains to the result at the expiration date of the options involved in the strategy. A "dynamic" break-even point is one that changes as time passes.

*Bullish*—describing an opinion or outlook in which one expects a rise in price, either by the general market or by an individual security. *See also* Bearish.

*Bull Spread*—an option strategy that achieves its maximum potential if the underlying security rises far enough, and has its maximum risk if the security falls far enough. An option with a lower striking price is bought and one with a higher striking price is sold, both generally having the same expiration date. Either puts or calls may be used for the strategy. *See also* Bear Spread.

*Butterfly Spread*—an option strategy that has both limited risk and limited profit potential, constructed by combining a bull spread and a bear spread. Three striking prices are involved, with the lower two being utilized in the bull spread and the higher two in the bear spread. The strategy can be established with either puts or calls; there are four different ways of combining options to construct the same basic position.

*Calendar Spread*—an option strategy in which a short-term option is sold and a longer-term option is bought, both having the same striking price. Either puts or calls may be used. A calendar combination is a strategy that consists of a call calendar spread and a put calendar spread at the same time. The striking price of the calls would be higher than the striking price of the puts. A calendar straddle would consist of selling a near-term straddle and buying a longer-term straddle, both with the same striking price.

*Calendar Straddle or Combination*—*see* Calendar Spread.

*Call*—an option which gives the holder the right to buy the underlying security at a specified price for a certain, fixed period of time. *See also* Put.

*Carrying Cost*—the interest expense on a debit balance created by establishing a position.

*CBOE*—the Chicago Board Options Exchange; the first national exchange to trade listed stock options.

*Class*—a term used to refer to all put and call contracts on the same underlying security.

*Closing Transaction*—a trade that reduced an investor's position. Closing buy transactions reduce short positions and closing sell transactions reduce long positions. *See also* Opening Transaction.

*Collateral*—the loan value of marginable securities; generally used to finance the writing of uncovered options.

*Combination*—any position involving both put and call options that is not a straddle. *See also* Straddle.

*Contingent Order*—an order to buy stock and sell a covered call option that is given as one order to the trading desk of a brokerage firm. Also called a "net order." This is a "not held" order. *See also* Market Not Held Order.

*Conversion Arbitrage*—a riskless transaction in which the arbitrageur buys the underlying security, buys a put, and sells a call. The options have the same terms. *See also* Reversal Arbitrage.

*Conversion Ratio*—*see* Convertible Security.

*Converted Put*—*see* Synthetic Put.

*Convertible Security*—a security that is convertible into another security. Generally, a convertible bond or convertible preferred stock is convertible into the underlying stock of the same corporation. The rate at which the shares of the bond or preferred stock are convertible into the common is called the conversion ratio.

*Cover*—to buy back as a closing transaction an option that was initially written.

*Covered*—a written option is considered to be covered if the writer also has an opposing market position on a share-for-share in the underlying security. That is, a short call is covered if the underlying stock is owned, and a short put is covered (for margin purposes) if the underlying stock is also short in the account. In addition, a short call is covered if the account is also long another call on the same security, with a striking equal to or less than the striking price of the short call. A short put is covered if there is also a long put in the account with a striking price equal to or greater than the striking price of the short put.

*Covered Call Write*—a strategy in which one writes call options while simultaneously owning an equal number of shares of the underlying stock.

*Covered Put Write*—a strategy in which one sells put options and simultaneously is short an equal number of shares of the underlying security.

*Covered Straddle Write*—the term used to describe the strategy in which an investor owns the underlying security and also writes a straddle on that security. This is not really a covered position.

*Credit*—money received in an account. A credit transaction is one in which the net sale proceeds are larger than the net buy proceeds (cost), thereby bringing money into the account. *See also* Debit.

*Cycle*—the expiration dates applicable to various classes of options. There are three cycles: January/April/July/October, February/May/August/November, and March/June/September/December.

*Debit*—an expense, or money paid out from an account. A debit transaction in one in which the net cost is greater than the net sale proceeds. *See also* Credit.

*Deliver*—to take securities from an individual or firm and transfer them to another individual or firm. A call writer who is assigned must deliver stock to the call holder who exercised. A put holder who exercises must deliver stock to the put writer who is assigned.

*Delta*—the amount by which an option's price will change for a corresponding change in price by the underlying stock. Call options have positive deltas, while put options have negative deltas. Technically, the delta is an instantaneous measure of the option's price change, so that the delta will be altered for even fractional changes by the underlying stock. Consequently, the terms "up delta" and "down delta" may be applicable. They describe the option's change after a full 1-point change in price by the underlying security— either up or down. The "up delta" may be larger than the "down delta" for a call option, while the reverse is true for put options. *See also* Hedge Ratio.

*Delta Spread*—a ratio spread that is established as a neutral position by utilizing the deltas of the options involved. The neutral ratio is determined by dividing the delta of the purchased option by the delta of the written option. *See also* Ratio Spread *and* Delta.

*Depository Trust Corporation (DTC)*—a corporation that will hold securities for member institutions. Generally used by option writers, the DTC facilitates and guarantees delivery of underlying securities if assignment is made against securities held in DTC.

*Diagonal Spread*—any spread in which the purchased options have a longer maturity than do the written options as well as having different striking prices. Typical types of diagonal spreads are diagonal bull spreads, diagonal bear spreads, and diagonal butterfly spreads.

*Discount*—an option is trading at a discount if it is trading for less than its intrinsic value. *See also* Intrinsic Value *and* Parity.

*Discount Arbitrage*—a riskless arbitrage in which a discount option is purchased and an opposite position is taken in the underlying security. The arbitrageur may either buy a call at a discount and simultaneously sell the underlying stock (basic call arbitrage) or may buy a put at a discount and simultaneously buy the underlying stock (basic put arbitrage). *See also* Discount.

*Discretion*—see Limit Order *and* Market Not Held Order.

*Dividend Arbitrage*—in the riskless sense, an arbitrage in which a put is purchased and so is the underlying stock. The put is purchased when it has time value premium less than the impending dividend payment by the underlying stock. The transaction is closed after the stock goes ex-dividend. Also used to denote a form of risk arbitrage in which a similar procedure is followed except that the amount of the impending dividend is unknown and therefore risk is involved in the transaction. *See also* Ex-Dividend *and* Time Value Premium.

*Downside Protection*—generally used in connection with covered call writing, this is the cushion against loss, in case of a price decline by the underlying stock, that is afforded by the written call option. Alternatively, it may be expressed in terms of the distance the stock could fall before the total position becomes a loss (an amount equal to the option premium), or it can be expressed as percentage of the current stock price. *See also* Covered Call Write.

*Dynamic*—for option strategies, describing analyses made during the course of changing stock prices and during the passage of time. This is as opposed to an analysis made at expriration of the options used in the strategy. A dynamic break-even point is one that changes as time passes. A dynamic follow-up action is one that will change as either the stock price changes or the option price changes or time passes. *See also* Break-even Point *and* Follow-up Action.

*Early Exercise (assignment)*—the exercise or assignment of an option contract before its expiration date.

*Equity Requirement*—a requirement that a minimum amount of equity must be present in a margin account. Normally, this requirement is $2,000, but some brokerage firms may impose higher equity requirements for uncovered option writing.

*Equivalent Positions*—positions that have similar profit potential, when measured in dollars, but are constructed with differing securities. Equivalent positions have the same profit graph. A covered call write is equivalent to an uncovered put write, for example. *See also* Profit Graph.

*Escrow Receipt*—a receipt issued by a bank in order to verify that a customer (who has written a call) in fact owns the stock and therefore the call is considered covered.

*Ex-Dividend*—the process whereby a stock's price is reduced when a dividend is paid. The ex-dividend date (ex-date) is the date on which the price reduction takes place. Investors who own stock on the ex-date will receive the dividend, and those who are short stock must pay out the dividend.

*Exercise*—to invoke the right granted under the terms of a listed options contract. The holder is the one who exercises. Call holders exercise to buy the underlying security, while put holders exercise to sell the underlying security.

*Exercise Limit*—the limit on the number of contracts which a holder can exercise in a fixed period of time. Set by the appropriate option exchange, it is designed to prevent an investor or group of investors from "cornering" the market in a stock.

*Exercise Price*—the price at which the option holder may buy or sell the underlying security, as defined in the terms of his option contract. It is the price at which the call holder may exercise to buy stock or the put holder may exercise to sell stock. For listed options, the exercise price is the same as the Striking Price. *See also* Exercise.

*Expected Return*—a rather complex mathematical analysis involving statistical distribution of stock prices, it is the return which an investor might expect to make on an investment if he were to make exactly the same investment many times throughout history.

*Expiration Date*—the day on which an option contract becomes void. The expiration date for listed stock options is the Saturday after the third Friday of the expiration month. All holders of options must indicate their desire to exercise, if they wish to do so, by this date. *See also* Expiration Time.

*Expiration Time*—the time of day by which all exercise notices must be received on the expiration date. Technically, the expiration time is currently 5:00 PM on the expiration date, but public holders of option contracts must indicate their desire to exercise no later than 5:30 PM on the business day preceding the expiration date. The times are Eastern Time. *See also* Expiration Date.

*Facilitation*—the process of providing a market for a security. Normally, this refers to bids and offers made for large blocks of securities, such as those traded by institutions. Listed options may be used to offset part of the risk assumed by the trader who is facilitating the large block order. *See also* Hedge Ratio.

*Fair Value*—normally, a term used to describe the worth of an option contract as determined by a mathematical model. Also sometimes used to indicate intrinsic value. *See also* Intrinsic Value *and* Model.

*Floor Broker*—a trader on the exchange floor who executes the orders of public customers or other investors who do not have physical access to the trading area.

*Follow-up Action*—any trading in an option position after the position is established. Generally, to limit losses or to take profits.

*Fundamental Analysis*—a method of analyzing the prospects of a security by observing accepted accounting measures such as earnings, sales, assets, and so on. *See also* Technical Analysis.

*Good Until Canceled (GTC)*—a designation applied to some types of orders, meaning that the order remains in effect until it is either filled or canceled. *See also* Limit, Stop, *and* Stop Limit.

*Hedge Ratio*—the mathematical quantity that is equal to the delta of an option. It is useful in facilitation in that a theoretically riskless hedge can be established by taking offsetting positions in the underlying stock and its call options. *See also* Facilitation *and* Delta.

*Holder*—the owner of a security.

*Horizontal Spread*—a option strategy in which the options have the same striking price, but different expiration dates.

*Implied Volatility*—a measure of the volatility of the underlying stock, it is determined by using prices currently existing in the market at the time, rather than using historical data on the price changes of the underlying stock. *See also* Volatility.

*Incremental Return Concept*—a strategy of covered call writing in which the investor is striving to earn an additional return from option writing against a stock position which he is targeted to sell— possibly at substantially higher prices.

*Institution*—an organization, probably very large, engaged in investing in securities. Normally a bank, insurance company, or mutual fund.

*In-the-Money*—a term describing any option that has intrinsic value. A call option is in-the-money if the underlying stock is higher than the striking price of the call. A put option is in-the-money if the stock is below the striking price. *See also* Out-of-the-Money *and* Intrinsic Value.

*Intrinsic Value*—the value of an option if it were to expire immediately with the underlying stock at its current price; the amount by which an option is in-the-money. For call options, this is the difference between the stock price and the striking price, if that difference is a positive number, or zero otherwise. For put options it is the difference between the striking price and the stock price, if that difference is positive, and zero otherwise. *See also* In-the-Money, Time Value Premium, *and* Parity.

*Last Trading Day*—the third Friday of the expiration month. Options cease trading at 3:00 PM Eastern Time on the last trading day.

*Leg*—a risk-oriented method of establishing a two-sided position. Rather than entering into a simultaneous transaction to establish the position (a spread, for example), the trader first executes one side of the position, hoping to execute the other side at a later time and a better price. The risk materializes from the fact that a better price may never be available, and a worse price must eventually be accepted.

*Letter of Guarantee*—a letter from a bank to a brokerage firm which states that a customer (who has written a call option) does indeed own the underlying stock and the bank will guarantee delivery if the call is assigned. Thus the call can be considered covered. Not all brokerage firms accept letters of guarantee.

*Leverage*—in investments, the attainment of greater percentage profit and risk potential. A call holder has leverage with respect to a stock holder—the former will have greater percentage profits and losses than the latter, for the same movement in the underlying stock.

*Limit Order*—an order to buy or sell securities at a specified price (the limit). A limit order may also be placed "with discretion"—a fixed, usually small, amount such as ⅛ or ¼ of a point. In this case, the floor broker executing the order may use his discretion to buy or sell at ⅛ or ¼ of a point beyond the limit if he feels it is necessary to fill the order.

*Listed Stock Option*—a put or call option that is traded on a national option exchange. Listed stock options have fixed striking prices and expiration dates. *See also* Over-the-Counter Option.

*Lognormal Distribution*—a statistical distribution that is often applied to the movement of stock prices. It is a convenient and logical distribution because it implies that stock prices can theoretically rise forever but cannot fall below zero—a fact which is, of course, true.

*Margin*—to buy a security by borrowing funds from a brokerage house. The margin requirement—the maximum percentage of the investment that can be loaned by the brokerage firm—is set by the Federal Reserve Board.

*Market-Maker*—an exchange member whose function is to aid in the making of a market, by making bids and offers for his account in the absence of public buy or sell orders. Several market-makers are normally assigned to a particular security. The market-maker system encompasses the market-makers and the board brokers. *See also* Board Broker *and* Specialist.

*Market Order*—an order to buy or sell securities at the current market. The order will be filled as long as there is a market for the security.

*Market Not Held Order*—also a market order, but the investor is allowing the floor broker who is executing the order to use his own discretion as to the exact timing of the execution. If the floor broker expects a decline in price and he is holding a "market not held" buy order, he may wait to buy, figuring that a better price will soon be available. There is no guarantee that a "market not held" order will be filled.

*Married Put and Stock*—a put and stock are considered to be married if they are bought on the same day, and the position is designated at that time as a hedge.

*Model*—a mathematical formula designed to price an option as a function of certain variables—generally stock price, striking price, volatility, time to expiration, dividends to be paid, and the current risk-free interest rate. The Black-Scholes model is one of the more widely used models.

*Naked Option—see* Uncovered Option.

*"Net" Order—see* Contingent Order.

*Neutral*—describing an opinion that is neither bearish or bullish. Neutral option strategies are generally designed to perform best if there is little or no net change in the price of the underlying stock. *See also* Bearish *and* Bullish.

*"Not Held"—see* Market Not Held Order.

*Open Interest*—the net total of outstanding open contracts in a particular option series. An opening transaction increases the open interest, while any closing transaction reduces the open interest.

*Opening Transaction*—a trade which adds to the net position of an investor. An opening buy transaction adds more long securities to the account. An opening sell transaction adds more short securities. *See also* Closing Transaction.

*Option Pricing Curve*—a graphical representation of the projected price of an option at a fixed point in time. It reflects the amount of time value premium in the option for various stock prices, as well. The curve is generated by using a mathematical model. The delta (or hedge ratio) is the slope of a tangent line to the curve at a fixed stock price. *See also* Delta, Hedge Ratio, *and* Model.

*Options Clearing Corporation (OCC)*—the issuer of all listed option contracts that are trading on the national option exchanges.

*Out-of-the-Money*—describing an option that has no intrinsic value. A call option is out-of-the-money if the stock is below the striking price of the call, while a put option is out-of-the-money if the stock is higher than the striking price of the put. *See also* In-the-Money *and* Intrinsic Value.

*Over-the-Counter Option (OTC)*—an option traded over-the-counter, as opposed to a listed stock option. The OTC option has a direct link between buyer and seller, has no secondary market, and has no standardization of striking prices and expiration dates. *See also* Listed Stock Option *and* Secondary Market.

*Overvalued*—describing a security trading at a higher price than it logically should. Normally associated with the results of option price predictions by mathematical models. If an option is trading in the market for a higher price than the model indicates, the option is said to be overvalued. *See also* Fair Value *and* Undervalued.

*Parity*—describing an in-the-money option trading for its intrinsic value: that is, an option trading at parity with the underlying stock. Also used as a point of reference—an option is sometimes said to be trading at a half-point over parity or at a quarter-point under parity, for example. An option trading under parity is a discount option. *See also* Discount *and* Intrinsic Value.

*Position*—as a noun, the specific securities in an account or strategy. A covered call writing position might be long 1,000 XYZ and short 10 XYZ January 30 calls. As a verb, to facilitate; to buy or sell—generally a block of securities—thereby establishing a position. *See also* Facilitation *and* Strategy.

*Position Limit*—the maximum number of put or call contracts on the same side of the market that can be held in any one account or group of related accounts. Short puts and long calls are on the same side of the market. Short calls and long puts are on the same side of the market.

*Premium*—the total price of an option contract. The sum of the intrinsic value and the time value premium.

*Profit Graph*—a graphical representation of the potential outcomes of a strategy. Dollars of profit or loss are graphed on the vertical axis, and various stock prices are graphed on the horizontal axis. Results may be depicted at any point in time, although the graph usually depicts the results at expiration of the options involved in the strategy.

*Profit Range*—the range within which a particular position makes a profit. Generally used in reference to strategies that have two break-even points—an upside break-even and a downside break-even. The price range between the two break-even points would be the profit range. *See also* Break-even Point.

*Profit Table*—a table of results of a particular strategy at some point in time. This is usually a tabular compilation of the data drawn on a profit graph. *See also* Profit Graph.

*Protected Strategy*—a position that has limited risk. A protected short sale (short stock, long call) has limited risk, as does a protected straddle write (short straddle, long out-of-the-money combination). *See also* Combination *and* Straddle.

*Public Book (of orders)*—the orders to buy or sell, entered by the public, that are away from the current market. The board broker or specialist keeps the public book. Market makers on the CBOE can see the highest bid and lowest offer at any time. The specialist's book is closed (only he knows at what price and in what quantity the nearest public orders are). *See also* Board Broker, Market-Maker, *and* Specialist.

*Put*—an option granting the holder the right to sell the underlying security at a certain price for a specified period of time. *See also* Call.

*Ratio Strategy*—a strategy in which one has an unequal number of long securities and short securities. Normally, it implies a preponderance of short options over either long options or long stock.

*Ratio Write*—buying stock and selling a preponderance of calls against the stock that is owned. (Occasionally constructed as shorting stock and selling puts.)

*Ratio Spread*—constructed with either puts or calls, the strategy consists of buying a certain amount of options and then selling a larger quantity of out-of-the-money options.

*Ratio Calendar Spread*—selling more near-term options than longer-term ones purchased, all with the same strike; either puts or calls.

*Ratio Calendar Combination*—a strategy consisting of a simultaneous position of a ratio calendar spread using calls and a similar position using puts, where the striking price of the calls is greater than the striking price of the puts.

*Resistance*—a term in technical analysis indicating a price area higher than the current stock price where an abundance of supply exists for the stock, and therefore the stock may have trouble rising through the price. *See also* Support.

*Return (on investment)*—the percentage profit that one makes, or might make, on his investment.

*Return If Exercised*—the return that a covered call writer would make if the underlying stock were called away.

*Return If Unchanged*—the return that an investor would make on a particular position if the underlying stock were unchanged in price at the expiration of the options in the position.

*Reversal Arbitrage*—a riskless arbitrage that involves selling the stock short, writing a put, and buying a call. The options have the same terms. *See also* Conversion Arbitrage.

*Reverse Hedge*—a strategy in which one sells the underlying stock short and buys calls on more shares than he has sold short. This is also called a synthetic straddle and is an outmoded strategy for stocks that have listed puts trading. *See also* Straddle *and* Ratio Write.

*Reverse Strategy*—a general name that is given to strategies which are the opposite of better known strategies. For example, a ratio spread consists of buying calls at a lower strike and selling more calls at a higher strike. A reverse ratio spread also known as a back-spread consists of selling the calls at the lower strike and buying more calls at the higher strike. The results are obviously directly opposite to each other. *See also* Reverse Hedge *and* Ratio Write.

*Risk Arbitrage*—a form of arbitrage that has some risk associated with it. Commonly refers to potential takeover situations where the arbitrageur buys the stock of the company about to be taken over and sells the stock of the company that is effecting the takeover. *See also* Dividend Arbitrage.

*Rolling*—a follow-up action in which the strategist closes options currently in the position and opens other options with different terms, on the same underlying stock. *See also* Roll Down, Roll Forward, *and* Roll Up.

*Roll Down*—close out options at one strike and simultaneously open other options at a lower strike.

*Roll Forward*—close out options at a near-term expiration date and open options at a longer-term expiration date.

*Roll Up*—close out options at a lower strike and open options at a higher strike.

*Rotation*—a trading procedure on the option exchanges whereby bids and offers, but not necessarily trades, are made sequentially for each series of options on an underlying stock.

*Secondary Market*—any market in which securities can be readily bought and sold after their initial issuance. The national listed option exchanges provided, for the first time, a secondary market in stock options.

*Series*—all option contracts on the same underlying stock having the same striking price, expiration date, and unit of trading.

*Specialist*—an exchange member whose function it is to both make markets—buy and sell for his own account in the absence of public orders—and to keep the book of public orders. Most stock exchanges and some option exchanges utilize the specialist system of trading.

*Spread Order*—an order to simultaneously transact two or more option trades. Typically, one option would be bought while another would simultaneously be sold. Spread orders may be limit orders, not held orders, or orders with discretion. They cannot be stop orders, however. The spread order may be either a debit or credit.

*Spread Strategy*—any option position having both long options and short options of the same type on the same underlying security.

*Standard Deviation*—a measure of the volatility of a stock. It is a statistical quantity measuring the magnitude of the daily price changes of that stock.

*Stop Limit Order*—similar to a stop order, the stop limit order becomes a limit order, rather than a market order, when the security trades at the price specified on the stop. *See also* Stop Order.

*Stop Order*—an order, placed away from the current market, that becomes a market order if the security trades at the price specified on the stop order. Buy stop orders are placed above the market while sell stop orders are placed below.

*Straddle*—the purchase or sale of an equal number of puts and calls having the same terms.

*Strategy*—with respect to option investments, a preconceived, logical plan of position selection and follow-up action.

*Striking Price*—*see* Exercise Price.

*Striking Price Interval*—the distance between striking prices on a particular underlying security. Normally, the interval is 5 points for stocks selling up to $50 per share, 10 points for stocks between $50 and $200 per share, and 20 points thereafter. There may, however, be exceptions to this general guideline.

*Suitable*—describing a strategy or trading philosophy in which the investor is operating in accordance with his financial means and investment objectives.

*Support*—a term in technical analysis indicating a price area lower than the current price of the stock, where demand is thought to exist. Thus a stock would stop declining when it reached a support area. *See also* Resistance.

*Synthetic Put*—a security which some brokerage firms offer to their customers. The broker sells stock short and buys a call, while the customer receives the synthetic put. This is not a listed security, but a secondary market is available as long as there is a secondary market in the calls.

*Synthetic Stock*—an option strategy that is equivalent to the underlying stock. A long call and a short put is synthetic long stock. A long put and a short call is synthetic short stock.

*Technical Analysis*—the method of predicting future stock price movements based on observation of historical stock price movements.

*Terms*—the collective name denoting the expiration date, striking price, and underlying stock of an option contract.

*Theoretical Value*—the price of an option, or a spread, as computed by a mathematical model.

*Time Spread*—*see* Calendar Spread.

*Time Value Premium*—the amount by which an option's total premium exceeds its intrinsic value.

*Total Return Concept*—a covered call writing strategy in which one views the potential profit of the strategy as the sum of capital gains, dividends, and option premium income, rather than viewing each one of the three separately.

*Trader*—a speculative investor or professional who makes frequent purchases and sales.

*Treasury Bill/Option Strategy*—a method of investment in which one places approximately 90% of his funds in risk-free, interest-bearing assets such as Treasury bills, and buys options with the remainder of his assets.

*Type*—the designation to distinguish between a put or call option.

*Uncovered Option*—a written option is considered to be uncovered if the investor does not have a corresponding position in the underlying security. *See also* Covered.

*Underlying Security*—the security which one has the right to buy or sell via the terms of a listed option contract.

*Undervalued*—describing a security that is trading at a lower price than it logically should. Usually determined by the use of a mathematical model. *See also* Overvalued *and* Fair Value.

*Variable Ratio Write*—an option strategy in which the investor owns

100 shares of the underlying security and writes two call options against it, each option having a different striking price.

*Vertical Spread*—any option spread strategy in which the options have different striking prices, but the same expiration dates.

*Volatility*—a measure of the amount by which an underlying security is expected to fluctuate in a given period of time. Generally measured by the annual standard deviation of the daily price changes in the security, volatility is not equal to the Beta of the stock.

*Write*—to sell an option. The investor who sells is called the writer.

# Formulae D

Chapter references are given in parentheses. The following notation is used throughout this appendix:

$x$ = current stock price
$s$ = striking price
$c$ = call price
$p$ = put price
$r$ = interest rate
$t$ = time (in years)
$B$ = break-even point
$U$ = upside break-even point
$D$ = downside break-even point
$P$ = maximum profit potential
$R$ = maximum risk potential

Subscripts indicate multiple items. For example $s_1$, $s_2$, $s_3$ *would designate three striking prices in a formula. The formulae are arranged alphabetically by title or by strategy.

## Annualized Risk (Ch. 25)

$$\text{Annualized risk} = \sum_i \text{INV}_i \ \frac{360}{H_i}$$

where $\text{INV}_i$ = percent of total assets invested in options with holding periods, $H_i$

$H_i$ = length of holding period in days

## Bear Spread

$s_1 < s_2$

### —Calls (Ch. 8)

$$P = c_1 - c_2$$
$$R = s_2 - s_1 - P$$
$$B = s_1 + P$$

### — Puts (Ch. 22)

$$R = p_2 - p_1$$
$$P = s_2 - s_1 - R$$
$$B = s_1 + P = s_2 + p_1 - p_2$$

## Black-Scholes Model (Ch. 28)

Theoretical call price $= xN(d_1) - se^{-rt}N(d_2)$

where $d_1 = \dfrac{\ln(x/s) + (r + \frac{1}{2}v^2)t}{v \sqrt{t}}$

and $d_2 = d_1 - v\sqrt{t}$

$\ln$ = natural logarithm

$N()$ = cumulative normal density function

$v$ = annual volatility

Delta $= N(d_1)$

## Bull Spread

$s_1 < s_2$

### —Calls (Ch. 7)

$$R = c_1 - c_2$$
$$P = s_2 - s_1 - R$$
$$B = s_2 - P = s_1 - c_2 + c_1$$

—Puts (Ch. 22)

$$P = p_2 - p_1$$
$$R = s_2 - s_1 - P$$
$$B = s_2 - P$$

## Butterfly Spread

A butterfly spread combines a bull spread using strikes $s_1$ and $s_2$ with a bear spread using strikes $s_2$ and $s_3$.

$$s_1 < s_2 < s_3$$

$$s_3 - s_2 = s_2 - s_1$$

—if using all calls (Ch. 10)

$$R = c_1 + c_3 - 2c_2$$

—if using all puts (Ch. 23)

$$R = p_1 + p_3 - 2p_2$$

—if using put bull spread and call bear spread (Ch. 23)

$$P = c_2 + p_2 - c_3 - p_1$$

—if using call bull spread and put bear spread (Ch. 23)

$$R = p_2 + c_2 - p_1 - c_3 - s_3 + s_2$$

Then

$$P = s_3 - s_2 - R \quad \text{or} \quad R = s_3 - s_2 - P$$
$$D = s_1 + R$$
$$U = s_3 - R$$

## Collateral Requirement for a Naked Option (Chs. 5 and 19)

Collateral requirement $= \$100 \max (1.3x - s, \ 2.5)$ for calls

$= \$100 \max (s - .7x, \ 2.5)$ for puts

---

| | | | |
|---|---|---|---|
| $x$ = current stock price | $p$ = put price | $B$ = break-even point | $P$ = maximum profit potential |
| $s$ = striking price | $r$ = interest rate | $U$ = upside break-even point | $R$ = maximum risk potential |
| $c$ = call price | $t$ = time (in years) | $D$ = downside break-even point | |

Subscripts indicate multiple items. For example $s_1$, $s_2$, $s_3$ would designate three striking prices in a formula. The formulae are arranged alphabetically by title or by strategy.

*Combination Buy* (Ch. 18)

$s_1 < s_2$

Out-of-the-money: $R = c_2 + p_1$

*In-the-money*: $R = c_1 + p_2 - s_2 + s_1$

$D = s_1 - R$

$U = s_2 + R$

*Combination Sale* (Ch. 20)

$s_1 < s_2$

Out-of-the-money: $P = c_2 + p_1$

In the money: $P = c_1 + p_2 - s_2 + s_1$

$D = s_1 - P$

$U = s_2 + P$

*Conversion and Reversal Profit* (Ch. 27)

Conversion: $P = s + c - x - p + \text{dividends} - \text{carrying cost}$

Reversal: $P = x + p - c - s - \text{dividends} + \text{carrying cost}$

where

$$\text{carrying cost} = \begin{cases} srt \ (\text{simple interest}) \\ s\,[1 - (1 + r)^{-t}] \ (\text{compound interest,} \\ \qquad\qquad\qquad\qquad \text{present worth}) \end{cases}$$

*Covered Call Write* (Ch. 2)

$$P = s + c - x$$
$$B = x - c$$

*Covered Straddle Write* (Ch. 20)

$$P = s + c + p - x$$
$$B = s - \tfrac{1}{2}P = \tfrac{1}{2}(x + s - p - c)$$

*Cumulative Normal Density Function* (Ch. 28)

Approximation by fifth-order polynomial

$a = 1 - z(1.330274y^5 - 1.821256y^4 + 1.781478y^3 - .3565638y^2 + .3193815y)$

where $y = \dfrac{1}{1 + .2316419|\sigma|}$

$z = .3989423e^{-s^2/2}$

Then

$$N(s) = \begin{cases} a & \text{if } s > 0 \\ 1 - a & \text{if } s < 0 \end{cases}$$

*Delta—see* Black-Scholes Model

*Delta Neutral Ratio:*

—stock versus option (Ch. 6)

$$\text{Neutral ratio} = \frac{1}{\text{Delta of option}}$$

—spread (Chs. 11 and 24)

$$\text{Neutral ratio} = \frac{\text{Delta of long option}}{\text{Delta of short option}}$$

*Equivalent Stock Position* (Ch. 28)

ESP = unit of trading × delta × number of options

where unit of trading is the number of shares of the underlying stock that can be bought or sold with the option (normally 100).

*Future Stock Price* (Ch. 28)

—lognormal distribution, assuming a movement of a fixed number of standard deviations

$$q = xe^{av_t}$$

where $q$ = future stock price

$v_t$ = volatility for the time period

$a$ = number of standard deviations of movement (normally $-3.0 \leq a \leq 3.0$)

---

$x$ = current stock price    $p$ = put price    $B$ = break-even point    $P$ = maximum profit potential
$s$ = striking price    $r$ = interest rate    $U$ = upside break-even point    $R$ = maximum risk potential
$c$ = call price    $t$ = time (in years)    $D$ = downside break-even point

Subscripts indicate multiple items. For example $s_1, s_2, s_3$ would designate three striking prices in a formula. The formulae are arranged alphabetically by title or by strategy.

*Probability of Stock Movement* (Ch. 28)

  —lognormal distribution

$$P(\text{below } q) = N \left\{ \frac{\ln(q/x)}{v_t} \right\}$$

$$P(\text{above } q) = 1 - P(\text{below } q)$$

where   $q =$ stock price in question
        $N() =$ cumulative normal density function
        $\ln =$ natural logarithm
        $v_t =$ volatility for the time period

*Put Pricing Model—Arbitrage Model* (Ch. 28)

  Theoretical put price $=$ theoretical call price $+ s - x +$ dividends $-$
                            carrying cost

where

$$\text{carrying cost} = \begin{cases} srt \text{ (simple interest)} \\ s\,[1 - (1 + r)^{-t}] \text{ (compound interest,} \\ \qquad\qquad\qquad\qquad \text{present worth)} \end{cases}$$

*Ratio Call Write* (Ch. 6)

  General case: long $m$ round lots of stock, short $n$ calls

$$P = m(s - x) + nc$$

$$U = s + \frac{P}{n - m}$$

$$D = s - \frac{P}{m}$$

  2:1 ratio (straddle sale)

$$P = s - x + 2c$$

$$U = s + p$$

$$D = s - p = x - 2c$$

*Ratio Spread*

  —*Calls (Ch. 11): buy $n_1$ calls at lower strike, $s_1$, and sell $n_2$ calls at
             higher strike, $s_2$*

$$s_1 < s_2$$

$$n_1 < n_2$$

$$R = n_1 c_1 - n_2 c_2$$

$$P = (s_2 - s_1)n_1 - R$$

$$U = s_2 + \frac{P}{n_2 - n_1}$$

Break-even cost of long calls for follow-up action (Ch. 11)

$$\text{Break-even cost} = \frac{n_2(s_2 - s_1) - R}{n_2 - n_1}$$

—Puts (Ch. 24): buy $n_2$ puts at higher strike, $s_2$, and sell $n_1$ puts at lower strike, $s_1$

$$s_1 < s_2$$

$$n_2 < n_1$$

$$R = n_2 p_2 - n_1 p_1$$

$$P = n_2(s_2 - s_1) - R$$

$$D = s_1 - \frac{P}{n_1 - n_2}$$

*Reversal*—*See* Conversion and Reversal Profit

*Reverse Hedge* (Ch. 4)—simulated straddle purchase

General case: short $m$ round lots of stock and long $n$ calls

$$R = m(s - x) + nc$$

$$U = s + \frac{R}{n - m}$$

$$D = s - \frac{R}{m}$$

2:1 ratio (straddle buy):

$$R = s + 2c - x$$

$$U = s + R$$

$$D = s - R = x - 2c$$

Using puts (long 100 stock, long 2 puts) (Ch. 18)

$$R = x + 2p - s$$

---

| | | | |
|---|---|---|---|
| $x$ = current stock price | $p$ = put price | $B$ = break-even point | $P$ = maximum profit potential |
| $s$ = striking price | $r$ = interest rate | $U$ = upside break-even point | $R$ = maximum risk potential |
| $c$ = call price | $t$ = time (in years) | $D$ = downside break-even point | |

Subscripts indicate multiple items. For example $s_1$, $s_2$, $s_3$ would designate three striking prices in a formula. The formulae are arranged alphabetically by title or by strategy.

$$U = s + R = x + 2p$$
$$D = s - R$$

*Straddle Buy* (Ch. 18)

$$R = p + c$$
$$U = s + R$$
$$D = s - R$$

*Straddle Sale* (Ch. 20)

$$P = p + c$$
$$U = s + p$$
$$D = s - p$$

*Synthetic Put Purchase*—short stock and long call (Ch. 4)

$$R = s + c - x$$
$$B = s - c$$

*Variable Ratio Write* (Ch. 6)

—long 100 shares of stock, short one call at strike $s_1$, short one call at strike $s_2$

$$s_1 < x < s_2$$

$$P = c_1 + c_2 + s_1 - x$$
$$D = s_1 - P = x - c_1 - c_2$$
$$U = s_2 + P$$

*Volatility*—Standard Deviation (Ch. 28)

$$v^2 = \frac{\sum_{i=1}^{n} (x_i - \bar{x})^2}{n - 1}$$

where $x_i$ = daily stock closing price

$\bar{x}$ = mean (average) of the $x_i$'s

$n$ = number of observations

—if $v$ is the annual volatility, then the volatility for a time period, $t$, is

$$v_t = v \sqrt{t}$$

APPENDIX

*Graphs* **E**

Chapter references are in parentheses.

A. Intrinsic Value—Call (Ch. 1)    B. Intrinsic Value—Put (Ch. 15)

C. Call Option Pricing Curve (Ch. 1)    D. Put Option Pricing Curve (Ch. 15)

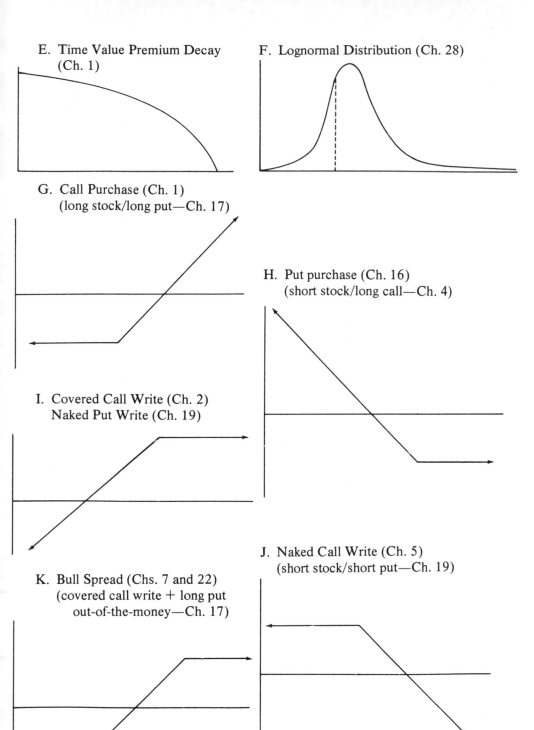

E. Time Value Premium Decay
   (Ch. 1)

F. Lognormal Distribution (Ch. 28)

G. Call Purchase (Ch. 1)
   (long stock/long put—Ch. 17)

H. Put purchase (Ch. 16)
   (short stock/long call—Ch. 4)

I. Covered Call Write (Ch. 2)
   Naked Put Write (Ch. 19)

J. Naked Call Write (Ch. 5)
   (short stock/short put—Ch. 19)

K. Bull Spread (Chs. 7 and 22)
   (covered call write + long put
    out-of-the-money—Ch. 17)

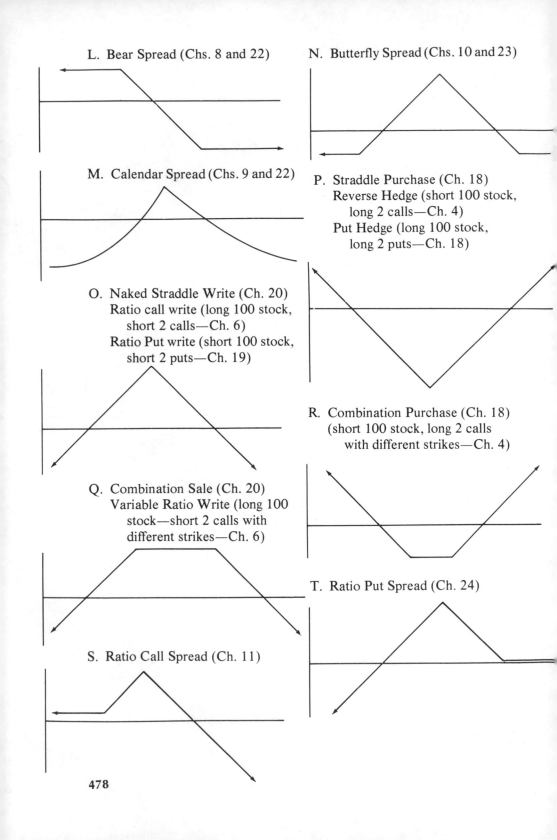

L. Bear Spread (Chs. 8 and 22)

N. Butterfly Spread (Chs. 10 and 23)

M. Calendar Spread (Chs. 9 and 22)

P. Straddle Purchase (Ch. 18)
   Reverse Hedge (short 100 stock,
      long 2 calls—Ch. 4)
   Put Hedge (long 100 stock,
      long 2 puts—Ch. 18)

O. Naked Straddle Write (Ch. 20)
   Ratio call write (long 100 stock,
      short 2 calls—Ch. 6)
   Ratio Put write (short 100 stock,
      short 2 puts—Ch. 19)

R. Combination Purchase (Ch. 18)
   (short 100 stock, long 2 calls
      with different strikes—Ch. 4)

Q. Combination Sale (Ch. 20)
   Variable Ratio Write (long 100
      stock—short 2 calls with
      different strikes—Ch. 6)

T. Ratio Put Spread (Ch. 24)

S. Ratio Call Spread (Ch. 11)

# Index

*484*